Time, Eternity, and the Trinity

Time, Eternity, and the Trinity

A Trinitarian Analogical Understanding of Time and Eternity

EUNSOO KIM

☙PICKWICK *Publications* • Eugene, Oregon

TIME, ETERNITY, AND THE TRINITY
A Trinitarian Analogical Understanding of Time and Eternity

Copyright © 2010 Eunsoo Kim. All rights reserved. Except for brief quotations in critical publications or reviews, no part of this book may be reproduced in any manner without prior written permission from the publisher. Write: Permissions, Wipf and Stock Publishers, 199 W. 8th Ave., Suite 3, Eugene, OR 97401.

Scripture quotations, unless otherwise noted, are from the Holy Bible, New International Bible (NIV). Copyright © 1973, 1978, 1984 by International Bible Society. Used by permission of Zondervan Publishing House. All rights reserved.

Pickwick Publications
An Imprint of Wipf and Stock Publishers
199 W. 8th Ave., Suite 3
Eugene, OR 97401

www.wipfandstock.com

ISBN 13: 978-1-60608-968-2

Cataloging-in-Publication data:

Kim, Eunsoo.

Time, eternity, and the trinity : a trinitarian analogical understanding of time and eternity / Eunsoo Kim.

viii + 368 p. ; 23 cm.

ISBN 13: 978-1-60608-968-2

1. Time. 2. Eternity. 3. Doctrine of the Trinity. 4. Barth, Karl, 1886–1968. 5. Balthasar, Hans Urs von, 1905–1988. I. Title.

BT131 K50 2010

Manufactured in the U.S.A.

Contents

Preface / vii

1 Introduction / 1

PART ONE: Time and Eternity in the Biblical, Historical, Philosophical, and Theological Debates

2 Biblical Understandings of Time and Eternity / 17

3 Time and Eternity in Classical Theism / 61

4 Contemporary Philosophical and Scientific Debates on the Nature of Time / 103

5 Contemporary Theological Debates on God's Eternity and Its Relation to Time / 146

PART TWO: Toward a Trinitarian Analogical Understanding of Time and Eternity

6 Time, Eternity, and the Trinity in the Theology of Karl Barth / 191

7 Time, Eternity, and the Trinity in the Theology of Hans Urs von Balthasar / 241

8 Toward an Alternative Trinitarian Analogical Understanding of Time and God's Eternity / 289

9 Conclusion / 339

Bibliography / 343

Preface

ONE OF THE RED-HOT ISSUES IN CONTEMPORARY CHRISTIAN THEOLogy is the problem of a renewed understanding of God's eternity and its relation to time. It is not merely a doctrinal issue, but sits at the heart of our understanding of God and human beings, and contributes to the total constitution of our world-view. Indeed, it is the place where most theological horizons converge and diverge. This study concerns a debate between two competing views on God's eternity: one focused on God's absolute timelessness in classical theism, and the other on God's temporal everlastingness in contemporary panentheism. The purpose of this study is to present an alternative Trinitarian analogical understanding of God's eternity and its relation to time, especially through a critical reflection on K. Barth's and H. U. von Balthasar's understandings of the issue. I maintain that this perspective can provide a helpful resource for thinking beyond the debate over whether God's eternity is timeless or everlasting.

That is, while critically reviewing very diverse contemporary views on the topic, my particular concern is how we can simultaneously grasp, in a theological perspective, not only the infinite qualitative difference but also the positive relationship between God's eternity and time. In my view, it can be accomplished by reconceiving, in a Trinitarian and analogical way, not only the nature of time but also that of God's eternity. In other words, neither *via negationis* (i.e., the timeless view) nor *via eminentiae* (i.e., the everlasting view) can properly comprehend the biblical teaching of the qualitative difference and the positive relationship between God's eternity and time. Therefore, a kind of *via analogia*—based on the Trinitarian triple analogy consisting of *analogia vitae*, *analogia relationis*, and *analogia communicationis*, which is centered on the only true God-given analogy, Jesus Christ—is a necessary for a proper conception of the biblical teaching of God's eternity and its positive relation to time. This analogical approach, which is based on the dynamic and dramatic concepts of God's Being-as-life-in-relation and of the Triune God's communicative action in eternity (i.e., the immanent Trinity) and time (i.e., the economic Trinity), can help us resolve the debate between absolute timeless eternity and temporal everlasting duration.

Without God's immeasurable love and grace and many sincere people's help, support, and prayer, this study could not have been completed. It would not be possible to acknowledge all of them here, so I express my appreciation only to those whose influence has been most decisive. First, my gratitude must be expressed to Dr. Kevin J. Vanhoozer, who was my mentor of doctoral study at Trinity Evangelical Divinity School (Trinity International University). He originally led me to the subject matter of this study, and always directed me with generous guidance and insightful comments throughout the whole process. More importantly, he has demonstrated for me the genuine virtues of a theologian, both in his own theological study and in the classroom. In addition, I want to give thanks to Dr. John S. Feinberg (Professor of Biblical and Systematic Theology at TEDS), who painstakingly read the entire manuscript, gave helpful comments, and helped me avoid many unclear expressions. I also thank Dr. Willem A. VanGemeren (the Director of Doctor of Philosophy in Theological Studies Program at TEDS) for his warm encouragement and hospitality during my stay there for research. I cannot forget the friendship and love of many other members of the faculty, staff, and student body at TEDS.

I deeply appreciate Dr. Cornelius Plantinga, Jr. (the President and Charles W. Colson Professor of Systematic Theology at Calvin Theological Seminary), Dr. John W. Cooper (Professor of Philosophical Theology at Calvin Theological Seminary), and Dr. Hae-Moo Yoo (Professor of Dogmatics at Korea Theological Seminary). They instructed me in the early stages of my theological study and laid the foundations of my theological thinking. Especially, I want to thank Dr. Jong-Yun Lee (the Senior Pastor of Seoul Presbyterian Church) and Dr. Yung-Han Kim (Professor of Christian Studies at Soongsil University) for their continuing spiritual and academic guidance and help.

Finally, I must turn my thankful mind toward my parents who are in the heavenly kingdom now, and sisters, brothers, and all other family members who have always been a source of self-sacrificing support and prayer for me throughout my life. My wife, Moon-Young Kim, deserves all of my heartful gratitude and love, because I could not have finished this project without her invaluable love and encouragement. I dedicate this work to all of them in memory of their love and devotion.

Soli Deo Gloria!
Eunsoo Kim
June 8, 2009.

1
Introduction

The Purpose

THE PURPOSE OF THIS STUDY IS TO PRESENT A TRINITARIAN ANALOGIcal understanding of God's eternity and its relation to time, especially, through a critical reflection of K. Barth's and H. U. von Balthasar's understandings, which can provide helpful resources for thinking further on the debate on the timeless/everlasting eternity of God. In this study, the main questions to pursue are as follows: *firstly*, to analyze and discern what are the essential problems of God's eternity and its relation to time in the biblical, historical, philosophical (and scientific), and theological debates; *secondly*, to analyze and expose two theologians' understandings of God's eternity and its real relation to time; *thirdly*, to examine the relevance of their views in light of the current theological discussions on the topic; that is to say, to what extent do the two theologians' Trinitarian analogical understandings of time and eternity help make a contribution towards a possible solution for the current debate on the problem of God's eternity and its relation to time; *finally*, while critically reviewing very diverse understandings on the topic, to present an alternative Trinitarian analogical understanding of God's eternity and its relation to time; in other words, to pursue how we can more properly understand the qualitative difference as well as its positive relationship between God's eternity and human time. It is possible in reconceiving not only the nature of time but also that of God's eternity in a Trinitarian and analogical way.

Therefore, my thesis statement of this study is as follows: There are helpful resources in dialogue with K. Barth and H. U. von Balthasar concerning a Trinitarian analogical understanding of time and eternity that would avoid the extreme tendencies of the absolute timeless and the temporal everlasting views of God's eternity which exaggerate the transcendence or immanence of God respectively. Neither the *via negativa* (i.e., timeless view) nor the *via eminentiae* (i.e., everlasting view) can properly conceive the perspectives of the infinite qualitative difference and the real and positive relationship between God's eternity and time simultaneously. Therefore, a kind of *via analogia* through the following Trinitarian triple analogy, *analogia vitae*, *analogia relationis*, and *analogia communicationis*, centered in the unique and the only true God-given analogy, Jesus Christ, is a key to grasp more properly the biblical teaching concerning God's eternity and its relation to time.

This Trinitarian analogical approach, which is based on a dynamic and dramatic concept of the Triune God's perfect Being-as-life-in-relation and His communicative action in eternity and time, can help us solve our own problem of the debates between traditional classical theism and contemporary panentheism, more specifically, of the views between absolute timeless eternity and temporal everlasting duration. Conclusively, a Trinitarian analogical understanding (i.e., *via analogia trinitatis*) can provide a more proper framework for Christian theology to conceive the relationship between God's eternity and time, divine transcendence and immanence, and thus God and the world in a broad sense.

The Problem

One of the red-hot issues in contemporary Christian theology is the problem of the renewed understanding of God's eternity and its relation to time. It is not merely a doctrinal problem as a part of the doctrine of God, as we shall see, but at the heart of our understanding of the biblical God and human beings (and the world), the meaning of salvation history including world history, and thus the whole structure of Christian theology. Indeed, it is the very place in which most of the horizons of the understanding of theological subject matters converge and diverge. Therefore, it is the problem of a total constitution of our world-view. In this sense, concerning the importance of this problem, J. S. Feinberg rightly points out that "this issue is actually an umbrella for a series of issues within the doctrine of God." He emphasizes it as follows:

"I believe, however, that anyone working within theology proper must engage in discussions about God's relation to time and eternity as we move toward the next millennium. I believe this is and will be a watershed issue for evangelical theism in the upcoming years."[1] Accordingly, in this study, although there are very diverse options in conceiving God's eternity and its relation to time, I will specifically focus on the debate between two alternative views of God's eternity: "the timeless eternal God" in traditional classical theism and "the temporal everlasting God" in contemporary panentheism. As N. Pike states, "the position that a theologian takes on the topic of divine eternity has a kind of controlling effect on the general shape and texture of his broad theological view about the nature of God" and His relation to the temporal world.[2]

A Crisis of Classical Theism and the Challenge of Panentheism

In this study, my particular concern is how to conceive the problem of God's eternity and its relation to time in the broad horizon of the God-world relationship from an evangelical point of view. It could be finally summarized as the problem of the relationship between divine transcendence and divine immanence. In a sense, one of the most significant factors which specifically characterizes one's theological paradigm is how to conceive the problem of the God-world relationship.[3] In many cases, therefore, a fundamental change of theological paradigm has been accompanied with a change of one's view of the God-world relation, and vice versa. Then, first of all, the concept of God is also specifically modified according to such a change of theological paradigm. In Christian theology, there can be many alternative options for conceiving the God-world relationship. For example, I. Barbour shows us eight different models for the God-world relationship as follows: Classical (Ruler-Kingdom), Deist (Clockmaker-Clock), Neo-Thomist (Workman-Tool), Kenotic (Parent-Child), Existentialist (None), Linguistic (Agent-Action), Embodiment (Person-Body), and Process model (Leader-Community).[4]

---

1. Feinberg, "New Dimensions in the Doctrine of God," 247.
2. Pike, *God and Timelessness*, ix.
3. Cf. Vanhoozer, "Effectual Call or Causal Effect?," 213.
4. Barbour, *Religion in an Age of Science*, 244. For a revised version of the argument, see his *Religion and Science*, 305–32.

In the contemporary situation of Christian theology, we are now confronted with a crisis of classical theism caused by various recent theological movements, for example: process theology, liberation theology, feminist theology, ecological theology, religious pluralism, and so on.[5] Among various new theological quests against classical theism, considering the topic of the study, I want to pay attention to a tendency toward a "panentheistic" approach to dissolve the problem of the God-world relationship.[6] More significantly, even though "panentheism"[7] is a fundamental strategy of process theology (cf. C. Hartshorne, J. B. Cobb, D. R. Griffin, S. M. Ogden, N. Pittenger, D. A. Pailin, J. A. Bracken, among others),[8] it is now accepted by ecological theology and other wide theological spectrums (cf. S. McFague, R. R. Ruether, J. Moltmann,

---

5. For a brief sketch on this issue, see Feinberg, "What Happens to God in Contemporary Thought," 81–148.

6. Considering this point, Vanhoozer rightly observes that "Christian theologians are today faced with a . . . choice between 'theism' and 'panentheism'. It may be only a slight exaggeration to say that we are in the midst of a paradigm revolution, but it is clear that the traditional doctrine of God (i.e., classical theism) is in crisis. Theologians of various denominational stripes, liberal and conservative, faced with the choice for or against classical theism, are increasingly abandoning ship." Idem, "Effectual Call or Causal Effect?," 214.

7. Recently, while rejecting classical theism, many theologians assert that panentheism is a more proper option to conceive God and the world relationship. "Panentheism" can be defined as follows: (1) C. Hartshorne: "God is not just the all of (other) things; but yet all other things are literally in him. . . . To be himself he does not need *this* universe, but only *a* universe, and only contingently does he even contain this particular actual universe." Idem, "Introduction: The Standpoint of Panentheism," 22. (2) F. D. Lindsey: "Panentheism is the view that God's being includes and penetrates the whole universe, so that every part of it exists in Him, but (as against pantheism) that His being is more than and not exhausted by the universe. If pantheism is the belief that 'God is all, and all is God,' then panentheism is the belief that 'God is in all, and all is in God.'" Idem, "An Evangelical Overview of Process Theology," 23. (3) P. Clayton: "[Panentheism is] the doctrine that the world is (in some sense) inside of God even though God is also more than the world." Idem, "The Case for Christian Panentheism," 201. For more detailed discussions on panentheism in various perspectives, see Clayton and Peacocke, *In Whom We Live and Move and Have Our Being*.

8. Hartshorne, "Introduction: The Standpoint of Panentheism," 1–25, and *Divine Relativity*; Cobb, *God and World*, and Cobb and Griffin, *Process Theology*; Griffin, *God, Power, and Evil*, and "Green Spirituality," 5–20; Ogden, *Reality of God and Other Essays*; Pittenger, *Divine Triunity*; Pailin and Sutherland, eds., *God and the Processes of Reality*; Bracken, *Society and Spirit* and "Panentheism from Trinitarian Perspective," 7–28. For some evangelical theologians' responses to process theology, see Nash, *Process Theology*; Lindsey, "Evangelical Overview of Process Theology," 15–32; and Feinberg, "Process Theology," 291–334.

A. Peacocke, P. Clayton, etc.).[9] In the evangelical theological circle, even though it is different from process theism, a seriously modified conception of God from classical theism was suggested by the so-called "openness of God" theology (i.e., open theism), which is represented by C. Pinnock, J. Sanders, and W. Hasker, among others.[10]

Generally speaking, panentheists and "openness of God" theologians criticize classical theism as a "deistic" theism which strongly emphasizes God's absolute transcendence over the world.[11] In their views, classical theism stresses a very static concept of God (i.e., divine simplicity, absolute immutability, impassibility, timeless eternity, omniscience, omnipotence, and so on, which are inseparably interconnected with one another). According to panentheists, such a very "static," "distant," "closed," "timelessly eternal," and "transcendent" concept of God is not at all consistent with the biblical teaching. Therefore, against it, panentheists emphasize a "personal," "dynamic," "relational," "open," "temporally everlasting," and "immanent" concept of God. Furthermore, they assert that it is a more biblically, logically, and scientifically consistent concept of God.[12] In his recent article, for example, P. Clayton asserts that "panentheism is able to solve certain contemporary philosophical problems in thinking the nature of God and God's relationship to the world better than any other 'live option' being advocated in the field

---

9. McFague, *Models of God* and *Body of God*; Ruether, *Gaia and God*; Moltmann, *God in Creation*; Peacocke, *Creation and the World of Science*, *Intimations of Reality*, and "God's Action in the Real World," 455–76; Clayton, *God and Contemporary Science* and "Case for Christian Panentheism," 201–8.

10. Hasker, *God, Time, and Knowledge*; Pinnock, et al., *Openness of God*; and Sanders, *God Who Risks*. A recent edition of *Christianity Today* (Feb. 7, 2000) reports a battle for the conception of God in evangelical theological circles between the 'openness of God' theologians and classical theists. See "God vs. God: Two Competing Theologies Vie for the Future of Evangelicalism," *Christianity Today* (Feb. 7, 2000) 34–35. In his critique of "the openness of God" theology, Geisler suggests to call it a "New Theism" or "Neotheism" because of its serious modification of the classical concept of God. Geisler, *Creating God in the Image of Man?*, 74. See also, Ware, *God's Lesser Glory*; Frame, *No Other God*.

11. However, panentheists' critiques of classical theism as a "deistic theism" is an oversimplification of the traditional view of God. For example, the Reformers, especially John Calvin, emphasized the God *pro nobis* (or *pro me*), not God *in se*. Considering this point, while responding to P. Clayton's proposal of panentheism, Vanhoozer rightly points out that we must distinguish "classical theological theism" from "classical philosophical theism." Idem, "A Case for Christian Panentheism?," 281.

12. Cf. Clayton, "Case for Christian Panentheism," 202.

today."[13] However, we must ask, is panentheism really a better theological paradigm than any other option?[14] Therefore, in order to examine the question, in this study, I want to focus on a recent vigorous debate on the understanding of God's eternity and its relation to time as a case study in the debate between classical theism and contemporary panentheism.

Actually, since a debate between Heraclitus and Parmenides in early Greek philosophy, the relationship between time and eternity has been one of the most problematic issues in philosophy as well as theology for a long time, and currently it is raised as a focal point for debate on the understanding of the nature of God's eternity and its relation to time. Concerning its difficulty, L. Berkhof once said that, "The relation of eternity to time constitutes one of the most difficult problems in philosophy and theology, perhaps incapable of solution in our present condition."[15] Concerning the debate between *timelessness* and *everlastingness*, even though all of the theologians who maintain the view of the everlastingness of God are not panentheists in a strict sense (cf. N. Wolterstorff), we can say that they are *temporalized* panentheists. That is to say, according to A. R. Peacocke, pan-en-theism (i.e., "all-in-God") is essentially a "spatial model" in terms of ontology, which means that "God's being is more than, and other than, the world, . . . [but] the world is 'in' God."[16] In a similar sense, therefore, if God is the Being-in-time, and if there is not any qualitative difference between God's time and the world's time, the everlasting view of God's eternity means that all of the world's finite time is *in* God's infinite time (i.e., all-in-God; pan-en-theism). Visually, it can be conceived as follows: $\{-\infty$ backward infinite time <<-------[finite world time]------->> forward infinite time $+\infty\}$. The only difference is the quantity of God's infinite time and the world's finite time. This is what I mean by the term a *temporal* model of panentheism: "all of world finite time is in God's infinite time."

---

13. Ibid., 201.

14. For some responses of evangelical theologians to Clayton's proposal, see "Case for Christian Panentheism?," 281–93. Recently, Cooper thoroughly persues and analyses the origin and concepts of panentheism in various philosophers and theologians from Palto to the present, and gives his own response to it; see idem, *Panentheism*.

15. Berkhof, *Systematic Theology*, 60.

16. Peacocke, *Creation and the World of Science*, 141.

As we have seen, in an ontological sense, panentheism is essentially a 'spatialized" concept of God, "all-in-God." However, we cannot separate space and time in this world. For example, in the view of Augustine, by the doctrine of *creatio ex nihilo*, not only *space* but also *time* is created together by God, and thus there was neither time nor space *before* creation. As he said, "We are not to try to conceive of infinite ages of time before the world, nor of infinite realms of space outside the world; for, just as there are no periods of time before it, so also are there no spatial locations outside it;" and, therefore, "The creation of the world and the beginning of time both occurred simultaneously, and the one did not come before the other."[17] In the twentieth century, A. Einstein came to the same conclusion in his Relativity Theory (1905 and 1915) that space and time cannot be separated. In addition, according to the contemporary orthodox Big-Bang theory, time has its own beginning and end. If we accept this view, although it can be distinguishable for the convenience of argument, we cannot separate the notions of space and time in conceiving the God-world relationship.[18] In this sense, we can say that time is the form of the creatures' existence and eternity is the mode of God's Being. Therefore, there is only a specific understanding of time/eternity which belongs to a specific ontological conceiving of the God-world relationship.

Recent Debates on God's Eternity: Timeless or Everlasting?

According to biblical teaching, Christian theology has unanimously affirmed that "God is eternal." However, regarding its relation to human time, the meaning of God's eternity has been interpreted in two fundamentally different ways: *timelessness* and *everlastingness*. In classical theism, God has been conceived as a timeless Being, who exists totally outside of time and has no temporal duration. Since time has been understood in the category of *change* and *movement*, it cannot

---

17. Augustine, *The City of God*, Book XI. 5 and 6 headings.
18. Cf. Sklar, *Space, Time, and Spacetime*; Craig, "God, Time, and Eternity," 497–503; and Pedersen, "The God of Space and Time," 14–20. For example, Helm asserts that "In saying that we ought to conclude that if God exists he is outside space and time. ... All that I am claiming is that the spacelessness of God seems to be a requirement of traditional theism and hence that the timelessness of God does." Idem, "God and Spacelessness," 221.

be applied to God as *the most perfect Being*. Therefore, God necessarily exists outside of time and transcends all of its limitations. For God, all of time exists in one eternal now. This view of timeless eternity has been maintained by Augustine, Boethius, Anselm, Aquinas, and most classical theists. Recent advocates of this view are P. Helm and B. Leftow among others.[19] Generally, in classical theism, Boethius' definition of eternity has been considered as one of the best: "Eternity is the complete possession all at once of illimitable life [*Aeternitas igitur est interminabilis vitae tota simul et perfecta possessio*]."[20] In this timeless interpretation of God's eternity, there are two distinct claims: (1) God's timelessness (the-Being-outside-of-time), and (2) God's simultaneity (i.e., God exists in one eternal now). God's timelessness is derived from the concept of divine perfection and simplicity and it is the basis of the doctrine of divine immutability and impassibility, and the simultaneity is the basis of divine omnipresence and omniscience.[21] All of those doctrines are inseparably interrelated to each other, and they are the irreducible divine attributes in classical theism. Accordingly, this view of God's timeless eternity eventually emphasizes the absolute transcendence of God over the temporal world.

There is, however, a very different view of God's eternity as everlasting duration, the infinite extension of time in both directions of backward and forward. Recently, this everlasting view of God's eternity is more widely accepted than the timeless view from process theologians to conservatives.[22] Contemporary proponents of this view of everlasting eternity include process theologians (cf. C. Hartshorne, S. Ogden, etc.), O. Cullmann, N. Pike, R. Swinburne, N. Wolterstorff,

---

19. Cf. Helm, *Eternal God*; and Leftow, *Time and Eternity*.

20. Cited in Stump and Kretzmann, "Eternity," 431.

21. In classical theism, while analyzing Anselm's conception of God's attributes, Feinberg insists that the logical derivation is as follows: divine perfection–aseity–simplicity–(timeless) eternity. However, the logical connection between eternity and immutability can be thought in the following two ways: simplicity–eternity–immutability or simplicity–immutability–eternity. Idem, "New Dimensions in the Doctrine of God," 250–51, and his *No One Like Him*, 385–86.

22. In this sense, Leftow rightly observes that, "The doctrine of divine timelessness was a nearly unchallenged orthodoxy for the millennium between Athanasius and Duns Scotus. Today the claim that God is temporal enjoys nearly as universal an acceptance among philosophers and theologians." Idem, *Time and Eternity*, 2–3.

C. Pinnock, and W. Hasker among many others.²³ In this view of God's everlastingness, the following two claims are significant: (1) God's temporality (the-Being-in-time), and (2) God's everlastingness (God exists in the infinite duration of time). Therefore, against traditional classical theism in which God was conceived as the "eternal, absolute, independent, unchangeable" abstract Being, process theologians insist that God is "temporal, relative, dependent, and constantly changing" in concrete Becoming.²⁴ However, we must remember that all of the proponents of a "temporal" God are not process theologians (cf. the theologians of the open theism, N. Wolterstorff, etc.). For example, while distinguishing from process theism, John S. Feinberg well presents an evangelical position of a "temporal" conception of God.²⁵

Among many significant related issues with the everlasting interpretation of God's eternity,²⁶ I want to focus on the concept of God's action in the temporal world. According to the Bible, God is a personal Being and a living and acting God, who created the world and time, continually sustains it, and brings us His salvation in time. Thus, we have a question that "if God is eternal in the sense of timelessness, how can He act in this temporal world?"²⁷ This is a key point for recent rejections of classical timeless eternity of God. Concerning this point, for instance, N. Wolterstorff asserts that "if we are to accept this picture of

23. Cullmann, *Christ and Time*; Pike, *God and Timelessness*; Wolterstorff, "God Everlasting," 181–203; Swinburne, *Coherence of Theism*; Hasker, *God, Time, and Knowledge*; Pinnock, "Systematic Theology," 101–25.

24. Cobb and Griffin, *Process Theology*, 47.

25. Feinberg, *No One Like Him*, 255–64 and 375–436, especially see 427–36.

26. For example, Brian Davies summarizes several major objections to the classical conception of God's timelessness as follows: "1. If God is timeless, he cannot be a person. 2. If God is timeless, his knowledge entails absurd consequences or is restricted. 3. If God is timeless, he cannot act. 4. If God is timeless, he cannot command our admiration or love. 5. There is biblical precedent for rejecting the view that God is timeless. 6. There is no good reason for supposing that if there is a God, then he is timeless." Idem, "Timeless God?," 215. According to the everlasting view, therefore, the following doctrines in classical theism are rejected: the doctrine of divine immutability, divine impassibility, divine simplicity, divine foreknowledge and omniscience, etc. For detailed arguments, see the followings: Hartshorne, *Omnipotence and Other Theological Mistakes*; Pinnock, et al., *Openness of God*; Basinger, *Case for Freewill Theism*; Nash, *Concept of God*; and Geisler, *Creating God in the Image of Man?*

27. For recent arguments on the concept of God's act in the world, see the following works: Wright, *God Who Acts*; Thomas, *God's Activity in the World*; Morris, *Divine and Human Action*; and Tracy, *God Who Acts*.

God as acting for the renewal of human life, we must conceive of him as everlasting rather than [timelessly] eternal. God the Redeemer cannot be a God eternal [in the timeless sense]. This is so because God the Redeemer is a God who changes."[28] In a similar sense, C. Pinnock underlines that "If God's eternity were timeless, God could not be related to our temporal world. In actual fact, though, the biblical symbols do not speak of divine timelessness but of God's faithfulness over time."[29] Therefore, Pinnock concludes as follows:

> The God of the Bible is not timeless. His eternity means that there has never been and never will be a time when God does not exist. Timelessness limits God. If he were timeless, God would be unable to work salvation in history, would be cut off from the world, have no real relationship with people and would be completely static.[30]

In these statements, their essential supposition seems to be that if there is someone who can act or do something in time, then he must be temporal. Conversely, however, we can ask whether the ability to act in the temporal world necessarily requires that God should be temporal as we are?[31] If not, is there any other option to allow God's action in this temporal world?

In addition, recently, one of the most powerful arguments against the timeless eternity of God comes form the analytic philosophical conception of the nature of time. Currently, in the area of philosophical theology, the debate on the nature of time is very significant for our understanding of God's eternity and its relation to time. As we shall see in chapter 4, there are two competitive theories of time, the tenseless (static, B-series) and the tensed (dynamic, A-series) theory of time. According to some philosophers and theologians, the traditional conception of God's timeless eternity is only consistent without any serious problems with the tenseless (static) theory of time (cf. P. Helm). However, according to the tensed (dynamic) theorists of time, along with some other reasons (cf. Brian Davies's summary of objections in footnote 26), God

---

28. Wolterstorff, "God Everlasting," 181–82 (italics original).
29. Pinnock, "Systematic Theology," 120.
30. Ibid., 121.
31. For an interesting attempt to answer the question, see Stump and Kretzmann, "Eternity," 429–58, and for a critique of the openness view of God, Geisler, *Creating God in the Image of Man?* especially chapter 5.

is temporal because the tensed theory of time is correct. As we shall see, proponents of this line of arguments are J. D. Lewis, A. G. Padgett, and W. L. Craig among many others.[32] For example, W. L. Craig insists that, "if the dynamic conception of time is correct, God is most plausibly understood to be temporal."[33] However, here again, if the tensed theory of time is correct, then must God be temporal as we are? Actually, this point of debate is another focal point for the proceeding study on how to reconcile the biblical and theological understanding of God's eternity and its relation to time and the philosophical and scientific conception of the tensed (dynamic) theory of time.

The Procedure

As previously mentioned, in the contemporary analytic philosophical understanding of time, time is conceived as "change" (cf. chapter 4). That is to say, they debate whether the nature of time is dynamic (tensed) or static (tenseless). In this case, the criterion is time as "change" (i.e., measured time). Therefore, in current theological debates on God's eternity (cf. chapter 5), the timeless view of God's eternity mainly appeals to the static (tenseless) theory of time (cf. P. Helm). However, dynamic (tensed) theorists assert that God is essentially temporal, besides other theological reasons, because, philosophically, the dynamic (tensed) theory of time is correct (cf. A. G. Padgett, W. L. Craig). Accordingly, in my judgment, the analytic philosophical theories of time, which essentially conceive time as change, seem to make an unpleasant demand on theologians to take a position either on a timeless or everlasting view of God's eternity. In this way, therefore, contemporary theologians make a mistake again in that they confine their understandings of God to the analytic philosophical conceptual frame, like the classical theologians wrongly confined their conception of God to the Greek ontological framework. However, in my view, the real problem is that both understandings of God's eternity (timeless and everlasting) cannot properly present the biblical understanding of God's eternity, i.e., its qualitative difference as well as its real and positive relation to time. In fact, as I will show in chapter 2, according to the Bible, it is true that not only God is

---

32. Cf. Lewis, "God and Time"; Padgett, *God, Eternity and the Nature of Time*; and Craig, *Time and Eternity*.

33. Craig, *Time and Eternity*, 115.

definitely beyond the limitation of the created time but also He really acts in time and thus has a positive relation to human time. Therefore, indeed, in this study, my essential intention is to show and to insist that, while defining time as "the form of life," a Trinitarian analogical understanding of time and God's eternity can break through the impasse between absolute timelessness and everlastingness.

This study is constituted in the following two parts: "Part One, Time and Eternity in Biblical, Historical, Philosophical, and Theological Debates," chapters 2 to 5, are an analytic part. In this section, I will analyze various understandings of God's eternity and its relation to time from the biblical conception of time to contemporary theological understandings. Then, "Part Two, Toward a Trinitarian Analogical Understanding of Time and Eternity," chapters 6 to 8, are a constructive part. In this section, I will present a Trinitarian analogical understanding of God's eternity and its relation to time from K. Barth's and H. U. von Balthasar's understandings and define my own view.

In chapter 2, I will analyze some key biblical terms and texts for grasping the biblical conception of time and eternity, and then some biblical scholars' understandings, for example: J. Marsh, J. Muilenburg, O. Cullmann, T. Boman, J. Barr, N. H. Snaith, P. Ricoeur, J. DeVries, E. C. Rust, and so forth. Finally, I will suggest my own view, which is a canonical approach. It will be constituted by the time of creation, the time of providence/redemption, and the time of consummation. According to the biblical conception of time and God's eternity, although it does not explicitly support either the timeless view or the everlasting view, it is clear that there is an infinite qualitative difference as well as a positive relationship between God's eternity and time. In chapter 3, I will pursue the historical background for the conception of God's timeless eternity in classical theism. The concept of timeless eternity can be traced through the Neo-Platonists and Plato, and finally up to the Eleatic philosopher, Parmenides. Therefore, I will briefly deal with the philosophical background of ancient Greek philosophy, from Parmenides to the Neoplatonist, Plotinus. Then, I will also analyze the conception of time and eternity in Augustine, Boethius, Anselm, and Thomas Aquinas.

In chapter 4, I will analyze contemporary philosophical and scientific debates on the nature of time between the dynamic (tensed) and the static (tenseless) theory of time. For this, I will deal with Einstein-Minkowski's revolutionary concept of space-time and McTaggart's paradox of time. Then, I will analyze and summarize the main conceptions of the two competitive theories of time: the dynamic (tensed) and the static (tenseless) theories. Finally, I will briefly present the nature of time and some significant theological implications. Then, in chapter 5, I will critically observe the contemporary theological debates on God's eternity and its relation to time. I will especially focus on the debates among evangelical theologians concerning the conception of God's eternity and its theological meaning; for example, P. Helm's absolute timeless conception of God's eternity, N. Wolterstorff's everlasting eternity, A. G. Padgett's relatively timeless eternity, and finally, W. L. Craig's timeless and omnitemporalism.

In chapters 6 and 7, I will deal with K. Barth's and H. U. von Balthasar's Trinitarian analogical understanding of God's eternity and its relation to time respectively. For this, I first analyze their conception of analogy, and then their Trinitarian analogical understanding of time and eternity, which is centered in the time of Jesus Christ. In this way, K. Barth made a Copernican turning point in conceiving God's eternity and time. Then, I will show that if Barth began the construction of the way, a Trinitarian analogical understanding of time and eternity, Balthasar paved it more concretely. Finally, in chapter 8, I will present my own view of God's eternity and its relation to time in an alternative Trinitarian analogical way. In order to do so, first of all, I will re-define time as "the form of *life*" in the biblical and theological perspective. In my view, a kind of *via analogia* alone can more properly conceive the biblical understanding of the infinite qualitative difference of God's eternity as well as its real and positive relation to time. It will be constituted by the following Trinitarian triple analogy, *analogia vitae*, *analogia relationis*, and *analogia communicationis*, centered in the unique and the only true God-given analogy, Jesus Christ. Such a Trinitarian analogical approach, which is based on a dynamic and dramatic concept of the Triune God's Being-as-life-in-relation and His communicative action in eternity (i.e., the immanent Trinity) and time (i.e., the economic Trinity), can provide an alternative way in solving our own problem of the debate between traditional classical theism and contemporary panentheism, absolute timeless eternity and temporal everlasting duration. In this *via analogia trinitatis*, in contrast to both the absolute timeless (*via negationis*) and the everlasting view (*via eminentiae*) of God's eternity, I will present my own view that there is an analogical relationship between God's time (i.e., eternity) and human time: God's time as the form of His existence and the created and fallen human time as the form of human existence. Finally, I will propose that we can call God's eternity (i.e., God's time) the "true time" as the mode of the true Living Triune God's existence.

PART ONE

Time and Eternity in the Biblical, Historical, Philosophical, and Theological Debates

2

Biblical Understandings of Time and Eternity

Introduction

OUR SUBJECT MATTER, THE PROBLEM OF TIME AND ETERNITY, IS ESsentially a theological study, though requires a vigorous interdisciplinary dialogue among theology, philosophy, and natural science (e.g., physics and cosmology). Therefore, it is necessary to begin our study with an investigation of Scripture, which is the ultimate norm for our theological discussion. However, because of limited space, my intention in this chapter is not a comprehensive study of biblical terminologies or texts concerning the subject matter of time and eternity, but a general observation of previous studies[1] and, more significantly, a discovery of significant biblical and theological insights for the following study. Indeed, the purpose of this entire thesis is to discern an adequate theological conceptual framework to meaningfully systemize those essential biblical insights and truth(s) concerning the relationship and difference between God's eternity and time in particular, and God's relation to the world in general.

---

1. Concerning some biblical understandings of God's eternity and time, see the following: Cullmann, *Christ and Time*; Marsh, *Fulness of Time*; Rust, "Time and Eternity in Biblical Thought," 327–56; Boman, *Hebrew Thought Compared with Greek*; Manek, "Biblical Concept of Time and Our Gospels," 45–51; Muilenburg, "The Biblical View of Time," 225–52; Jenni, "Time," 642–49; Snaith, "Time in the Old Testament," 175–86; Wilch, *Time and Event*; Barr, *Biblical Words for Time*; DeVries, *Yesterday, Today and Tomorrow*; and Ricoeur, "Biblical Time," 167–80.

Some Significant Biblical Terminology and Texts for Time and Eternity

First of all, we need a preliminary knowledge of the biblical terms and their actual usage in order to properly understand some previous biblical scholars' studies on the biblical conception of time and eternity.[2] Yet, as we shall see, we must remember that the biblical terms do not give us a concrete or abstract (biblical) concept of time and eternity. In the Old Testament, even though we cannot find a definitive biblical term for time and eternity,[3] there are various lexical data from which we can determine the biblical conception of time and eternity: *yôm* (daylight, day, eschatological day, or today), *'ōpen* (right time, proper time), *'ēt* (a specific time, moment, or time in general), *'atth* (the present, now, at this time), *mô'ēd* (appointed time, meeting place or time, or time of feast), *zmn* (a specific time or hour), *r'š* (beginning of a certain time period), *qṣ* (end time), *qdm* (ancient time), *nēṣaḥ* (lastingness, perpetuity, or forever), *'ad* (eternity), *ôlām* (remote time, long time, duration, perpetuity, eternity, age, or world), *'lm* (hidden time or remote time), and so forth. However, our attention lies in the following two important words: *'ēt* and *ôlām*.

'Ēt

At first, the term *'ēt* is the most essential word in conceiving the Israelites experience of time.[4] The etymology is uncertain, but it is used in various meanings, "time, a point of time, a period of time, or the right time." According to A. Tomasino, the two conceptions of time as cyclical and linear, which are common in the ancient Near East and ancient

---

2. In this section, generally, I am indebted to the following works: Verhoef, "Time and Eternity," 1252–55; Tomasino, "*ôlām*," 345–51, and "'*ēt*," 563–67; Preuss, "*ôlām*," 530–45; and Kronholm, "'*ēt*," 434–51. In this study, without a special notice, I will use the translation of the biblical texts from *New International Version* (NIV), and all of Hebrew and Greek terms are transliterated.

3. Cf. Guhrt and Hahn, "Time," 841.

4. Cf. Tomasino, "'*ēt*," 563–67. For an extensive study of the term, *'ēt*, see Wilch, *Time and Event*. However, according to DeVries, since *'ēt* is not "the primary Hebrew term for expressing pure time relationships," rather the term *yôm* (the day) must be considered as "an essential clue in an understanding of the Hebraic concept of time." Idem, *Yesterday, Today and Tomorrow*, especially chapter 1, heading and 41–42.

Greece, were presented by the word, *'ēt*, in the OT. First of all, it usually does not mean "duration," but a "specific moment" or "a point of time" at which something happens, like *Zeitpunkt* in German.[5] That is to say, the essential meaning of *'ēt* is neither a natural division of time nor a special situation in the course of history, i.e., the chronological time. In the OT, therefore, time is not an abstract concept, but specific and concrete events and occurrences, for example: the time of her death (1 Sam 4:20—"when she is dying"), the time of the burnt sacrifice (2 Chr 29:27—"when the offerings were finished"), the time of old age (Ps 71:9—"Do not cast me away when I am old;" cf. 1 Kgs 11:4). In this sense, it is generally used to refer to "a specific occasion of peculiar quality and content."[6]

However, more significantly, according to P. A. Verhoef's observation, "Characteristic for the OT understanding of time is the faith in the eternal living God (Exod 15:18; Ps 90:1-2; Isa 40:28; Dan 12:7) as the Creator and Lord of time in all its dimensions;" for instance, "in the realm of nature (Lev 26:4; Deut 28:12; Job 5:26, 38:32; Ps 1:3), of Israel's cult (Exod 23:14-19), of the life span of humanity (Ps 31:15; Eccl 3:2, 7:17), and in general of Israel's past experiences of God's dealings with them, as well as of their future expectations."[7] In this sense, for the Israelites, the time of *'ēt* denotes specific events and concrete moments of God's providence in the course of history as a whole.

According to S. J. DeVries, a common phrase, "*bā 'ēt hāhi* (at that time)"[8] is frequently used in historical narratives for the past events (e.g., Gen 21:22—"At that time Abimelech and Phicol the commander of his forces said to Abraham;" Deut 1:9—"At that time I said to you," and 1:16—"And I charged your judges at that time;" cf. Deut 2:34; Josh

---

5. Cf. Jenni, "Time," 643.

6. Wilch, *Time and Event*, 102, cf. 32-33. After a full-length study, however, Wilch concludes that, "the word *'ēt* was used in the OT in order to indicate the relationship or juncture of circumstances, primarily in objective sense and only secondarily in a temporal sense, and to direct attention to a specifically definite occasion or situation" (p. 164).

7. Verhoef, "Time and Eternity," 1253.

8. In the OT, the parallel phrase, "*Bāyyôm hāhu* (in that day)" is also frequently used as a similar sense, see DeVries, *Yesterday, Today and Tomorrow*, 40-41. Through this whole work, in order to figure out the Hebraic relational concept of time, the author extensively analyzes the usage and the meaning of the phrase *Bāyyôm hāhu* (used to refer to the past as well as to the future), *hāyyôm* (used to refer to the present).

5:2, 6:26; 1 Kgs 8:65; 1 Chr 21:28), and for the future and eschatological events in prophetic narratives (e.g., Jer 4:11—"At that time this people and Jerusalem will be told;" Mic 3:4—"Then they will cry out to the Lord, but he will not answer them. At that time he will hide his face from them;" cf. Isa 18:7; Jer 33:15; Dan 12:1). Especially, in the eschatological context, the word designates the coming hour of judgment (e.g., Isa 13:22—"Her time is at hand;" Jer 46:21—"the day of disaster is coming upon them, the time for them to be punished;" cf. Jer 50:31, 51:33; Ezek 30:3). It is also used to designate the right time or the suitable favorable time for an event (e.g., 2 Sam 11:1—"In the spring, at the time when kings go off to war;" cf. Hag 1:2; Eccl 3:1–9), and a chronological time in some cases (e.g., 1 Sam 9:16—"About this time tomorrow I will send you a man;" 1 Sam 20:12—"I will surely sound out my father by this time the day after tomorrow;" cf. 1 Kgs 19:2; 20:6). In the LXX, it is generally translated by *kairos* (198 times), *hora* (24 times), and so forth.

Ôlām

In the OT, the terms which can denote the concept of eternity are *nēṣah*, *'ad*, *ôlām* (Hebrew) and *alām* (Aramaic), but the most important term is *ôlām / alām*.[9] The Aramaic term, *alām* (20 times in the OT) means "a remote time,"[10] and the various meanings of *ôlām* (440 occurrences in the OT) are similarly "farthest time, most distant time" or "a long time, constancy, forever, for all time."[11] However, in the latest biblical Hebrew and in Middle Hebrew, because of the influence of the Greek *aiōn*, *ôlām* was also used to denote some new meanings like "space of time, age, aeon, and world."[12] Therefore, according to the *NIV Exhaustive Concordance*, *ôlām* is actually translated in various ways: "forever, everlasting, eternal,

---

9. For this section, see Tomasino, "*ôlām*," 345–51; Verhoef, "Time and Eternity," 1254–55; and Preuss, "*ôlām*," 530–45. For a comprehensive study of the word, *ôlām*, see Jenni, "Das Wort *ôlām* im Alten Testament," 197–248 and 1–35, which are summarized in his article "Time," 642–49.

10. This term appears 20 times in the OT, mostly in the book of Daniel, and its meanings are "forever" (Dan 2:4, 44, 3:9, 5:10, 6:6, 21, 26), "forever and ever" (Dan 2:20), "eternal" (Dan 4:3, 34), and "everlasting" (Dan 7:14, 27). Cf. Verhoef, "Time and Eternity," 1254.

11. Cf. Jenni, "Time," 644; Preuss, "*ôlām*," 531; and Tomasino, "*ôlām*," 346.

12. Jenni, "Time," 644.

eternity, ancient, long ago, always, permanent, old, age-old."[13] In its essential meaning, however, the term does not clearly support any philosophical or theological interpretations of eternity between *everlasting* and *timeless* eternity.[14] That is, there are the two concepts of eternity, but the rest is a word study which tells us how the term *ôlām* is used in various contexts.

The term, *ôlām* is usually used to describe events extended into the most distant past as well as the most distant future from the present.[15] On the one hand, when it refers to the past, it generally means "ancient" in its construct phrases with other nouns such as in, "Your father's blessings are greater than the blessings of the ancient mountains" (Gen 49:26; cf. Hab 3:6), "Lift up your heads, O you gates; be lifted up, you ancient doors" (Ps 24:7, 9), and "Remember the days of old; consider the generations long past" (Deut 32:7). The expression with a proposition, *me ʿôlām* means "from ancient times, from antiquity," for example: Gen 6:4—"The Nephilim were on the earth in those days–and also afterward" and Ps 25:6—"Remember, O Lord, your great mercy and love, for they are from of old" (cf. Jer 2:20, 31:3; Mic 5:2). On the other hand, *ôlām* is also used more frequently to refer to the future (over 260 times). In many cases, it means "a future of limited duration" or "a single life span;" for example, "Then he will be his servant for life" (Exod 21:6; cf. Deut 15:7; 1 Sam 27:12), and "When the storm has swept by, the wicked are gone, but the righteous stand firm forever" (Prov 10:25). In this sense, according to J. Guhrt, the term is used characteristically to denote the whole duration of a man's life. Thus, he asserts that the essential meaning of *ôlām* is not remote antiquity, but rather an extent of time, a life span (e.g., Exod 21:6, 29:9; Deut 15:17; 1 Sam 1:22).[16]

---

13. Cf. Verhoef, "Time and Eternity," 1254.

14. Cf. Tomasino, "*ôlām*," 346.

15. In this sense, DeVries asserts that the Hebrews have two dimensional linguistic systems in respect to time. "That is to say, many of their words for the past and for the future were essentially the same. Unspecified time either in the past or in the future could be referred to as *ʿaz* or by means of the prepositional phrase, *baʿet hahi*. A particular time either in the past or future could be referred to by using *bayyom hahu*. Remote time either in the past or future could be *ôlām*. Thus, time does not move through a series of points from past through present to future; it simply diverges in two directions, past and future, from the present." Idem, *Yesterday, Today and Tomorrow*, 40.

16. Guhrt and Hahn, "Time," 827–28.

In many cases, *ôlām* means "unceasingness or perpetuity" of something. This can be seen in the description of different aspects of creation–the earth and the heavens (Ps 78:69—"He built his sanctuary like the height, like the earth that he established forever;" cf. Eccl 1:4; Ps 148:6), "the city of God"—Zion (Ps 48:8—"in the city of our God: God makes her secure forever"), the temple (1 Kgs 8:13—"I have indeed built a magnificent temple for you, a place for you to dwell forever"), the nations (Isa 47:7—"I will continue forever—the eternal queen"; cf. Ps 81:15), and God's anger/enmity (Mal 1:4—"They will be called the Wicked Land, a people always under the wrath of the Lord"). In the same sense, God's covenant with His people is described as perpetual or eternal by the phrase *běrît ôlām* (everlasting covenant) as seen in the covenant with Noah (Gen 9:12, 16—"I will see it and remember the everlasting covenant between God and all living creatures of every kind on the earth"); the covenant with Abraham (Gen 17:7—"I will establish my covenant as an everlasting covenant between me and you," cf. Gen17:13, 19; cf. Judg 2:1; 2 Sam 7:24; 1 Chr 16:15); and in the covenant with David (2 Sam 7:13, 16, 22:51; 1 Kgs 2:33, 45; 2 Chr 13:5), and so forth.

In some cases, the term *ôlām* is also used to denote divine titles and attributes, for instance: the divine title, *'el ôlām* (Gen 21:33—"there he called upon the name of the Lord, the Eternal God" [NIV] or "the everlasting God" [NASB]; cf. Isa 40:28; Dan 7:9) means "the Ancient One" or "Eternal One," which is a common epithet for the divine being in the ancient Near East.[17] In the similar sense, God's word (Isa 40:8—"The grass withers and the flowers fall, but the word of our God stands forever"; cf. Ps 119:89), His covenant (1 Chr 16:34; Ezra 3:11; Ps. 89:2; Jer 33:11), His protection for Israel (Deut 33:27), His righteousness (Isa 51:6), and His reign (Exod 15:18; Ps 9:7; Jer 10:10) are all described as eternal. In addition, it is also used to directly describe God Himself by the phrase *me ôlām 'ad ôlām* (from everlasting to everlasting) in Ps 90:2—"Before the mountains were born or you brought forth the earth and the word, from everlasting to everlasting you are God" (cf. Ps 41:13,

---

17. Tomasino, "*ôlām*," 346. Cf. Preuss, "*ôlām*," 537–38.

103:17; Neh 9:5).[18] In the LXX, the term *ôlām* (236 times) is translated as *aiōn / aiōnis* (95 times), *chronos* (4 times), *arche*, and so on.[19]

In the NT, too, we can find various terms for time and eternity:[20] *chronos* (time, period of time), *kairos* (time, a point of time, moment), *aiōn* (age, life-span, long time, eternity), *aiōnis* (eternal, forever), *aidios* (eternal), *hōra* (hour, time, a point of time), *hōraios* (at the right time, seasonable), *ēmera* (day), *sēmeron* (today), *nyn* (now), *arti* (just, immediately), *euthus* and *eutheōs* (at once, immediately). Among them, I will focus on the following three important words: *chronos*, *kairos*, and *aiōn*.

Chronos

We will first give attention to the Greek word *chronos*, which in general terms means "time, a period of time." According to G. Delling, in the Greek world, time is generally conceived in physical or cosmological perspective. We see this in Plato, Aristotle, and others.[21] In this sense, H.-C. Hahn says that *chronos* mainly denotes "the quantitative, linear expanse of time, a space or period of time, and is thus a term of the formal and scientific conception of time."[22] In classical Greek, *chronos* is used to denote "time" in the general sense either a longer or a shorter time. In the LXX, it is used about 100 times (e.g., for *yôm* 29, for *'ēt* only 4), with its chief occurrence in Maccabees, Isaiah, Daniel, and Job. Although *chronos* can denote a point of time like *hōra* and *kairos* (e.g., Jer 45:28; Neh 10:34, 13:31), it is generally used to designate a long period of time, a life-span, or a course of time (e.g., Josh 4:24, 24:29—"After these things, Joshua son of Nun, the servant of the Lord, died at the age

---

18. For a full study of the usage of the phrase, *'ad ôlām*, see Long, "Notes on the Biblical Use of *'ad ôlām*," 54–67.

19. Preuss, "*ôlām*," 533.

20. For this part, I am indebted to Sasse, "*aiōn*," 197–209; Delling, "*kairos*," 455–64, and "*chronos*," 581–93; and Guhrt and Hahn, "Time," 826–50.

21. Delling, "*chronos*," 585.

22. Guhrt and Hahn, "Time," 826. According to Jenni, "This word is clearly used for time as a measurable quantity, as is shown, indeed, by the quantitative adjectives such as *polus*, 'much,' or *mikros*, 'small,' which often accompany with it" (cf. Matt 25:19, "a long time"; Rev 20:3, "a little while"). Idem, "Time," 645.

of a hundred and ten;" Isa 23:15—"the span of a king's life;" cf. Isa 38:5; Job 32:6, 32:7), but never used for a timeless or other-worldly eternity.[23]

In the NT, *chronos* (54 occurrences, especially in the writings of Luke) generally means "a span of time," and thus it is used to denote a longer or shorter duration of a condition or an activity; for example, a long illness (John 5:6—"he had been in this condition for a long time"; cf. Luke 8:27, 29), a long time absence (Matt 25:19—"After a long time the master of servants returned;" cf. Luke 20:9), the period of activity (Acts 1:21—"the whole time the Lord Jesus went in and out among us"), any actual or projected length of stay (Acts 19:22—"while he stayed in the province of Asia a little longer"; cf. Acts 14:3, 15:33; 1 Cor 16:7), and the whole or parts of one's life-time (1 Cor 7:39—"A woman is bound to her husband as long as he lives"; cf. Gal 4:1). However, like *kairos* and *nyn*, it is also used to describe a short time (John 7:33, 12:25) or a point of time (Luke 4:5; Acts 1:6). According to H.-C. Hahn, however, a more theologically significant fact is that *chronos* is used to describe the salvation-history formula (cf. Acts 13:18, God's redemptive activity of forty years in the desert) and Christ centered understanding of time, "the *chronos*—pronouncements," which is described by the phrase, *to plērōma tou chronou* ("the fullness of time," Gal 4:4).[24] H. Schlier interprets the phrase, "the fullness of time," that "the moment in which the *chronos* is complete, in which time (in the sense of the passing time) reached its full measure, i.e., came to its end."[25]

Kairos

In a general sense, *kairos* denotes "time, a point of time, or a decisive moment." In classical Greek, the word is used to denote "the decisive or crucial place or point, whether spatially, materially or temporally."[26] In its temporal sense, it means a suitable time, the right time, or a favorable moment. It can be also used synonymously with other temporal terms, like *chronos, hōra, nyn,* or *semeron*. In the LXX, *kairos* is used primarily for *'ēt* 198 times among 300 occurrences. Although it refers to a decisive

23. Cf. Guhrt and Hahn, "Time," 841

24. Ibid., 843.

25. H. Schlier, *Der Brief an die Galater*, KEK 7 (1965), 194. As cited in Guhrt and Hahn, "Time," 843.

26. Delling, "*kairos*," 455. Cf. Jenni, "Time," 645.

or a more general moment of time, its usages illustrate an important characteristic aspect of the OT understanding of time. That is, "the creator, Yahweh, has created the whole of time and fills it in accordance with his will, and also fixes the individual *kairoi* (cf. Gen 1:14)."[27] God directs and allots *kairoi* for the natural creatures (cf. the heavenly bodies—Job 38:32; the weather—Lev 26:4; seasons for plants—Job 5:26; for animals–Job 39:1; and the time of feast and festivals—Exod 23:14) as well as for human activities (cf. one's life-span—Sir 17:2; the hour of birth—Mic 5:3; and of the death—Eccl 7:17). Furthermore, it is frequently used to describe God's saving activity in the past historical experiences (e.g., Deut 1:9—"At that time I said to you"; 1:16—"I charged your judges at that time"; cf. Deut 2:33; 6:6; 1 Chr 21:28; 2 Chr 7:8) and in the future (Isa 18:1; Jer 3:17; Dan 12:1; Joel 3:1) by the phrase, *en to kairo ekeino* (at that time).

In the NT, the word *kairos* is used 85 times to denote a particular point of time (e.g., Matt 11:25—"At that time Jesus said"; cf. Luke 13:1; Acts 7:20) as well as a shorter or longer time-span (Mark 10:30; Luke 18:10; 21:24; Eph 2:12; Rom 8:18) as is its usage in the OT. According to H.-C. Hahn, however, "The decisively new and constitutive factor for any Christian conception of time is the conviction that, with the coming of Jesus, a unique *kairos* has dawned, one by which other time is qualified" (e.g., Matt 8:29—"Have you come here to torture us before the appointed time?"; cf. Matt 26:18; 1 Tim 6:15; 1 Pet 1:11).[28] Thus, *kairos* is used to describe the decisive time of salvation and of grace; for instance, Mark 1:15—"The time is fulfilled (*hoti peplērōtai ho kairos*), and the kingdom of God is at hand; repent and believe in the gospel" (NASB); 2 Cor 6:2—"Behold, now is the acceptable time (*nyn kairos euprosdektos*), behold, now is the day of salvation (*nyn hēmera sōtērias*)" (NASB). Accordingly, with the time of Jesus Christ, the old age has passed away, and a new epoch, the fulfillment of the times, has begun. It will be finally and fully revealed in the last time (*en kairō eschatō*), at the time of Jesus Christ's return in glory (cf. 1 Pet 1:5; 1 Tim 6:14), and thus it also designates the time of the last and final judgment (cf. 1 Cor 4:5; 1 Pet 4:17–18; Rev 11:18).

27. Guhrt and Hahn, "Time," 835.
28. Ibid., 837.

Aiōn

The term, *aiōn*, generally means "long time, life-span, epoch, age, or eternity," and its related words are *aiōnios* (eternal, forever) and *aidios* (eternal). In classical Greek, it is used to denote a lifespan or a generation as well as the distant past (the beginning of the world) and the far future (eternity). In Plato's *Timaeus*, however, the meaning of *aiōn* was developed to describe a "timeless, ideal eternity, in which there are no days or months or years, [in contrast to] *chronos* as the time which is created with the world as a moving image of eternity (*eikō kinēton tina aiōnos*, Tim., 37d)."[29] Although Aristotle tried to conceive *aiōn* as "the relative period of time allotted to each specific thing," Plato's idea was succeeded to Philo, Plutarch, and Stoic philosophers.[30] In the LXX, *aiōn* is used over 450 times for the Hebrew word, *'ôlam*, to designate a long time, duration, or one's whole life-span (e.g., for individual men—Deut 15:17; Exod 21:6; 1 Sam 1:22; for generations—Exod 40:15; Ps 18:51; or for the whole nation—Josh 4:7; Judg 2:1), which is distinguished from *chronos* (a course of time) and *kairos* (a point of time for a unique event). In the inter-testamental Judaism, however, we can find a new conception of *aiōn* as a spatial sense like the doctrine of the worlds (*aeōns*).[31]

In the NT, *aiōn* is used over 100 times to describe "a long time, duration of time," "an age, epoch, era of the world" (e.g., Matt 13:39—"The harvest is the end of the age;" cf. Matt 28:20; Heb 9:26), or "the world in the spatial sense" (e.g., Mark 4:19—"the worries of this life;" 1 Cor 2:6—"but not the wisdom of this age or of the rulers of this age;" cf. Heb 1:2). It can also denote "a long distant time" in the past (Luke 1:70—"as he said through his holy prophets of long ago") as well as in the future (John 4:14—"But whoever drinks the water I give him will never thirst. Indeed, the water I give him will become in him a spring of water up to eternal life") like *'ôlam* in the OT. According to J. Guhrt, therefore, the usages of *aiōn* in the NT show its two sources, the OT and inter-testamental Judaism.[32] That is, on the one hand, the prepositional usages of

---

29. Sasse, "*aiōn*," 198.
30. Ibid.
31. Guhrt and Hahn, "Time," 829.
32. Ibid., 829. According to Jenni, "Temporal and spatial meanings cross over into one another in the Jewish apocalyptic doctrine of the two aeons; the existence of this doctrine has been attested ever since the first century BC. In addition to II Esdras and the rabbinical literature (*hzh ôlam*, 'this aeon'; *hb 'ôlam*, 'the coming aeon'], the NT also

aiōn reflect the usages of *ʿōlam* in the OT to designate the distant past (e.g., Luke 1:70, 3:21; Acts 3:21) or the future (Matt 21:19; Mark 3:29; John 4:14, 13:8; 1 Cor 8:13). On the other hand, when it is used as a noun, which means aeon, age (Matt 13:39–40, 49), epoch, or the world (Mark 4:19; 1 Cor 2:6), it can be considered as an influence of the Jewish apocalyptic thought. However, even in these latter cases, the usages of *aiōn* show the NT writers' characteristic understanding of history and eschatology. It is especially clear in the eschatology of Matthew and Paul in that they distinguished between "this age" and "the age to come" (Matt 12:32—"but anyone who speaks against the Holy Spirit will not be forgiven, either in this age or in the age to come;" cf. 2 Cor 4:4; Heb 9:9-10). In addition, John's characteristic use of *zoe aionios* (eternal life) reflects the meaning of *ʿōlam* (lifetime) in the OT, which essentially belongs to God.[33] Accordingly, J. Guhrt concludes that, "Surveying the usage of the word *aiōn, aeōn*, and the connected eschatology, one can establish that, with all the varied accentuations, *the NT speaks of eternity in the categories of time.*"[34]

Understandings of the Biblical Conception of Time

Concerning the biblical understandings of time and eternity, some significant classical studies are as follows: C. von Orelli (1871),[35] J. Schmidt

---

uses these concepts (Matt 12:32; Eph 1:21: 'not only in this age but also in that which is to come')." Idem, "Time," 645–46.

33. Guhrt and Hahn, "Time," 832.

34. Ibid., 833 (italics mine).

35. Conrad von Orelli, *Die hebräischen Synonyma der Zeit und Ewigkeit* (Leipzig: Lorentz, 1871). In this study, however, Orelli's exegetical analysis of the various biblical words was distorted by Friedrich A. Trendelenburg's Aristotelian philosophical conception of time, which is only conceivable through change and motion. In addition, Orelli's work is based on the principles of Max Müller's linguistic method, which maintains that, in language, there lies a petrified philosophy. Thus, it is essentially an etymological comparative study with other languages rather than an analysis of the actual usage of the words in the text itself. For criticisms on von Orelli's view, Barr, *Biblical Words for Time*, 86–100; Wilch, *Time and Event*, 2–4; and DeVries, *Yesterday, Today and Tomorrow*, 31–32.

(1940),[36] O. Cullmann (1950), and J. Marsh (1952) among many others.[37] Here, I will begin my investigation with J. Marsh's *The Fulness of Time*,[38] which may be the first full-length study of the biblical conception of time in English.

Realistic vs. Chronological Time

In *The Fulness of Time*, J. Marsh distinguishes between the concepts of "realistic" and "chronological" (i.e., measured or clock) time. According to him, the latter is essentially the conception of the modern Western man, and the former is the characteristic biblical conception of time.[39] It is clear in the NT by the distinction made between *kairos* and *chronos*, as well as in the OT, *realistic* time is represented by the term, *'ēt*. Chronological time is only a late development in the Hebrew thought, which was an influence of the Babylonians.[40] As he says,

> The contrast between "chronological" and "realistic" is exhibited in the NT distinction between *chronos* (measured time, duration) and *kairos* (time of opportunity and fulfillment). *Chronos* may refer to a short time ("a moment of time," Luke 4.5) or a

---

36. J. Schmidt, *Der Ewigkeitbegriff im Alten Testament* (Munich: Aschendorff, 1940). Although this work still provides useful exegetical sources for our subject, its weaknesses are its outdated etymological methodology and the dominated dogmatic concerns of the Roman Catholic Church. Cf. Padgett, *God, Eternity and the Nature of Time*, 24–26.

37. For a brief observation of the previous biblical study on the subject matter of time and eternity, see Wilch, *Time and Event*, 1–17; and DeVries, *Yesterday, Today and Tomorrow*, 31–39.

38. John Marsh, *Fulness of Time*. His view is summarized in his article, "Time, Season," 258–67.

39. Many biblical scholars agree with this "realistic" view of biblical conception of time; for example, before J. Marsh, H. Wheeler Robinson also asserted the same view that, in the OT, time is conceived "in the concrete, in its filled content, and not as an abstract idea. 'Time' is that which meets you on your path through life." Robinson, *Inspiration and Revelation in the Old Testament*, 109–11. For the similar view, see von Rad, *Old Testament Theology*, 99–119. In the NT, Manek analyzes the difference between the writing methodology and contents of the writings of Luke and the other Gospels by the different concepts of time, "realistic" (Mark, Matthew, and John) and "chronological" (Luke-Acts). See also, Manek, "Biblical Concept of Time and Our Gospels," 45–51.

40. According to Jenni, however, "The Egyptians and the Babylonians also know only expressions for the right, established point of time or for the long, unlimited duration, and use the word 'day(s)' for the most varied designations of time. The abstraction 'time' belongs among the accomplishments of Greek culture." Idem, "Time," 646.

long time ("time of forty years," Acts 13.18). The characteristic meaning of *kairos* can be seen in such phrase as "time of temptation" (Luke 8.13) and "time of harvest" (Matt 13.30). The OT has a word (*'ēt*) which can translate *kairos*; indeed, it has a rather rich variety of words with this meaning; but it has no word which can properly translate *chronos*.[41]

According to Marsh, therefore, "throughout the Bible the word 'time' is used realistically," which is closely linked to specific events (e.g., natural, social, religious, and of human life) and its contents (cf. Eccl 3:1–8).[42] It means an opportunity (a time, *'ēt* or *kairos*) for man's appropriate action. The more significant fact is that God the Creator ordains, provides, controls, and maintains all times of opportunity in the course of events for His own purposes (cf. Deut 11:14; Hos 2:11; Ps 104:27, 145:15; Jer 33:20). Thus, through an analysis of the usage of the phrases, "at that time" (*bā 'ēt hahi*) and "in that day" (*bāyyôm hāhu*) in the OT, Marsh says that "the whole of history, past, present and future, consists of times that are all, in the Psalmist's phrase, 'in God's hands' (Ps 31:15)."[43] According to Marsh's analysis, not only the usage of the word "time" (*'ēt* or *kairos*) but also the other temporal designations like "day," "year," "season," "moment," "now," "hour" are all defined by their content of God's action, which means a "concrete" or "realistic" conception of time of the Bible rather than chronological time. Indeed, as we have

---

41. Marsh, "Time, Season," 258. In his *Fulness of Time*, Marsh asserts that, "An examination of the Old Testament reveals one important fact–that there is no word for 'time' as chronological, ... The characteristic word for 'time' is, as we have seen, *'ēt*, which, like *kairos* in the New Testament, has no chronological meaning in itself. The abstract, chronological conception of time is foreign to the Bible" (p. 179, cf. pp.19–21). Rust also maintains the same view in saying that, "The Hebrew view of time we shall find to be realistic and existential." Idem, "Time and Eternity in Biblical Thought," 328.

42. Marsh, "Time, Season," 258, and see also, his *Fulness of Time*, 20–21. In the same sense, Pedersen says that, "For the Israelite time is not merely a form or frame. Time is charged with substance, or, rather, it is identical with substance; time is the development of the very events." Idem, *Israel: Its Life and Culture*, I–II, 487. Jenni also maintains the same view as follows: "The OT, and also the NT, does not know this abstract phenomenon 'time' as an idea of general validity. 'Time' is understood there essentially from the point of view of time content, not as a dimension in itself, which is filled with all kinds of content." Idem, "Time," 643. Cf. DeVries, "Meaning of Time," 1347. However, Kronholm warns to such a 'realistic' conception of time that "'*ēt* per se does not denote time having a definable content or quality. The actual content or quality of the time in question can be determined only from the particular context." Idem, "'*ēt*," 447.

43. Marsh, "Time, Season," 260.

seen, Marsh's view of a *realistic* understanding of biblical time against a "chronological" or "abstract" time seems to present an insightful aspect of the biblical concept of time. However, it is also true that, as J. R. Wilch rightly points out, "instead of demonstrating the true meaning of the historical event, Marsh robs it of its historicity by removing it from its unique place in chronological time and relegating it to a timeless category that is foreign to man's experience in his finite existence."[44]

Some years later, in following H. W. Robinson, J. Marsh, and J. Pedersen,[45] J. Muilenburg, too, asserts a "realistic" view in saying that, in contrast to the surrounding peoples in the ancient Near East and the Greeks, the Israelites believe that:

> [T]he mystery and meaning of time is not resolved by appeal to the cosmic world of space; among the other nations the heavenly bodies are deified and *chronos* spatializes time into extension and duration. In the one, time is grasped in terms of purpose, will, and decision; in the other the secrets of the stars are determined by "those who divide the heavens, who gaze at the stars, who at the new moons predict what shall befall you." (Isa. 47:13. Cf. also and especially 44:24ff)[46]

In Muilenburg's view, the biblical time is *concrete time*, thus there is "an interior, psychic relationship" between man and time.[47] Accordingly, for the Israelite, any speculation of an abstract idea of time or a precise measuring of the extent of time as the distance of duration are not their main concerns. Rather the essence of time lies in the concrete happenings or events and its specific content as a living relation. As he says,

---

44. Wilch, *Time and Event*, 9. In the same sense, Steensgaard points out that, for Israel, "Time was always the time of some particular thing, it was the course of event itself.... but we should note that there is no logical contradiction between the two views of time, the chronological and the concrete, filled-with-events. The Israelites, too, were able to subdivide time, and genealogy and chronology are important elements of the Biblical writings." Idem, "Time in Judaism," 64. Cf. Jenni, "Time," 646. Like Steensgaard and Jenni, Wolff, too, observes that there are not only realistic time but also chronological time in the OT. See, idem, *Anthropology of the Old Testament*, especially Chapter 10, "The Old Testament Concept of Time," 83–92. Westermann also emphasizes the significance of historicity in the OT. See his *Elements of Old Testament Theology*, 9–15.

45. Cf. Muilenburg, "Biblical View of Time," 234–35.

46. Ibid., 231. According to Muilenburg, there is a characteristic distinction between the spatial mentality of ancient Greece and the time mentality of Israel. Cf. idem, "Biblical View of Time," 229, 230, and 232.

47. Ibid., 236.

"Biblical time is comprehended not by its extent but by its immediacy, not by its quantitative measurements, but by its quality, by the nature of the content with which it is filled."[48] However, Muilenburg also emphasizes the significance of historicity for Israel, which is symbolized by "the *way* or *road*," the ongoing movement of time within Israel's life and its history from Egypt to Zion, from the beginning to the end. On this road of history, Yahweh is the Leader: "As the people of God, Israel moves through history under his lordship and sovereignty, his righteous leading and grace."[49]

In addition, more significantly, Muilenburg points out that, as the servant of God's word, the Israelite's characteristic grasping of the mystery of time lies in a dynamic, living experience of speaking and hearing, the communicative relationship between "I and Thou," between divine and human. First of all, to the Israelites, God always appears as the acting God, who is "active in time and event."[50] Therefore, Muilenburg insists that, "The concreteness of time in event is matched by the concreteness of speech in the word. What the eye was to the ancient Greek, the ear was to the man of Israel. The realm of maximum reality was that of speaking-hearing" (cf. Isa 1:2; Deut 32:1–2; Amos 3:1; Jer 1:4, 12).[51] In the Bible, there is an inseparable interrelationship between word and event, speech and time, because God's Word performs action and event, and "words move . . . only in time."[52] As Muilenburg says,

---

48. Ibid., 238. Cf. Jenni, "Time," 646.

49. Muilenburg, "Biblical View of Time," 234.

50. Ibid., 231.

51. Ibid, 239. While appealing to Boman and Straus, Muilenburg contrasts the *eye* for the ancient Greek to the *ear* for Israel. Cf. T. Boman, *Hebrew Thought Compared with Greek*. Concerning this point, Boman says that, "For the Hebrews who have their existence in the temporal, the content of time plays the same role as the content of space plays for the Greeks. As the Greeks gave attention to the peculiarity of things, so the Hebrews minded the peculiarity of events" (139); and "We *see* the spatial and *hear* the temporal" (142, italics original). Erwin W. Straus, "Aesthesiology and Hallucination" in *Existence: A New Dimension in Psychiatry and Psychology*, ed. R. May (New York, 1958): "The eye is the agent for identification and stabilization, the ear an organ for perceiving the actuality of happenings. There exist in phenomena a temporal co-existence of sound and hearing, whereas the visible is peculiarly time-less with respect to the gaze which can rest on it, turn from it, and turn to it" (p. 158). As cited in Muilenburg, "Biblical View of Time," 239 n. 24.

52. Muilenburg, "Biblical View of Time," 241. For the importance of the relationship between time and language, see Ebeling, "Time and Word," 261–66.

> Thus throughout the Bible the mystery of time is related to the mystery of life lived in speech.... God's Word rules and controls all of Nature, and the whole movement of history from beginning to end is understood by the activity of his Word. From creation to redemption His Word goes forth to accomplish his will and purpose.[53]

Linear vs. Cyclical Time

Another extensive study of the biblical conception of time was provided by O. Cullmann's celebrated work, *Christ and Time*.[54] In this work, Cullmann conceived of the characteristic biblical understanding of time as "linear time" in contrast to the "cyclical time" of Hellenism.[55] He says that, "the conception of the course of time which the New Testament presupposes by stating it in opposition to the typically Greek idea, . . . is the *upward sloping line*, while in Hellenism it is the *circle*."[56] Accordingly, for the Greeks, since time is conceived as "the eternal circular course in which everything keeps recurring," they seek redemption as to be freed from time itself, which is to transfer from this time-bounded world to the timeless beyond. In this way, in Greek thought, time is spatialized. However, for biblical and primitive Christianity, salvation is only accomplished within time itself. The following statement by Cullmann

---

53. Muilenburg, "Biblical View of Time," 241. Indeed, according to Muilenburg, throughout the Bible, "Nature, worship, personal experience; past, present, future; creation, revelation, eschatology; life, death, and responsibility are all of them interpreted and appropriated in the reality of [God's] words spoken and heard" (240).

54. Cullmann, *Christ and Time*, for our purpose, especially see 37–80.

55. Cf. ibid., 51–60. In his revised edition, against various criticisms, even though Cullmann emphasized the fact that time *per se* is not his main interest as well as the NT itself, he still maintains the conception of time as "linear structure" in the NT as the "framework" for his understanding of Christ-centered *Heilsgeschichte*, which is his main subject-matter in this work. See his "Foreword to the Third Edition" in *Christ and Time*.

56. Ibid., 51 (italics original). Against cyclical time as Eliade's mystic time and Mowinckel's understanding of time in cultic festival cycle, Rubenstein also insists that the ancient Israel, Rabbinic Judaism, and Christianity all conceived time as a linear or historical fashion, not cyclical fashion. Rubenstein, "Mythic Time and the Festival Cycle," 157–83. Cf. Eliade, *Cosmos and History*, 1–130, and Rudavsky, *Time Matters*, 2–3. However, according to Steensgaard, we can find both concept of time in the OT: the concept of historical (linear) time and the mythical time (cyclical) time. Steensgaard, "Time in Judaism," 63–108.

succinctly describes his understanding of redemptive history in the linear structure of biblical time:

> The New Testament knows only the linear concept of Today, Yesterday, and Tomorrow; all philosophical reinterpretation and dissolution into timeless metaphysics is foreign to it. It is precisely upon the basis of this rectilinear conception of time that time in Primitive Christianity can yield the framework for the divine process of revelation and redemption, for those kairoi which God in his omnipotence fixes, for those ages into which he divides the whole process. Because time is thought of as an upward sloping line, it is possible here for something to be "fulfilled"; a divine plan can move forward to complete execution; the goal which beckons at the upper end of the line can give to the entire process which is taking place all along the line the impulse to strive thither; finally, the decisive mid-point, the Christ-deed, can be the firm hold that serves as guidepost for all the process that lies behind and for all that lies ahead.[57]

Such a linear concept of the biblical time is based on Cullmann's understanding of the two typical terms, *kairos* and *aiōn*, which are the key words for understanding redemptive history. According to him, while *kairos* means "a definite point of time" which has a fixed content, *aiōn* designates "a duration of time," which is a defined or undefined extent of time. In the NT, on the one hand, *kairos* as a decisive point of time determined by the "sovereign divine power" has a special place in the execution of God's redemptive plan (cf. Acts 1:7, "the *kairoi* which the Father in his sovereign power has fixed"). The term, *kairos*, is used to designate not only the present (cf. Matt 8:29, 26:18; John 7:6; 1 Pet 4:17; Col 4:5) but also the past event (cf. Titus 1:3; 1 Pet 1:11) and the decisive moment of the eschatological drama (cf. Rev 1:3, 11:18; Luke 19:44, 21:8). Thus, the joining of *kairoi*, the specific moments or decisive periods of time in the light of God's plan forms "a meaningful time line," which constitutes redemptive history.

On the other hand, even though *aiōn* (like in the OT) has various meanings (e.g., age, world, universe, and eternity), its essential meaning is the extension of time and duration. Therefore, according to Cullmann, *aiōn* (eternity) has essentially "a time meaning," not the timelessness in Platonism.[58] Accordingly, he asserts that, "It means rather endless time

---

57. Cullmann, *Christ and Time*, 53–54.
58. Ibid., 47 and 61.

and therefore an ongoing of time which is incomprehensible to men; or, as it may be still better expressed, it means the linking of an unlimited series of limited world periods, whose succession only God is able to survey."[59] Accordingly, in Cullmann's view, there is not any opposition between time and eternity, rather both are complementary concepts as "limited time and unlimited endless time," which, as a whole, constitute "the upward sloping time line" for *Heilsgeschichte*. Conclusively, he insists that "time is not a thing opposed to God, but is rather the means of which God makes use in order to reveal his gracious working."[60]

However, in T. Boman's *Hebrew Thought Compared with Greek*, we can see a very different understanding of the Hebrew and the Greek conceptions of time.[61] First of all, according to Boman, the Greek conception of time is not "cyclical," but a "straight line." Indeed, the Greeks were interested in the precise measuring of time by the movement of the heavenly bodies (especially the sun), which is represented as "a straight time-line." Thus, Aristotle states that "time is the continuous dimension of successive movement" (*Physics*, iv. 11, 220a. 25f).[62] Accordingly, in contrast to Cullmann, Boman asserts that "the popular time conception of the Greeks is as rectilinear as our own," which is reflected in the verb-forms of the Greek language as "a straight time-line": the past—the present—the future.[63] Boman says,

---

59. Ibid., 46.

60. Ibid., 51. For critical examinations of Cullmann's view of "linear time" and "*aion* as the endless time," see Marsh, *Fulness of Time*, "Appendix," 174–81, and Malina, "Christ and Time: Swiss or Mediterranean?," 1–31.

61. Boman, *Hebrew Thought Compared with Greek*, for our purpose, especially see "Chapter III. Time and Space," 123–83.

62. Ibid., 125. However, Plato's conception of time is different from Aristotle's in that while the latter's interest is the physical time, the former's is the religious time. For Plato, the problem of the relation of time and eternity is a very significant one: "eternity for him is not endless astronomical time, but the life-form of the divine world to which God also belongs. Time designates for him the life-form of the world of nature, the world produced by God. By way of analogy with the origin of the world, which he defines as a reflection of divinity, Plato calls time a moving image of eternity (*Timaeus* 38). . . . This time can be divided into days, nights, months, and years; all these are *parts* of time. The past and the future are merely *forms* of time. We can see here how Plato already distinguishes between physical time and psychological time: divisible time is physical time, but present, past, and future are psychological categories. Yet both physical and psychological time belong to the sensible and transitory world in the same way as time, divine time, the archetype of time, is called eternity" (p. 127).

63. Ibid., 125. In this work, Boman especially pays attention to the tense system of

According to Aristotle, therefore, we must represent time by the image of a line (more accurately: by the image of movement along a line), either a circular line to indicate objective, physical, astronomical, and measurable time, or a straight line as demanded by the grammatical time of past, present, and future in which are laid those actions that we express in temporal terms. It is an illusion to believe that these two ways of looking at time are so different that they cancel each other out; they do have in common the principal feature, conception of time by the metaphor of a line, and what form the line takes is epistemologically of no importance or, in any case, only incidental.[64]

In Boman's view, however, the Hebrews grasped time not by the movement of the heavenly bodies as the Greeks did, but by its content: "The heavenly luminaries emit differing intensities of light and warmth, and in that way they define time" (cf. Gen 1:16, 18:1; 1 Sam 11:9; Neh 7:3). Thus, the Israelites thought that "time is determined by its content. Time is the notion of the occurrence; it is the stream of events."[65] According to Boman, the Hebrews believed that the determinants of time are "time-rhythms rather than time-cycles or time-lines," as we feel it in the rhythmic alteration between light and darkness, warmth and cold, the phase of the moon, and the seasons of the year.[66] For the Hebrews, therefore, all of the isolated units of time have their own "rhythm;" for example, the rhythm (period) of *a day*: "dull—bright—

---

verb in order to grasp the difference between the Hebrew and the Greek conception of time. That is, according to him, in Indo-Germanic languages and the Greek, the verb-forms have a straight time-line as "*the past*-(the pluperfect)-(the imperfect)-(the perfect)-*the present*-(the exact future)-*the future*." However, the Hebrew has only two tenses: "complete (perfect, *factum*) and incomplete (imperfect, *fiens*)." Cf. idem, *Hebrew Thought Compared with Greek*, 124–26 and 143–51.

64. Ibid., 125–26.

65. Ibid., 139. In the same sense, E. C. Rust more clearly explains this point as follows: "Even the matter of the division of the day, it is the realistic and not the abstract chronological motif that is found. It is not equal lengths of duration that matter. The sun has a life of its own, and the day is characterized in its parts by the contents of the sun's life. . . . In a similar way the months are differentiated on the basis of content in relation to the life of the moon and the life of nature. A month will be known by its content—the month of rain, the month of flowering, the month of ingathering. From seed time to harvest, month follows month in the course of year. As year follows year, the times, months and days which are differentiated by contents associated with the cycles of nature, recur." Idem, "Time and Eternity in Biblical Thought," 330–31. Cf. DeVries, "Meaning of Time," 1347–49.

66. Boman, *Hebrew Thought Compared with Greek*, 133–34.

dull" or "evening—morning—evening"; *a week*: "rest day—week day—rest day"; *a month*: "new moon—full moon (or moon phases)—new moon"; *a year*: "beginning—the months—return to the beginning"; *a human life*: "the earth—life–return to the earth." Accordingly, in the Hebrew thought, the general time-rhythm has the form of ~ - ~ (i.e., the pattern like A–B–A).[67] In addition, each of the lower time-rhythms passes into the higher time-rhythm: a day –> a week –> a month –> a year, and so forth. However, in the biblical conception of time, a long duration of time can be imagined as a successive straight line of the repetition of cyclical periods. In connection with this, Boman insists that the biblical concept of "eternity" (*ʿôlam*) is not timeless, but a "boundless time." He concludes that, therefore, "Even when *ʿôlam* is used of God, it suggests only unbounded time and does not refer to his being beyond time or to his transcendence."[68]

James Barr's Criticism of the Previous Studies

We have observed some classical understandings of the biblical conception of time. Their methodology, however, is basically an etymological study, which is now considered an outdated method of study. Since it is believed that the meaning of words is determined not in etymology, but in actual usage in specific textual contexts, there have been many recent criticisms concerning the etymological approach.[69] Accordingly,

---

67. Cf. ibid., 135.

68. Ibid., 151–52. While comparing the spatial structure of the Greeks and the temporal structure of the Hebrews, Boman says that, "Our notion of eternity (*Ewigkeit*) inherited from Plato is at base the same thing as the divine beyond (*Jenseits*), and is therefore rather more spatial than something temporal. The Hebrew language has no word for the same notion" (p. 151). Therefore, Boman corresponds the Hebrew *ʿôlam* to Anaximander's *apeiron* as a conceptual equivalent: "Anaximander called *to apeiron* the Infinite or more correctly the boundless, 'the undefined, eternal, and immutable first cause of all things whence they all arise and whither they return'. Thus the Greeks mean to define by *to apeiron* the first cause of all *things*, and the Israelites by *ʿôlam* mean to define the beginning and the end of all *becoming* or *having become*: *to apeiron* is the spatially extended boundless, but *ʿôlam* is the temporally extending unbounded. For the Greeks the content of the world was eminently spatial, for the Israelites it was principally temporal" (p. 153).

69. For criticisms of etymological approach in the biblical theology, see Barr, *Semantics of Biblical Language*, and *Biblical Words for Time*; and DeVries, *Yesterday, Today and Tomorrow*, 31–33 and 335–50. For example, concerning the etymological methodology, J. Barr rightly points out that, "The main point is that the etymology of a

traditional conclusions about the Hebrew view of time—"that the Hebrews were the first ancient culture to have a realistic view of history, or that the Hebrews conceived time as linear while other cultures such as the Egyptians and the Greeks conceived of time as cyclical, or that the Hebrews viewed time as substantial rather than chronological"—are now considered to be highly problematic.[70] We can see an exegetical and systematic criticism in J. Barr's *Biblical Words for Time*.[71]

J. Barr strongly criticized the earlier investigations, especially the studies of J. Marsh and O. Cullmann, which were focusing on lexical methodology rather than on the actual usages of the temporal words in the Bible (cf. his semantic principles). As we have seen, J. Marsh insisted that the biblical understanding of time is essentially *realistic*, not *chronological* time, which is clearly exhibited by the distinction between *kairos* (and *'ēt*, time of opportunity and fulfillment) and *chronos* (measured time, duration). However, according to Barr, the actual usage in the NT does not clearly show such a difference between the two words: cf. Mark 1:15//Gal 4:4; Acts 3:20//Acts 3:21; 1 Pet 1:5//1 Pet 1:20//Jude 18. In this comparison, Barr asserts that, "If there is a difference between *chronos* and *kairos* in the New Testament usage, it is clear that it cannot correspond to the distinction between *chronological* and *realistic* time as expounded by Marsh and Robinson."[72] Furthermore, Barr complains that the distinction of the two thinking modes about time as chronological and realistic contains inner contradictions. A more important fact is that it neglects the significance of the chronological system and the historicity in the Bible.[73]

The next analysis in Barr's work mainly lies in O. Cullmann's understanding of biblical time on the distinction and relationship be-

---

word is not a statement about its meaning but about its history; it is only as a historical statement that it can be responsibly asserted, and it is quite wrong to suppose that the etymology of a word is necessarily a guide to either its 'proper' meaning in a later period or to its actual meaning in that period." Barr, *Semantics of Biblical Language*, 109.

70. DeWeese, "God and the Nature of Time," 105.

71. James Barr, *Biblical Words for Time*.

72. Ibid., 23. For Barr's own research on the usage of the terms, *chronos* and *kairos*, see pp. 33–49. Actually, as he shows, the term *kairos* has been used in the post-classical Greek, the LXX and the NT for the general sense of "time," "period," or "course of time" rather than the specific meaning of "point of time" or "opportune time."

73. Cf. ibid., 24–33.

tween *kairos* (a point of time) and *aiōn* (a duration or extent of time).[74] In Barr's view, it is true that there seems to be a difference between the two terms, but kairos was also used as to mean an age or period in many cases (cf. Dan 9:27; Heb 9:9; Mark 10:30). Therefore, Barr asserts that "in biblical Greek usage it is impossible to state the distinction between *kairos* and *aiōn* as that between 'moment' and 'age' or 'period.'"[75] In this sense, we cannot simply determine by a word study "*the concept* of a biblical time" (e.g., the NT *kairos* concept as "decisive moment") because it has various meanings in its actual usages in the Bible. In this connection, it is more dubious that Cullmann figures out the essence of the NT understanding of time on the basis of the distinction between the two words, *kairos* and *aiōn*. Furthermore, these facts "greatly weaken or entirely destroy the connection between his theory of time and the facts of lexical usage in the New Testament," and thus the whole structure of his distinctive theology of *Heilsgeschichte*, too.[76] According to Barr, therefore, "The basic fault in the whole procedure is the assumption that the vocabulary stock is laid out in a pattern which correlates exactly with the mental pattern of New Testament thinking about time."[77]

Topological Approach to the Conception of the Biblical Time

While recognizing the valid aspects of J. Barr's criticism of the previous biblical studies of time, N. H. Snaith tries to suggest a topological approach to the biblical conception of time rather than an etymological word study: namely, "Circular Time, Horizontal Time, Vertical Time."[78] At first, according to Snaith, *Circular time* is a common conception of

74. Cf. ibid., 50–85. While analyzing Cullmann's work, Barr also deals with K. Delling (pp. 57–62) and C. von Orelli (pp. 86–100).

75. Ibid., 51.

76. Ibid., 54.

77. Ibid., 84.

78. Snaith, "Time in the Old Testament," 175–86. According to Snaith, "both Circular and Horizontal are proper and natural human ways of thinking about time, both inside and outside the Bible; but Vertical Time is the essentially Biblical element, and this in the way in which it is continuously impinging upon, invading and transforming the other two types of time. The first two are of the earth, earthy; the third is of the Lord and of heaven. The first two are 'natural' (*phuchikos*); the third is 'spiritual' (*pneumatikos*)" (p. 176). Interestingly, Snaith corresponds the following three Hebrew verbs, *naqaf* (come round), *'abar* (pass), and *paqad* (visit), to the Circular, Horizontal, and Vertical time respectively (cf. p. 176).

time not only for both the Hebrew and the Greek thought but also for the natural man in all the world. Circular time seems to be an obvious fact as we observe the apparent circular movement of the heavenly bodies in every day and the recurrence of the seasons in every year. More specifically even, is the close relationship between the annual cyclic movement of nature and the agricultural feasts in the OT (cf. Isa 29:1; 2 Sam 11:1). This circular time is therefore "pastoral and agricultural time." More significantly, for the Hebrews, circular time functions as "religious" time and "cult" time, and thus "with the development of religious institutions it becomes 'ecclesiastical' time"; for example, "Tishri 1, the festival of Trumpets; Tishri 10, the Day of Atonement; Tishri 15 (full moon of Tishri), the Feast of Tabernacles; later, Hanukkah and Purim; Nisan 14, Passover; Nisan 15, Unleavened Bread; seven weeks later, the Feast of Weeks: i.e., the three feasts and the festivals."[79] All of these denote the annual circular time also is the form of religious time.

Secondly, *Horizontal time* involves the passage of the years, which adds up one by one: "It is the ever-rolling stream of time, the straight line which goes on and on."[80] It can be described by the two words, *chronos* and *aiōn*. In the OT, the chronological time is important to fix the precise date of the significant past events and a datum-line of "regnal years" of the kings in 1, 2 Kings and 1, 2 Chronicles. We especially see this in Kings where the editor tried to synchronize the dates of the two kingdoms, Judah and Israel. For example, combining "The four hundred and eightieth year after the children of Israel were come out of the land of Egypt"(1 Kgs 6:1) with the fourth year of Solomon gives us a precise date of the year of the Exodus in the chronological sense.[81] More significantly, for the Hebrews, "time as a horizontal movement" is described by *'ôlam* and *aiōn*. In the OT, in its basic sense, "*'ôlam* means 'on and on and on,' or 'back and back and back.'"[82] Accordingly, it means "a long duration" for the indefinite past as well as for the indefinite future, and thus it means an ongoing continuing history. However, in light of Persian and ancient Zoroastrian eschatology, we can more adequately

---

79. Ibid., 177–78. Snaith insists that, "All these ceremonies belong to the original natural rites of the circular time of the seasons" (p. 179).

80. Ibid., 179.

81. Cf. ibid., 180.

82. Ibid.

understand the later usage and meaning of *'ôlam, aiōn* as "this age," "the age to come," or "world" in the Bible.

According to Snaith, finally, the idea of *Vertical time* is particularly the Hebrew contribution, and it is closely related to God's direct action and involvement in the world for His peoples.[83] Therefore, it can reveal the way of God's relation to human time. In the OT, God appears essentially not as "He who is," but rather "He who acts," and God is the One who continually "visits"(*paqad*) this world which He has made (cf. Ps 65:9). God continually visits peoples with His salvation (cf. Exod 3:16, 4:31; Ps 106:4; Luke 1:68). Snaith says that, therefore, "The Vertical downward motion continually invades both Circular and Horizontal time."[84] That is, for the Israelites, the circular time in the annual feast and festivals was changed in its meaning by God's "vertical action" from agricultural to religious; for instance, the Passover (cf. Exod 12:27; Deut 16:1), the Feast of Unleavened Bread (cf. Exod 12:33–34; Deut 16:3), the Feast of Weeks (Deut 16:9–12), and the Feast of Ingathering (cf. Lev 23:43).[85] In addition, God's visitations, the divine vertical actions into the horizontal time-line, take place not only in the great events of Israel's history but also in every day and detail of life. In this way, the circular and horizontal time are regularly and continuously invaded by God's vertical time. Thus, for the Israelites, the Vertical time, the divine NOW, is the decisive moment for the visitation of the living God, the Savior of Israel.[86] Accordingly, Snaith concludes as follows:

> [A]lways there is the now and NOW and *NOW* of the Visitation of God. But it is not momentarily that God "visits" the world of nature and of man, since the impetus of each Now infiltrates into the stream, both the circular stream of time and the horizontal stream of time. *Kairos* merges into *chronos* and *aiōn*;

---

83. Cf. ibid., 181.
84. Ibid., 182.
85. Ibid., 182–83.
86. Cf. ibid., 186. Snaith helped to clarify the idea of Vertical time understood by the Aristotelian concept of the Now in saying that: "This Now is . . . Vertical time, though properly it is not 'time' at all, nor is it 'space.' It is different from Circular time, which belongs to the world of created things, the movement of the earth and the cycle of the seasons. It is different from Horizontal time, which is subservient to cause and effect, and always within this same horizontal scheme. It is Now, neither circular nor horizontal, but, for the Israelites, infusing, animating and *saving* both. . . . It divides all time; it joins all time. It is 'of God,' and it is in and through this Now that He governs, directs, and saves this world of things and men" (p. 186).

more accurately, *paqad* enters into and gives life to both *naqaf* and *'ôlam*. The action of God in His world is ever renewing, ever continuing; always into and always in. Every point of the circle is a NOW of divine action. Every point of the horizontal line is a NOW of divine action. And both the circle itself and the line itself are the sphere of divine action.[87]

Paul Ricoeur's Understanding of the Biblical Time

Recently, Paul Ricoeur, too, criticizes the previously received view, "the radically dichotomous thesis," as we have seen in Boman's and Cullmann's conception of the biblical time in comparison with that of the Greek's, like linear vs. cyclic time or biblical *kairos* vs. Greek *chronos*, and their methodology of semantics and etymology which is used similarly in Kittel's dictionary.[88] According to his analysis, "the question itself was badly posed," and thus there are misunderstandings on both sides. For the Greeks, we must distinguish between popular religion and the mystery cults, and also between these and Greek philosophical thought. That is to say, the cyclic time of festivals and rites can be found in other cultures too, but not in the Greek thinkers. Secondly, the conceptions of time are very diverse among Greek thinkers: the poets, the historians, and the philosophers. Furthermore, in the ancient Greek historiography, there is no evidence for a conception of time as a whole of history nor a systematic inquiry of the relationship between the process of events and a universal chronology. Thirdly, then, we must not confuse the implicit conceptions of time in the epic or tragic poets with an explicit definition of time in the philosophers like Plato or Aristotle. Therefore, Ricoeur says that,

> Hence, when we speak of a Greek conception of time we must avoid the threefold error of reducing the cultural dimension to a literary factor, this literary factor to some philosophical expression, and this philosophical expression to some explicit thesis, even that of Plato or Aristotle.[89]

---

87. Ibid., 185.
88. Ricoeur, "Biblical Time," 167.
89. Ibid., 168.

This situation can also be said to be true in finding an understanding of the biblical conception of time. That is to say, according to Ricoeur, even though we can find a cyclic conception of time in the Hebrew culture on the cultural level, there are also many differences. Furthermore, on the level of nonphilosophical and philosophical formulations, there is "a total asymmetry." This means that we cannot compare directly the Hebrew and the Greek conceptions of time. Ricoeur therefore suggests an alternative understanding of biblical time according to the literary genres, the characteristic acts of discourse of the Bible: "narrative, legislations, prophecies, wisdom sayings and literature, hymns and psalms."[90] He believes that the interweaving of the different temporal qualities in the literary genres can properly designate "biblical time."

At first, the narrative genre (cf. Pentateuch) is a telling story, and thus it may emphasize the linearity in a single line of narrative time; for example, the narrative from the creation through the fall of human beings to the election of Abraham, and the narrative from the deliverance from Egypt through the desert and Sinai to the promise land. However, the narrative is not purely a narrative structure in which the writers add one by one, for there is the intersection of the law between narratives. Thus, the whole is constituted by the laws and the narratives. Accordingly, "this union results both a narrativization of ethics and an ethicization of the narratives."[91] In doing so, on the one hand, the history of the Israelites is ethicized under the law of God. Yahweh's law affected and was reinterpreted by generations again and again. On the other hand, the law also has "the dimension of an irrevocable anteriority," and this affects the "narrative anteriority." In this way, the narrative becomes something more than pure linearity, that is to say, it presents the "structure of a cumulative history."[92]

Secondly, if we look back toward the past in the tradition, the prophets look forward toward the future. The prophets are an interruption of the narrative temporal linear structure in anticipation of the catastrophic end of history and an eschatological new reversal of salvation. However, the prophecy is related to the narrative tradition in that "it is in relation to this illusionary projection of the tradition

---

90. Ibid., 170.
91. Ibid., 172.
92. Ibid., 173.

about the future that the prophet takes his hand."[93] Therefore, in the temporal structure, it is not foresight but "the irruption of real history" or "the confrontation of an ideological use of tradition with a truthful discernment of historical actuality."[94] In this sense, the anticipated something new in the future is not a radically different one, but "a sort of creative repetition of the old."[95] Hence, there is a temporal dialectic in the prophets between the old and the renewed.

Thirdly, there are other forms of nonnarrative writings: the Wisdom and the Hymn. Even though the wisdom writings are not interested in history, they conjoin everyday life and "immemorial" time (i.e., an eternal or everlasting time), which has always existed as an eternal one. In this way, the wisdom is presented in the form of proverbs as immemorial. Or, in Job, we are confronted with the immemorial human limit conditions as an ageless problem like the struggle of evil and good, the fault, failure, or suffering (i.e., the problem of theodicy), and so forth. According to Ricoeur, however, the wisdom writings are related to the narratives and the laws in their rejoining of ethical anteriority and reinforcing the archetypal traditional narratives. Accordingly, he says that, "In all these ways, the immemorial time of wisdom reinforces all the nonlinear feature of the great Yahwist narrative."[96]

Finally, the time of the psalms and of the Hymn envelopes all the other forms of temporality. That is to say, that in worship, all of the great narratives like creation, exodus, the law, salvation and wisdom are re-actualized today. Meaning, therefore, that the time of hymn, the psalms, is the same as that of today and everyday. In this way, according to Ricoeur, biblical time can be properly conceived in the interweaving throughout the canonical texts in various genres, which is a synchronic and inter-textual reading of the Hebrew Bible. In doing so, it presents that "the model of biblical time rests on the polarity between narrative and hymn and on the meditation brought about between telling and praising by the law and its temporal anteriority, prophecy and its eschatological time, and by wisdom and its immemorial time."[97]

---

93. Ibid., 174.
94. Ibid.
95. Ibid., 175.
96. Ibid., 178.
97. Ibid., 180.

Understandings of the Biblical Conception of God's Eternity

We can find various interpretations of the biblical conception of God's eternity among biblical scholars: timeless eternity (H. Sasse), everlasting eternity (O. Cullmann, S. J. DeVries), the primeval time (E. C. Rust), and an undetermined conclusion (J. Marsh, J. Muilenburg).

God's Eternity as "Timelessness"

First of all, according to H. Sasse, "*aiōn* has the full significance of eternity when it is linked with the concept of God. Apart from the doxologies, this is the case in the description of God as the eternal God."[98] That is to say, even though there is a very simple conception of God's eternity in the older writings of the OT as *'el 'ôlam*, "the God of old" (Gen 21:33), we can find a developed idea of God's eternity; for example, Isa 40:28, *'elōhim 'ôlam (theos aiōnios)*—"the eternal God," Rom 16:26, *ho aiōnios theos*—"the eternal God," and 1 Tim 1:17, *ho basileus tōn aiōnōn*—"the eternal king" (cf. Jer 10:10). Furthermore, in view of Sasse, the phrase "I am the first and the last" (cf. Isa 44:6) clearly describes the eternity of God. Therefore, he insists as follows:

> As the Creator and Consummator God is the eternal One. His eternal being stretches beyond the time of the world. He is from eternity to eternity. Before the world was created, He was; and when heaven and earth have vanished, He will be. Thus the unending eternity of God and the time of the world, which is limited by its creation and conclusion, are contrasted with one another.... the eternal being of God is represented as pre-existence and post-existence. Yet in later Judaism there are also attempts to make eternity the complete antithesis of time.... Here eternity is thought of as *timelessness*, as in Plato.[99]

According to Sasse, there is a conceptual development for God's eternity in the later writings of the OT and the later Judaism, and it is carried over into the NT. Thus, in the NT, God's eternity is conceived as "the opposite of this cosmic time which is limited by creation and conclusion." Yet, in the NT, there is a new development in that the con-

---

98. Sasse, "*aiōn, aiōnios*," 200.
99. Ibid., 201–2 (italics mine).

ception of God's eternity was extended to Jesus Christ, as we see in the notions of the pre-existence of Him (cf. Heb 1:10–12, 13:8; Rev 1:17–18, 2:8, 22:13). Accordingly, for Sasse, "In the NT, too, eternity is thought of as the opposite of this cosmic time which is limited by creation and conclusion. Statements concerning the eternal being and action of God are thus expressed in terms of pre- and post- (cf. *pro* and *apo tōn aiōnōn*, 1 Cor 2:7; Col 1:26; Eph 3:9; *pro kataboles kosmou*, John 17:24; Eph 1:4; 1 Pet 1:20)."[100] However, it is noteworthy that, recently, there is a tendency for some biblical scholars to reject the idea of the timeless eternity of God, while maintaining an undetermined conclusion of the meaning of God's eternity, as to whether or not it is timeless or everlasting.

God's Eternity as "Everlasting Time"

Notably, as we have seen, it was O. Cullmann among many other contemporary biblical scholars who clearly interpreted God's eternity in the temporal sense as "everlasting time." Cullmann thoroughly understands the meaning of *aiōn* in a temporal sense against Platonic timelessness. As Cullmann states, "Eternity, accordingly, is designated by the term *aiōn*, which carries a time meaning."[101] In his view, we cannot discover the concept of timeless eternity from biblical linguistic usage, and thus it comes only the influence of Platonic philosophy. He asserts that,

> To Primitive Christianity, as to Judaism, the Greek manner of distinguishing between time and eternity is quite foreign. . . . Eternity is the endless succession of the ages (*aiōnes*). . . . Thus time and eternity share this time quality. Primitive Christianity knows nothing of a timeless God. The "eternal" God is he who was in beginning, is now, and will be in all the future, "who is, who was, and who will be" (Rev 1:4). Accordingly, his eternity can and must be expressed in this "naïve" way, in terms of *endless* time.[102]

---

100. Ibid., 202.

101. Cullmann, *Christ and Time*, 46–47.

102. Ibid., 62–63 (italics mine). He also says that, "eternity, as meant in this linguistic usage, is not to be interpreted in the Platonic and modern philosophical sense, where it stands in contrast to time; it must rather be taken as endless time. . . . It means rather endless time and therefore an ongoing of time which is incomprehensible to men; or, as it may be still better expressed, it means the linking of an unlimited series of limited world periods, whose succession only God is able to survey" (45–46).

According to Cullmann, therefore, eternity is an endless time as an entire unending extension, which is unlimited in both the backward and the forward direction. The only difference between eternity and time is the fact that the former is unlimited endless time, and the latter is limited. In the following statements, Cullmann succinctly summarizes his view of time and eternity:

1. Time in its entire unending extension, which is unlimited in both the backward and the forward direction, and thus is "eternity."

2. Limited time, which lies between Creation and the eschatological drama, and thus is identical with the "present" age, "this age."

3. Periods of time that are limited in one direction but unlimited in the other, and specifically:

   a. The period to which the phrase *ek tou aiōnos*, "out of the age," points back, i.e., the time that lies before the Creation. On the side of Creation it has an end and so a limit; but in the backward direction it is unlimited, unending, and only in this sense is it eternal.

   b. The time that extends beyond the end of the present age (*aiōn mellōn*, the "coming age"). It thus has in the so-called eschatological drama its beginning and so a limit; but in the forward direction it is unlimited, unending, and only in this sense is it eternal.[103]

Simon J. DeVries also follows this approach of interpreting the OT and NT idea of God's eternity as everlasting.[104] According to him, Scripture does not know and participate in the abstract speculation on eternity in which God lives as a splendid isolation state. The idea of timelessness is borrowed from ancient Greek philosophy. For DeVries, therefore, "to the people of the Bible—Israelites and Jewish Christians living out of the Hebraic heritage—it would have been impossible to even think of eternity as a timelessness before and after time."[105] The Hebrew words and their equivalents in the NT, which are translated "eternal" and "eternity," only mean an endlessness or perpetuity, and do

---

103. Ibid., 48.
104 Cf. DeVries, "Meaning of Time," 1347.
105. Ibid.

not have the negative conditionedness as a mark of every finite creature. Accordingly, DeVries insists that,

> To say God is eternal from biblical standpoint means that His existence brackets cosmic time. He was there at the beginning of all created things; He will be there when temporal reality ends; and He is present at every moment in between. This is the true meaning of eternity. Before, above, and beyond all creaturely existence, God is; yet He is intimately close in every temporal experience—not passively but actively—governing all His creatures and calling each person, to whom He has given the power of free choice, to obey and believe.[106]

God's Eternity as "the Primeval Time"

E. C. Rust also essentially understands eternity in the temporal sense, but sees a difference between God's eternity and our time. According to him, our time is characterized by its transience, and filled with pain, anxiety and death. As he says, concerning our human time, that:

> It is a broken and separated time, in which the transient present alone has reality, separating on its razor edge the past from the future. The future is continually committing suicide upon that razor edge and tumbling into the realm of the "already become." Only in the "now," in this flux of becoming, is decision possible, and yet its pattern is the pattern of death. To some measure we are able to rise above it, to hold to the past by memory and anticipate the future in imagination, yet true and full integration eludes the natural man. He is slave of *chronos*, of the deadly succession of "nows" in which his hopes are frustrated and his pasts seem irrecoverable.[107]

However, God's mode of being is far different from our form of existence in that "God is no slave of time, no victim of transience and succession, like his creation. It is he who orders the times of men, and all times are under his control."[108] That is to say, there is a qualitative dif-

---

106. Ibid.

107. Rust, "Time and Eternity in Biblical Thought," 351.

108. Ibid., 343. Rust also says that, "Time is, indeed, ours because God grants it to us. On the other hand, God's eternity is entirely his. He does not need time as something outside himself in order to live. His eternity is very life, the expression of his activity" (p. 354). He further explains the difference between God's eternity and our time as

ference between God's time (i.e., eternity) and our created world time. Therefore, Rust insists this as follows:

> [God's] eternity is time with a difference, and the difference is more than a quantitative one. Eternity is more than the mere summation of "times"; it is *the primeval time* in which all have their ground. In this sense, too, eternity would quite clearly be expressive of God life, for it is he who controls and grants all times. He is to be characterized by "everlastingness," but his "everlastingness" is the primeval whole of time that embraces all times.[109]

Accordingly, for Rust, since God's eternity embraces all times, time has a place in eternity. That is to say, even though God's eternity transcends our human time, it does not negate our world-time. Therefore, "He is Lord of his eternity as he is Lord of our time, ordaining our *kairoi* and filling them with his presence."[110]

God's Eternity and Undetermined Conclusion

J. Marsh maintains an undetermined conclusion on the meaning of God's eternity in the Bible. Since the Bible does not have an abstract term (cf. the word, *'ôlam*, is also a temporal term in its essential sense) to depict the being and existence of God, in spite of its limits, it cannot but describe God's being and His eternity by limited words in various formulae. Thus, in Marsh's view, the various phrases of *'ôlam*, "throughout generations," "from everlasting to everlasting," or the plural form of *'ôlam*, must not be thought of as a literal addition of unbounded temporal duration in a quantitative sense (contra. O. Cullmann), but rather

---

follows: "God's eternity is time without limits. Yet it is not subject to the ambiguities, transitoriness, and frustrations of creaturely time. It is significant that his eternal being is pictured in the images of pre-existence and post-existence. He was before the world created (Ps 89:2), and he will be when heaven and earth are gone (Ps 101:26ff). Thus his unending eternity stands over against the time of the world, limited by creation and the Day of Jehovah. Furthermore, there is a permanence in God which persists behind the changes of our temporal existence" (p. 341).

109. Ibid., 342 (italics mine).

110. Ibid., 353. Cf. Ebeling's the following statement, "Eternity, theologically understood, is God's lordship of time getting linguistically expressed in the Word of God." Idem, "Time and Word," 261.

it must be read as a poetic emphasis which is to designate "a qualitative difference."[111] Considering Ps 90:2, therefore, he says,

> The Psalmist is not saying, we think, that God's time is the same as ours, only of infinite duration; He is saying that God's time is not as ours, and that while the hyperbolic use of our temporal language may bring us near to the point of apprehension, the wonder and mystery of his being lie beyond our full apprehension. If this be so (and the point, I admit, is an appeal to poetry), then the appearance of aio3nes in the New Testament is to be understood not as an indication that time is endless, but God's time is other than ours, and that the expresses of poetic speech are a better instrument of apprehension than the dull sobriety of prose.[112]

We can find various biblical texts concerning God's eternity in the Bible, and some significant texts are as follows:

—Exod 15:18, "The Lord will reign for ever and ever."

—Ps 90:2, "Before the mountains were born or you brought forth the earth and the world, from everlasting to everlasting you are God."

—Ps 145:13, "Your kingdom is an everlasting kingdom, and your dominion endures through all generations."

—Eccl 3:11, "He has made everything beautiful in its time. He has also set eternity in the hearts of men; yet they cannot fathom what God has done from beginning to end."

—Isa 44:6, "This is what the Lord says—Israel's King and Redeemer, the Lord Almighty: I am the first and I am the last; apart from me there is no God."

---

111. Marsh, "Time, Season," 266. He continues that, "Thus the OT uses a temporal term to show that throughout the course of time there is active a supra-temporal being whose beginning and end baffle our comprehension, but whose effective reality we may know in his control of events, as of the world in which they occur" (Ibid.). See also Henry, "Eternity," 372.

112. Marsh, *Fulness of Time*, 175. He also says, "Neither is there any compelling reason for interpreting 'ôlam in the Old Testament or aiōn in the New in terms either of a timeless eternity or of an endless ('eternal') time. What is asserted in the New Testament is that no duration, no 'age' is 'outside' God; he rules over all ages, and in particular he has ruled in human history to accomplish the promised end of history while the process is still going on" (p. 180).

—Eph 1:4, "For he chose us in him before the creation of the world to be holy and blameless in his sight."

—1 Tim 1:17, "Now to the King eternal, immortal, invisible, the only God, be honor and glory for ever and ever."

—1 Pet 1:20, "He was chosen before the creation of the world, but was revealed in these last times for your sakes."

As we see, all of these biblical texts can be interpreted as involving either timeless eternity or everlasting eternity, but the reversal is also true and does not clearly support both views. After a study of biblical teaching on God's eternity, therefore, J. S. Feinberg concludes as follows:

> First, no specific word or phrase in itself necessitates either atemporal or temporal eternity. Second, various assertions about God's eternity might at first glance seem to necessitate an everlasting or sempiternal God, rather than an atemporally eternal deity. However, no passage which discusses God's eternity addresses the metaphysical question of the nature of that eternity, i.e., whether it is temporal or atemporal. In fact, many passages about God's eternity actually intend to teach something other than God's relation to time—such as God's sovereign authority or his dependability. Consequently, I conclude that while Scripture affirms divine eternity and teaches that this means unending existence always, we cannot answer from the Bible alone whether God's eternity is temporal or atemporal in nature.[113]

In the same sense, J. Muilenburg, too, reserves a clear conclusion on the meaning of God's eternity. According to him, in the Bible, it is clear enough that "God is transcendent to man's time" because God created man's time and will end it. However, the qualitative difference between time and eternity does not directly mean that "the contrast is between time and non-time" or "God is timeless."[114] Muilenburg even states that, therefore, "What God's reality is like apart from time is a mystery not only forever veiled from us, but one which does not belong to the givenness of revelation."[115] We can finally conclude that, in my judgment, what is clear in the Bible is that the mode of God's existence as

---

113. Feinberg, *No One Like Him*, 263–64.
114. Muilenburg, "Biblical View of Time," 250–51.
115. Ibid., 251.

eternity is different from the mode of the creature's existence as time. For example, it is expressed in 2 Pet 3:8 as follows: "With the Lord a day is like a thousand years, and a thousand years are like a day" (cf. Ps 90:4). However, to pursue the question of the exact meaning of God's eternity beyond this is just a theological or a philosophical problem, not a biblical study.

A Canonical Approach to the Biblical Conception of Time and Eternity

Up to now, we have seen various contemporary understandings of the biblical conception of time and eternity. However, in my view, in order to properly understand this, we must first establish a canonical approach to the biblical conception of time and eternity alongside the theological exegeses of the concrete biblical texts. The canonical approach means that we must deal with the Bible as a whole. Then, it reveals the whole structure of the biblical time as well as the meaning of God's eternity. It can be briefly constituted as the following three aspects: the time of creation, the time of providence and redemption, and the time of consummation.

The Time of Creation

The Bible, the Word of God, begins with the following declaration: "In the beginning God created the havens and the earth" (Gen 1:1). Concerning this passage, we have two significant problems for our study. At first, does the Bible clearly teach the doctrine of *creatio ex nihilo*?[116] If so, secondly, does the doctrine of *creatio ex nihilo* mean the absolute beginning of time itself, and thus, does it necessarily mean the timeless God's eternity? In other words, more specifically, the problem is whether God's creation of the world is *in* or *with* time? According to J. S. Feinberg, "Creation *ex nihilo* is one of the trademarks of the Christian

---

116. For discussions on this topic, see Donnelly, "Creation *ex nihilo*," 200–217; Goldstein, "Origins of the Doctrine of Creation *Ex Nihilo*," 127–35; Currid, "Examination of the Egyptian Background of the Genesis Cosmogony," 18–40; Young, "*Creatio Ex Nihilo*," 139–51; Senor, "Divine Temporality and Creation *Ex Nihilo*," 86–92; May, *Creatio Ex Nihilo*; Copan, "Is *Creatio Ex Nihilo* a Post-Biblical Invention?," 77–93; Copan and Craig, *Creation out of Nothing*.

doctrine of creation."[117] In the history of theology, it was Augustine who seriously struggled with the problems and gave for the first time a systematic theological explanation for it. Concerning the origin of the universe (cosmogony), against Platonic dualism and Plotinian emanationism, Augustine asserted the doctrine of *creatio ex nihilo* based on his exegesis of Gen 1:1 in his *Confessions*.[118] According to Augustine, before creation, there was nothing (xi.4). God created the heaven and the earth (the whole universe) not from "a material already existent," but "out of nothing" by His Word, the Son of God (xi.5, 6, 7; xii.7; xiii.33). Then, what does *berēšît* (in the beginning) mean? It means the very beginning of time itself. As Augustine says, "Thou hast made all time; and before all times Thou art, nor in any time was there not time. At no time, therefore, hadst Thou not made anything, because Thou hadst made time itself. And no times are co-eternal with Thee, because Thou remainest for ever" (xi.13, 14). In his *The City of God*, Augustine more clearly affirms that "the creation of the world and the beginning of time both occurred simultaneously, and that the one did not come before the other."[119] In this way, Augustine insisted on not only *creatio ex nihilo* (creation from nothing) but also *creatio cum tempus* (creation with time).[120]

Recently, however, there is a tendency to reject the doctrine of *creatio ex nihilo* as a biblical teaching in theological as well as scientific perspectives.[121] For instance, a philosopher of science, I. G. Barbour asserts that "Creation 'out of nothing' is not a biblical concept," but a post-biblical development against gnosticism.[122] Gerhard May proposed the same idea in his *Creatio Ex Nihilo*.[123] According to May, the

---

117. Feinberg, *No One Like Him*, 552.

118. Augustine, *Confessions*, especially, books 11 and 12.

119. Augustine, *City of God*, xi.7.6 (heading).

120. Cf. Gunton, *Triune Creator*, 73–86.

121. This topic, creation *ex nihilo*, is a red-hot issue in discussions between theology and science. See Hawking, *Brief History of Time*; Russell, et al., eds., *Physics, Philosophy, and Theology*; Peters, ed., *Cosmos as Creation*; Drees, "Quantum Cosmologies and the 'Beginning,'" 373–96; Deltete, "Hawking on God and Creation," 485–506; Russell, et al., eds., *Quantum Cosmology and the Laws of Nature*; Craig and Smith, *Theism, Atheism, and Big Bang Cosmology*; Zycinski, "Metaphysics and Epistemology," 269–84.

122. Barbour, *Issues in Science and Religion*, 384. Cf. Gilkey, *Maker of Heaven and Earth*, 45–76; Peacocke, *Creation and the World of Science*, 77–85; McMullin, "Natural Science and Belief in a Creator," 49–79.

123. Gerhard May, *Creatio Ex Nihilo*.

idea of *creatio ex nihilo* in itself is "not demanded by the text of the Bible," but it was invented by the second century Church Fathers (e.g., Tatian, Theophilus of Antioch, Irenaeus) because of a theological need to prevent the Church from gnosticism and the Greek metaphysical cosmology.[124] Yet, as P. Copan points out, May's work is essentially a patristic study, which is not based on biblical exegesis.[125]

Thus, now, we must turn to the biblical evidences for the subject matter. According to G. J. Wenham, in Gen 1:1, "*berēšît* refers to the beginning of time itself, not to a particular period within eternity (cf. Isa 40:21; 41:4)."[126] However, for him, considering the verb *bārā* (to create), even though it is used solely for God's activity in Hebrews, the text itself does not necessarily mean "creation out of nothing." Yet, Wenham says, "That God did create the world out of nothing is certainly implied by other OT passages which speak of his creating everything by his word and his existence before the world (Ps 148:5; Prov 8:22–27)."[127] A. Neher affirms that "the biblical narrative of the Creation which simultaneously relates two births, that of the cosmos and that of time."[128] Thus, even

---

124. Cf. May, *Creatio Ex Nihilo*, 24, 26–38, and 148–78. However, at least, we can find a clear affirmation of the idea of creation *ex nihilo* in 2 Macc. 7:28. According to Ellingworth, it "strongly affirms *creatio ex nihilo*: 'God made [the sky and the earth] out of nothing' (*ex ouk onto3n*)." Idem, *Epistle to the Hebrews*, 569. On the other hand, Goldstein suggests that the origin of creation of *ex nihilo* is "the belief in bodily resurrection" of Jews and Christians. Idem, "Origins of the Doctrine of Creation *Ex Nihilo*," 129. For the Jewish Rabbinic conception of time and creation, see Winston, "Book of Wisdom's Theory of Cosmogony," 185–202. According to Winston, the doctrine of *creation ex nihilo* is missing in Jewish-Hellenistic literature, and, in rabbinic literature, it appears only in a polemical context (p. 186). Thus he concludes that it is not Jewish but the influence of Christian-Muslim thought (p. 199). Cf. Rudavsky, "Creation and Temporality in Medieval Jewish Philosophy," 458–77, and his *Time Matters*, 4–10 and 23–57.

125. Copan, "Is *Creation Ex Nihilo* a Post-Biblical Invention?" 87.

126. Wenham, *Genesis 1–15*, 14. Cf. Currid, "An Examination of Egyptian Background of Genesis Cosmogony," 30.

127. Wenham, *Genesis 1–15*, 14. For a similar view, see Eichrodt, *Theology of the Old Testament*, vol. 2, 101, and Westermann, *Genesis*, 7. For more biblical evidences, see Copan, "Is *Creatio Ex Nihilo* a Post-Biblical Invention?" 89–92.

128. Neher, "View of Time and History in Jewish Culture," 149. He continues that, "the very term with which the account begins, *bereshit*, indicates that what seemed essential to the narrator of Genesis was not what was at the beginning, but the fact that there was a beginning. *Bereshit* does not mean 'at the beginning,' but 'in a beginning.' The creative act occupies a period of time. God begins to create, and he spreads creation over seven days. The primordial element is 'time' itself. Creation was manifested

though the word itself, just like the term "Trinity," does not appear in the written biblical text, other biblical evidences like Heb 11:3, Rom 4:17 (cf. 2 Macc 7:28) lead us to conclude that the doctrine of *creatio ex nihilo* and *creatio cum tempus* is a concrete biblical teaching.[129]

However, for our purpose, one more significant question remains. That is, could we logically assume that the doctrines of *creatio ex nihilo* and *creatio cum tempus* necessarily entail the idea of the "timeless" eternity of God? We normally think, as did Augustine, that it is *prima facie* a timeless eternity.[130] However, the answer is unfortunately uncertain. For example, according to W. P. Alston among many others, the doctrine of *creatio ex nihilo* logically and necessarily entails the idea of the timelessness of God, since the idea of a temporal God and the doctrine of *creatio ex nihilo* are incompatible.[131] However, while distinguishing between "standard" and "accidental" temporalism, T. D. Senor suggests that the latter position, still, can maintain the idea of a "temporal" God with the doctrines of *creatio ex nihilo* and *creatio cum tempus*. That is to say, according to "accidental temporalism," since time is an aspect of the created order, God is simply timeless before creation, but after that God has chosen "temporality" as His own.[132]

Furthermore, E. Jenni also asserts the idea of *creatio cum tempus* in saying that, "God's dominion over time is most clearly revealed by the fact that he created time along with the universe as its creature form of existence. Time has its beginning, from which point the days can be numbered (Genesis 1) . . . Together with the created world, earthly time, determined by the stars (Gen 1:14), will also end or be absorbed in

---

in the appearance of time. This time is entirely new. That is the significance of the verb *bara*, which designates the creative act. Throughout the Bible this verb is reserved for God. Only God can 'create,' i.e., bring forth in a sudden and sovereign manner. Creation expressed as *bara* is indeed *ex nihilo*, since it is a break with all that went before. The anterior is inexistent by comparison with the *novum* that is creation" (p. 149–50).

129. For a theological-exegetical argument on this topic, see Feinberg, *No One Like Him*, 550–57, and, for the biblical evidences, see Copan and Craig, *Creation out of Nothing*, 29–91.

130. Cf. Feinberg, *No One Like Him*, 391.

131. Cf. Alston, "Hartshorne and Aquinas," 132–33.

132. Senor, "Divine Temporality and Creation *Ex Nihilo*," 87–89. Indeed, we can find a full version of such an "accidental temporalism" in Craig's view on time and eternity. For a brief summary of his view, see Craig, "Timelessness and Omnitemporality," 129–60, and his *Time and Eternity*. I will fully discuss Craig's view in chapter 5 in this study.

God's eternity (Isa 60:19-20)."[133] Yet, for Jenni, *creatio cum tempus* does not mean necessarily God's timelessness, as he says, "in any case, it is not the same as timelessness."[134] According to him, we cannot find a metaphysical timelessness in the Bible. The idea of *creatio cum tempus* means that, in its best sense, God, the Creator, is the Lord over time: "God reveals himself now and then *in* time as the sole Lord and thereby also as Lord *over* time."[135] In the same sense, Colin E. Gunton also emphasizes that the creation "out of nothing" only means "an absolute qualitative distinction between creator and creation" and therefore between "the divine eternity and the worldly time," but it does not mean necessarily God's timelessness.[136]

The Time of Providence/Redemption and Consummation

According to biblical teaching, God not only created the world but also sustains and will consummate it. The biblical God is not the God of Deism, like a clockmaker, who does not directly engage in the world and its history after creation. Rather, the biblical doctrine of providence affirms "an ongoing divine concern for and activity in the world subsequent to its original creation," and thus "apart from the doctrine of providence, the idea of God would be largely irrelevant to what is happening in the word."[137] However, concerning our subject matter, the problem is how God acts and works in the temporal world. How does God relate with time? In my view, God's providence of the world and its history is none other than His providence of time. In this way, the essential form is God's promise and fulfillment structure. In Scripture, there is God's grand design for redemption: creation and the fall, and then, the promise of redemption (cf. Gen 3:15, 9: 25-27, 12:1-3, 17:7-8), its

---

133. Jenni, "Time," 647. Nash maintains the same view: "As Gen. 1 makes clear, the creation of time is part of the creation of the universe. The measurements and divisions of time come about as God separates day from night (Gen 1:3-5) and creates the sun, moon, and stars which 'mark the fixed times, the days and the years, and serve as lights in the firmament of the sky' (vv.14-15). Israel recognized that it is God not only had created but also continued to sustain this temporal rhythm along with the meteorological cycle." Idem, "Time," 1309.

134. Jenni, "Time," 647.

135. Ibid.

136. Cf. Gunton, *Triune Creator*, 83-86.

137. Vanhoozer, "Providence," 641.

fulfillment in Jesus Christ (cf. Gal 4:4; John 19:30), and its final eschatological consummation in the new heaven and the new earth (cf. Rev 21:1–5).[138]

In this grand structure of divine promise and fulfillment for the redemption of His people, there are multi-faceted promises and fulfillments, up to every moment of history. In this sense, W. Kaiser says that, "the promise-plan of God is indeed multi-faceted and all inclusive," and all of them sum up in "the Promise" for the Messiah, Jesus Christ.[139] In His promise and fulfillment, God allots His right and favorable time (*kairos*) for that, and, in doing so, God rules, controls, and leads the whole history (*chronos*) to its unique *telos* in His own way according to His own good will. Therefore, time is the medium of *Heilsgeschichte*, the redemptive history, for God's promise and fulfillment.

As we have seen in the doctrine of *creatio ex nihilo*—*creatio cum tempus*, time (*chronos*), as historical, physical, chronological, or measured time, is not eternal in itself. It was created by God with the world as the form of human as well as nature's existence. Thus, it has not only its beginning with creation (Gen 1:1, 4) but also its end as the *eschatos*, the consummation (Rev 21:1, 6). However, in spite of its limited characteristics of transitory, contingency, and ever brokenness as past, present, and future, the *continuum* of time, as *chronos*, is a gracious gift of God for us. Indeed, the preservation of the created world is possible through God's sustaining action of time. Thus, we can say that God's providence of the world is actually the providence of time.

In addition, because of God's ever redeeming and renewing activity *in*, *through*, and *for chronos*, the whole of history as the *continuum* of times (cf. as we can see in the biblical narrative as a whole and, specifically, in the various *tôldōt* in Genesis, the genealogies of 1 Chr 1:1—9:44; Matt 1:1–17; Luke 3:23–38) does not fall into a mere meaningless repetition of cyclic movement of nature or of human birth and death (cf. Gen 5:3–32). But, it has its unique *telos*, which is fulfilled in Jesus Christ and finally in eschatological consummation. Time itself is

---

138. Cf. VanGemeren, *Progress of Redemption*. In this work, VanGemeren traces God's grand redemptive plan "in telling the story of redemption, the Bible reveals the progression of God's plan for his people; both Old and New Testaments witness to the glory prepared for the new people of God in Jesus Christ" (ibid., 15). Kaiser also sees a "Canonical theological center" in the Old and the New Testament as "the promise" of God. Idem, *Toward an Old Testament Theology*, 33, cf. pp. 20–40.

139. Kaiser, *Toward Rediscovering the Old Testament*, 89–91.

neither a majestic flow from beginning to end, nor is it a tyrant over all things. Rather, with other creature, it also is under the control of God, its Creator.[140] In this sense, in the Bible, time is regarded as "a created sphere in which God's redemptive plan is actualized."[141]

Therefore, time *per se* is not opposed to God, rather it is the means of God's mighty communicative action in this world. In His favorable time, God made His covenant with His people and has fulfilled it through time. Actually, in the Bible, all of time is filled with the history of God's promises and fulfillments in His covenant with His people.[142] Thus, all times ultimately belong to God and serve to accomplish His purposes. As we have seen, in its essential meaning, *kairos* is usually used to denote the time for action and decisive moment, and thus specifically for God's action in this world for us. As J. Calvin grasped, the created world is "the theater of God's Glory [*theatrum gloria dei*], the arena of divine reflection and action."[143] If the universe is the space (stage) for God's action and human existence, we can say that time is the form or means for the performance of God's creative dramatic action and human responsive activities in the course of events. Thus, the biblical history as a whole appears to us as a grand "Theo-Drama," which is filled with God's

---

140. See the following Muilenburg's statements: "Time is not dependent upon the creation of the heavenly bodies of sun and moon; they are not only created on the fourth day, but they themselves exist under the sovereignty of a God who assigns to them their special work and function. They are created for history." Idem, "Biblical View of Time," 231.

141. Henry, "Time," 1094. Henry says, "The interconnected redemptive *kairoi* supply the threadline of salvation history. Yet the divine *kairoi* at the same time secretly enfold the entire secular movement of time (Acts 17:26) for the fulfillment, often unwittingly, of God's ultimate purposes" (p. 1095). Buckwalter also points out that, "Chronological time is of greatest importance in both Testaments as a way of tracing God's redemptive interventions in history. The most out standing Old Testament example of this is Israel's redemption from Egypt (Neh 9:9–25; Ps 78:12–55; Hos 11:1); in the New Testament it is the coming of Jesus as Messiah, Savior, and Lord (Acts 3:12–26; 10:34–43; 13:16–41)." Idem, "Time," 774.

142. According to Henry, "As the *kairos* is a decisive momentary unveiling of the eternal, so the *aio3n* discloses the Lord of ages who divides the long sweep of time according to his own purposes. The *kairoi* are decisive turning points within the larger *aiōna*. The Bible brackets history with an eye on the age of promise, the age of fulfillment, and the age to come." Idem, "Time," 1905.

143. Cf. Schreiner, *Theater of His Glory*, 7. According to DeVries, in a similar sense, for Israel, "time" was conceived as "the arena within which Yahweh acts purposefully; temporal event was the vehicle of his self-disclosure." Idem, *Yesterday, Today and Tomorrow*, 35.

initiative communicative action with His creatures' proper responses. In its course, every *kairos* is the decisive moment, the Now, for God's presence and His mighty action. This is the very reason why the present (the now) is also called 'the present' (the gift), for it is the time of God's gracious presence for us. More precisely, it is the time for a communicative relationship between God and His creatures.

Accordingly, God is not only the Creator and the Consummator of time, " the Alpha and the Omega, the Beginning and the End" (Rev 21:6, cf. 1:8), "the First and the Last" (Isa 41:4, 44:6; Rev 2:8), but also the Director of time (cf. Eccl 3:1-11; Rev 1:8). Therefore, God is the Lord of time.[144] Thus, God ordains, allots, controls, and maintains not only the *kairoi* for the natural time as "seedtime and harvest, cold and heat, summer and winter, day and night"(Gen 8:22) and the right times for all activities of human life (cf. Eccl 3:1-8), but also *kairoi* for salvation and grace (cf. Isa 49:8; Hos 10:12; Mark 1:15; 2 Cor 6:2). Indeed, "He has made everything appropriate in its time" (Eccl 3:11; cf. Acts 1:7). Therefore, we cannot but praise the only true living God, the Lord of time, with the Psalmist, "My times are in your hand!" (Ps 31:15). Finally, we must pay attention to the *kairos* of Jesus Christ, for "His time is God's special *kairos.*"[145] In Him, time is fulfilled in the unique sense (cf. Mark 1:15; Gal 4:4), and it is the turning point in history from "this *aiōn*" to "the *aiōn* to come," which is the final consummation of time in His *parousia*, the Second Coming in the *eschaton*.

Conclusion

So far, I have tried to grasp some key clues for the understanding of the biblical conception of time and God's eternity from the biblical terminology and texts as well as from some biblical scholars' studies on the topic. However, as we have seen, there is not a definite understanding or universal consensus on the subject matter. There are very diverse understandings and interpretations. Generally speaking, in my

---

144. According to Buckwalter, the following phrases point out God's lordship over time: "the First and Last" (Isa 41:4, 44:6, 48:12), "the Beginning and End" (Rev 21:6), "the one who is, was, and is to come" (Rev 1:4, 8), "King of the Ages" (1 Tim 1:17; Rev 15:3). In the NT, this lordship over time is extended to Jesus Christ, who is also called "the Alpha and Omega, the First and Last, the Beginning and End" (Rev 22:13). Idem, "Time," 774.

145. Rust, "Time and Eternity in Biblical Thought," 345.

view, the biblical conception of time and eternity depends on how we understand and grasp the differences and relationships of biblical terminology, *'ēt*, *'ôlam*, *chronos*, *kairos*, and *aiōn* among many others and their meanings through a study on the actual usages in specific biblical texts. As we have seen, however, there are no clear-cut interpretations of these words in their contexts and usages, and thus we must view them not as contrary, but as complementary in their combined forms in order to fully understand biblical time and eternity.

As J. Barr shows us, while recognizing the overlap in their meanings and usages which is, I think, a very normal phenomenon in every actual language, there is a need to characterize the meaning of the terms according to their usages as follows: the word, *kairos* is basically used to denote the time for concrete actions, events, occurrences or its specific content in qualitative sense; but, *chronos* describes the *continuum* of time as the series of action and events or a linear expanse of time, which can be quantitatively measured by physical time; and finally, *aiōn* basically designates an unestimatable, unthinkable time for the most distant past as well as the future, and the totality or the wholeness of time as we see in its usages for "a life span," "this age" (the age to come), or "this world." In this sense, God's eternity can be described by the word *aiōn* in an analogical way, for it is actually an unthinkable, unestimatable time which is beyond our human imagination. In addition, more significantly, we need a canonical approach to Scripture as a whole, which can show the whole structure of biblical history and its meaning, from creation through redemption in Jesus Christ to its eschatological consummation.

Finally, for conceiving God's eternity, the meaning of the words, *'ôlam* and *aiōn* in actual usages is crucial. As previously stated, the Bible uses these terms to describe the unestimatable, unthinkable time, or the totality of time. In this study, our main concern is how we can properly conceive not only the relationship but also the qualitative difference between God's eternity and human time. As we have seen, it seems that God's real relationship with the world-time is quite obvious in the Bible,[146] although it needs an adequate theological scheme to

---

146. Here, I want to posit God's "real relationship" to the world and time in contrast to the "relation in reason" in classical theism. According to Bruce A. Ware, "Much of classical theology so stressed God's absolute immutability that his relationship to the contingent and changing world could only be conceived, if at all, as a relation of rea-

understand it properly. Yet, the main difficulty lies in how to conceive the difference between our human time and God's eternity. What, then, is God's eternity? A timeless eternity? Or, an everlasting time? Does Scripture clearly state this? Unfortunately, even though there are some different understandings on the meaning of God's eternity, there is now a consensus among most of biblical scholars that we cannot find a definite meaning of God's eternity either "everlasting" or "timeless" in the Bible. Indeed, it is true that there is not an abstract conceptualization of God's eternity, nor is there a special word for it in the Bible as we can see in the ancient Greek philosophy.[147]

However, although Scripture does not give us a clear and direct form, it is clear that there is not only a positive relationship but also a difference between human time and God's eternity. We can most clearly see this in the time of Jesus Christ, the Incarnation, the Life, the Cross and the Resurrection. Indeed, as the God-and-man, He is the Revealer of God's eternity as well as the Redeemer of our fallen time. Accordingly, as we shall see in later chapters of this study, in order to properly conceive it, we need a Trinitarian analogical understanding of time and eternity. In addition, as P. Helm states, we need a "second-order" reflection on the subject-matter.[148] After an extensive critical study on "biblical words for time," J. Barr suggests that the problem should be handled in the area of philosophical theology rather than biblical theology. As he states, "We may conclude therefore that the prominence of philosophical-theological considerations, both in the posing of the problems about time and in solutions offered, suggests that the question should be handled much more frankly and more completely within the area of philosophical theology."[149] Thus, in order to best clarify our subject matter, we must engage in a vigorous interdisciplinary dialogue between theology, philosophy, and contemporary natural science. Finally, we must find an adequate systematic theological understanding which can combine the interdisciplinary dialogue with the biblical insights and truths. This is the very reason why we need this study.

---

son—i.e., a relation that is not real in God but obtains only insofar as God knows from all eternity that creatures will be really related to him." Ware, "Evangelical Reformulation of the Doctrine of the Immutability of God," 431 n. 1. Cf. Hill, "Does the World Make a Difference to God?," 146–64.

147. Cf. Jenni, "Time," 644.

148. Helm, *Eternal God*, 5.

149. Barr, *Biblical Words for Time*, 158.

3

Time and Eternity in Classical Theism

Introduction

IN CONTEMPORARY THEOLOGY, BECAUSE OF VARIOUS CRITICISMS AND challenges from very diverse perspectives to the traditional classical theism, there have been attempts to moderate and reformulate the concept of God.[1] First of all, however, what on earth is classical theism? Recently, while classifying two competing concepts of God, R. H. Nash identified the older, traditional view as classical theism, Christian theism, or simply theism. The other, which is a contemporary challenging view to classical theism, is generally called panentheism, neoclassical theism, or Process theology.[2]

Accordingly, classical theism can be attributed to the traditional concept of God, which was mainly formulated in the period from Augustine to Thomas Aquinas.[3] Hence, it is sometimes called Thomistic theism because it was systematized and synthesized in the theology of Thomas Aquinas and in medieval Scholasticism. David R. Griffin, a process theologian, characterized "the essential core of Thomistic theism" by the following eight attributes of God: (1) eternity or non-temporality, (2) immutability, (3) impassibility, (4) actus purus (pure actuality), (5) simplicity, (6) necessity, (7) omniscience, and finally,

---

1. The criticisms of classical theism come from various sources; for example, Process theology, Feminist theology, Liberation theology, even within Evangelical theology (e.g., the open theism).

2. Cf. Nash, *Concept of God*, 19.

3. Cf. Owen, *Concepts of Deity*, 1–2, and for a summary of Thomistic theism, see pp.1–48.

(8) omnipotence.[4] According to Griffin and other process theologians, however, the Thomistic package of divine attributes does not fit with the biblical God of love, who directly acts with human beings in the temporal world.[5] Especially concerning God's timelessness, R. H. Nash states this problem as follows:

> True, most classical Christian theologians like Augustine and Aquinas understood God's eternity in the sense of timelessness. . . . It means that God exists totally outside of time; that is, God has neither temporal duration nor temporal location. God does not exist at any particular moment of time and His existence does not occur during any period of time. He is "outside" of time. For a timeless God, all time exists in one eternal present; there is no past or future for God.[6]

Indeed, in the history of Christian theology, one of the most difficult problems lies in how to conceive God's eternity and its relation to our ever-transient-temporal world. In classical theism, God is eternal in the sense of "timeless," and at the same time God both created and sustains the whole universe as well as continually acts in this temporal world. However, as some philosophers and theologians (e.g., N. Pike, R. G. Swinburne, C. Pinnock, N. Wolterstroff among many others) insist, in classical theism, the following two fundamental tenets, God's timelessness which implies an absolute transcendence over the world and His real and positive relatedness to the temporal world are fatally inconsistent with each other.[7] For example, J. C. Yates succinctly describes this severe tension in classical theism as follows,

> *Prima facie* we would seem to be faced with an almost all-embracing inner tension between the two component poles of classical theism. On the one hand its *a priori* emphasis on perfect being would seem to lead us towards a wholly transcendent deity detached from the world, whereas its adherence to putative

---

4. Griffin, *God, Power, and Evil*, 73–77. Similarly, Owen gives a definition of classical theism as follows, "[Classical] Theism may be defined as belief in one God, the Creator, who is infinite, self-existent, incorporeal, eternal, immutable, impassible, simple, perfect, omniscient and omnipotent." Idem, *Concepts of Deity*, 1. For an open theist's criticism of classical theism, see Pinnock, "Systematic Theology," 101–25.

5. Nash, *Concept of God*, 20. See also, Kärkkäinen, *Doctrine of God*, 53–55.

6. Nash, *Concept of God*, 21.

7. Cf. Pike, *God and Timelessness*; Swinburne, *Coherence of Theism*; Wolterstorff, "God Everlasting," 181–203, and "Unqualified Divine Temporality," 187–213.

revelation draws us to an undeniable immanence or action in the world. That the one being could be both timeless/eternal and personal-creative-incarnate seems acutely unlikely.[8]

In order to properly resolve this tension, we must first understand the problem in classical theism. In this chapter, therefore, I will briefly survey the philosophical origin or background of the ancient Greek philosophies, and then, the process of formulation of classical theism in general and that of the concept of God's timeless eternity and its relation to the temporal world in particular.

Time and Eternity in Ancient Greek Philosophy

As we have seen in chapter 2, we cannot define a definitive concept of the absolute timeless God's eternity in the Bible. Then, in classical theism, where does it come from? Many theologians and philosophers concur that its origination was ancient Greek philosophy. That is to say, they assert that the concept of *timeless* eternity can be traced through the Neo-Platonists and Plato, and finally to the Eleatic philosopher, Parmenides.[9]

Heraclitus and Parmenides

One of the primary concerns for ancient Greek philosophers was the problem of change in the natural world. Yet, for them, though time is inseparably inter-connected with the problem of change and motion, it is still a subsidiary aspect of the latter (cf. the ancient Greek myth of Kronos and Ouranos).[10] After some developments in ancient Greek cosmology (e.g., Anaximander, Empedocles, Pythagoras, etc), a Presocratic thinker, Heraclitus of Ephesus (ca. 544–484 BC) insisted that, "everything [i.e., 'all sensible things'] is in a state of becoming and flux" (*panta*

---

8. Yates, *Timelessness of God*, 5.

9. Cf. Yates, *Timelessness of God*, 11; Sorabji, *Time, Creation and the Continuum*, 98; Padgett, *God, Eternity and the Nature of Time*, 38. For a brief introduction of the conception of time in ancient Greek philosophy, see Kneale, "Time and Eternity in Theology," 87–108; Lloyd, "Views on Time in Greek Thought," 117–48; Ariotti, "Conception of Time in Late Antiquity," 526–52; and Cushman, "Greek and Christian Views of Time," 254–65.

10. Cf. Turetzky, *Time*, 5–6.

64 Time, Eternity, and the Trinity

rhei).¹¹ He declared that, therefore, "You cannot step twice into the same river, for fresh waters are ever flowing in upon you."¹² According to him, everything is coming-to-be in eternal change, therefore nothing really is, but all things flow, as he said, "All things are in motion, nothing steadfastly is."¹³ Reality is in flux in this temporal world. Hence, for Heraclitus, the only unchanging fact is that everything is change, but flux itself is everlasting duration.¹⁴

However, it is worth mentioning that, according to F. Copleston, in the philosophy of Heraclitus, we can find a conception of unity in diversity, difference in unity. In the view of Heraclitus, reality is one, but at the same time it is essentially many. That is, the One, the Logos as a personal God, controls the whole order of the ever-becoming world.¹⁵ According to Heraclitus, time has no beginning and is an infinite duration. That is to say, for Heraclitus, time is neither identified with change itself nor the *logos*, but functions as a unifying rational principle of things in the ever-changing world.¹⁶

In contrast to Heraclitus, however, Parmenides (ca. 520–430 BC) asserted that substance (i.e., "what is"—the real object, the One Being) is eternal, neither coming into being nor perishing. The real object (Being) is unique and whole, and thus completely indivisible, immovable and immutable.¹⁷ Accordingly, for the nature of reality, becoming and perishing, motion in space and change in quality are all unreal and a mere shadow of appearance. Thus, according to him, time is unreal because nothing can change.¹⁸ Also he sees constancy as real, and there-

---

11. Cited in Guthrie, *History of Greek Philosophy*, vol. I, 450 and 451. For the life and philosophy for Heraclitus, see ibid, 403–92, and Kirk, *Heraclitus* (Cambridge: Cambridge University Press, 1954).

12. Cited in Copleston, *History of Philosophy*, vol. I, 39.

13. Ibid.

14. Cf. Turetzky, *Time*, 8–9, and Brabant, *Time and Eternity in Christian Thought*, 6.

15. Cf. Copleston, *History of Philosophy*, vol. I, 39–46.

16. Cf. P. Turetzky, *Time*, 8–9,

17. Cf. Guthrie, *History of Greek Philosophy*, vol. II, 28–40. Concerning this point, we can say that, in a sense, the contemporary debate on the nature of time between the tenseless (static) theory and the tensed (dynamic) theory of time is a renewal of the debate between Heraclitus (Becoming) and Parmenides (Being).

18. Cf. Cornford, "Elimination of Time by Parmenides," 137–42. For this point, Turetzky says that, "Parmenides was the first to express and argue for a stringent form of what has continued to be a major view of time in the West, that time is unreal. Parmenides eliminated time from his ontology." Idem, *Time*, 10.

fore change is unreal and a mere appearance. In his *The Way of Truth*, Parmenides stated, "[S]ince it [i.e., Being or the One] exists it is unborn and imperishable, whole, unique, immovable and without end. It *was* not in the past, nor yet *shall* it be, since it now *is*, all together, one and continuous."[19] That is to say, for Parmenides, simply and absolutely, "It is," and therefore, becoming (or change) is an illusion. Concerning this famous passage, however, although the majority view maintains the "timeless" interpretation, there are very diverse interpretations including the concept of "immutable everlasting duration."[20] In view of Parmenides, therefore, the meaning of eternity is unclear yet whether it is or is not timeless. Yet, it is clear that Parmenides provided a conception toward a timeless eternity by eliminating time with change and appearances from his ontology.

Plato and Aristotle

In the philosophy of Plato (ca. 428–347 BC), however, we can see an attempt to reconcile Being and Becoming (i.e., between Parmenides and Heraclitus).[21] In doing so, Plato's philosophy is characterized as an ontological dualism–the well-known two worlds theory. For Plato, the totality of existence is divided into two modes of being: the eternal Being (*ousia*) and the temporal becoming (*genesis*), or the supernatural and the natural.[22] That is to say, on the one hand, there is an eternal, indivisible, and changeless world of the *idea* (the Forms—*eidos*), which has reality, and thus it is being itself. On the other hand, there

---

19. Cited in Guthrie, *History of Greek Philosophy*, vol. II, 26 (italics original).

20. For this passage, Sorabji gives eight different interpretations including his own "timeless" interpretation. Cf. idem, *Time, Creation and the Continuum*, 99–108. See also Yates, *Timelessness of God*, 12, and Padgett, *God, Eternity and the Nature of Time*, 38–41. The timeless interpretation is supported by the following Parmenides' statement: "What is cannot have come into being. If it did, it came either from what is or what is not. But it did not come from what is, since it is existent it did not come to be but already is; nor from what is not, for the non-existent cannot generate anything." As cited in Guthrie, *History of Greek Philosophy*, vol. II, 28.

21. Cf. Benjamin, "Ideas of Time in the History of Philosophy," 10.

22. According to Yates, Plato's shaping of the dualistic world-view is the most important factor for Western philosophy and theology. See, idem, *Timelessness of God*, 15. Cf. Passmore, *Philosophical Reasoning*, especially chapter 3, "The Two-Worlds Argument," 38–57.

is also a temporal, divisible, and changeable world of appearances (the particulars—*eidoron*).

According to Plato, between the two worlds, the Demiurge brought the cosmos (the visible world) into being, and modeled it according to the ideal Forms, which are eternal. This is Plato's formation theory of the world. In other words, the ideal forms are unchanging perfect entities, which are patterns and standards, but all other things of the actual universe come from them as their copies in the multiplicity of changing appearances (e.g., the form of "tree-ness" -> oaks, maples, pines, etc.). More significantly for our subject, Plato insisted that time was co-created with the world of appearance. As Plato says, "Time, then, came to be together with the universe so that just as they were begotten together."[23] Unlike most of his predecessors, Plato believed time had its beginning with the world, and therefore if the world were to vanish, time would vanish, too.[24] Thus, in Plato's view, while reality (the *Idea*) is in eternity, time (*chronos*), which is the mode of being for the world of appearance, is defined as "a moving image of eternity (*aion*)."[25]

For Plato, therefore, while eternity is remaining in unity, time is moving according to number in the realm of appearances. Plato says, "This number, of course, is what we call 'time'."[26] P. Turetzky summarizes Plato's view of time and eternity as follows:

> The Demiurge created the world according to the model of the forms. . . . To this end he created time. Since, unlike the forms, time is created, it belongs to the realm of appearances, a derivative order of being. For the created universe to be as much like its eternal model as possible, the Demiurge created time as an image of eternity. Plato writes that time is a moving image of eternity that moves according to number. Thus time differs from

---

23. Plato, *Timaeus*, 38c, in *Plato: Complete Works*, 1241.

24. According to Praser, "Plato regarded time as coeval with the world; it was created when the world was, and if the world were ever to vanish, time would vanish with it." Idem, *Of Time, Passion, and Knowledge*, 18. Cf. Turetzky, *Time*, 16–17.

25. Plato, *Timaeus*, 37d, in *Plato: Complete Works*, 1241. According to Turetzky, "Plato was the first on record to treat time as distinct from change." Idem, *Time*, 18.

26. Here is the full text: "Now when the Father who had begotten the universe observed it set in motion and alive, a thing that had come to be as shrine . . . . And so he began to think of making a moving image of eternity: at the same time as he brought order to the universe, he would make an eternal image, moving according to number, of eternity remaining in unity. This number, of course, is what we now call 'time'." Plato, *Timaeus*, 37d, in *Plato: Complete Works*, 1241.

the eternity of the forms in two respects: it moves, i.e. it partakes of change; and it moves according to number, its movement is rationally ordered. Time is an image of eternity because, while time moves and changes, its movement is the movement of the sphere of the universe. This is circular motion, in which after each complete cycle the sphere returns to its original position. We are told that "was" and "will be" apply only to processes of becoming which are in time. Time itself encompasses all such processes; it follows that time as a whole does not change and thus resembles eternity.[27]

That is to say, in Plato's view, while time is identified with the whole duration and the celestial motions in the created world, the forms (*Idea*) in eternity remain static and are "always" in the same state. Plato says,

> What is *that which always is* and has no becoming, and what is *that which becomes* but never is? The former is grasped by understanding, which involves a reasoned account. It is unchanging. The latter is grasped by opinion, which involves unreasoning sense perception. It comes to be and passes away, but never really is. Now everything that comes to be must of necessity come to be by the agency of some cause, for it is impossible for anything to come to be without a cause. So whenever the craftsman looks at what is always changeless and, using a thing of that kind as his model, reproduces its form and character, then, of necessity, all that he so completes is beautiful.[28]

However, Plato's meaning of "always" for the unchanging ideal Forms is still unclear whether it is timeless or everlasting duration. Therefore, even though Plato's conception of eternity of the Forms can be conceived as "timeless" (majority view), it does not exclude the interpretation of everlasting duration (minority view).[29] At any rate, philosophers

---

27. Cf. Turetzky, *Time*, 14–15. He continues that, for Plato, "As an image of eternity, time links the order of the eternal world of forms and unchanging reality with the order of the natural world of changing things. This link makes the created universe into a rational, intelligible harmony that exemplifies the purpose of the Demiurge to make it as beautiful and good as possible. Time belongs in the realm of appearances because it moves. Moreover, it moves according to number, which makes its motion intelligible. Time can be counted and regularly segmented, and so it appears as a numerical order" (p. 15).

28. Plato, *Timaeus*, 28a, in *Plato: Complete Works*, 1234–35.

29. According to Sorabji, "Plato did not decide between making eternity timeless and giving it everlasting duration." Idem, *Time, Creation and the Continuum*, 112. Actually, however, Sorabji himself takes the timeless interpretation (cf. ibid., 109), but

and theologians generally attribute to Plato the first concrete doctrine of eternity in western thought.[30]

Concerning the two worlds problem, Aristotle (384–322 BC) replaced Plato's scheme of "the ideal Forms and appearance" by his own relationship of "form and matter." According to Aristotle, everything is "form in matter" or "formed-matter." In this sense, "what is" is all the unity of form and matter. In other words, "matter" (*dynamis*, potentiality) is actualized by "form" to "actuality" (*energia*). This relationship of "potentiality-actuality" can be described as a movement, development, and change (e.g., seed –> tree). Therefore, Aristotle believed that all things which come into being are subject to this motion in time. Aristotle was probably the first philosopher who argued and provided a systematic analysis of the nature of time in the sense of natural science rather than metaphysics.[31]

According to Aristotle, time itself is clearly not movement or change, but neither does time exist without change; as he says, "time is neither movement nor independent of movement."[32] Time can be apprehended or measured only by movement and change, marking it by "before" and "after." Therefore, Aristotle defined time in a more actual sense as the "number of motion in respect of 'before' and 'after.'"[33] That is to say, time is not movement itself, but it is, at the same time, "what exactly it has to do with movement."[34] For him, however, time is a more essential concept than movement. Everything which is changing is in time: "[T]ime is thought to be in everything, both in earth and in sea and in heaven. It is because it is an attribute, or state, of movement (since it is the number of movement) and all these things are moveable (for they are all in place), and time and movement are together, both in respect of potentiality and in respect of actuality."[35]

Whittaker insists the interpretation of everlasting duration, see idem, "'Eternity' of the Platonic Forms," 131–44. Cf. Owen, "Plato and Parmenides on the Timeless Present," 317–40.

30. Yates, *The Timelessness of God*, 15.

31. For Aristotle's conception of time, see his *Physics*, Book 4. 10. 217b30–14. 224a15, in *Complete Works of Aristotle*, vol. I, 369–78; and Owen, "Aristotle on Time," 3–27.

32. Aristotle, *Physics*, 4.11. 219a1 (p. 371).

33. Ibid., 11. 219b1 (p. 372).

34. Ibid., 11. 219a3 (p. 371).

35. Ibid., 14. 223a16–21 (p. 377).

While Plato thought of time in relation to eternity, Aristotle tried to understand time in the natural sense with the concept of movement and change, but without any connection with eternity. Eternity is not part of Aristotle's discussion of time. As we have seen, he defines time with the number of motion, that is to say the movement of the bodies of heaven.[36] According to Aristotle, therefore, "it is clear that there is neither place nor vacuum nor time outside the heavens."[37] Outside of the spherical shell of the universe, there is no time, since there are no bodies and no motions. He continues that,

> outside the heaven, as we have shown, body neither exists nor comes to exist. Hence whatever is there, is of such a nature as not to occupy any place, nor does time age it; nor is there any change in any of the things which lie beyond the outermost motion, they continue for their entire duration unalterable and unmodified, living the best and most self-sufficient of lives. As a matter of fact, this word duration possessed a divine significance for the ancients, for the fulfillment which included the period of life of any creature, outside of which no development can fall, has been called its duration. On the same principle the fulfillment of the whole heaven, the fulfillment which includes all time and infinity, is "duration"—a name based upon the fact that it "is always"—duration—immortal and divine.[38]

Therefore, if there is a God outside of heaven, in Aristotle's view, God is "the Unmoved Mover" or "the Prime Mover," who is the initiator of motion and thus the pure actuality in eternity. However, for the meaning of eternity in Aristotle, scholars generally have thought that he conceived eternity as "everlasting duration"[39] or "a special sort of omnitemporality,"[40] but not timelessness. In his *Metaphysics*, Aristotle describes God's life as follows,

> It is a way of life the best we ever have for a short time. For he is *always* in that state, which for us is impossible. . . . If, then, God

---

36. In this sense, Ariotti characterized Aristotle's conception of time as "celestial reductionism of time." Idem, "Conception of Time in Late Antiquity," 526–28.

37. Aristotle, *De Caelo* 1.9. 279a12–b3, as cited in Sorabji, *Time, Creation and the Continuum*, 127.

38. Aristotle, *De Caelo* 1.9. 279a12–b3, as cited in Yates, *Timelessness of God*, 16–17.

39. Cf. Sorabji, *Time, Creation and the Continuum*, 127; and Padgett, *God, Eternity and the Nature of Time*, 41.

40. Yates, *Timelessness of God*, 18.

is always in that good state in which we are sometimes that is wonderful.... God's self-dependent actuality is a life most good and everlasting. We say then that God is a living being, everlasting and most good, so that life and continuous, everlasting *aion* belong to him. For that is what God is.[41]

Middle-Platonism (Plutarch) and Neo-Platonism (Plotinus)

Although there are some controversies in interpreting Parmenides' and Plato's conception of eternity as "timelessness," we can find a definitive idea of "timeless" eternity in the Middle Platonist Plutarch (ca. AD 45–125). More significantly, according to A. G. Padgett, Plutarch applied timelessness to God, not simply the Being (Parmenides) or the Forms (Plato).[42] Plutarch says, "But God (if there be need to say so), and He exists for no fixed time, but for the everlasting ages (*kat'aiona*) which are immovable, timeless (*achronos*), and undeviating, in which there is no earlier no later, no future nor past, no older nor younger; but He, being One, has with only one 'Now' completely filled 'For ever'; and only when Being is after His pattern is it in reality Being, not having been nor about to be, nor has it had a beginning nor is it destined to come to an end."[43] In this sense, according to Plutarch, temporal terms cannot be applied to God, for He exists in eternity which is timeless. In ancient Christianity, this Middle Platonism strongly influenced Alexandrian theology, which is a blend of Platonism and Christian thought (e.g., Origen, ca. AD 185–254).[44]

---

41. Aristotle, *Metaphysics*, 12.7, 1072b13–1073a13, as cited in Sorabji, *Time, Creation and the Continuum*, 127.

42. Padgett says, "This is the first instance known to me where a timeless eternity is directly associated with God. Furthermore, this is the first instance of an *absolute* concept of timeless eternity . . . In Platonism, then, we discover the origin of the subtle concept of a timeless and non-durational divine eternity." Idem, *God, Eternity and the Nature of Time*, 42.

43. Plutarch, *On the E at Delphi*, 393 A-B, as cited in Yates, *Timelessness of God*, 19–20. Cf. Padgett, *God, Eternity and the Nature of Time*, 42.

44. For example, in *On First Principles*, Origen asserts that, "[T]he statements we make about the Father and the Son and the Holy Spirit must be understood as transcending all time and all ages and all eternity" (4.4.1). Accordingly, Padgett says that, "It is from the Platonism of Alexandrian theology, then, that the doctrine of divine timelessness first enters into Christian theology." Padgett, *God, Eternity and the Nature of Time*, 42.

In this era, however, probably a Neo-Platonist, Plotinus (ca. AD 205–270) was one of the most important philosophers for our subject matter, since he critically clarified Plato and Aristotle again, and profoundly influenced Augustine's and then Boethius' understanding of time and eternity, and thus the whole of classical theism.[45] While criticizing Aristotle's natural and empirical understanding of time, Plotinus thought of, like Plato, that eternity is the origin and the source of time. Thus, for him, time can be understood only in relation with eternity, and actually the former comes from the latter. Yet, in contrast to Plato's dualism and formation theory of the world, based on his monism, Plotinus insisted on an "emanation theory" which means that everything emanated from "the One" in the following ontological hierarchy: the One –> the Intellect (Nous, Divine Mind) –> the [World] Soul –> the Changing World (Individual souls –> Matter –> Non-being).[46]

We can find Plotinus' understanding of time and eternity in his *The Enneads*, III. 7, "Time and Eternity."[47] It is here that Plotinus first most consistently and fully discussed the absolute timelessness of "the One," which is the source of being in unity and self-identity beyond all thought and all being, and without change, succession, and extension. Then, according to Plotinus, in the series of emanations of hypostases (i.e., the order of beings), while describing time as "the life of the Soul" as the third hypostasis,[48] Plotinus defined eternity as "the life of Nous" (Divine Mind or the Intellect, which corresponds to Plato's Forms) in the realm of the second hypostasis:[49]

---

45. For the influence of Plotinus on Christianity, see Rist, "Plotinus and Christian Philosophy," 386–413.

46. Cf. Plotinus, *The Enneads*, 5.2 (pp. 436–38), and Turetzky, *Time*, 47.

47. Plotinus, "Time and Eternity" in *The Enneads*, 3.7 (pp. 253–72). For a helpful discussion for Plotinus' understanding of time and eternity, see Callahan, *Four Views of Time in Ancient Philosophy*, 88–148; Plass, "Timeless Time in Neoplatonism," 1–19; Smith, "Eternity and Time," 196–216.

48. Plotinus defines time as "the Life of the Soul in movement as it passes from one stage of act or experience to another" (*The Enneads*, 3.7.11, p. 266), and thus "a certain expanse (a quantitative phase) of the Life of the Soul" (3.7.12, p. 266). Concerning the relationship between the Soul and time, Plotinus says that, "the Soul begot at once the Universe and Time; in that activity of the Soul this universe sprang into being; the activity is Time, the Universe is a content of Time." *The Enneads*, 3.7.12 (p. 267).

49. Accordingly, Smith says that, for Plotinus, "The identification of eternity with the intelligible substance is seen as a counterpart to the identification of time with the whole heaven and the universal order (cosmos)." Idem, "Eternity and Time," 198–99.

> We know it [i.e., eternity] as a Life changelessly motionless and ever holding the Universal content in actual presence; not this now and now that other, but always all; not existing now in one mode and now in another, but a consummation without part or interval. All its content is in immediate concentration as at one point; nothing in it ever knows development: all remains identical within itself, knowing nothing of change, for ever in a Now, since nothing of it has passed away or will come into being, but what is now, that it is ever. . . . That which neither has been nor will be, but simply possesses being; that which enjoys stable existence as neither in process of change nor having ever changed—that is Eternity. Thus we come to the definition: *the Life—instantaneously entire, complete, at no point broken into period or part—which belongs to the Authentic Existent by its very existence, this is the thing we were probing for—this is Eternity.*[50]

Here we can find a significant definition of eternity: viz. "Eternity is the instantaneously entire, complete life which belongs to the Authentic Existent (Divine Mind, *Nous*–i.e., God)." According to Plotinus, there is an infinite qualitative difference, not simply quantitative, between eternity and time, in that the eternity of Nous is timeless (*achronos*)–"it is outside of time"–and durationless–it is an unextended instant like a point.[51] He says,

> Now the life of Authentic-Existence is measurable not by time but by eternity; and eternity is not a more or a less or a thing of any magnitude but is the unchangeable, the indivisible, is timeless Being. We must not muddle together Being and Non-Being, time and eternity, not even everlasting time with the eternal; we cannot make laps and stages of an absolute unity; all must be taken together, wheresoever and howsoever we handle it; and

---

In this sense, Plotinus says, "Time . . . is not to be conceived as outside of soul; Eternity is not outside of the Authentic Existent [i.e., Nous]: nor is it to be taken as a sequence or succession to Soul, any more than Eternity is to the Divine. It is a thing seen upon Soul, inherent, coeval to it, as Eternity to the Intellectual Realm" *The Enneads*, 3.7.11 (p. 266).

50. Plotinus, *The Enneads*, 3.7.3 (pp. 255–56, italics mine).

51. According to Plotinus, "the conception of Eternity demands something which is in its nature complete without sequence; . . . it requires something immediately possessed of the due fullness of Being, something whose Being does not depend upon any quantity (such as instalments of time) but subsists before all quantity. Itself having no quantity, it can have no contact with anything quantitative since its Life cannot be made a thing of fragments, in contradiction to the partlessness which is its character; it must be without parts in the Life as in the essence." *The Enneads*, 3.7.6 (p. 259).

it must be taken at that, not even as an undivided block of time but as the Life of Eternity, a stretch not made up of periods but completely rounded, outside of all notion of time.[52]

In some places, Plotinus used a center-circle analogy in order to explain a non-durational, point-like timeless eternity as follows:

> Time in its ceaseless onward sliding produces parted interval; Eternity [which is outside of time] stands in identity, pre-eminent, vaster by unending power than Time with all the vastness of its seeming progress; Time is like a radial line running out apparently to infinity but dependent upon that, its center, which is the pivot of all its movement; as it goes it tells of that center, but the center itself is the unmoving principle of all the movement.[53]

It is helpful to understand Plotinus' concept of eternity by what W. Beierwalters says in his commentary on *The Enneads*, 3.7:

> Eternity therefore is the unchangeable life of the Mind, abiding the selfsame in itself, being the Whole or All at once (because it is without past or future), which is alone with itself "continually" thinking without interval or extension. This eternal self-presence of thought in being through life resembles a point, in which everything is collected at once in thinking, but which nevertheless does not relinquish its unextended unity, that is moved and lives in itself through thought, in that it "proceeds out of itself into flux." Eternity is precisely this "constantly" moved, unextended, timeless NOW, which collects everything at once in itself as in a point. NOW is identical with the "Timeless-Present-Being." Since Eternity is determined neither through the WAS nor through the WILL BE, "the earlier" nor the "later," the "before" nor the "after," it remains only that "Eternity is in that which is Being": in the IS is always already NOW in that it is the "full-

---

52. Plotinus, *The Enneads*, 1.5.7 (p. 62).

53. Plotinus, *The Enneads*, 6.5.11 (p. 611), He continues, "A circle related in its path to a center must be admitted to owe its scope to that center; it has something of the nature of that center in that the radial lines converging on that one central point assimilate their impinging ends to that point of convergence and of departure, the dominant of radii and terminals: the terminals are of one nature with the center, feeble reproductions of it, since the center is, in a certain sense, the source of terminals and radii impinging at every point upon it; these lines reveal the center; they are the development of that undeveloped" (6.8.11, p. 693). As we shall see, Boethius and Thomas Aquinas used the same analogy of the center-circle for the relationship between time and God's eternity.

ness" of Being always already thinking. Precisely in this characterization of Eternity as IS and NOW the Being of Eternity reveals itself to human thought as paradoxical: that Eternity, though it is not time, yet due to language's being interwoven with temporality, must be assigned terms which originally had a temporal sense. IS and NOW, therefore, must in relation to Eternity be conceived atemporally, just as in the concepts of duration and motion one must in each case also conceive their negation, if they are to capture adequately the Being of Eternity. Thus, Eternity is—like the highest concept of Plotinian philosophy, the ONE itself—only accessible to a negative dialectic, and this again only in an analogical sense: as the negation of time, as that which is dissimilar to time.[54]

Finally, for the relationship between God and eternity, Plotinus insists that, "Eternity, thus, is of the order of the supremely great; intuition identifies it with God: it may fitly be described as God made manifest, as God declaring what He is, as existence without jolt or change, and therefore as also the firmly living.... Thus a close enough definition of Eternity would be that it is a life limitless in the full sense of being all the life there is and a life which, knowing nothing of past or future to shatter its completeness, possesses itself intact for ever."[55] Consequently, in Plotinus' view, we can find the fullest and clearest conception of a "durationless" and "absolute timeless" eternity of God in ancient non-Christian philosophy, which profoundly influenced Classical theism, as we shall see, especially through Augustine, Boethius, Anselm, and Thomas Aquinas.[56]

---

54. Plotin, *Über Ewigkeit und Zeit*, trans. with an Introduction and Commentary by Werner Beierwalters, Klostermann Texte Philosopie (Frankfurt am Main: Vittorio Klostermann, 1967) 41–43. As cited and translated in Craig, *The Problem of Divine Foreknowledge and Future Contingents from Aristotle to Suarez*, 94–95.

55. Plotinus, *The Enneads*, 3.7.5 (pp. 257–58, italics mine).

56. Cf. Yates, *Timelessness of God*, 23. In this sense, Padgett also states that, "Plotinus wrote the fullest and most influential philosophical discussion of absolute timelessness in his day. His discussion influenced both Augustine and Boethius, thereby influencing Anselm, Thomas, and the entire medieval tradition.... In Plotinus, then, we find the seed of the fully developed notion of an eternal Now coexisting will all earthly nows; an immutable, timeless, and non-durational life which is God." Idem, *God, Eternity and the Nature of Time*, 43. Cf. Plass, "Timeless Time in Neoplatonism," 1–19.

The Way to Classical Theism

According to Henry Chadwick, the history of Christian philosophy began with Philo Judaeus (ca. 30 BC—AD 45).[57] In Judaism, Philo asserted timeless eternity for the God of the Bible on the basis of Platonism.[58]

> God is withdrawn from both ends of time. For His life is not so much Time as Eternity (*aion*), the archetype and pattern of time. And in Eternity there is nothing past and nothing future, but only present.[59] The one who alone is eternal and the Father of all things visible and invisible.[60]

In ancient Christian theology, the Apostolic Fathers (e.g., Ignatius, Justin, Tatian, Athenagoras), Clement of Alexandria, Tertullian, the Alexandria theologian Origen, the Greek Church Fathers (e.g., Hilary, Athanasius, Basil of Caesara, and Gregory of Nyssa) also insisted on the timelessness of God, but not in detail.[61] Therefore, in this section, my concern mainly focuses on the meaning of God's eternity and its relation to time according to Augustine, Boethius, Anselm, and Thomas Aquinas.

Augustine

Under the influence of Plotinus' Neoplatonism,[62] Augustine (354–430) accomplished a great classical synthesis in ancient Christian theology. In so doing, Augustine paved the way for Classical Theism in medieval

---

57. Cf. Chadwick, *Cambridge History of Later Greek and Early Medieval Philosophy*, 137.

58. Cf. Yates, *Timelessness of God*, 19.

59. Philo, *Quod Deus Immutabilis Sit* 6. 32, L. Cohn and P. Wendland edition of Philo, 1896, vol. 2, p. 63, as cited in Yates, *Timelessness of God*, 19.

60. Philo, *De Virtutibus*, 39. 214, as cited in Yates, *Timelessness of God*, 19.

61. Cf. Yates, *Timelessness of God*, 20 and 25. For the conceptions of time and God's eternity in Patristic Theology, see Wolfson, "Patristic Arguments against the Eternity of the World," 351–67; Azkoul, "On Time and Eternity," 56–77; Plass, "Transcendent Time and Eternity in Gregory of Nyssa," 180–92, and "Concept of Eternity in Patristic Theology," 11–25.

62. Augustine himself mentioned the influence of Neoplatonism in his thought, see the following: *Confessions*, VIII.2; *City of God*, VIII.5 and12; IX.10. Cf. Padgett, *God, Eternity and the Nature of Time*, 43; Yates, *Timelessness of God*, 26; and Quispel, "Time and History in Patristic Christianity," 104. However, as we can see in his doctrine of *creatio ex nihilo*, Augustine attempted to overcome the weakness of Neoplatonism in Christian perspective.

theology.[63] We can find Augustine's main conception of time and eternity in his *Confessions*, Book XI, and *The City of God*, Book XI and XII.[64] Like Plato and Plotinus, Augustine attempts to clarify the origin and the nature of time in its relationship to eternity and God. For this reason, his conception of the nature of time begins with the exploration of the eternal Word, especially Gen 1:1–3. Accordingly, Augustine's thinking of time lies in the line of his doctrine of creation. In his interpretation of Genesis, Augustine accepted Plato's theory of *creatio cum tempus*. The center of his synthetic thought, however, is biblical Christianity. That is to say, Augustine asserted the doctrine of *creatio ex nihilo* in biblical and Christian perspective, against Plato's formation theory (i.e., dualism) and Plotinus' emanation theory (i.e., monism). Thus, concerning the problem of the creation of the world, Augustine asserted the doctrine of "creation out of nothing," without any pre-existing matter or other things outside God (i.e., the problem of "out of what"), and thus "the absolute beginning of time" (i.e., the problem of "when") by the eternal God in the biblical perspective. Actually, the Christian doctrine of "creation out of nothing" is a revolutionary thought, which is distinguished from Greek philosophy and any other ancient world-view.[65]

First of all, in his thinking about time, Augustine well knew the subtlety and difficulty in saying that,

> What, then, is time? Is there any short and easy answer to that?
> Who can put the answer into words or even see it in his mind?
> Yet what commoner or more familiar word do we use in speech

---

63. In this sense, Leftow says, "Augustine's thinking [especially his concept of divine eternity] was the core that determined the broad outlines of all that later medieval philosophical theology made of the concept of God." Idem, *Time and Eternity*, 73.

64. Augustine, *Confessions*, 209–31, and *City of God*, 449–540. For a general introduction for Augustine's conception of time and eternity, see Callahan, "Augustine: Time, a Distention of Man's Soul," in *Four Views of Time in Ancient Philosophy*, 149–87; Jess, "Divine Eternity in the Doctrine of St. Augustine," 75–96; McEvoy, "St. Augustine's account of Time and Wittgenstein's Criticism," 547–77; Polk, "Temporal Impermanence and the Disparity of Time and Eternity," 63–82; Leftow, "Augustine: Eternality as Truest Existence," in *Time and Eternity*, 73–111; Knuuttila, "Time and Creation in Augustine," 103–15.

65. The concept of "the creation out of nothing (*creatio ex nihilo*)" appeared in 2 Macc 7:28, and is implied in Rom 4:17 and Heb 11:3. Before Augustine, some Church Fathers (e.g., Origen, Tertullian, Irenaeus, and Athanasius) asserted this doctrine. For a full study on the doctrine of *creatio ex nihilo* in early Christianity, see May, *Creatio Ex Nihilo*; Copan, "Is *Creatio Ex Nihilo* a Post-Biblical Invention?" 77–93; Copan and Craig, *Creation out of Nothing*, 93–145.

than time? Obviously when we use it, we know what we mean, just as when we hear another use it, we know what he means. What *is* this time? If no one asks me, I know; if I want to explain it to a questioner, I do not know.[66]

Augustine's conception of time is based on his doctrine of *creatio ex nihilo* and the mutability of the world. As we have already seen, Augustine asserted the doctrines of *creatio ex nihilo* and *creatio cum tempus*. Augustine says that, "They [i.e., the world] were made by You of nothing–not of Yourself, not some matter not made by You or of some matter previously existent: but of a *concreated* matter, that is a matter created by You in the same act [as the things You made of it], because You gave form to its formlessness without any interval of time."[67] At first, Augustine asserts that God created the world "with" time, not "in" time. Time itself has its beginning because it is created with the world, and its origin is *ex nihilo*. It means that time has its absolute beginning. Augustine states,

> [W]hen the sacred and wholly truth-laden Scriptures say that "In the beginning God created the heavens and the earth," this is so that we may know that nothing was made before the heavens and the earth; for if something was made before them, it is this something that would then be said to have been made "in the beginning." Beyond doubt, then, the world was made not in time but simultaneously with time.[68] [Therefore,] at no time then had You not made anything, for time itself You made.[69]

Augustine concluded that, therefore, "the creation of the world and the beginning of time both occurred simultaneously, and that the one did not come before the other."[70]

In addition, since everything was created out of nothing, it always has a tendency to fall toward non-being, and thus it necessarily has a characteristic of mutability. According to Augustine, time is inseparably related to change (i.e., mutability): "Obviously it could not, for where there is no change of movement there is no time."[71] Therefore, for him,

66. Augustine, *Confessions*, XI.14 (p. 219).
67. Ibid., XIII.33 (p. 284).
68. Augustine, *City of God*, XI.6 (p. 456).
69. Augustine, *Confessions*, XI.14 (p. 219).
70. Augustine, *City of God*, XI.6 (p. 456).
71. Augustine, *Confessions*, XII.11 (p. 241).

such mutability is a logical foundation of time. And its ultimate foundation is "not-being," for time, as the mode of the existence of the created being, comes from not-being (i.e., *creatio ex nihilo*). In this sense, Augustine insists that, "time *is* only in that it tends towards not-being."[72] It means that time comes from not-being (the future, which is "not yet") and passes away to not-being (the past, which "no longer" exists), and thus the present *is* the only real time, but it will cease to be because it flows away into the past. Whereas, "if the present were always present and never flowed away into past, it would not be time at all, but eternity."[73] He concludes that, therefore, "eternity and time are rightly distinguished by the fact that time does not exist without some movement and change, whereas in eternity there is no change."[74]

Before turning to God's eternity, concerning Augustine's doctrine of time, it must be emphasized that, in following Plotinus, he reduced time to a matter of man's soul (i.e., consciousness)—"a psychological theory of time."[75] First of all, for Augustine, time is always in flux. It flows from the future through the present to the past. In this sense, Augustine's view of time can be thought of as a dynamic (tensed) theory of time.[76] Concerning the direction of time's arrow, according to Augustine, it always flows from the future through the present into the past. We can find such a notion in various places; for example,

> time comes forth from some secret place when from future it becomes present, and departs into some secret place when from present it becomes past.[77]
>
> Where is it from?—obviously from the future. By what way does it pass?—by the present. Where does it go?—into the past. In other words it passes from that which does not yet ex-

---

72. Ibid., XI.14 (p. 219).

73. Ibid.

74. Augustine, *City of God*, XI.6 (p. 456).

75. Concerning Augustine's psychological theory of time, Edmund Husserl says, "For no one in this knowledge-proud modern generation has made more masterful or significant progress in these matters than this great thinker who struggled so earnestly with the problem." Idem, *Phenomenology of Internal Time-Consciousness*, 21, as cited in Polk, "Temporal Impermanence and the Disparity of Time and Eternity," 78.

76. For the dynamic (tensed) theory and the static (tenseless) theory of time, see the next "Chapter 4. Contemporary Philosophical Debates on the Nature of Time" in this work.

77. Augustine, *Confessions*, XI.17 (p. 221).

ist, by way of that which lacks extension, into that which is no longer.[78]

However, in Augustine's view, ever-passing time raises some difficulties. That is, concerning the reality of time, the future is not yet and the past is no longer. Even the present, which is the only real *is*, is also unclear because it always passes away into the past. As Augustine says,

> But at any rate this much I dare affirm I know: that if nothing passed there would be no past time; if nothing were, there be no present time. But the two times, past and future, how can they *be*, since the past is no more and the future is not yet? On the other hand, if the present were always present and never flowed away into the past, it would not be time at all, but eternity. But if the present is only time, because it flows away into the past, how can we say that it *is*? For it is, only because it will cease to be. Thus we can affirm that time is only in that it tends towards not-being.[79]

In this statement, Augustine's view of time is a presentism, in the sense that the past and the future do not exist objectively and thus the present alone is real. The following his statement clearly shows this: "it might be said that there are not three times, past, present and future, . . . but only present, because the other two do not exist."[80] Therefore, for Augustine, future time, as well as past time, does not have length, for they are not existent (i.e., non-being). However, at the same time, the present time, too, does not have a length because it lacks extension. If the present has a length, it must be divided into the future and the past. Thus the present is only a point of time, which cannot be divided into even the minutest parts of moments.[81] This means that the present is a durationless instant, like a mathematical point. Accordingly, for Augustine, we cannot objectively measure the periods of time.

In order to solve such a paradox of time, Augustine focused on the human mind, consciousness (i.e., a psychological approach). If the future and the past exist, they are only in the present of the mind. That is to say, the past is in the present as memory, and the future is in the present as expectation. He says,

78. Ibid., XI.21 (p. 224).
79. Ibid., XI.14 (p. 219).
80. Ibid., XI.17 (p. 221).
81. Cf. ibid., XI.15 (pp. 219–21).

> At any rate it is now quite clear that neither future nor past actually exists. Nor is it right to say there are three times, past, present and future. Perhaps it would be more correct to say: there are three times, a present of things past, a present of things present, a present of things future. *For these three exist in the mind, and I find them nowhere else: the present of things past is memory, the present of things present is sight, the present of things future is expectation.* If we are allowed to speak thus, I see and admit that there are three times, that three times truly are.[82]

In conclusion, according to Augustine, time is real, but it can be conceived only in the human mind, the consciousness. Thus, Augustine asserts that, "time is certainly extendedness ... of the mind itself" (i.e., a distention of the soul, *distentio animae*).[83] Accordingly, in his argument on the problem of the measurement of time, Augustine declears, "It is in you, O my mind, that I measure time."[84] In this sense, Augustine believes that human consciousness and time are inevitably inter-related, hence time is a subjective time in mind. Augustine's such a conception of a subjective time profoundly influenced modern philosophies, especially in the concept of Immanuel Kant's "subjective time" and that of Edmund Husserl's "immanent time."

Concerning the meaning of God's eternity, Augustine clearly maintained the idea of God's timeless eternity. As we have seen, for Augustine, God, the Creator and Ordainer of time, is outside of time and prior to all of times. In relation to this, Augustine's conception of the timeless eternity comes from the doctrine of divine simplicity and immutability in a logical sense. According to Augustine, God is the perfect Being, who is in perfection, completeness, and fullness, and thus He cannot be in change and motion in time. In this sense, Augustine insists that, "eternity is the very substance of God Himself" (*aeternitas, ipsa Dei substantia est*).[85] God exists in an eternal "Now" (today) because He is the self-existent Being and the self-same Substance. Augustine says,

---

82. Ibid., XI.20 (p. 223, italics mine).
83. Ibid., XI.24 (p. 227) and 26 (p. 227).
84. Ibid., XI.27 (p. 229).
85. Augustine, *Enarr. In Ps.* CI, *Sermo* ii, 10; *PL* 36, 1311, as cited in Jess, "Divine Eternity in the Doctrine of St. Augustine," 75. In his *Confessions*, Augustine says that "if something arose in the substance of God which was not there before, that substance could not rightly be called eternal" (11.10).

> [God's] Being is a name for immutability. For all things that are changed cease to be what they were, and begin to be what they were not. Nobody has true being, pure being, real being except one who does not change.... What does "I am who am" mean but "I am eternal ... I cannot be changed"?[86]

Augustine believed that God truly exists because of His immutability, since every mutable being eventually falls into nothing in time.[87] Concerning this point, he says, "You are eternal, *who only have immortality*: for you change neither in form nor by motion, nor is your will changed as the times change."[88] Therefore, for Augustine, divine eternity is derived from divine immutability, and further ground is a divine simplicity based on the perfect Being of God.[89] Augustine says that in God's eternity, "there is no change of any kind."[90] And also, without change, there is no time.[91] In this sense, time cannot be co-eternal with God, for God is changeless. Rather, as he asserts, if time is changeless, it would be not time, but eternity.[92] In Augustine's view, therefore, eternity, which lacks time, is the mode of God's existence.

> *Thou art always the self-same, and Thy years shall not fail.* Your years neither go nor come.... Your years abide all in one act of abiding: for they abide and the years that go are not thrust out by those that come, for none pass.... Your years are as a single day; and Your day comes not daily but is today, a today which does not yield place to any tomorrow or follow upon any yesterday. In You today is eternity.[93]

Augustine thus sees the difference between God's eternity and time as a qualitative difference between the immutability of God and the mutability of creatures (i.e., the world). That is to say, all creatures are mutable

---

86. Augustine, *Sermon*, 7.7, in J. P. Minge, *Patrologia Latina* (Paris, 1841), vol. 38, 65. As cited in Leftow, *Time and Eternity*, 73.

87. As Augustine says, "God ... truly exists because he is unchangeable." Augustine, *Nature of Good*, in *S. Aur. Augustini: Opera omnia* (Paris: Gaume Fratres, 1836), vol. 8, 780, as cited in Leftow, *Time and Eternity*, 74.

88. Augustine, *Confessions*, XII.11 (p. 239, italics original).

89. Cf. Jess, "Divine Eternity in the Doctrine of St. Augustine," 93–95; Padgett, *God, Eternity and the Nature of Time*, 42; and Leftow, *Time and Eternity*, 73–111.

90. Augustine, *City of God*, XI.6 (p. 456).

91. Cf. Augustine, *Confessions*, XII.11 (p. 241).

92. Cf. ibid., XI.14 (p. 219).

93. Ibid., XI.13 (pp. 218–19).

being because they are created from nothing, but God is immutable and thus eternal because He is the Creator and the immutable, perfect and self-existent Being.

The relationship between eternity and time, according to Augustine, is that eternity is prior to all times (*ante omnia tempora*). As he says,

> It is not in time that You are before all time: otherwise You would not be before all time. You are before all the past by the eminence of Your ever-present eternity: and You dominate all the future in as much as it is still to be.[94]

In this statement, when Augustine speaks of "before all the times," it does not mean temporal "before" but it is a logical priority, pre-temporality, or transcendence over time, because there is no time before creation. In addition, for Augustine, God's eternity is "ever-present" (*nunc stans*), as he says that, "in eternity nothing passes but all is present, where time cannot be present all at once . . . and . . . time with its past and future must be determined by eternity, which stands and does not pass, which has in itself no past or future."[95]

Finally, for the meaning of God's eternity, Augustine insists that God created all things by uttering of His Word, which is "all in one act, yet abiding eternally"[96] as a single point in the excellency of an ever-present eternity. Therefore, according to Augustine, eternity is always immutable and an indivisible whole which is ever-present, the eternal Now, without any succession of past and future. Elsewhere, he says that, "we are not to try to conceive of infinite ages of time before the world, nor of infinite realms of space outside the world; for just as there are no periods of time before it, so also are there no spatial locations outside it."[97] Consequently, we can conclude that Augustine's conception of God's eternity is timeless, no temporal duration and no temporal location.[98]

---

94. Ibid., XI.13 (p. 218).

95. Ibid., XI.11 (p. 217).

96. Augustine, *Confessions*, XI.7 (p. 215), and 13 (p. 190), trans. J. G. Pilkington in *Basic Writings of Saint Augustine*, ed. W. J. Oates (Grand Rapids: Baker, 1992).

97. Augustine, *City of God*, XI.5 (p. 454).

98. Concerning a more detail discussion for the meaning of God's eternity in Augustine, see Leftow, *Time and Eternity*, 73–111; Feinberg, *No One Like Him*, 381; DeWeese, "God and the Nature of Time," 128–56; Jess, "Divine Eternity in the Doctrine of St. Augustine," 75–96.

Boethius

In Christian theology, it was probably Anicius Manlius Severinus Boethius (ca. 480–525) who gave one of the most important definitions of God's eternity, which is a definitive conception of divine eternity in classical theism, even up to now.[99] In his *The Consolation of Philosophy*, while attempting to reconcile divine foreknowledge and human freedom, Boethius defines God's eternity as follows:

> Now that God is eternal is the common judgment of all who live by reason. Therefore let us consider, what is eternity; for this makes plain to us both the divine nature and the divine knowledge. *Eternity, then, is the whole, simultaneous and perfect possession of boundless life* [*Aeternitas igitur est interminabilis vitae tota simul et perfecta possessio*], which becomes clearer by comparison with temporal things. For whatever lives in time proceeds in the present from the past into the future, and there is nothing established in time which can embrace the whole space of its life equally, but tomorrow surely it does not yet grasp, while yesterday it has already lost. And in this day to day life you live no more than in that moving and transitory moment. Therefore whatever endures the condition of time, although, as Aristotle thought concerning the world, it neither began ever to be nor ceases to be, and although its life is drawn out with the infinity of time, yet it is not yet such that it may rightly be believed to be eternal. For it does not simultaneously comprehend and embrace the whole space of its life, though it be infinite, but it possesses the future not yet, the past no longer. Whatever therefore comprehends and possesses at once the whole fullness of boundless life, and is such that neither is anything future lacking from it, nor has anything past flowed away, that is rightly held to be eternal, and that must necessarily both always be present to itself, possessing itself in the present, and hold as present the infinity of moving time.[100]

---

99. Concerning this point, Leftow rightly states that, "Boethius definition was a staple of medieval discussions of eternity." Idem, "Roots of Eternity," 191. And according to Yates, "It is universally agreed that he is the most important transmitter of the Neoplatonic concept of eternity to the Christian Middle Ages." Idem, *Timelessness of God*, 30 n. 90. For some recent examinations of Boethius' concept of time and eternity, see the following: Ford, "Boethius and Whitehead on Time and Eternity," 38–67; Stump and Kretzmann "Eternity," 429–58; Dales, "Time and Eternity in the Thirteenth Century," 27–45; Quinn, "On the Mereology of Boethian Eternity," 51–60; Rogers, "Eternity Has No Duration," 1–16.

100. Boethius, *Consolation of Philosophy*, 5.6 (pp. 423–25, italics mine). Feinberg says, "Boethius saw the question of human freedom and divine foreknowledge as a

In this statement, two things are clear. First, like Augustine, Boethius seems to hold a dynamic theory of time and presentism, in saying that, "time proceeds in the present from the past into the future," "in this day to day life you live no more than in that moving and transitory moment," and "tomorrow surely it does not yet grasp, while yesterday it has already lost." In the flow of time, therefore, temporal life is an ever-transitory moment of the present, because the past and the future are not real. It is only the ever-moving present which is real. At this point, it is interesting to note the direction of time's arrow. As we have seen, for Augustine, passing time always flows from the future through the present into the past (i.e., the future –> the past). However, Boethius says that "time proceeds in the present from the past into the future" (i.e., the past –> the future).

Secondly, in contrast to temporal life, God's eternity "comprehends and possesses at once the whole fullness of boundless life." That is to say, in eternity, all time (past, present and future) is present to God at once simultaneously (*tota simul*). In this sense, Boethius gives a famous definition of divine eternity: "Eternity ... is the whole, simultaneous and perfect possession of boundless life (*aeternitas igitur est interminabilis vitae tota simul et perfecta possessio*)." In Boethius' definition of eternity, as in Augustine's, we can find a strong influence of Neoplatonism, especially that of Plotinus, in that he defined eternity as a "divine life." Actually, as we have seen, Boethius' definition of God's eternity came from Plotinus' words: "the Life–instantaneously entire, complete, at no point broken into period or part–which belongs to the Authentic Existent [i.e., *Nous*, Divine Mind, God] by its very existence, this is the thing we were probing for–this is Eternity."[101]

---

genuine problem, and he seems to have been the first to think it could be resolved by applying the notion of timeless eternity to it." Idem, *No One Like Him*, 381.

101. Plotinus, *Enneads*, III.7.3 (p. 256). In this sense, for Boethius, Sorabji rightly points out that, "It was he above all who transmitted to the Christian middle ages the Neoplatonist concept of eternity." Idem, *Time, Creation and the Continuum*, 119. Leftow even says that, however, "Boethius simply took this definition over from pagan Neoplatonist philosophers. He did nothing to integrate it with his Christian theology. It occurs, if fact, only in his *Consolation of Philosophy*, a work whose Christianities are so minimal that some have doubted that Boethius wrote it. The definition became standard for medieval Christian theologians. But there too, there was nothing especially Christian about it. It was simply a bit of useful philosophy." Idem, "Response to *Mysterium Trinitatis*," 194. See also Stump and Kretzmann, "Eternity," 431, footnote 6; Padgett, *God, Eternity and the Nature of Time*, 45; Yeats, *Timelessness of God*, 31; DeWeese, "God and the Nature of Time," 164–68.

According to Boethius' definition of eternity, God is timelessly "eternal," but He has His own divine "life." Concerning this definition, however, one of the most controversial problem is the interpretation of the nature of God's "eternal life." At first glance, there seems to be an inconsistency between "possession all at once" (i.e., a point-like non-extended instant) and "boundless, illimitable life" (i.e., an endless infinite duration). In a reasonable sense, a "life" must entail some duration, for a point-like instant cannot be a life. Recently, therefore, Eleonore Stump and Norman Kretzmann interpret it as a special duration, an "atemporal duration" not "a frozen" or "an isolated, static instant," as *nunc stans*.[102] First, they hold that God's eternity entails a life, so numbers or propositions are not eternal but sempiternal (i.e., everlasting) in a good sense. Secondly, it is "boundless" (illimitable) life, which is an infinite duration without a beginning and an end. It cannot be limited. Thirdly, eternal life entails a special sort of duration. Finally, for them, "the complete possession all at once" means a kind of atemporality. Therefore, according their interpretation, Boethius' definition means that, the divine eternal life, God's mode of existence, is an "atemporal duration." That is to say, in Stump/Kretzmann's view, it is clear that the eternal God has a life, but it is "the complete possession all at once" (*vitae tota simul et perfecta possessio*), which means timeless. Thus, for them, God's eternity is an "atemporal duration." However, the real problem is that, how can it be an "infinitely extended duration" at the same time? Concerning the meaning of "atemporal duration," they give the following explanation:

> Because an eternal entity is atemporal, there is no past or future, no earlier or later, *within* its life; that is, the events constituting its life cannot be ordered sequentially from the standpoint of eternity. But in addition, no temporal entity or event can be earlier or later than past or future with respect to the whole life of an eternal entity, because otherwise such an eternal life or entity would itself be part of a temporal series.... the existing of an eternal entity is a duration without succession, no eternal entity has existed or will exist; it *only* exists.... the eternal, pastless, futureless present is not instantaneous but extended, because eternity entails duration. The temporal present is a durationless instant,.... The eternal present, on the other hand, is by definition an infinitely extended, pastless, futureless duration.[103]

102. Stump and Kretzmann, "Eternity," 430–34.
103. Ibid., 434–35.

Atemporal duration is duration none of which is not—none of which is absent (and hence future) or flowed away (and hence past). Eternity, not time, is the mode of existence that admits of fully realized duration.[104]

However, K. A. Rogers criticizes Stump/Kretzmann's concept of "atemporal duration" as being "*prima facie*, quite a puzzling notion," since in ordinary sense "duration" must involve an "extension in time."[105] In the same sense, P. Fitzgerald also criticizes it as being inconsistent in that "duration" (i.e., limitless extension) without any "temporal parts" is impossible.[106] God's eternity cannot be an extended duration, for the simplicity of God cannot entail any temporal parts, and therefore it is "all at once" (*tota simul*) like a single point. As Boethius himself says, "whatever endures the condition of time, . . . it does not simultaneously comprehend and embrace the whole space of its life," but "whatever therefore comprehends and possesses *at once* the whole fullness of boundless life, . . . that is rightly held to be eternal, and that must necessarily both always be present to itself, possessing itself in the present, and hold as present the infinity of moving time."[107] In this sense, Fitzgearld asserts, "God's timeless, eternal mode of being seems to me to admit of the 'point' interpretation, ... This 'nondurational' or 'point' interpretation fits the '*totum simul*' formula."[108] According to B. Leftow, however, if we suppose the tenseless (i.e., static) view of time, Boethius' concept of God's eternity as "a timeless durational life" and at the same time "eternal now" (*tota simul*) can be understandable. As he says, "Perhaps, then, Boethian eternity is like an extension in the tenseless time. Perhaps, that is, it involves earlier and later, any yet none of it 'passes away' or is 'yet to come,' as tensed theories say that phases of time do. If this is so, then an eternal being could be one that somehow lives at once (*tota simul*) all moments of a life whose moments are ordered as earlier and later."[109]

---

104. Ibid., 445.

105. Rogers, "Eternity Has No Duration," 6.

106. Fitzgeald, "Stump and Kretzmann on Time and Eternity," 260–69. For a similar criticism on Stump/Kretzmann's durational interpretation, see Craig, *Problem of Divine Foreknowledge*, 91–96, and DeWeese, "God and the Nature of Time," 157–68.

107. Boethius, *Consolation of Philosophy*, V.6 (pp. 423–25).

108. Fitzgeald, "Stump and Kretzmann on Time and Eternity," 264.

109. Leftow, *Time and Eternity*, 120.

For Boethius, in my view, it seems clear that God's eternity is a kind of "life" as His own mode of existence, but it is also "the perfect possession of boundless life" *all at once (tota simul)*, like a single point. According to W. L. Craig, the term of the "eternal life" in Boethius' view means no more than "existence" or "being" which is used in contrast to the temporal world's life.[110] Boethius himself says that, "it is a different thing to have embraced at once the whole presence of boundless life, . . . by his own simplicity of nature."[111] In another place, Boethius states the following concerning God's eternity:

> But what is said of God, "ever is," signifies only one thing, that he was, as it were, in all the past, is in all the present—however that term be used—and will be in all the future. According to the philosophers this may be said of the heavens and of other immortal bodies, but of God it is said in a different way. He is ever, because "ever" is with him a term of present time, and there is this great difference between the present of our affairs, which is now, and the divine present: our "now" connotes changing time and sempiternity; but God's "now," abiding, unmoved, and immovable, connotes eternity.[112]

In these statements, it is clear that God's eternity is "ever present" (i.e., divine *Now*), a life lived all "at once," which is timeless and nondurational in the sense of lacking any temporal extension.[113] In order to understand this, it is helpful to understand Boethius' view concerning God's eternal providence and temporal fates in the world as follows:

> For providence embraces all things together, through they are different, though they are infinite; but fate arranges as to their motion separates things, distributed in place, form and time; so that this unfolding of temporal order being united in the foresight of divine mind is providence, and the same unity when distributed and unfolded in time is called fate. . . . *God by providence disposes what is to be done in a single and unchanging way, but by fate accomplishes those same things he has disposed in a manifold and temporal way*. . . . [Therefore,] this surely is clear, that the unmoving and simple form of the way things are done is providence, and fate is the movable interlacing and temporal

---

110. Craig, *Problem of Divine Foreknowledge*, 92.
111. Boethius, *Consolation of Philosophy*, V.6 (p. 425).
112. Boethius, *De Trinitate*, 4 in *Boethius*, LCL, vol. 74 (pp. 21–23).
113. Cf. Padgett, *God, Eternity and the Nature of Time*, 46.

ordering of those things which the divine simplicity has disposed to be done.[114]

Here, we can find a scheme of Neoplatonic metaphysics, "*complicatio-explicatio*, enfolding–unfolding" model.[115] According to Boethius, the relationship between God's eternal providence and the fate of the temporal world is the same as of God's eternity and time. That is to say, all temporal things are enfolded already in God's one, eternal providence. As T. P. McTighe states, "For him, the temporal is, indeed, truly present in the eternal. All temporal moments are present there, not divided off from each other, but identical to the other in the encompassing (*complectens*) identity of eternity . . . time is an unfolding. . . . It is the divine unity unfolded into plurality."[116] Similarly, concerning divine knowledge of all time, Boethius says, God sees "all things as though from the highest peak of the world."[117] Therefore, considering the strong influence of Neoplatonic metaphysics as well as Plotinus' view of a non-durational and unextended timeless eternity, we can suppose that God's eternity is timeless in Boethius' view.[118]

In addition, in order to conceive the relationship between eternity and time, Boethius uses an analogy of a center-circle as follows: "For just as, of a number of spheres turning about the same center, the in-

114. Boethius, *Consolation of Philosophy*, IV.6 (pp. 359–61, italics mine).

115. Yates, *Timelessness of God*, 34.

116. Thomas P. McTighe, "Eternity and Time in Boethius," in *History of Philosophy in the Making*, ed. L. J. Thro (Washington: University of America, 1982), 53. As cited in Yates, *Timelessness of God*, 34–35.

117. Boethius, *Consolation of Philosophy*, V.6 (p. 427).

118. See the following statement of Plotinus, "So <the life of that which has real being> must not be counted by time, but by eternity. And this is neither more and less (*pleon, elatton*), nor of any length (*mekos*), but a 'this', and unextended (*adiastatos*) and not temporal (*ou chronikon*). You must not then join what has being to what does not, nor time or the temporal always (*to chronikon de aei*) to eternity, nor must you stretch out (*parekteinein*) the unextended (*adiastatos*). But you must take it all as a whole (*pan holon*), if you take it at all, and take not the indivisibility which is found in time, but the life of eternity which is not made up of many times, but is all together (*pasa homou*) from the whole time." *Enneads*, 1.5.7, as cited in Sorabji, *Time, Creation and the Continuum*, 113. In interpreting the statement, Sorabji says that, "These denials of duration, which are repeated again and again by the later Neoplatonists, seem to me to exclude most of the rival interpretations of eternity, including the idea of *enduring present. Indeed, the only surviving alternatives to the 'timeless' interpretation would seem to be those which treat eternity as a mere instant.*" Ibid., 113 (italics mine). See also Sorabji's non-durational interpretation on Boethius, ibid., 119–20.

nermost one approaches the simplicity of middleness... and if anything is joined or associates with that center, it is gathered into its simplicity. ... Therefore, as reasoning, as that which becomes is to that which is, *as time is to eternity, as the circle is to its center,* so is the moving course of fate to the unmoving simplicity of providence."[119] In this analogy, all the spheres and all the points of circumference of the circle (i.e., all the fates, all the temporal events in the moving course) are simultaneously present at the center-point of the circle (i.e., the one, simple God's providence and eternity) at once (*tota simul*). Therefore, we can conclude that, for Boethius, God's eternity is an absolute timeless eternity at a point-like. In addition, it is worth noting that, in some statements of Boethius, we can find an implication for the static understanding of the nature of time (e.g., the center-circle analogy for time and eternity).[120] In this way, Boethius established an influential definition of God's eternity in Medieval Christian theology.

Anselm

Anselm of Canterbury (1033–1109) was mainly influenced by Augustine, Boethius, and Aristotle's philosophy. We can find Anselm's discussions of God's eternity in his *Proslogion* 19 and 20, *Monologion* 18 to 24, and *De Concordia* 5.[121] However, at first, let's begin with Anselm's definition of God. As we well know, Anselm gives a famous ontological argument on God's existence. In his *Monologion*, Anselm says that, "God truly exists," since God is "the greatest, hightest Being—the Supreme Being" and "the existence of one Being through himself (*esse per se*)."[122] In *Proslogion* 2,

---

119. Boethius, *Consolation of Philosophy*, IV.6 (pp. 361–63, italics mine). As we have seen, Plotinus used the same analogy of center-circle for time and eternity relationship, see *Enneads*, 6.5.11 (p. 611).

120. Cf. DeWeese, "God and the Nature of Time," 168–71.

121. Anselm, *Proslogion, Monologion*, and *De Concordia* in *Anselm of Canterbury: The Major Works*, ed. Brian Davies and G. R. Evans (Oxford: Oxford University Press, 1998). For discussions on Anselm's concept of time and eternity, see Leftow, *Time and Eternity*, 183–216; DeWeese, "God and the Nature of Time," 172–80; Holt, "Timelessness and the Metaphysics of Temporal Existence," 149–56.

122. Cf. Anselm, *Monologion*, 1–6 (pp. 11–14). In *Monologion* 3, Anselm concludes that, "Therefore, there is on thing (being) which alone exists most greatly and most highly of all" (*Est igitur unum aliquid, quod solum maxime et summe omnium est*). Hopkins, *Companion to the Study of St. Anselm*, 68.

however, Anselm defined God another way: "You are something than which nothing greater can be thought."[123] He explains that as follows,

> Lord, not only are You that than which a greater cannot be thought, but You are also something greater than can be thought. For since it is possible to think that there is such a one, then, if You are not this same being something greater than You could be thought—which cannot be.[124]

According to such a definition of God, for Anselm, God is limitless and timelessly eternal, as he says, "All that which is enclosed in any way by place or time is less than that which no law of place or time constrains. Since, then, nothing is greater than You, no place or time confines You but You exist everywhere and always. And because this can be said of You alone, You alone are unlimited and eternal."[125]

Furthermore, according to Anselm, God is identical with all of His attributes because of His simplicity.[126] As he says, "The supreme nature is simple; thus, all the things which can be said of its essence are simply one and the same thing in it. And things can only be said of it in respect of substance with respect to what it is."[127] That is to say, "God is eternal" does not mean a mere possessing of the attribute of eternity. But, for Anselm, God is precisely identical to His eternity itself, i.e., God = eternity (and all other attributes: goodness, justice, etc.). He explains this as follows,

> Life and wisdom and other [attributes], then, are not parts of You, but all are one and each one of them is wholly what You are and what all the others are. Since, then, neither You nor Your eternity which You are have parts, no part of You or of Your eter-

---

123. Anselm, *Proslogion*, 2 (p. 87).

124. Ibid., 15 (p. 96).

125. Ibid., 13 (p. 94).

126. Anselm explains this as follows, "The supreme nature is what it is—good, great, existing—precisely through itself and nothing else. So then, it is just through justice and it is just through itself. And if so, then what is more necessarily and clearly the case than that the supreme nature is justice itself? Thus 'just through justice' is and means the same as 'just through itself,' and vice versa. And so if you ask 'what is this supreme nature we are talking about?,' you may answer 'justice.' What could be truer? . . . And since the supreme nature is strictly said not to possess, but to be, justice, when it is said to be just strictly it is intelligibly thought of as 'being justice,' and not as 'possessing justice.'" *Monologion*, 16 (p. 29).

127. Anselm, *Monologion*, 17 (p. 30).

nity is anywhere or at any time, but You exist as a whole everywhere and Your eternity exists as a whole always.[128]

In this way, Anselm identified God with His eternity on the basis of His simplicity. That is to say, God is supremely simple and supremely immutable, and thus cannot have temporal parts, but must be at once as a whole, which is eternity. Therefore, eternity is God Himself by definition.

What, then, exactly is Anselm's concept of God's eternity? First of all, God's eternity has no beginning or end. He explains,

> This simple nature, that creates and sustains all things—when did it begin? . . . if A begins to be out of (and through) B, B must be some thing other than A. The supreme nature, therefore, does not begin to be out of (or through) itself. So we have excluded all three possibilities (nothing, something else, and itself). Therefore, it does not have a starting point. Nor will it come to end. For if it has an end, it is not supremely immortal or supremely incorruptible. But it is supremely immortal and incorruptible. Therefore it does not have an end.[129]

Anselm's argument goes further, "It has no past, or future. It has no temporal present (not, that is, the transitory present that we experience). Its life span—its eternity—which is simply itself, is unalterable and partless."[130] That is to say, God's eternity is without beginning and end as well as without the temporal succession of past, present, and future. His Life, the mode of existence of the Suprem Being (i.e., the perfect Being), is absolutely simple and immutable, that is eternity. Anselm gives his own defintion of God's eternity as follows:

> Suppose, then, we say that it [i.e., the Supreme Being] always exists. What we take this to mean, then, is that it exists eternally. And since for it to exist is to be alive, that it lives eternally. It has, that is, unending life, perfectly, simultaneously and as a whole. Nothing makes better sense. It would seem that its *eternity is life unending, simultaneous, whole, and perfectly existing.* Now its substance simply is its life, and its life simply is its eternity. Its eternity is quite without end; it is nothing but simultaneous and perfect existence. This is already sufficiently clear. True eternity,

---

128. Anselm, *Proslogion*, 18 (p. 98).
129. Anselm, *Monologion*, 18 (p. 31).
130. Ibid., 24 (p. 40).

> the eternity that applies to this on esubstance alone—what is it if it is not life unending, simultaneous, whole, and perfectly existing? True eternity pertains to one substance only—the uncereated Creator.[131]

In this statement, we can find Boethius' words again that "*eternity is the whole, simultaneous and perfect possession of boundless life.*" In this way, Anselm clearly maintains the view of absolutely timeless divine eternity. This is also clear in the following statement by Anselm:

> That He is not in place or time but all things are in Him.... You were not, therefore, yesterday, nor will You be tomorrow, but yesterday and today and tomorrow You *are*. *Indeed You exist neither yesterday nor today nor tomorrow but are absolutely outside all time.* For yesterday and today and tomorrow are completely in time, however, You, though nothing can be without You, are nevertheless not in place or time but all things are in You. For nothing contains You, but You contain all things.[132]

In Anselm's view, if God exists in time, then, He must be temporally composite, be temporally contained, and subject to temporal change, but the simple God cannot be so. Since God is supremely simple and immutable and eternity is nothing but His essence, it is timeless. Therefore, God is timelessly eternal in the sense that He exists absolutely outside of time.

Finally, for Anselm, if the eternal God exists absolutely outside of time, then, how can God relate to human time? Concerning the relationship between God's eternity and time, Anselm insists that, "Indeed within eternity, in which there is no past or future but only a present, ... [However,] although in eternity there is only a present, nevertheless it is not a temporal present as ours is, only an eternal one in which all periods of time are contained.... For eternity has its own unique simultaneity which contains both all things that happen at the same time and place and that happen at different times and places."[133] Therefore, eternity exists altogether with every part of time and all the times at once. As Anselm states, "In eternity there is no time before or after. Something in eternity exists unceasingly now, since in eternity there is no temporary existence.... This is due to the nature of eternity which embraces

---

131. Ibid., 24 (p. 40–41, italics mine).
132. Anselm, *Proslogion*, 19 (p. 98, italics mine).
133. Anselm, *De Concordia*, I.5 (p. 443).

all time and all that occurs at any point in time."[134] That is to say, God exists everywhere and always (i.e., in every place and every time), but at the same time He exists simultaneously as a whole only in the sum of all places and times.[135]

In my view, however, there is an inconsistency in Anselm's conception of God's eternity and its relation to time. That is, in Anselm's view, God as eternity exists absolutely outside of time, but at the same time He exists all the time. Such a paradox in Anselm's conception of God's eternity and its relation to time seems to imply a tenseless (static) view of time as in the case of Boethius. Or in other words, B. Leftow, while interpreting Anselm's concept of timeless eternity and its relation to time, insists that Anselm's eternity is "a supertemporal dimension." This means that, "For given this supertime, God is temporally omnipresent even if no ordinary time exists for Him to be present to: even without ordinary time, He still exists in eternity's 'supertime.'"[136] Consequently, for Anselm, God's eternity can be thought as a "supertime," which means that He exists outside of time, but at the same time He can exist at all the times at once (*tota simul*).

Thomas Aquinas

In the theology of Thomas Aquinas (1225–1274), classical theism reaches its zenith. We can find his main arguments on God's eternity and its relation to time in his *Summa Theologiae*, 1a.10.1–4 and *Summa Contra Gentiles*, I.15.[137] Like Augustine, Boethius, and Anselm, Aquinas' logical and ontological basis of God's eternity is God's simplicity and immutability. That is, God's simplicity entails His immutability, and His immutability entails His eternity.[138] In the theology of Aquinas, therefore,

---

134. Ibid., I.5 (p. 444).

135. Cf. Anselm, *Monologion*, 20 and 21 (p. 33 and 34).

136. B. Leftow, *Time and Eternity*, 215.

137. Here I use the following edition: Thomas Aquinas, *Summa Theologica*, vol. 1, trans. Fathers of the English Dominican Province (Westminster: Christian Classics, 1981) or *Summa Theologiae*, vol. II, 1a.2–11, trans. Timothy Mcdermott (New York: Blackfriars, 1964), and *Summa Contra Gentiles*, Book One: *God*, trans. Anton C. Pegis (Notre Dame: University of Notre Dame Press, 1975).

138. Cf. Leftow, "Root of Eternity," 192; DeWeese, "God and the Nature of Time," 184; Yates, *Timelessness of God*, 39; and Broussard, "Eternity in Greek and Scholastic Philosophy," 8. According to Feinberg's analysis, "whereas Anselm moves

eternity is not an isolated doctrine, but a part of his scientific knowledge of God. Among his arguments on the divine essence, "simplicity" is the first and the most important attribute in the divine nature.[139] For him, as for Augustine, God is one and unity, "the substance of God is therefore his existence," thus He does not have any parts, but "God is truly and absolutely simple."[140]

Furthermore, according to Aquinas, all of God's attributes are identical with the essence of God, as he says, "God is nowise composite, but is altogether simple."[141] Therefore, as in Anselm, "God ... is identical with his own eternity just as he is identical with his own nature" (i.e., God = eternity).[142] Because of His simplicity (*Summa Theologiae*, 1a.2) and perfection (1a.4), God is immutable (1a.9). As Aquinas says,

> Now God, being limitless and embracing within himself the whole fullness of perfection of all existence, cannot acquire anything, nor can he move out towards something previously not attained. So one cannot in any way associate him with change.[143]

Therefore, in the view of Aquinas, only God, as the perfect Being, is absolutely immutable, and thus, because of His immutability, is eternal (1a.10): "the notion of eternity derives from unchangeableness in the same way the notion of time derives from change. Eternity therefore principally belongs to God, who is utterly unchangeable."[144] He continues,

> From what we have said it is further apparent that God is eternal. Everything that begins to be or ceases to be does so through motion or change. Since, however, we have shown that God is absolutely immutable, He is eternal, lacking all beginning or

---

from God's perfection to his eternity in the *Proslogium* and from God's simplicity directly to his eternity in the *Monologium*, Aquinas's basic line of thought moves from simplicity to immutability and from immutability to timeless eternity." Idem, *No One Like Him*, 384.

139. Cf. Burns, "Divine Simplicity in St. Thomas," 271, and Padgett, *God, Eternity and the Nature of Time*, 49.

140. Aquinas, *Summa Theologiae*, Ia.3.4 (p. 31) and *Summa Theologica*, Ia.3.7 (p. 19).

141. Aquinas, *Summa Theologica*, Ia.3.7 (p. 19). Aquinas says, "God is to be identified with his own essence or nature." Ibid., Ia.3.3 (p. 29).

142. Ibid., Ia.10.2 (p. 139).

143. Ibid., Ia.9.1 (pp. 127–28).

144. Ibid., Ia.10.2 (p. 139).

end.[145] Eternity, in the true and proper sense, belongs to God alone, for eternity, we said, follows upon unchangeableness, and God alone, as we showed, is altogether unchangeable.[146]

That is to say, Aquinas believes that God is eternal because He is altogether immutable. God exists without beginning and end, for He is the self-existent perfect Being. Therefore, God cannot be in time, because time is the measure of change (motion).

As a matter of fact, Aquinas' first way of proof of God's existence is based on change (motion). His argument continues as follows,

> The first and more manifest way is the argument from motion. It is certain in the world some thing are in motion. Now whatever is in motion is put in motion by another, for nothing can be in motion, whereas a thing moves inasmuch as it is in act. For motion is nothing else than the reduction of something from potentiality to actuality.... Therefore, whatever is in motion must be put in motion by another... But this cannot go on to infinity. ... Therefore, it is necessary to arrive at a first mover, put in motion by no other; and this everyone understands to be God.[147]

There is no potentiality (*potentia*) in God, but He is pure actuality and pure act (*actus purus*) in eternity.[148] Accordingly, for Aquinas, God is "the First Mover" or "Unmoved Mover," and "the First Cause of Change" or "the Uncreated Creator," and, therefore, He is the eternal God. In this way, the logical foundation of God's eternity is as follows: the perfect self-existent Being-divine simplicity-divine immutability-divine eternity, and thus God is eternal.

According to Aquinas, eternity is completely different from time, "which is merely the *numbering of before and after in change*."[149] As he says, "Time and eternity clearly differ. Now this is ... an intrinsic difference [in] that eternity is an instantaneous whole whilst time is not, eternity measuring abiding existence and time measuring change."[150]

---

145. Aquinas, *Summa Contra Gentiles*, I.15.1 and 2 (p. 98).

146. Aquinas, *Summa Theologiae*, Ia.10.3 (p. 141).

147. Ibid., Ia.2.3 (p. 13).

148. Cf. ibid., Ia.3.1 (p. 21).

149. Ibid., Ia.10.1 (p. 137, italics original). Aquinas' understanding of time largely depends on Aristotle's *Physics* 4. Cf. Davies, *Thought of Thomas Aquinas*, 105. For Aquinas' concept of time, see Quinn, *Doctrine of Time in St. Thomas*.

150. Aquinas, *Summa Theologiae*, Ia.10.4 (p. 145).

What, then, is Aquinas' concept of God's eternity?[151] For argument, first of all, Aquinas accepted Boethius' definition of eternity: "eternity is the instantaneously whole and perfect possession of unending life (*aeternitas est interminablis vitae tota simul et perfecta possessio*)."[152]

In defending the definition, Aquinas characterizes eternity as follows: "First, anything existing in eternity is unending (*interminabile*), that is to say, lacks both beginning and end (for both may be regarded as ends). Secondly, eternity itself exists as an instantaneous whole (*tota simul*) lacking successiveness."[153] Eternity does not have a beginning/end and succession of change in time, and therefore it is interminable and instantaneously whole. Then, while comparing eternity to time, Aquinas defines eternity in a negative way,

> For just as we are aware of time by becoming aware of the flowing instant (*fluxum nunc*), so we grasp the idea of eternity by grasping the idea of an abiding instant (*nunc stans*).... Eternity and God are the same thing. So calling him eternal does not imply his being measured by something extrinsic; the notion of measurement arises only in our way of conceiving the situation.[154]
> ... eternity is an instantaneous whole (*tota simul*) whilst time is not, eternity measuring abiding existence and time measuring change.... The "now" remains unchanged in substance throughout time, but take on different forms ... But eternity remains unchanged both in substance and in form. Eternity therefore differs from the "now" of time. Just as eternity is properly the measure of existence as such, so time is properly the measure of change.[155]

According to Aquinas, eternity does not simply differ from time, but absolutely lacks it. Therefore, God is timelessly eternal. However, in his *Summa Contra Gentiles*, Aquinas presents eternity in a positive way as follows,

---

151. For Aquinas' concept of God's eternity, see Broussard, "Eternity in Greek and Scholastic Philosophy," 5–94; Davies, *Thought of Thomas Aquinas*, 103–17; Hughes, *On A Complex Theory of A Simple God*, 114–20; and La Croix, "Aquinas on God's Omnipresence and Timelessness," 391–99.

152. Aquinas, *Summa Theologiae*, Ia.10.1 (p. 134).

153. Ibid., Ia.10.1 (p. 137).

154. Ibid., Ia.10.2 (pp. 139–41).

155. Ibid., Ia.10.4 (pp. 145–47).

> We must therefore posit something that is a necessary being. Every necessary being, however, either has the cause of its necessity in an outside source or, if it does not, it is necessary through itself. But one cannot proceed to infinity among necessary beings the cause of whose necessity lies in an outside source. We must therefore posit a first necessary being, which is necessary through itself. This is God, since, as we have shown, He is the first cause. God, therefore, is eternal, since whatever is necessary through itself is eternal.[156]

In this statement, Aquinas characteristically identifies God's necessity for eternity. That is to say, God's eternity is a necessary attribute, not an accidental. Concerning this fact, he says, "Necessity is a mode of truth. Now truth, according to Aristotle, resides in the mind. So necessary truths are eternal only if they exist in the eternal mind, which is nothing other than God's mind. So it does not follow that anything outside God is eternal."[157] In sum, Aquinas' argument goes as follows:

(a) There must be a necessary Being, which is God
   (God = necessity); and then,
(b) A necessary being is eternal (necessity = eternity);
   and therefore,
(c) God is eternal (God = eternity).

In this sense, Aquinas says that, "Eternity and God are the same thing."[158]

In order to understand Aquinas' concept of God's timeless eternity, the following statement is probably helpful:

> Moreover, God's understanding has no succession, as neither does His being. He is therefore an ever-abiding simultaneous whole—which belongs to the nature of eternity. On the other hand, the duration of time is stretched out through the succession of the before and after. Hence, the proportion of eternity to the total duration of time is as the proportion of the indivisible to something continuous; not, indeed, of that indivisible that is the terminus of a continuum, which is not present to every part of a continuum (the instant of time bears a likeness to such an indivisible), but of that indivisible which is outside a continuum

---

156. Aquinas, *Summa Contra Gentiles*, I.15.5 (p. 99).
157. Aquinas, *Summa Theologiae*, Ia.10.3 (p. 143).
158. Ibid., Ia.10.2 (p. 141).

> and which nevertheless co-exists with any given part of a continuum or with a determinate point in the continuum. For, since time lies within motion, eternity, which is completely outside motion, in no way belongs to time. Furthermore, since the being of what is eternal does not pass away, eternity is present in its presentiality to any time or instant of time.[159]

In this statement, it is clear that God has neither "temporal succession" nor "temporal duration," i.e., extension. Rather, God's eternity is "an ever-abiding simultaneous whole" outside the temporal continuum. Therefore, Aquinas believes that God's eternity is a timeless eternity not only without beginning and end, but also whithout duration and temporal location. Conclusively, as B. Letow rightly points out, for Aquinas, eternity is surely the mode of life of the simple Being of God.[160] However, it does not have any temporal duration of succession—past, present, and future; or before and after—as in a temporal being, and thus it is a possession of the whole life at once. As Aquinas states, the eternal God is "not only existent but living" in an instantaneously whole life at once (*tota simul*).[161]

Concerning the problem of God's eternity and its relation to time, Aquinas also uses Boethius' "center-circle" analogy:

> We may see an example of sorts in the case of a circle. Let us consider a determined point on the circumference of a circle. Although it is indivisible, it does not co-exist simultaneously with any other point as to position, since it is the order of position that produces the continuity of the circumference. On the other hand, the center of the circle, which is no part of the circumference, is directly opposed to any given determinate point on the circumference. Hence, whatever is found in any part of time co-exists with what is eternal as being present to it, although with respect to some other time it be past or future. Something can be present to what is eternal only by being present to the whole of it, since the eternal does not have the duration of succession. The divine intellect, therefore, sees in the whole of its eternity, as being present to it, whatever takes place through the whole course of time. And yet what takes place in a certain part of time was not always existent. It remains, there-

---

159. Aquinas, *Summa Contra Gentiles*, I.66.7 (pp. 218–19).

160. Cf. Leftow, *Time and Eternity*, 150.

161. Aquinas, *Summa Theologiae*, Ia.10.1 (p. 137). Cf. Davies, *Thought of Thomas Aquinas*, 106.

fore, that God has a knowledge of those things that according to the march of time do not yet exist.[162]

In this vision, all the events—past, present, and future—in a continuous temporal series (i.e., the circumference of the circle) are present to God in eternity (i.e., the center of the circle). According to G. J. DeWeese, however, "It does not entail . . . that God sees all events as simultaneous with each other. It is God's seeing of the events, not the events themselves, that are simultaneous."[163] Elsewhere, Aquinas says that, "God . . . is wholly outside the order of time, stationed as it were at the summit of eternity, which is wholly simultaneous, and to Him the whole course of time is subjected in one simple intuition."[164] Therefore, we can conclude that Thomas Aquinas' concept of God's eternity is an absolute timeless eternity. In timeless (i.e., "wholly outside the order of time") eternity, God knows all temporal events—past, present, and future—at once. In this sense, W. L. Craig says that such an understanding of Aquinas' divine foreknowledge and future contingents (i.e., the relationship between God's eternity and time) can properly fit with the static (tenseless) view of time.[165] It seems clear in the following Aquinas' "traveler-watchtower" analogy:

> Furthermore, although corporeal and temporal particulars do not exist simultaneously, God surely has simultaneous knowledge of them. For He knows them according to His manner of being, which is eternal and without succession. . . . This also makes it clear that He has certain knowledge of contingent things. Even before they come into being, He sees them as they

---

162. Aquinas, *Summa Contra Gentiles*, I.66.7 (p. 219). Elsewhere, Aquinas explains God's timeless knowledge of the whole temporal events in using another analogy: "Were someone to see many travelers along a road successively, over a certain period of time, in each part of that time he would see some passers by as present, so that over the whole time of his vision he would see every traveler as present. He would not see all as present at once because the time of his seeing is not all-at-once. If his seeing were able to exist all at the once, he would see at once all as present, although they do not all pass by as present at once. Whence because the vision of God's knowledge is measured by eternity, which is all at once and yet includes all of time . . . God sees what happens in time not as future but as present." Idem, *De Veritate*, 2.12. As cited in Leftow, *Time and Eternity*, 181–82.

163. DeWeese, "God and the Nature of Time," 182.

164. Aquinas, *In Perihermeias*, 14.20. Cited in Craig, *Problem of Divine Foreknowledge*, 107.

165. Cf. Craig, "Was Thomas Aquinas a B-Theorist of Time?," 475–83.

actually exists, and not merely as they will be in the future and as virtually present in their causes with a claim to future existence, are not sufficiently determinate to admit of certain knowledge about them; but, regarded as actually possessing existence, they are determinate, and hence certain knowledge is possible.... For His eternity is in present contact with the whole course of time, and even passes beyond time. We may fancy that God knows the flight of time in His eternity, in the way that a person standing on top of a watchtower embraces in a single glance a whole caravan of passing travelers.[166]

Conclusion

In this chapter, I surveyed, though very briefly, various theologians to establish a consensus in classical theism that God's eternity is an absolute timelessness, from its metaphysical background in ancient Greek philosophy, and then through Augustine, Boethius and Anselm, and finally to Thomas Aquinas. In doing so, we can clearly see that there is a strong influence of Greek metaphysics, especially Neo-Platonism (i.e., Plotinus), which can be traced back to Plutarch, Plato, and finally to Parmenides. It seems clear that, in establishing the concept of God's absolute timeless eternity, classical theists used the Greek philosophers' concepts and understandings of time/eternity. That is, the concept of absolute timeless eternity is basically constituted according to the Greek ontological paradigm: the Perfect Being—simplicity—immutability—timeless eternity. However, it is also true that, in doing so, they held fast to the biblical and Christian perspective, leaving an excellent theological heritage for Christian theology today.

Meanwhile, Augustine clearly shows by his doctrine of *creatio ex nihilo et creatio cum tempus* that there is a qualitative difference between time and eternity. Time is created from nothing as are the created beings by the eternal God, and thus, time as such is the mode of the created entities' existence. In addition, it is worth noting that, even though classical theologians recognized well the negative difference between time and God's eternity, they also indicated a motif which implies a positive relationship between them. That is to say, in borrowing Plotinus' idea of time and eternity, Boethius, and thus Anselm and Aquinas as well,

166. Aquinas, *Compendium of Theology*, 142.

defined God's eternity as "the whole, simultaneous and perfect possession of boundless life (*aeternitas igitur est interminabilis vitae tota simul et perfecta possessio*)." In this definition, they conceived God's own life in His being, which implies a partial correspondence within an infinite qualitative difference to the eventful temporal life of the creatures. However, they did not develop such a significant idea for understanding God's eternity and its relation to time in its full sense. The reason for this seems to be that they were too much captivated by the concept of the one, simple, and thus immutable God alone (i.e., *Deo Uno*).

Concerning the use of Greek metaphysics in classical theism, I want to mention theological methodology. Generally speaking, one of the main tasks of Christian theology is, first of all, a systematic formulation of biblical truth and, at the same time, its contextualization in order to bear witness to the world in response to contemporary intellectual challenges and questions concerning ultimate truth claims. Accordingly, especially, in the area of systematic theology, when we study a theological subject matter like the problem of the relationship between God's eternity and time, we always need a proper "conceptual frame" or methodological framework in order to develop the subject into a coherent system as a whole. The reason for this is that Christian theology is not a mere collection of biblical proof-texts or doctrinal statements on various theological subject matters but a "faith seeking understanding," always seeking understanding beyond a confusing paradox in the fragments of truth claims. Therefore, concerning the use of a philosophical conceptual frame in order to figure out biblical truth, like Augustine's use of Platonism and Aquinas' use of Aristotelian philosophy, (though we can criticize the methodological inadequateness) we need not to simply insist that it is unbiblical and thus should be discarded, as many do, but we must find a more proper theological methodology (or world view) for the biblical truth claim. That is to say, the biblical content itself determines its proper methodology, not vice versa. In this sense, theologians can use a proper philosophical concept for theological clarity, but a philosophical framework should not confine its theological content and its agenda.

In this sense, even though the understandings of God's eternity and its relation to time in classical theism are not completely wrong, there is a methodological flaw in that there is a one-sided emphasis on the absolute difference between time and eternity because of the unity of God (i.e., *Deo Uno*). In my view, therefore, a positive relationship between God's eternity and time, along with the qualitative difference between them, can be fully conceived in Trinitarian thinking (i.e., *Deo Trino*). As we have seen in chapter 2, according to the biblical perspective, there must be a look at not only qualitative differences but also the positive relationship between God's eternity and time, since God Himself created and sustains time. Furthermore, time is the arena of God's revelation and the medium of His mighty redemptive actions in the works of the Son and the Holy Spirit. In truth, the unity of God (*Deo Uno*) and the Trinity (*Deo Trino*) are inseperable. The only true biblical God, who is the living God, is the Triune God in one unity. The Trinity *ad intra* (i.e., immanent Trinity of the self-existent Being in eternity) and the Trinity *ad extra* (i.e., the economic Trinity of revelation and redemption in time) cannot be separated (cf. K. Rahner's Rule).[167] We shall see such an indepth study of the Trinitarian understanding of time and God's eternity in "Part II, Toward a Trinitarian Understanding of Time and Eternity."

---

167. K. Rahner's Rule is as follows: "The economic Trinity is the immanent Trinity and the immanent Trinity is the economic Trinity." Rahner, *Trinity*, 22.

4

Contemporary Philosophical and Scientific Debates on the Nature of Time

Introduction

IN THIS WORLD, EVERYTHING WHICH EXISTS ESSENTIALLY RELATES TO time. Time is our human mode of existence and the very condition of limitation. Nothing happens out of time. Therefore, time is the horizon embracing all existences in this world. As J. Muilenburg says, "To live is to live in time, and our consciousness and thinking are so commingled with its movement, so intimately involved in its flux and the inexorability of temporal changes that the quest for serenity and interior tranquility never ceases to occupy us."[1] Accordingly, it is not a surprising fact that time is a central subject of almost all academic disciplines, not only theology but also philosophy, natural science, history, social science, literature, ethics, among many others, which are "all engaged in a common encounter with the mystery of this basic givenness of our human existence."[2] Thus, human beings have energetically pursued the meaning and the nature of time from the dawn of history.[3] However, even in this twenty-first century, which is now proceeding to the era of

---

1. Muilenburg, "Biblical View of Time," 226.

2. Ibid., 225.

3. In this sense, Coveney and Highfield point out, "Time is one of the greatest sources of mystery to mankind. Throughout history, human beings have restlessly puzzled over time's profound yet inscrutable nature. It is a subject which has captivated poets, writers, and philosophers of every generation." Idem, *Arrow of Time*, 23. For the history of the understanding of time, see Capek, "Time," 389–98; Sorabji, *Time, Creation and Continuum*; Turetzky, *Time*; and Lippincott, et al., *Story of Time*. For a helpful bibliography on the study of time, see Fraser and Soulsby, "Literature of Time," 145–60.

intelligent revolution beyond the era of scientific revolution, we still do not and cannot exhaustively understand the nature of time, "the familiar stranger."[4]

What, then, is time? Even though time is the very mode of existence for human beings as well as the other creatures in this world, the ways of understanding time are very different in every human culture and every area of human activities.[5] Indeed, if we think more about time, it appears more and more as an unsolvable mystery and enigma. Therefore, as frequently cited, Augustine's lamentation clearly shows its difficulty: "If no one asks me, I know; if I want to explain it to a questioner, I do not know."[6] However, in spite of its difficulty, if we bravely try to figure out the nature of time, we must first understand its multi-aspects, the complexity of time.[7] Accordingly, when we try to study on time, we must not forget its very diverse meanings, functions, and aspects in various perspectives.[8] The many aspects of time are demonstrated in the following various conceptions: metaphysical time, physical (or measured) time, cosmological time, biological time, psychological time, historical time, social time, and so forth.[9] There are very diverse concepts and competitive theories and explanations in conceiving the nature of time. In this sense, E. J. Lowe rightly says that time is "the most puzzling and paradoxical feature of the world."[10] However, in order to

---

4. Cf. the book title of Fraser, *Time: The Familiar Stranger*.

5. In the following works, we can see very diverse understandings of time in various world-wide cultures and human activities, Gardet, et al., *Cultures and Time*; Balslev and Mohanty, eds., *Religion and Time*; and Fraser, *Voices of Time*, which is a collection of articles concerning various aspects of time from the historical, cultural, linguistic, musical, psychological, biological, and physical perspectives.

6. Augustine, *Confessions*, xi.14.

7. For this reason, Craig rightly points out that, "Too often the question of the nature of time has been prematurely answered by some philosopher and physicist simply because he is largely ignorant of relevant discussions outside his chosen field of expertise." Idem, *Tenseless Theory of Time*, ix.

8. Cf. Boslough, "Enigma of Time," 109–32. Why has time been "a perennial source of puzzlement and perplexity"? The reason is that, as R. Gale states, "the problem of time is a group of intimately related questions having to do with the nature of the concepts of truth, events, things, knowledge, causality, identification, action, and change." Gale, *Philosophy of Time*, vii.

9. Cf. Whitrow, *Natural Philosophy of Time*; Harris, *Reality of Time*; Horvath, "New Notion of Time," 35–55.

10. Lowe, *Possibility of Metaphysics*, 84.

properly comprehend our subject matter, the problem of God's eternity and its relation to time, we must first understand the nature of "time" itself. Therefore, before turning to our issue, I want to briefly survey the following two alternative conceptions of the nature of time in contemporary philosophy and science: the tenseless (static) and the tensed (dynamic) theory of time.

The Beginning of Contemporary Debates on the Nature of Time

In reconceiving the nature of time, vigorous contemporary debates were provoked by the following three very significant works in physics and metaphysics in the early 20th century: A. Einstein's Special Theory of Relativity (1905) and General Theory of Relativity (1915),[11] H. Minkowski's "Space and Time" (1908),[12] and J. M. E. McTaggart's "The Unreality of Time" (1908).[13] Actually, they made a watershed for recent debates on the nature of time between the two rival conceptions of time, the tenseless (static) theory and the tensed (dynamic) theory. As we shall see, their conception of time also affected vital discussions in other areas: metaphysics, philosophy of science, philosophy of logic, philosophy of language, philosophy of mind, philosophy of religion, among many others.[14] Accordingly, in ongoing discussions, all of those works have profoundly influenced the recent understandings of time in that they provided not only the logical foundations and vocabularies but also the essential concepts for the debates on the nature of time. As a matter of fact, since the present debates on the nature of time were brought about from those works, we cannot properly understand the former without some knowledge about the latter. Therefore, it will be in proper order to review, though briefly, those works first.

11. Einstein, "Elektrodynamik bewegter Körper," 891–921, and it was reprinted as "On the Electrodynamics of Moving Bodies," 140–71. Cf. idem, *Meaning of Relativity*.

12. Minkowski, "Space and Time," 75–91.

13. McTaggart, "Unreality of Time," 457–74. It was reprinted in Keeling, *Philosophical Studies*, chapter 5, "The Unreality of Time," 110–31, and an extended form in Broad, *Nature of Existence*, vol. 2, chapter 33, "Time," 9–31. This extended article was also partly reprinted in Le Poidevin and MacBeath, *Philosophy of Time*, 23–34. I used Broad's edition here.

14. For the importance of the debate between tenseless and tensed theory of time in related areas, see Smith, "General Introduction," 1–14.

Einstein-Minkowski's Concept of Space-Time

In the beginning of the 20th century, A. Einstein's Special Theory of Relativity (cf. hereafter STR, 1905) can be considered as another "Copernican turning" not only for physics in general but also for the concept of time in particular in that it made a revolutionary turning point in the understanding of time.[15] In classical physics, time is conceived as "absolute time" which in itself exists without relation to anything external and flows equably.[16] However, by his STR, Einstein dispelled the idea of Newtonian concept of absolute time. Especially, the Michelson-Morley experiment (1887), which was to measure the ether effect on the speed of light by the earth's movement, showed that there is no such kind of "ether" in the space of the universe. It means that there is not a universal standard reference, absolute space, and absolute time. In the STR, therefore, the only uniqueness in the universe is the speed of light (a universal constant, c), which is a universally homogeneous speed for every reference frame (i.e., the principle of constancy).[17] This idea of the invariance of the speed of light functions as a foundational

---

15. For the history of the concepts of space and time and various theories in recent discussions, see the following: Putnam, "Time and Physical Geometry," 240–47; Stein, "On Einstein-Minkowski Space-Time," 5–23; Van Fraassen, *Introduction to the Philosophy of Time and Space*; Capek, *Concepts of Space and Time*; Sklar, *Space, Time, and Spacetime*; Earman, et al., *Foundations of Space-Time Theories*; Friedman, *Foundations of Space-Time Theories*; Nerlich, *What Spacetime Explains*.

16. In his *The Principia*, I. Newton states as follows: "Absolute, true, and mathematical time, in and of itself and of its own nature, without reference to anything external, flows uniformly and by another name is called duration. Relative, apparent, and common time is any sensible and external measure (precise or imprecise) of duration by means of motion; such a measure—for example, an hour, a day, a month, a year—is commonly used instead of true time." Idem, *Principia*, 408–9. In this statement, Newton distinguished the "absolute" (i.e., universal) time and space from the "relative" (i.e., measured or clock) time and space. Accordingly, Newton also recognized the idea of relativity in our actual world. According to French, "the basic concept of relativity is as old as the mechanics of Galileo and Newton." Idem, *Special Relativity*, 3. Thus, in my view, the only difference between Newton and Einstein is that the former presupposed the "absolute" universal time, but the latter did not. In his Relativity Theory, Einstein used measured, clock time. Furthermore, Einstein applied the idea of relativity to all of our physical experience.

17. Einstein asserted that, "in empty space light is always propagated with definite velocity V which is independent of the state of motion of the emitting body." Idem, "On the Electrodynamics of Moving Bodies," 140.

principle in the STR.[18] At the same time, according to Einstein's famous equation, $E = mc^2$, it is the marginal speed in the universe in that nothing can reach it.[19]

More significantly for our subject, according to the STR, space and time are intrinsically linked together. Thus, there cannot be a "simultaneous" event for the observers in different moving frames.[20] Accordingly, local time in any moving system is relative to the time of the other frames of reference. In the STR, one of the most significant characteristics is the fact that "simultaneity" is relative, and therefore there cannot be the absolute "Now," for all observers are in different frames of reference from each other. In addition, according to the STR, time itself is flexible, and thus it can be stretched or shrunk by motion. That is to say, if the speed of motion approached the speed of light, the timewarp (i.e., time-dilation effect) escalates (cf. the paradox of twins).[21] In this way, Einstein restored time as an essential part of physics again, and thus it is inseparable from concrete physical events.[22] According to the General Theory of Relativity (cf. hereafter GTR, 1915), time is also affected by gravity. If there is more gravity, time passes more slowly

18. Cf. Friedman, *Foundations of Space-Time Theories*, 163.

19. Hawking explains it as follows: "Because of the equivalence of energy and mass, the energy which an object has due to its motion will add to its mass. In other words, it will make it harder to increase its speed. . . . As an object approaches the speed of light, its mass rises ever more quickly, so it takes more and more energy to speed it up further. It can, in fact, never reach the speed of light, because by then its mass would have become infinite, and by the equivalence of mass and energy, it would have taken an infinite amount of energy to get it there. For this reason, any normal object is forever confined by relativity to move at speeds slower than the speed of light. Only light, or other waves that have no intrinsic mass, can move at the speed of light." Idem, *Brief History of Time*, 20–21.

20. Einstein says, "we must not ascribe *absolute* meaning to the concept of simultaneity; instead, two events that are simultaneous when observed from some particular coordinate system can no longer be considered simultaneous when observed from a system that is moving relative to that system." Idem, "On the Electrodynamics of Moving Bodies," 145 (italics original).

21. Cf. Davies, *God and the New Physics*, 120–23.

22. According to Davies, "Before Galileo and Newton, time was an organic, subjective thing, not a parameter to be measured with geometrical precision. Time was part and parcel of nature. Newton plucked time right out of nature and gave it an abstract, independent existence, robbing it of its traditional connotations. It was included in Newton's description of the world merely as a way of keeping track of motion mathematically; it didn't actually *do* anything. Einstein restored time to its rightful place at the heart of nature, as an integral part of the physical world." Idem, *About Time*, 17.

because of the gravitational time-dilation effect. Therefore, the four dimensional curvature of space-time appears as a flexible curve according to gravity of matter.

Although Einstein's STR was published in 1905, it was H. Minkowski who gave its clearest interpretation in the concrete four-dimensional space-time geometry.[23] According to him, substantive physical reality can be described in the four-dimensional manifolds of space-time. As Minkowski states, "Henceforth space by itself, and time by itself, are doomed to fade away into mere shadows, and only a kind of union of the two will preserve an independent reality."[24] Thus, a position of substance in the world can be described by the four-dimensional coordinates—x, y, z (space) with t (time), and it is called "a world-point." Then, the everlasting career of the substantial point, dx, dy, dz, and dt (if we take the parameter t, from $-\infty$ to $+\infty$) constitutes "a curve in the world, a *world-line*," which is the space-time continuum.[25] Accordingly, in this view, the whole universe can be described by these world-lines of the four-dimensional arena of world events in indissoluble space-time.

Therefore, for Minkowski, space-time is the set of events in the static four-dimensional geometry. From these conceptions, Minkowski introduced a fundamental axiom: "*The substance at any world-point may always, with the appropriate determination of space and time, be looked upon as at rest.*"[26] This means that all world-points always exist as a fixed form along with the straight world-line of the static four-dimensional space-time continuum. In this concept of space-time, time does not flow, for it is fixed with space. Accordingly, there is no passage of time as in common sense. As a result, Einstein-Minkowski's space-time seemed to entail a static (tenseless) view of time. In this sense, as early as 1914, E. Cunningham wrote as follows:

> With Minkowski space and time became particular aspects of a single four-dimensional concept; the distinction between

---

23. According to Craig, Einstein originally conceived a 3+1 dimensional theory, but after Minkowski's interpretation of his STR in the 4-dimensional space-time theory, he preferred the latter for his own Relativity Theory. Cf. idem, *Tenseless Theory of Time*, 12. See also Friedman, *Foundations of Space-Time Theories*, 16. Actually, Minkowski was Einstein's occasional mathematical mentor at Zurich. Cf. Swenson, *Genesis of Relativity*, 177.

24. Minkowski, "Space and Time," 75.

25. Ibid., 76.

26. Ibid., 80 (italics original).

them as separate modes of correlating and ordering phenomena is lost, and the motion of a point in time is represented as a *stationary curve in four-dimensional space*. Now if all motional phenomena are looked at from this point of view they become *timeless phenomena* in *four-dimensional space*. The whole history of a physical system is laid out as a *changeless whole*.[27]

McTaggart's Paradox

In the very same year as Minkowski's article on "Space and Time" in science, another very significant and disputative article was published in philosophy by J. M. E. McTaggart, "The Unreality of Time" (1908).[28] In this famous work, McTaggart's essential intention was to prove the unreality of time. In order to do so, he begins his argument by distinguishing between the two different ways in which we ordinarily conceive and talk about time. He named them the "A-Series" and "B-Series" of time. That is, according to McTaggart, events are capable of being ordered in two different ways: (1) The "B-series" means that events can be ordered in respect to their relationship to other events as "earlier than" and "later than"; (2) otherwise, "A-series" means they are ordered in respect to past, present, and future. However, McTaggart thought that there is a paradox in our understanding of time, as follows,

> Since distinctions of the first class [i.e., B-series] are permanent, it might be thought that they were more objective, and more essential to the nature of time, than those of the second class [i.e., A-series]. I believe, however, that this would be a mistake, and that the distinction of past, present, and future is as *essential* to time as the distinction of earlier and later, while in a certain sense it may, as we shall see, be regarded as more *fundamental* than the distinction of earlier and later. And it is because the

---

27. Cunningham, *Principle of Relativity*, 191. Cited in Capek, *Concepts of Space and Time*, 501 (italics original).

28. A number of articles and books have been published concerning McTaggart's view of the unreality of time. Among them, see the following: Broad, *Examination of McTaggart's Philosophy*; Gale, *Language of Time*; King-Farlow, "Positive McTaggart on Time," 169–78; Zeilicovici, "(Dis)solution of McTaggart's Paradox," 175–95; Lowe, "Indexical Fallacy in McTaggart's Proof of the Unreality of Time," 62–70; Farmer, *Being in Time*; Oaklander and Smith, *New Theory of Time*; Oaklander, "McTaggart's Paradox and Smith's Tensed Theory of Time," 205–21; Rochelle, *Behind Time*; Craig, *Tensed Theory of Time*.

distinctions of past, present, and future seem to me to be essential for time, that I regard time as unreal.[29]

That is to say, in McTaggart's view, according to our common and natural conception of time, the essential reality of time lies in the A-series of time in which events run from the past through the present to the future. However, by a "careful consideration," it appears as "merely subjective" and "only a constant illusion of our minds."[30] Therefore, the real nature of time contains only the B-series (i.e., the series of positions that constitutes time-relations as "earlier than" and "later than" in the order of events). Yet, this B-series is also untenable. The reason is that, according to McTaggart, time always involves change. That is, if nothing changed, there could not be time, but if anything changes, then all other things change with it.[31] Accordingly, on the one hand, in the B-series, the order of events (e.g.,–M–N–O–P–) is permanently there; i.e., it was, is, and will be in that order as a tenseless sense. In this sense, there is no temporal passage, for there is no change. As a result, "there can be no B series when there is no A series, since without an A series there is no time."[32] Therefore, McTaggart accepts A-series as the more fundamental property of time. On the other hand, according to McTaggart, there is also no A series of time, for its determinants of the past, the present, and the future are incompatible and self-contradictory.[33] Consequently, McTaggart asserts that time is unreal.[34] However, as we shall see, al-

---

29. Broad, *Nature of Existence*, vol. 2, 10 (italics original).
30. Ibid., 11.
31. Cf. ibid.
32. Ibid., 13.

33. Ibid., 16. McTaggart explains the contradiction of A-series as follows: "Every event must be one or another, but no event can be more than one. If I say that any event is past, that implies that it is neither present nor future, and so with the others. And this exclusiveness is essential to change, and therefore to time. For the only change we can get is from future to present, and from present to past. The characteristics, therefore, are incompatible. But every event has them all. If M is past, it has been present and future. If it is future, it will be present and past. If it is present, it has been future and will be past. Thus all three characteristics belong to each event" (p. 20).

34. See the following conclusion of McTaggart: "The reality of the A series, then, leads to a contradiction, and must be rejected. And, since we have seen that change and time require the A series, the reality of change and time must be rejected. And so must the reality of the B series, since that requires time. Nothing is really present, past, or future. Nothing is really earlier or later than anything else or temporally simultaneous with it. Nothing really changes. And nothing is really in time. Whenever we perceive

though the tensed and the tenseless theorists accept McTaggart's concepts of A- and B-series of time as their own analytic conceptual frame, all of them reject his conclusion of the unreality of time.

The Static (Tenseless) Theory of Time

After Einstein-Minkowski and McTaggart, throughout ongoing debates on the nature of time, more specifically concerning the problem of "the temporal becoming" or "the passage of time," the debaters have been generally divided into the following two essentially rival theories: A-theory vs. B-theory, Tensed theory vs. Tenseless theory, or Dynamic theory vs. Static theory.[35] Although the nomenclatures are different, generally, they have been used interchangeably because the essential conceptions of time are very similar in each group: Tensed theory (A-theory and Dynamic theory) and Tenseless theory (B-theory and Static theory).[36] However, we must remember that there is not "the" tenseless theory or "the" tensed theory, for there are very diverse versions on each side. Here, because of space limitations, I will only briefly summarize a typical conception of time for both theories. We can classify some important theorists in both groups as follows:[37] (1) tenseless theorists— B. Russell, N. Goodman, W. V. O. Quine, D. C. Williams, J. J. C. Smart, A. Grünbaum, H. Putnam, D. Parfit, D. H. Mellor, L. N. Oaklander, and

---

anything in time—which is the only way in which, in our present experience, we do perceive things—we are perceiving it more or less as it really is not." Ibid., 22.

35. Davies succinctly describes the difference between the tensed (dynamic) vs. the tenseless (static) theory of time as a conversation between a physicist and a sceptic in his *God and the New Physics*, 128–32.

36. Concerning the nomenclatures, some theorists understand them as the same, but some others do not. As we have seen, the distinction of A- vs. B-theory was originated from McTaggart, but Mellor changed it as tensed vs. tenseless theory in his *Real Time* (1981), and Lowe used this distinction because of some conceptual confusion, naming as dynamic vs. static theory. However, for example, Tooley prefers to use the third one, but Craig wants to use the traditional A- vs. B-theory terminology, and Mellor recently returned to this naming in his *Real Time II* (1998). Concerning such a problem of the nomenclatures, see Craig, *Tensed Theory of Time*, ix; and Lowe, *Possibility of Metaphysics*, 85–86.

37. Even though I provided this list by my own study, it does not include all of the significant scholars who are involved in the debates between the tensed vs. the tensless theory of time, and, furthermore, some have changed their view in the course of their debates.

R. Le Poidevin;[38] (2) tensed theorists—C. D. Broad, A. N. Whitehead, H. Reichenbach, A. N. Prior, M. Capek, R. M. Gale, S. McCall, G. T. Whitrow, G. N. Schlesinger, J. R. Lucas, Q. Smith, M. Tooley, E. J. Lowe, and W. L. Craig.[39]

First, I will begin with the Tenseless (Static/B) theory of time. The essential tenets of the tenseless view of time can be summarized as follows: (1) Time itself is real, but our experience of the flow of time is a mere mind-dependent illusion. Therefore, the notions of past, present and future as the temporal passage are merely epistemological or subjective properties, not ontological or objective reality.[40] (2) The common-sense view of time, which holds that the past (things ceased to exist) and the future (things do not yet exist) are not real but the only real is the present (things now really exist), is wrong. As Einstein's STR shows, all times–past, present, and future–are essentially and equally real, for there are not any intrinsic ontological differences between the temporal properties of past, present, and future. Eventually, it leads to determinism for the future. (3) Finally, the A-determinants, *pastness*, *presentness*, and *futurity* are not essential to understanding the reality of time, but rather the reality lies in the B-relations of time as *earlier than*, *simultaneous with*, and *later than*. Such a tenseless (static) theory of time has been generally supported by (1) a metaphysical rejection

---

38. Cf. Russell, "On the Experience of Time," 212–33; Williams, "Myth of Passage," 457–72; Goodman, *Structure of Appearance*; Quine, *Word and Object*; Smart, "River of Time," 213–27; Putnam, "Time and Physical Geometry," 240–47; Grünbaum, "Meaning of Time," 195–228, and *Philosophical Problems of Space and Time*; Parfit, "Personal Identity," 3–27, and *Reasons and Persons*; Mellor, *Real Time*, and *Real Time II*; Oaklander, *Temporal Relations and Temporal Becoming*; Le Poidevin, *Change, Cause and Contradiction*.

39. Cf. Broad, *Scientific Thought*, and *Examination of McTaggart's Philosophy*; Whitehead, *Process and Reality*; Reichenbach, *Philosophy of Space and Time*; Prior, *Past, Present and Future*, and *Papers on Time and Sense*; Gale, *Language of Time*; Capek, "Relativity and the Status of Becoming," 607–17, and idem, *Concepts of Space and Time*; Lucas, *Treatise on Time and Space*, and idem, *Future*; McCall, "Objective Time Flow," 337–62, and *Model of the Universe*; Whitrow, *Natural Philosophy of Time*; Schlesinger, *Aspects of Time*, and *Timely Topics*; Smith, *Language and Time*; Tooley, *Time, Tense, and Causation*; Lowe, *Possibility of Metaphysics*; Craig, *Tensed Theory of Time*, and *Tenseless Theory of Time*.

40. Smith rightly points out that, "One of the central issues in the 20th century philosophy of time is whether temporal becoming is a mind-dependent feature that events acquire or seem to aquire by virtue of being apprehended, or whether it is a mind-independent feature that inheres in events irrespectively of their relation to a conscious organism." Idem, "Mind-Independence of Temporal Becoming," 109.

of the objective reality of temporal becoming, (2) scientific arguments from the deterministic interpretation of the STR, and (3) arguments from the tenseless theory of linguistic-analytic philosophy. These arguments are closely interrelated to each other.

The Mind-Dependence of Temporal Becoming

We normally say that "time flows like a river" or "time flies like an arrow." However, according to the tenseless (static) view, such an idea of the passage of time as a stream is a confused and absurd illusion.[41] In order to avoid such a confusion in conceiving the nature of time, B. Russell distinguished two kinds of time-relations between the relation of subject-object (*mental time*) and the relation of object-object (*physical time*). According to him, the former is our immediate experience of time that appears as a temporal passage of past, present and future, but the latter is objective time-relation that is in the order of earlier and later. Russell insists that, therefore, "In a world in which there was no *experience* there would be no past, present, or future, but there might well be earlier and later."[42]

While appealing to the four-dimensional space-time manifold theory, D. C. Williams also emphatically states that the various notions of temporal passage; for example, "the passing present," "the moving present," "the traveling now," "the act of becoming," or "the surge of process," are all just "a myth," which is wrong in that it is not a mere metaphorical sense but a fundamentally false and deceptive idea.[43] In the same sense, J. J. C. Smart asks that if there is a passage of time like a flowing river, how fast is it moving? It is an absurd question because in that case we need a second time-scale in order to measure the first time-dimension,

---

41. Smart says that, "It is clear, then, that we cannot talk about time as river, about the flow of time, of our advance through time, or of the irreversibility of time without being in great danger of falling into absurdity." Idem, "River of Time," 216.

42. Russell, "On the Experience of Time," 212 (italics mine).

43. Cf. Williams, "Myth of Passage," 460–61. He says, "I believe that the universe, without residue, of the spread of events in space-time, and that if we thus accept realistically the four-dimensional fabric of juxtaposed actualities we can dispense with all those dim non-factual categories which have so bedeviled our race: the potential, the subsistential, and the influential, the noumenal, the numinous, and the non-natural" (p. 458).

and then a third one for the second, and so forth.[44] However, there cannot be such a "super-time." According to Smart, therefore, events are the facts in temporal relations of 'before and after and of simultaneity.' As he says, "Events do not come into existence; they occur or happen. 'To happen' is not at all equivalent to 'to come into existence.'"[45] Thus, there is not a passage of time like an ever-rolling stream. Recently, while appealing to McTaggart's view of the self-contradictory nature of A-properties of time, D. H. Mellor insists that, "There is no flow of time. The tensed view of time is self-contradictory and therefore untrue."[46] In his interpretation of the STR, K. Gödel also maintained the same view in saying that, "it seems that one obtains an unequivocal proof for the view of those philosophers who, like Parmenides, Kant, and the modern idealists, *deny the objectivity of change and consider change as an illusion or an appearance due to our special mode of perception.*"[47]

For the thesis of the mind-dependence of temporal becoming, however, A. Grünbaum is considered as "the most prominent advocate" among others.[48] Grünbaum's essential thesis is as follows: "Becoming is mind-dependent because it is not an attribute of physical events per se but requires the occurrence of certain *conceptualized conscious experiences* of the occurrence of physical events."[49] However, what does "becoming" or "passage" mean? According to him, becoming is "occurring *now* or coming into being of previously future events and their subsequent belonging to the past."[50] In a strict sense, therefore, the problem of the passage of time turns on the problem of the transiency of the present (i.e., "becoming present," "occurring now") or the problem of

---

44. Cf. Smart, "River of Time," 215. For contra arguments to Smart, see Prior, "Time after Time," 244–46, and Markosian, "How Fast Does Time Pass?" 829–44.

45. Smart, "River of Time," 217.

46. Mellor, "History without the Flow of Time," 69.

47. Gödel, "Remark about the Relationship," 557 (italics mine).

48. Baker, "On the Mind-Dependence of Temporal Becoming," 341.

49. Grünbaum, "Meaning of Time," 197 (italics original). This article was reprinted in various places in different titles, "Status of Temporal Becoming," 322–53; and "Exclusion of Becoming from the Physical World," 471–500. For a further argument to defense the thesis of the mind-dependence of temporal becoming, see Baker, "Temporal Becoming," 218–36, and, for some criticisms of Grünbaum's thesis, see Lacey, "Causal Theory of Time," 332–54; Ferré, "Grünbaum on Temporal Becoming," 426–45; Smith, "Mind-Independence of Temporal Becoming," 109–19.

50. Grünbaum, "Meaning of Time," 195.

"the status of the adverbial attribute now." First of all, for Grünbaum, in contrast to the common-sense view, "*becoming* is not a feature of the temporal order of physical events with respect to earlier and later."[51] He says,

> The temporal relations of earlier (before) and later (after) can obtain between two physical events independently of the transient now and of any minds. On the other hand, the classification of events into past, present, and future, which is inherent to becoming, requires reference to the adverbial attribute now as well as to the relations of earlier and later.[52]

That is, in Grünbaum's view, according to Einstein-Minkowski's spacetime theory, all events have a temporal betweenness relation in each world-line like the spatial betweenness of the points in an Euclidean straight line. Actually, in the Minkowskian world, events simply "are" in the tenseless sense, not "were," "are," or "will be" in the tensed sense.

For Grünbaum, the ideas of "the arrow of time" or "the irreversibility of time" can be explained by the concept of "*anisotropic* time."[53] Accordingly, the idea of the *arrow* of time does not relate to "becoming now." Then, how can Grünbaum explain the transiency of the present? He answers that, the necessary condition to qualify a physical event (at a time *t*) as "occurring now" is nothing other than the human (or other *mind-possessing* organism *M*'s) *conceptual awareness* of experiencing it.[54] In this sense, temporal becoming as a "*present* happening or occurring *now*" is just a result of a human awareness of experiencing a physical event, *E*, at a time *t* as a simultaneous event with his/her time of *now* in the tensed conceptual framework, not an intrinsic nature of physical

---

51. Ibid., 196 (italics mine).

52. Ibid., 197.

53. Cf. ibid., 198–201. However, for Grünbaum, the becomingless physical world does not necessarily imply determinism of the future. See pp. 219–27.

54. Grünbaum further explains this as follows: "What then is the content of *M*'s conceptual awareness at time *t* that he *is experiencing* a certain event *at that time*? *M*'s experience of the event at time *t* is coupled with an awareness of the temporal coincidence of his experience of the event with a state of *knowing* that he has that experience at all. In other words, *M* experiences the event at *t* and knows that he is experiencing it. Thus, presentness or nowness of an event requires conceptual awareness of the presentational immediacy of either the experience of the event or, if the event is itself *un*perceived, of the *experience* of another event simultaneous with it." Idem, "Meaning of Time," 207 (italics original).

events *per se*.⁵⁵ Therefore, temporal becoming is essentially a mind-dependent phenomenon and a psychological (mental) event. In this sense, in the tenseless view, without a conscious observer, there is not the flow of time in reality, for the physical world is ordered in McTaggart's B-relations of earlier and later events. It is, in D. C. Williams's words, a "four-dimensional fabric of juxtaposed actualities."⁵⁶

Arguments form the Deterministic Interpretation of the STR

In the area of the philosophy of science, deterministic interpretations of the STR were provided by C. W. Rietdijk and H. Putnam among many others.⁵⁷ First, according to Rietdijk, if there are at least two different observers ($W1$ and $W2$) who are their own inertial frames in four-dimensional space-time, and when the two frames are crossing at a point, there is an event ($E1$, or some events) which is already a past event for $W2$, but, at the same time, which is an 'absolute' future event for $W1$.⁵⁸ Thus, for him, the past (or present) event $E1$ *for only one* inertial system ($W2$) is already determined *in all other* systems, even it is "predetermined" still in the future for $W1$. In this sense, Rietdijk concludes that

> there is determinism (which is, of course, not the same thing as causality), also in micro-physics. Also there is no free will; from this it follows, e.g., that the whole philosophy of existentialism is untenable. In the same way, of course, we can conclude that theories, intending to save free will with the aid of "indeterminism" in micro-physics, cannot be tenable.⁵⁹

H. Putnam presents the same view in more general explanation. He begins with a premise, which is the "man on the street's" view of the nature of time is as follows: "All (and only) things that exist *now*

---

55. Davies maintains the same view in saying that, "We cannot escape that the qualities of time we regard as the most vital—the divisions into past, present and future, and the forward movement of each division—are purely subjective. It is our own existence that endows time with life and motion. In a world devoid of conscious observers, the river of time would cease flowing." Idem, *Other Worlds*, 46.

56. Williams, "Myth of Passage," 458.

57. Cf. Rietdijk, "Rigorous Proof of Determinism," 341–44, and Putnam, "Time and Physical Geometry," 240–47. Cf. Mellor, "Special Relativity and Present Truth," 74–77.

58. For a clearer understanding Rietdijk's argument, see his figure and further explanation in "Rigorous Proof of Determinism," 341–42.

59. Ibid., 343.

are real" (i.e., future and past things are not real).⁶⁰ From this premise, at least two different observers, I-now and you-now, are real in relative world-lines to each other. Then, because of the principle that "there are no privileged observers," "all and only things," which stand in a certain physical relation R to me-now and to you-now, are equally real in a tenseless sense. According to the STR, at a simultaneous point, I find that not only everything in the relation R to me-now but also everything in the relation R to you-now is real at the same time. Then, there are some events which lie in "the future" for I-now in my coordinate system, and at the same time, which lie in "the present" for you-now in your coordinate system. For this reason, Putnam asserts: "All things that exist now are real."⁶¹ This means, according to him, that "*all* future things are real ('things' includes 'event'), and likewise that all *past* things are real, even though they do not exist *now*."⁶² Therefore, all things (events) of the past, the present, and the future are equally real in a tenseless sense, and thus future events already have a truth value (i.e., they are determined). This means that at least the STR is not compatible with the idea of temporal becoming and indeterminism. Finally, Putnam declares as follows:

> I conclude the problem of the reality and the determinateness of future events is now solved. Moreover, it is solved by physics and not by philosophy ... Indeed, I do not believe that there are any longer any *philosophical* problems about Time; there is only the physical problem of determining the exact physical geometry of the four-dimensional continuum that we inhibit.⁶³

Tenseless Linguistic Arguments

One of the most vigorous debates on conceiving the nature of time lies in the area of the philosophy of language, especially focusing on

---

60. Putnam, "Time and Physical Geometry," 240.

61. Ibid., 243.

62. Ibid., 246 (italics original).

63. Ibid., 247. For a criticism of Rietdijk and Putnam, see Stein, "On Einstein-Minkowski Space-Time," 5–23, and concerning the problem of STR and determinism of the future, see Maxwell, "Are Probabilism and Special Relativity Incompatible?," 23–43; Dieks, "Special Relativity and the Flow of Time," 456–60; and H. Stein, "On Relativity Theory and Openness of the Future," 147–67.

the semantic content of ordinary tensed sentences.[64] The problem is whether or not *tense* in our ordinary language usage is essential to understanding temporal reality. As we shall see, according to the tensed theory, the fact that every language has a linguistic tense system reflects "our experience of the world as being tensed, as having a past, present, and future."[65] For example, as a tensed theorist W. L. Craig asserts that the linguistic tense is "a window on the world: Our language is tensed because reality is tensed. That is to say, there are tensed facts which are objective features of the world."[66]

In the view of tenseless theorists, however, the A-determinants of pastness, presentness, and futurity are not at all the reality of the world. The tenseless view can be broadly divided into the old and the new tenseless theory. According to the old tenseless theory (cf. B. Russell, A. J. Ayer, N. Goodman, W. V. O. Quine, J. J. C. Smart, C. Williams), every tensed sentence in A-determinants (the past, the present, and the future) can be translated into a tenseless sentence in B-relations (earlier than, simultaneous with, and later than) without losing its meaning. For instance, J. J. C. Smart succinctly states the old-tenseless view as follows:

> That is, a language could be devised in which temporal copula did not exist, but in which we used the words "earlier than," or "simultaneous with" in combination with a non-temporal copula and the expression "this utterance." This language would not contain words like "past," "present," and "future." For example "is past" would be translated by "is earlier than this utterance."[67]

In the old tenseless theory, there are two distinctive theories, "the date-sentence theory" and "the token-reflexive theory." The date-sentence theorist asserts that any tensed sentence, "It is *now* snowing" can be translated into "It *is* snowing at noon, Dec. 15, 2001" (tenseless sense). According to the token-reflexive theory, it can be translated into "It *is* snowing simultaneous with this utterance" (tenseless sense). In this

---

64. For this issue, see the following works: (1) the tensed view—Gale, *Language of Time*; Smith, *Language and Time*; Craig, *Tensed Theory of Time*; (2) the tenseless view—Mellor, *Real Time*, and *Real Time II*; (3) some collections of important articles from both sides—Oaklander and Smiths, *New Theory of Time*; Le Poidevin, *Questions of Time and Tense*.

65. Craig, *Time and Eternity*, 115.

66. Ibid., 115–16.

67. Smart, "River of Time," 224. Cf. Quine, *Word and Object*, 170–76; Goodman, *Structure of Appearance*, 359–71.

view, there are primitive temporal relations, e.g., earlier and later, which are the ontological status of the reality, and they are irreducible to tensed properties.[68] However, according to the evidence in the area of philosophy of language, this old-tenseless theory is now considered a failed project.[69] The reason is that tenseless sentences cannot properly perform all the functions of tensed sentences.[70]

Therefore, while recognizing the weakness of the old-tenseless theory, D. H. Mellor among others (cf. J. J. C. Smart, M. MacBeath, P. Fitzgerald, M. Beer, L. N. Oaklander) suggests a new-tenseless theory, which is "the token-reflexive truth condition theory."[71] According to the new tenseless theory, A-sentences cannot be translatable to B-sentences, but the latter gives the tenseless truth conditions of the former. That is, since all tensed sentences have tenseless token-reflexive truth conditions, the reality itself is tenseless.[72] For example, the tensed sentence "It is now snowing" (cf. 'now' is at noon, Dec. 15, 2001) is true if and only if the tenseless truth condition "it is snowing at noon, Dec. 15, 2001" is true. In this sentence, the tensed "is" does not have an eternal truth-value. It depends on only its tenseless truth condition of "at the tenseless time, t, of the utterance" (i.e., at noon, Dec. 15, 2001). Thus, according

---

68. Cf. the following Goodman's statement, "The 'past,' 'present,' and 'future' name no times. Rather 'is past at,' 'is present at' and 'is future at' are tenseless two-place predicates that may respectively be translated by the tenseless predicates 'is earlier than,' 'is at,' and 'is later than.'" Idem, *Structure of Appearance*, 295.

69. Cf. Craig, *Time and Eternity*, 118, and Smith, "Problems with the New Tenseless Theory of Time," 371–72.

70. Cf. Yates, *Timelessness of God*, 68–70.

71. Cf. Mellor, *Real Time*. For example, a new tenseless theorist, Oaklander states, "For a variety of reasons, . . . recent defenders of the tenseless view have come to embrace the thesis that tensed sentences cannot be translated by tenseless ones without loss of meaning. Nevertheless, recent detensers have denied that the ineliminability of tensed language and thought entails the reality of temporal properties. According to the new tenseless theory of time, our need to think and talk in tensed terms is perfectly consistent with its being the case that time is timeless. Tensed discourse is indeed necessary for timely action, but tensed facts are not, since the truth conditions of tensed sentences can be expressed in a tenseless metalanguage that describes unchanging temporal relations between and among events." Idem, "Defence of the New Tenseless Theory of Time," 26–27. See also Oaklander, *Temporal Relations and Temporal Becoming*. For the debates on the new tenseless theory, see the articles in Oaklander and Smith, *New Theory of Time*. For criticisms of the new tenseless theory, see Smith, *Language and Time*; Priest, "Tense and Truth Conditions," 162–66; Craig, "Tense and the New B-Theory of Language," 5–26, and "New B-Theory's *Tu Quoque* Argument," 249–69.

72. Cf. Mellor, "Tense's Tenseless Truth Conditions," 167–72.

to Mellor, tense (the A-properties of pastness, presentness, and futurity) is unreal, for the real facts are only the tenseless B-facts. Accordingly, D. H. Mellor states that

> The sole function of tensed facts is to make tensed sentences and judgments true or false. But that job is already done by the tenseless facts that fix the truth-values of all tensed sentences and judgment tokens. Provided a token of "*e* is past" is later than *e*, it is true. Nothing else about *e* and it matters a jot: in particular no tensed fact about them matters. It is immaterial, for a start, where *e* and the token are in the A-series; and if that is not material, no more *recherché* tensed fact can be. Similarly for tokens of all other tensed types. Their tenseless truth conditions leave tensed facts no scope for determining their truth-values. But these facts by definition determine their truth-values. So in reality there are no such facts.[73]

W. L. Craig summarizes the gist of Mellor's new-tenseless theory as follows: "the tenseless truth conditions [are] what makes the tensed sentences true. Since those conditions are tenseless, no tensed facts are necessary to make tensed sentences true. All that is needed is tenseless facts."[74] However, in facing some criticisms against the new-tenseless theory, Mellor recently revised his theory in his *Real Time II* more as an "indexical theory."[75]

The Dynamic (Tensed) Theory of Time

In contrast to the Tenseless (Static) theory, there is a very different understanding of the nature of time, the Tensed (Dynamic/A) theory of time. Its essential tenets are as follows: (1) Time is real, and the idea of temporal becoming, the flow of time, is not a mere mind-dependent subjective illusion, but an ontologically objective reality of the world. (2) Our common tensed experience of time is quite right, that, as someone holds, the existence at "now" is only real, for the past ceased to exist and the future does not yet exist (e.g., presentism),[76] or some others take the view that the past and the present are real, but the future is not (e.g.,

---

73. Mellor, *Real Time*, 102.
74. Craig, *Time and Eternity*, 120.
75. Cf. Mellor, *Real Time II*, 32.
76. Cf. Smith, *Language and Time*.

the causal theory of time).⁷⁷ (3) Therefore, the A-properties of pastness, presentness, and futurity are essential to understanding the reality of time, for there are ontological differences between the temporal properties. Such a tensed (dynamic) theory of time has been supported by (1) the metaphysical understanding of the objective reality of temporal becoming, (2) arguments form the indeterministic interpretation of the STR, (3) arguments from the tensed theory of linguistic-analytic philosophy, and finally (4) the arguments for "the arrow of time" in thermodynamics, quantum physics, cosmology, biology, causation theory, and so forth.

The Mind-Independence of the Temporal Becoming

Although H. Bergson, A. N. Whitehead, and many others point out the significance of "becoming" in reality of the world, I will begin with C. D. Broad. According to Broad, physicists generally conceive time very much like space. The most general analogy is that duration in time is similar to extension in space, and thus the relation of two events can be thought of as two points on a straight line in space. For Broad, however, there is a peculiarity of series of events in time in that "it has not only an intrinsic *order* but also intrinsic *sense*."⁷⁸ In other words, the intrinsic order of events on the straight line of events-series has an "arrow-head" in the fixed sense: "the intrinsic sense of a series of events in Time is essentially bound up with the distinction between past, present, and future."⁷⁹ Another obvious analogy is that "*Now* in Time is *Here* in Space." Yet, according to Broad, there is also a difference between Now and Here. That is, the meaning of "here" designates different regions according to the different speakers' places, but "now" has an essential reference to Now. Thus, we must "treat past, present, and future on their own account, without expecting any help from spatial analogies."⁸⁰ Then, Broad distinguishes the meaning of change as follows: "The changes of things are changes *in* Time; but the change of event or of moments from future,

---

77. Recently, Tooley proposed a causal theory of time, see his *Time, Tense, and Causation*.

78. Broad, *Scientific Thought*, 57. For a fuller exposition of Broad's view of time, see Mundle, "Broad's View about Time," 353–74.

79. Broad, *Scientific Thought*, 58.

80. Ibid., 59.

through present, to past, is a change *of* Time."[81] But, there is another kind of change, which is the most fundamental: "change from future to present." Broad calls this third kind of change "becoming," which means "the coming into existence of events."[82] For him, the future is quite different from the past and the present, for the latter are real but the former is nothing at all until it comes into existence (i.e., "the future events are non-entities").[83] Consequently, according to Broad, temporal becoming is essentially an objective reality of the world, not a mere mind-dependent illusion.[84]

Similarly, against J. J. C. Smart's attack on the absurdity of the idea of temporal passage (cf. his criticism of the rate of the passing time), A. N. Prior replies that time really passes, and, in that case, "the rate of this change is one time-unit per time-unit" (i.e., second per second, minute per minute, hour per hour, or year per year). If one became one year older, then time passed exactly one year. Therefore, we don't need any "mysterious super-time" to measure it.[85] Concerning this problem, another answer is provided by P. J. Zwart as follows, "in the relational view of time the concept of a hyper-time is completely without meaning because the flow of time is, in this view, the flow of *all* events."[86]

---

81. Ibid., 64–65.

82. Ibid., 67.

83. Cf. ibid., 68. Broad says, "Nothing has happened to the present by becoming past except that fresh slices of existence have been added to the total history of the world. The past is thus as real as the present. On the other hand, the essence of a present event is, not that it precedes future events, but that there is quite literally *nothing* to which it has the relation of precedence. The sum total of existence is always increasing, and it is this which gives the time-series a sense as well as an order" (pp. 66–67). He continues, "the future does not exist so long as it is future.... [However,] whatever is has become, and the sum total of the existent is continually augmented by becoming. There is no such thing as *ceasing* to exist; what has become exists henceforth for ever" (p. 69, italics original).

84. A few years later, Eddington also emphasized that, "The great thing about time is that it goes on. But this is an aspect of it which the physicist sometimes seems inclined to neglect.... Something must be added to the geometrical conceptions comprised in Minkowski's world before it becomes a complete picture of the world as we know it. We may appeal to consciousness to suffuse the whole—to turn *existence* into *happening*, *being* into *becoming*." Idem, *Nature of the Physical World*, 68.

85. Cf. Prior, "Time after Time," 244. Recently, Markosian gives a similar criticism on Smart's argument on the rate of the time-flow. Idem, "How Fast Does Time Pass?," 829–44. See also Schlesinger, "How Time Flies," 501–23.

86. Zwart, *About Time*, 67.

However, then, what on earth does the flow of time mean? According to Prior, it is just a metaphor, but its literal truth denotes the fact that time itself moves from the future to the present, from the present to the comparatively near past, and then to the further and further distant past. He says, "Then whatever is happening, has happened, or will happen is all the time 'becoming more past' in this extended sense; and just this is what we mean by the flow or passage of time."[87]

Furthermore, according to M. Capek, the tenseless (static) theory has a serious problem. He asks that, "If true reality is timeless, *where does the illusion of succession come from?* If time has no genuine reality, why does it appear to be real?"[88] For this question, Capek says,

> If the illusionary reality of time is nothing but a gradual raising the curtain of ignorance which separates our mind from a complete and timeless insight, then at least *this process of raising is still a process which unfolds itself gradually without being given at once*; but, by conceding this, we admit the reality of time either in our mind or *between* our mind and the allegedly timeless reality.[89]

Accordingly, although Minkowski eliminated "succession" or "temporal becoming" in the physical world, there is at least "the *movement of our consciousness* to the future." Yet, for Capek, this dualism of the timeless physical world and mind conscious temporal becoming world is absurd and unintelligible, for it is nothing but a result of "the alleged spatialization of time."[90] In the same sense, N. Markosian also emphatically states that,

> There are no genuine, monadic, spatial analogous to pastness, presentness and futurity; there are certainly no such properties as *being north, being south* or *being west*.... [However,] times and events successively possess different A-properties as *the*

---

87. Prior, *Papers on Time and Tense*, 1–2.
88. Capek, *Philosophical Impact of Contemporary Physics*, 164 (italics original).
89. Ibid.
90. Ibid., 165. In elsewhere, Capek insists that "the denial of becoming in the physical world generates enormous epistemological difficulties in creating an intolerable dualism of two completely heterogeneous realities without any possibility to relate them in any intelligible way: the becomingless realm of 'true' reality and the temporally incomplete realm of the phenomenal 'flux'; basically it is a relapse into ancient Eleatic myths with all their weird and superfluous paradoxes." Idem, "Relativity and the Status of Becoming," 616.

> *pure passage of time*.... [Therefore,] there are certain properties possessed by time, but not possessed by any dimension of space, in virtue of which it is true to say that time passes.[91]

In contrast to the tenseless view, therefore, Markosian asserts that the A-properties (i.e., pastness, presentness, and futurity) and the objective passage of time are "the essential, metaphysical core of the view that time passes."[92]

While appealing to the indeterminism of quantum physics, H. Reichenbach also emphasizes the objective temporal becoming and the directionality of time. He asserts that the "essential property of time is its directionality" in that the undetermined future events are becoming the determined past ones. He says,

> This specific feature is based on the fact that time—and time alone—is the dimension of the *causal chains* upon which we have based our theory of space and time. Time is the direction of the grain of the manifold along which the causal chains extend, whereas space reflects only the neighborhood relations between the coexisting causal chains. The direction of the causal chains is also the direction of the world-lines of objects which remain identical with themselves and which therefore represent special cases of causal chains.[93]

For Reichenbach, therefore, indeterminism entails the directionality of time and a tensed (dynamic) view of the nature of time.[94] S. McCall presents a similar view. In his article, "Objective Time Flow," S. McCall offerring the "objective" temporal passage "in the sense that time flow characterizes the universe independently of the existence of conscious beings."[95] By his "tree model," McCall suggests a dynamic universe theory in which time flows. In this model, at any time *t*, there are many future branches, which represent the possible future histories or courses of events as the four-dimensional spatio-temporal manifolds. However, a possible branch realized as an actual one at time *t*, and then, the other set of branches is cut off from the main trunk of treelike history of

---

91. Markosian, "How Fast Does Time Pass?" 835.
92. Ibid., 836.
93. Reichenbach, *Philosophy of Space and Time*, 270.
94. Cf. Reichenbach, *Direction of Time*.
95. McCall, "Objective Time Flow," 337. He further developed this project in his book, *Model of the Universe*.

the universe. Thus, the complete universe is different at every different time through the ongoing process of the passage of time. Accordingly, as McCall says, "Each moment of time, therefore, defines a separation of the universe into past and future that is ontological rather than epistemological."[96] In this dynamic model of the world, the flow of time is an objective and ontological reality, not a mere subjective illusion or myth. Therefore, what the tensed theorists emphasize is the fact that there is objective temporal becoming reality in the world.

Arguments from the Indeterministic Interpretation of the STR

Among many others, M. Capek suggests a different interpretation of Einstein-Minkowski's four-dimensional space-time manifold theory.[97] As we have seen, the classical deterministic interpretation of the STR conceives that not only the past and the present but also the future events are equally real. Future events already exist prior to and independently of human awareness. Therefore, Minkowski's conception of space-time is incompatible with the objective status of temporal becoming in the deterministic physical world (cf. C. W. Rietdijk and H. Putnam).[98] As M. Capek points out, the key point of the becomingless interpretation of Minkowski's space-time is "the relativization of simultaneity."[99] That is, if there is no objective or absolute "Now," then there is no absolute separation between the past and the future. This leads to the becomingless relative physical world in that there is no absolute distinction between successive states of the world. However, in Capek's view, such a deterministic interpretation of the STR is a "superficial and unwarranted conclusion," and instead the STR eventually "strengthened" the objective status of becoming.

According to Capek's interpretation of the STR, (1) in the relativistic space-time, "there are some types of succession which are *absolute*

96. Ibid., 343.
97. Cf. Capek, "Inclusion of Becoming in the Physical World," 501–24; Stein, "On Einstein-Minkowski Space-Time," 5–23, and "On Relativity Theory and Openness of the Future," 147–67; Dieks, "Special Relativity and the Flow of Time," 456–60.
98. Cf. Capek, "Relativity and the Status of Becoming," 607. However, although eliminating the objective temporal becoming in the physical world, there is a significant difference between Grünbaum and Rietdijk/Putnam in that the former does not assert determinism for the future events, but the latter does (pp. 608 and 610–15).
99. Ibid., 608.

since they remain successions in *all* frames of reference." Thus, it is "a network of world lines each of which consists of a succession of irreversible, causally related events."[100] (2) More significantly, for him, there is a difference between time and space. Therefore, the following three phrases—"the class of absolutely simultaneous events," "absolute instantaneous space," and "absolute juxtaposition"—have quite the same meaning. If there are no juxtapositions (i.e., instantaneous spatial relations), then "there are certain types of succession which remain such in all frames of reference."[101] Accordingly, Capek's characterization of Minkowski's space-time is as follows: "There is a four-dimensional process of gradually unfolding causal lines separated not by instantaneous distance, but by four-dimensional loopholes of causal independence."[102] Furthermore, while distinguishing between "the genuine (i.e., causal or absolute) and the nominal (noncausal) future," Capek asserts an indeterminism for the future events in the casual (absolute) sense. As Capek says, "The events constituting my absolute future are *unobservable in principle by any conceivable observer*. . . . [More generally,] No event future with respect to *any* particular Here-Now can be perceived by *any* then conceivable observer."[103] The reason is that it is actually impossible without violating the principle of the STR (i.e., nothing greater than the speed of light) that the other distant observer can receive a signal of my absolute future event before it appears to my Here-Now. More radically, on the basis of his "presentism" (which maintains the view that only the present is real) and his conception of metaphysical time, Q. Smith asserts that the STR is a false theory.[104]

The Tensed Linguistic Arguments

According to tensed theorists of time (cf. A. N. Prior, R. M. Gale, Q. Smith, R. Swinburne, W. L. Crag, etc.), the pervasive tensed system of all languages and the ineliminability of tense from our ordinary use of language reflect the fact that *tense* is an objective feature of reality in

100. Ibid., 609 (italics original).
101. Ibid., 609–10.
102. Ibid., 610.
103. Ibid., 611.
104. See Smith, *Language and Time*, especially Chapter 7, "Absolute Presentness and the Special Theory of Relativity," 225–50.

the world. Therefore, a tenseless theorist D. H. Mellor states as follows: "Tense is so striking an aspect of reality that only the most compelling argument justifies denying it."[105] However, in the view of tensed theorists, there are not any convincing arguments to eliminate tense. Accordingly, based on the correspondence theory of truth, tensed theorists maintain that if a tensed sentence is true, then it corresponds with tensed reality of the world. Then, reality itself must be tensed.[106] In this view, the old-tenseless theorists' assertion of the translatability from a tensed sentence to a tenseless one is implausible.[107] For example, A. N. Prior provided a classical argument for the reality of tensed facts as follows, (someone is released from a painful situation, e.g., a dental treatment or a final exam),

> One says, e.g. "thank goodness that's over!," and not only is this, when said, quite clear without any date appended, but it says something which it is impossible that any use of a tenseless copula with a date should convey. It certainly doesn't mean the same as, e.g., "Thank goodness the date of the conclusion of that thing is Friday, June 15, 1954," even if it be said then. (Nor, for that matter, does it mean "Thank goodness the conclusion of that thing is contemporaneous with this utterance." Why should anyone thank goodness for that?)[108]

However, as we have seen, the new tenseless theorists assert that a mere assertion of the untranslatability of A-sentences to B-sentences is not sufficient to defeat the tenseless theory, for the B-relations of time provide the sufficient truth conditions for A-sentences. However, against such a new tenseless theorists' attack, Q. Smith strongly insists as follows: "no A-sentence or A-sentence-token has the same truth conditions as any B-sentence or B-sentence-token and that this implies that the new tenseless theory of time is false."[109] According to Smith, all A-sentences express only A-propositions and events (and facts) pos-

105. Mellor, *Real Time*, 4–5.
106. Cf. Craig, *Time and Reality*, 117.
107. Cf. Smith, *Language and Time*, 3–66.
108. Prior, "Thank Goodness That's Over," 17. For further debates on this topic, see Kiernan-Lewis, "Not Over Yet: Prior's 'Thank Goodness' Argument," 241–43, and Oaklander, "Thank Goodness It's Over," 256–58.
109. Smith, *Language and Time*, 12. For his further discussion on this theme, see chapter 3, "Untranslatability of A-Sentences by Tenseless Token-Reflexive Sentences," 67–93.

sess A-properties of presentness, present pastness, or present futurity.[110] Furthermore, Smith insists that, "Not only are the tenseless truth *conditions* A-sentence-tokens 'reducible' to their tensed truth conditions, but their tenseless *truth* is 'reducible' to their tensed truth."[111]

For this reason, Smith proposes his own tensed theory of time as an absolute "presentism," which means that all of reality is unified in presentness. According to Smith's definition, "Presentism is the theory *that every possibly true sentence has presentness for a logical subject and that every state of affairs has presentness for a metaphysical subject.*"[112] That is to say, according to Smith, presentism is not merely a linguistic problem, but it is an all inclusive conception of time which embraces all objective physical and metaphysical states of affairs, for "presentness inheres in the infinite totality of beings."[113] Finally, based on his presentism, Smith suggests a "metaphysical time," which is a "primitive, absolute, all-embracing and is the only time series, all other time concepts being reductively definable in terms of nontemporal n-adic properties or in terms of these properties and the primitive temporal properties of metaphysical time."[114]

The Arguments for the Arrow of Time

For the tensed theory of time, more supportive arguments come from the existence of "the arrow of time" in the physical world. Even though Newtonian mechanics gives a dazzling mathematical description of motion from apples to the heavenly bodies, it cannot give any information about the direction of the time of our universe. Thus, as P. Coveney and R. Highfield rightly point out, "The enigma of time's direction remained a flaw at the centre of science."[115] Nowadays, however, there is wide recognition of the existence of "the arrow of time" in the natural world, which means that time has a unique directionality, asymmetry,

---

110. Cf. ibid., 94.

111. Ibid., 100.

112. Ibid., 133.

113. Ibid., 136. For Smith's detailed argument for his "presentism," see "Part II. The Argument for Presentism," in *Language and Time*, 133–259.

114. Ibid., 251.

115. Coveney and Highfield, *Arrow of Time*, 21.

or irreversibility.[116] For the question, "Is there an arrow of time in the physical world?" I. Prigogine emphatically insists that, "the arrow of time is *an exact property* of important classes of dynamical systems."[117] In the physical world, for him, all evidences of our experience seem to denote the fact that time flows in a single direction, from the past through the present toward the future. Here I will briefly describe the following five basic arrows of time in thermodynamics, quantum physics, cosmology, biology, and causation theory.[118]

The Second Law of Thermodynamics and Entropy

First of all, the argument of time's arrow comes from the second law of thermodynamics, which is the most fundamental and important argument for the arrow of time in the physical world.[119] Thermodynamics is originally concerned with the performance of a heat engine. According

---

116. The term, "time's arrow" was probably first used by Eddinton, an astrophysicist, in his Gifford Lectures at the University of Edinburgh in 1927. Cf. idem, *Nature of the Physical World*, 68. For recent discussions on this topic, see Prigogine, *From Being to Becoming*; Morris, *Time's Arrows*; Flood and Lockwood, *Nature of Time*; Coveney and Highfield, *Arrow of Time*; Savitt, *Time's Arrows Today*; Davies, *About Time*; Price, *Time's Arrow and Archimedes' Point*; Schulman, *Time's Arrows and Quantum Measurement*; Zeh, *Physical Basis of the Direction of Time*.

117. Prigogine, "Foreword," in Coveney and Highfield, *Arrow of Time*, 16 (italics mine).

118. For example, Penrose suggests the following seven possible 'arrows' in nature: (1) Decay of the K0-meson particle; (2) Quantum-mechanical observations; (3) General entropy increase; (4) Retardation of radiation; (5) Psychological time; (6) Expansion of the Universe; and (7) the existence of the Black holes and the possibility of the White holes. See idem, "Singularities and Time-asymmetry," 581–638. However, Hawking denotes the following three basic arrows: (1) the thermodynamic arrow of time–the increase of entropy; (2) the psychological arrow of time; and (3) the cosmological arrow of time–the expansion of the universe. Cf. idem, *Brief History of Time*, 143–53. Recently, Zeh also gives five arrows of time in the physical world: (1) the time arrow of radiation; (2) the thermodynamical arrow of time; (3) the quantum mechanical arrow of time; (4) the time arrow of spacetime geometry; and (5) the time arrow in quantum cosmology. See idem, *Physical Basis of the Direction of Time*.

119. Concerning the importance of the second law of thermodynamics, Eddington states as follows: "The law that entropy always increases—the second law of thermodynamics—holds, I think, the supreme position among the laws of Nature . . . if your theory is found to be against the second law of thermodynamics I can give you no hope; there is nothing for it but to collapse in deepest humiliation." Idem, *Nature of the Physical World*, 74. For a recent excellent argument on the problem of time (or becoming) in thermodynamics and physics, see Prigogine, *From Being to Becoming Sciences*.

to thermodynamics, heat can only flow from a hotter body to a cooler one, and, in any process of energy transformation, it is irreversibly scattered. While the first law of thermodynamics states that the total energy of the universe is always constant (i.e., the law of the conservation of the sum of energy), the second law shows us the fact that, in a closed system, the total entropy of the universe is always increasing toward its maximum value. For the second law of thermodynamics, in 1865, R. Clausius defined the concept of "entropy" as "a quantity that relentlessly grows with dissipation and attains its maximum value when all the potential for further work is spent."[120]

According to I. Prigogine, "There is no real system in nature that can go through a cycle of operations and return to its initial state without increasing the entropy of the exterior, or more generally the 'universe.' The increase of entropy distinguishes the future from the past: there exists an arrow of time."[121] Furthermore, in an isolated system (or a closed universe), since entropy always increases toward its maximum value, it implies that the isolated system (or the closed universe) ultimately faces the dead state of thermodynamic equilibrium (i.e., the "heat death" of the universe). In the following statement, P. Coveney and R. Highfield succinctly explain the relationship between the second law of thermodynamics and the arrow of time as follows:

> Time is linked by thermodynamics to ideas about organisation and randomness. The flow of time becomes apparent because there is an inexorable tendency in any system left to its own devices for organisation to diminish and randomness to increase. If milk is added to black tea, the milk molecules mingle and diffuse with those of the tea. Eventually, both are evenly distributed, giving tea its characteristic murky brown appearance; when the mixing is complete, no further change occurs. Within the tea in its final state, the molecular randomness—or to be thermodynamically accurate the entropy—has reached a maximum value. This is equilibrium state, when molecules of milk and tea are to be found uniformly throughout the mixture and the capacity for more mixing is lost. We never see the reverse process, in which the uniform brown liquid spontaneously separates into white milk and black tea. For in order to do that, we would have to travel back in time. The arrow of time is

---

120. Coveney and Highfield, *Arrow of Time*, 151.
121. Prigogine, *Modern Thermodynamics*, 83.

made explicit in the so-called *Second Law of Thermodynamics*, which states that all physical processes are irreversible because some energy is always dissipated as heat.[122]

However, in spite of the principle of entropy, I. Prigogine and others recently showed us the possibility of spontaneous self-organization from the planets to cells in the irreversible non-equilibrium universe. Prigogine calls it "dissipative structure." However, as we shall see, it does not violate the second law of thermodynamics in broad sense.

The Arrow of Time in Quantum Physics

Quantum physics is another new revolutionary physics alongside Einstein's Relativity Theory in the twentieth century. While the latter concerns the macro-world, the former focuses upon the atomic and sub-atomic micro-world. Like Newtonian classical physics and Einstein's relativity theory, quantum physics as well is essentially reversible with respect to time (i.e., time-symmetric system).[123] However, there are two peculiar phenomena, which denote the directionality of time, the problem of quantum measurement and the existence of the *neutral K-meson* (K^0-*meson* or *kaon*) sub-atomic particle.[124] The term "quantum" was originated from M. Planck's explanation of electromagnetic radiation of "black body" by "quantum," which is a certain packet of energy (1900). In 1905, A. Einstein showed this fact that light is constituted as energy packets of "light quanta" (i.e., "photon") by his experiment of "the photoelectric effect." However, a strange aspect of the photon is that it has the following dual properties at the same time: wave and particle. In 1923, L. de Broglie generalized this in saying that all particles that have the properties of a wave at the same time, and the reverse is also true. Such quantum mechanics can be described by Schrödinger's wave equation (1926), which is basically deterministic and time-symmetric. However, according to W. Heisenberg's famous "uncertainty principle"

---

122. Coveney and Highfield, *Arrow of Time*, 147–48.

123. Cf. ibid., 29–32, and Morris, *Time's Arrow*, 45–64.

124. Coveney and Highfield describe these facts as follows, "Quantum mechanics gives us tantalizing hints of the presence of time's arrow. As we shall see, it suggests that the passage of time is guaranteed by something very simple: our own observation of change. And by opening up the secret world of the *atom*, it reveals one tiny particle whose existence indicates that time is irreversible." Idem, *Arrow of Time*, 108.

(1927), we cannot precisely know the position and the momentum of an electron at the same time. Since Schrödinger's equation gives us only the "probability" of the position of particles, the problem of measurement arises in the quantum world. The relationship between the act of measurement and the arrow of time is as follows:

> It thus seems that if we turn our backs and do not peek, a wave-function evolves in a reversible and deterministic manner. Yet one measurement of the location of the electron on the screen alters the behaviour irreversibly. When the wave-function collapse occurs, all the many possibilities reduce to a single real event. This removes the symmetry between the past state of the system (potentiality) and the present state (actuality). Indeed, if one tries to use the method to retrodict the past from a given measurement result, one gets incorrect results. Thus *the very act of measurement introduces an arrow of time into the phenomena described by quantum mechanics.*[125]

According to P. Coveney and R. Highfield, such a wave-function collapse by the act of measurement is "irreversible and fully objective."[126]

Another arrow of time in quantum (particle) physics is found in the time-asymmetry phenomenon of the decay of an unstable particle called "the long-lived *kaon* (K^0)."[127] In common decay, K^0 is transformed into three *pions* (a negative *pion*, a positron, and a *neutrino*). However, in very rare cases (about once in 10^9 decays), it can be transformed into a positive *pion*, an electron, and an anti-*neutrino*. In this decay process, *CP* violation is observed, and thus, as a consequence of *CPT* invariance, there is a *T* (time reversal invariance) violation. It can be used to define the arrow of time. Concerning this phenomenon, R. Penrose says its significance as follows:

> [T]he tiny effect of an almost completely hidden time-asymmetry seems genuinely to be present in the K^0-decay. It is hard to believe that Nature is not, so to speak, "trying to tell us something" through the results of this delicate and beautiful experiment, which has been confirmed several times . . . I believe that it is a feature of key significance.[128]

125. Ibid., 129.
126. Ibid., 134.
127. Ibid., 140.
128. Penrose, "Singularities and Time-asymmetry," 583.

The Arrow of Time in Cosmology

In the early twentieth century, astronomers had observed the phenomenon of red-shift by the Doppler effect from the spectrum of the light of stars. This means that the stars (or galaxies) are moving away from us. In 1929, E. Hubble discovered that the size of a galaxy's red-shift is directly proportional to its distance from us (cf. the Hubble parameter, H0). This has been regarded as a strong evidence for the fact that the universe is dynamic and expanding, not static. Actually, in 1922, A. Friedmann, a Russian physicist, predicted this fact from Einstein's GTR (cf. Einstein himself missed predicting this fact by introducing "the cosmological constant" because of his trust in the conception of a static universe). Therefore, S. W. Hawking points out that, "The discovery that the universe is expanding was one of the great intellectual revolutions of the twentieth century."[129] This expanding universe implies the cosmological arrow of time.

Furthermore, in 1948, R. Alpher and G. Gamow (with H. Bethe) published a paper about the "Big Bang," which describes the earlier state of the universe. Finally, in 1965, A. Penzias and R. Wilson accidentally discovered an all-pervasive microwave radiation in the universe, which was considered as "an echo of the birth of the universe" (cf. the satellite COBE's measurement of cosmic microwave background radiation in 1992).[130] Therefore, according to contemporary orthodox cosmology, the universe has its beginning with the so-called "Big-Bang" from a *singularity*, which is a space-time point of zero volume and infinite mass.[131] This means that "time had a beginning at the big bang."[132] And then, if ours is a closed universe, after enough time, the whole universe will be contracted to a huge final *singularity* of a "Big Crunch" because of gravitational force. In the same sense, "black holes" can be considered as an evidence of the final *singularity* (i.e., the end of the universe) in which every space-time disappears because of its strong gravitational force. The term, "black hole" was first used by J. Wheeler in 1969, and

129. Hawking, *Brief History of Time*, 39.

130. Cf. Coveney and Highfield, *Arrow of Time*, 98.

131. Around 1965–70, Penrose and Hawking proved that there must be a big bang singularity based on the GTR. Cf. Hawking, *Brief History of Time*, 49–50. However, after that, Hawking himself ironically rejects the idea of singularity of the Big Bang based on his quantum cosmology.

132. Hawking, *Brief History of Time*, 46.

was predicted by S. Chandrasekhar (1930) and R. Oppenheimer (1939) among others. Black holes are made by the collapse of stars, which are more massive than the "Chandrasekhar limit." Nowadays, the existence of black holes is generally considered as a "proved" fact by the "pulsar," which was first discovered by J. Bell in 1967 (cf. Cynus X-1 is a good evidence). According to R. Penrose, the structures of the singularities of the Big Bang and the Big Crunch are different. That is to say, the entropy of the former is lower than that of the latter, and thus the thermodynamical arrow and the cosmological arrow are compatible.[133]

The Arrow of Time in Biology

Every living creature possesses the process of birth, growth, and death. In this sense, P. Coveney and R. Highfield point out that the irreversibility of time is revealed "as the ultimate source of the pathos of human life. . . . the fact that every living creature dies is the most tangible evidence for the flux of time."[134] They continue as follows,

> Aspects of time in biology are analogous to both cyclical and linear cultural experience. Cyclical time appears in cell division and the orchestra of different rhythms in our bodies, ranging from high-frequency nerve impulses to leisurely cycles of cell turnover. And the notion of irreversible time is manifested by ageing in the passage from birth to death.[135]

According to P. Davies, two characteristics of living systems are "complexity and organization."[136] In the creative activities of biological organisms, we can observe a production of order. Is this in contradiction to the second law of thermodynamics? However, in this case too, the amount of increased entropy in the exterior system (i.e., environment of the biological organism) is always more than that of negative entropy in the organisms. Thus, the total system's entropy is always increasing.

---

133. Cf. Coveney and Highfield, *Arrow of Time*, 178–81. "Irreversibility and entropy also seem to be unavoidably linked with the greatest happening of all, the birth of time and of the universe itself. This event to begin all events—the process of creating a universe from nothing—is irreversible, being inextricably bound up with the production of entropy" (pp. 290–91).

134. Ibid., 25.

135. Ibid., 26–27.

136. Davies, *God and the New Physics*, 59.

> [T]here need be no contradiction at all between biology and the second law. The latter refers always to the *total* system. It is possible for order to accumulate in one place at the price of entropy generated elsewhere. Now an essential feature of living systems is that they are "open" to their surroundings: they are not completely sealed off or self-contained in any way. They can only survive by exchanging energy and material with their environment. When a proper entropy balance sheet is drawn up one finds that the growth of order in an organism is paid for by entropy in the wider environment. In all cases there is a net entropy increase.[137]

Therefore, in the terms of I. Prigogine, all living systems as "self-organizing structures" are kinds of "dissipative structures" in that their surrounding entropy is always increasing. Accordingly, we can conclude that the arrow of life denotes the arrow of time along with the second law of thermodynamics.

The Arrow of Time in Causal Relations

The theory of causation is one of the central issues in metaphysics, philosophy of language, philosophy of mind, and philosophy of science. In addition, it is also closely related to arguments about the arrow of time and the dynamic conception of the world. Among many others, M. Tooley recently presented a causal theory of time in his *Time, Tense, and Causation*.[138] In this work, Tooley attempts to synthesize the tensed and the tenseless theories of time as an "intermediate approach" based on his realistic understanding of causation. He says as follows,

> [T]here are two crucial differences between tenseless approaches to the nature of time and *standard* tensed accounts. On the one hand, tenseless approaches to time involve both a static conception of the world and the idea that tensed facts are logically supervenient upon tenseless facts. Traditional tensed approaches, on the other hand, incorporate a dynamic conception of the world, together with the claim that tenseless facts are supervenient upon tensed facts. The tensed view of time that I shall be defending, by contrast, represents an intermediate position, since it combines the idea that the world is dynamic with

---

137. Ibid., 65.
138. Tooley, *Time, Tense, and Causation*.

the thesis that tensed facts are logically supervenient upon what tenseless facts are actual as of different times.[139]

As he says, his "non-existent future" theory of time eventually describes a tensed (dynamic) theory of time, for events can be causally related only in a dynamic world, in which the past and the present are real, but the future is not.[140] According to Tooley, there is a fundamental difference between the past (fixed and settled) and the future (open and undetermined). Therefore, the world is essentially characterized by "a deep asymmetry" between the past and the future, and time is also characterized by "an intrinsic direction." While appealing to C. D. Broad, Tooley maintains that the past and the present are real, but the future is not, and "the present lies at the cutting edge of reality, with the world growing through the addition of new facts."[141]

Based on his causal theory, Tooley asserts that, "Time flows, and as it does, enduring entities such as ourselves move forward in time, while events that have taken place recede ever further into the past."[142] However, Tooley's theory of time is different from the traditional tensed theory in that he insists that "tenseless concepts and facts are more basic than the tensed ones."[143] Then, how can the two assertions be compatible with each other? In Tooley's view, not only the direction of time but also the tense of the state of affairs can be defined by the direction of *causation*, for causal relations are identical with the order of temporal relations and the passage of time.[144] Therefore, the world is dynamic in its reality "because, and only because, what tenseless states of affairs are now actual changes with the passage of time."[145] Finally, Tooley concludes that,

> [I]n grounding the dynamic nature of the world upon causation, ... time, understood as involving the coming into existence of events, is a totally objective feature of the world that is not

---

139. Ibid., 1–2.

140. Cf. ibid., 3. For Tooley's realistic understanding of causation, see his *Causation*, and "Causation: Reductionism versus Realism," 172–92.

141. Tooley, *Time, Tense, and Causation*, 31.

142. Ibid., 11.

143. Ibid., 29. For Tooley's detail arguments, see "Part III: Tensed Facts" (pp. 157–251).

144. Cf. ibid., 255–300.

145. Ibid., 377.

dependent in any way upon the experiences of humans, or other conscious (or self-conscious) beings. In this respect, it contrasts sharply with those tensed accounts that assign a central and crucial role to the phenomenology of the experience of time.[146]

The Nature of Time and Its Theological Implications

So far, we have briefly reviewed the two rival conceptions of the nature of time in contemporary debates in metaphysics and natural science. As we have seen, in the debates between the tenseless theories and the tensed theories, one of the key points is how to conceive the passage of time. How on earth does time flow? Is it a mere mind-dependent illusion or an objective reality? Which theory is correct between the tenseless (static) and the tensed (dynamic) theory of time? Indeed, as M. Tooley points out, it is "the most fundamental question in the philosophy of time."[147] Unfortunately, as we have seen, there is not yet any consensus on the real nature of time between these two rival theories. However, for this study, my intention is not to prove which theory is correct, rather my concern focuses upon the following question: If the tensed (dynamic/A) theory of time is correct, how can we properly conceive God's eternity, its relation to world time, and God's action in this time-bounded dynamic world? Therefore, for my study, I will assume a relational and dynamic (tensed) conception of time as correct.[148]

Being (Substance) and Time: An Objective and Relational Conception of Time

At first, for this study, my concern mainly focuses on objective (real) and relational time, not on subjective and absolute time.[149] If we take

146. Ibid., 379.

147. Ibid., 13.

148. Similarly, in recent debates concerning the understanding of God's eternity, Padgett, Yates, and Craig among many others hold this relational-dynamic conception of time. See Padgett, *God, Eternity and the Nature of Time*, 82–121; Yates, *Timelessness of God*, 95; and Craig, "God, Time, and Eternity," 497–503.

149. Cf. Bunge, "Physical Time," 355–88. Bunge classifies the following four possible consistent theories of time: "*AS*: Time is absolute and subjective (Kant). *AO*: Time is absolute and objective (Newton). *RS*: Time is relative and subjective (Berkeley). *RO*: Time is relative and objective (Lucretius)" (p. 355). While preferring the relational-objective

Kantian subjective time as an epistemological *a priori* condition,[150] our main issue of God's relation to time would be an empty question.[151] In this sense, I suppose that time is real and objective. In addition, in my view, being and time are inseparably interrelated to each other. That is to say, without being (and things), there is no time. Time in itself is not a being (i.e., an independent ontological substance), but it is the mode of existence for the created universe and everything in it. In saying that, I want to posit my stance of an objective and relational view of time. However, as I already briefly mentioned, I. Newton maintained the view of "absolute time," which flows uniformly without any external relations.[152] According to him, time is real, but it is neither substance nor accident. Time has its own peculiar mode of existence because of God's existence, thus it has independent ontological status without any relation to other physical objects. For Newton, time is an "eminent effect of God."[153] In other words, according to him, time itself is not created, but is a consequence that emanates from God's sempiternal existence, and thus God is temporal in this absolute time. In Newton's view, "Time, then, acts as a boundary condition between God's person and the created world of nature. It is identical neither with God nor with nature, and yet is a necessary condition for the existence of nature and natural processes."[154]

In contrast to Newtonian "absolute time," there is a different conception of the nature of time as "relational." That is, as Lucretius points

---

view of time, he insists that, "Time is not out there, by itself and ready-made, as the absolute view of time had it: time is in making alongside happenings" (p. 375).

150. In contrast to objective or real time, I. Kant insisted on a conception of ideal and subjective time as follows: "Time is nothing but the form of inner sense, that is, of the intuition of ourselves and of our inner state.... Time is the formal *a priori* condition of all appearances whatsoever.... It is no longer objective, if we abstract from the sensibility of our intuition, that is, from that mode of representation which is peculiar to us, and speak of *things in general*. Time is therefore a purely subjective condition of our (human) intuition (which is always sensible, that is, so far as affected by objects), and in itself, apart from the subject, is nothing." Idem, *Critique of Pure Reason*, 77–78 (italics original).

151. Cf. Yates, *Timelessness of God*, 58.

152. Cf. the footnote 16 in this chapter.

153. Newton, *Unpublished Scientific Papers of Isaac Newton*, 131–32. As cited in Turetzky, *Time*, 72.

154. Turetzky, *Time*, 73.

out, "time is nothing by itself,"[155] for it cannot be separated from concrete changes of things and events occurring in it. Thus, even though time is not identical with change, a relational view of time comes from our awareness of time in the changes of things and happenings of events. Time *per se* is not a substance or entity in that apart from objects and events "it can be given no meaning or existence,"[156] but rather we can say that it is the way of being or the trajectory of substance. More specifically, time is the form of the relationship between beings (things) and events, and with the other beings. In this sense, S. Hackett says, "Time is . . . a relational among objects that are apprehended in an order of succession or that objectively exist in such an order: time is a form of perceptual experience and of objective processes in the external (to the mind) world."[157] In the same way, F. Guy also asserts that "any modern conception of time must recognize that it is a relationship, not an existent entity; it is a 'metrical frame' for designating one of the ways in which events and things are related to each other. Time is . . . a genuinely ontological relationship."[158]

Cambridge Change and Real Change

As we have seen, in McTaggart's view, time presupposes change, and events presuppose time, but, for him, time is unreal. Similarly, M. Capeck points out that, "The consciousness of time is inseparable from that of change. . . . Just as it was difficult to separate space conceptually from its concrete content, it required a considerable effort of abstraction to differentiate from changes and events 'taking place' in it."[159] In this sense, most philosophers of time reject McTaggart's view of the "unreality of time" in that time is real, not merely a subjective illusion. However, at this very point, recent views of the nature of time are divided between the tenseless (static) and the tensed (dynamic) theory. M. Tooley succinctly summarized it as follows:

---

155. Lucretius, *De rerum natura*, I, 459–60. As cited in Capek, "Time," 389.
156. Yates, *Timelessness of God*, 60.
157. S. Hackett, *Theism*, 263. Cited in Craig, "God, Time and Eternity," 500.
158. Guy, "Man and His Time," 405 and 439.
159. Capek, "Time," 389.

> According to a static conception, what states of affairs there are does not depend upon what time it is. Change, consequently, cannot be a matter of a change, over time, in what states of affairs exist. It must be a matter simply of the possession, by an object, or by the world as a whole, of different intrinsic properties at different times. According to a dynamic conception of the world, by contrast, what states of affairs exist does depend upon what time it is. As a consequence, the totality of monadic states of affairs which exist as of one time, and which involve a given object, may differ from the totality that exists as of some other time, and it is precisely such a difference that constitutes change in an object, rather than merely the possession by an object of different properties at different times. Similarly, change in the world as a whole is a matter of a difference in the totality of states of affairs that exists as of different times, and not merely a matter of the possession of different properties by different temporal slices of the world.[160]

Accordingly, we can clearly see that the conception of the nature of *time* and that of *change* are inseparable. However, in following P. Geach, we can distinguish the concept of change in time in following two forms: Cambridge (relative) change and real (ontological qualitative) change.[161] Geach characterized some Cambridge philosophers' (like Russell and McTaggart) view of change as "Cambridge change," which is defined as follows: for a thing x, if F(x) has a different truth-value at different times, t_1 and t_2, then, the thing x is changed. For example, the death of Socrates causes a Cambridge change for his wife, Xanthippe, for it made her a widow. However, Socrates suffered a real change, death, for himself. Another example is change in my daughter, *Seulki*: now she is smaller than me, but she is growing. At some time she will be grow and will be taller than me. In this case, while Seulki has really changed in her height, it is a mere Cambridge change for me. Therefore, Cambridge change is a relational concept. If there is a qualitative or ontological change in the objects, we can call it a "real" change.[162] According to Geach, every real

---

160. Tooley, *Time, Tense, and Causation*, 16

161. Geach, *God and the Soul*, 71–72. Cf. McCall, *Model of the Universe*, 44–47; and Padgett, *God, Eternity and the Nature of Time*, 10–12.

162. According to Padgett, the difference between a qualitative and a relative change, and their relationship with a real change are as follows: "A changes in object Q is qualitative if and only if a quality of Q is either gained or lost (or Q comes into existence or ceases to exist) in the change. A change in Q is relative if and only if a relative property

change entails a Cambridge change, but not vice versa.[163] However, in this created universe, everything undergoes a real, genuine, or ontological qualitative change with the Cambridge change. In this sense, time is real and dynamic in this actual world.

However, for God, there is only Cambridge change in a relational sense, but not real change in His Being and His nature. In the same sense, an evangelical theologian, B. A. Ware recently discusses God's "relational mutability," while asserting God's ontological and ethical immutability.[164] That is to say, first of all, according to Ware, God is not ever changed in His Being and His intrinsic nature. Then, as a corollary and "a second-order type of changelessness," God is immutable in a moral sense in that God is also "unchangeable in his unconditional promises and moral obligations to which he has freely pledged himself."[165] Yet, God is mutable in respect to His relationship with His peoples and creatures. Ware argues this as follows:

> Anselm observed long ago that one's essence need not change as a result of changing relationships with others. He argued that though another person is born, to whom one now has numerous relations which can develop or cease and all of which were formerly nonexistent, this can occur without causing any necessary changes in one's own person. This point is vital for our present discussion. God freely involves himself within the spatio-temporal structure in which humans live, and he does so not as a mere passive observer. God's involvement in history is pervasive and comprehensive. . . . In the light of the Scriptural evidence that God indeed changes in relationship with his creatures, . . . [but] these changes of relationship neither entail nor involve incidentally changes in God's intrinsic nature . . . God [is] made neither better nor worse by his relational changes. He neither increases nor decreases in excellence since he is, as already stated, the fullness of all excellence. Indeed God can-

---

of Q is either gained or lost in the change. What, then, about 'real' change? . . . [A] real change will take place in an object at a time if a qualitative change takes place in that object during that time, which is the basis for the relative change. A change is a merely relative one in an object if there is a possible world in which the change takes place in that object at a time and no qualitative change occurs in that object during that time." Idem, *God, Eternity and the Nature of Time*, 11.

163. Cf. Geach, *God and the Soul*, 72.

164. Cf. Ware, "Evangelical Reformulation of the Doctrine of the Immutability of God," 434–40.

165. Ibid., 436.

not change for the better or the worse, but he can change in some sense nonetheless. He changes from anger to mercy, from blessing to cursing, from rejection to acceptance. Each of these changes is real in God, though no such change affects in the slightest the unchangeable supremacy of his intrinsic nature. God's relational mutability only expresses in time and in personal relationship the changelessness of his intrinsic nature and free word."[166]

J. S. Feinberg, too, maintains a very similar view in saying that "God must be immutable in his person [i.e., being and attributes], purposes, will (decree), and ethical rules," but He can change in "administration of God's plan of salvation," "Cambridge properties" (i.e., relational sense), and the "knowledge of the truth of indexical propositions" in time's flow.[167]

The Nature of Time and Some Theological Implications

In a theological perspective, the problem of the nature of time is not merely a subsidiary one, but how to conceive it has a fundamental importance for almost all subject matters of systematic theology, from the doctrine of creation to eschatology. The following are some examples with respect to the problem of the nature of time. Of course, for every case, we can expect various intermediate positions, but I will describe only the radically rival conceptions in each case here.

The Doctrine of Creatio ex Nihilo and Time

Is God's creation of the world *in* time or *with* time? If we take the conception of absolute time (cf. I. Newton), God created the world *in* time, and this implies sempiternalism for God's eternity. Accordingly, God is temporal as I. Newton conceived. However, if we take a relational view of physical time, *creatio ex nihilo* means God's creation of the world *with* time. Thus, time itself has its beginning and will have its end with the world. This can imply God's atemporality, the timeless eternity of God. However, even in the relational view of time, as we shall see in later

---

166. Ibid., 439–41.

167. Feinberg, *No One Like Him*, 271–72. For his detailed biblical, theological, and philosophical arguments on God's immutability, see 264–76.

chapters, there can be various arguments for the beginning of time and the timeless understanding of God's eternity.

Divine Immutability/Omniscience/Foreknowledge and Time

If we take the tenseless (static) theory of time, there is no problem with the doctrine of divine omniscience and foreknowledge, for all events and facts of the past, the present, and the future are equally real and everything is already determined permanently. In addition, the doctrine of divine immutability fits very well with the tenseless theory time, for in this view there are no real changing facts even in this created world. However, according to the tensed (dynamic) theory of time, at least future facts are undetermined, for they do not exist yet, and thus, some theologians assert that the orthodox doctrines of divine omniscience and foreknowledge seem to be logically untenable and inconsistent (cf. contra this, the doctrine of divine decree). Furthermore, things undergo real change in the dynamic world of tensed time. Therefore, if we hold the idea of God's real relation to our ever transient time-bounded dynamic world, we need more reasoning to conceive properly divine immutability, omniscience, and foreknowledge.

Anthropology and Time

Recently, one of the hottest battles between the tenseless and the tensed theory of time lies in the problem of personal identity and the nature of time.[168] Even though there are some exceptions, while the tenseless

---

168. For this problem, see the following: Wiggins, *Identity and Spatial-Temporal Continuity*; Chisholm, "Identity Through Time," 163–82; Shoemaker, "Persons and Their Pasts," 269–85; Parfit, "Personal Identity," 3–27; Perry, "Can the Self Divide?," 463–88; Hoy, "Becoming and Persons," 269–80; Hirsch, *Concept of Identity*; Shoemaker and Swinburne, *Personal Identity*; Oaklander, "Temporal Passage and Temporal Parts," 79–84; Oderberg, *Metaphysics of Identity over Time*; Merricks, "On the Incompatibility of Enduring and Perduring Entities," 523–31; Sider, "Four-Dimensionalism," 197–231; Rea, "Temporal Parts Unmotivated," 225–60; Balashov, "Persistence and Space-Time: Philosophical Lessons of the Pole and Barn," 321–40; Brogaard, "Presentist Four-Dimensionalism," 341–56; Le Poidevin, "Continuants and Continuity," 381–98; Parsons, "Must a Four-Dimensionalist Believe in Temporal Parts?," 399–418; Simons, "How to Exist at a Time When You Have No Temporal Parts," 419–36; Van Inwagen, "Temporal Parts and Identity across Time," 437–59.

theorists generally maintain the "perdurance" theory for personal identity over time, the tensed theorists hold the "endurance" theory.[169] That is to say, based on four-dimensional spatio-temporal relations, tenseless theorists prefer the temporal-parts theory for personal identity in static time. But, in the tensed theorists' view, it is an absurd idea that a concrete person (or object) and its history are different. In this sense, a tensed theorist, D. Lewis, recently insisted, that the tenseless view of the temporal parts theory of personal identity cannot be reconciled with the moral agent. He says that, "if the tenseless view is correct, there are no agents which persist while performing any action."[170]

Conclusion

In classical theism, God's eternity has been conceived as timeless eternity. This timeless eternity of God is consistent with the tenseless theory of time without any serious problem. Recently, therefore, P. Helm, among others, strongly defends the timeless eternity of God on the basis of the tenseless theory of time.[171] However, some philosophers and theologians assert, if we take the tensed theory of time, the timeless eternity of God is not plausible. Indeed, recently, one of the most powerful arguments against the timeless eternity of God comes form the tensed theory of time. As we shall see, the proponents of this line of arguments are J. D. Lewis, A. G. Padgett, and W. L. Craig among many others.[172] For example, W. L. Craig emphatically insists that, "if the dy-

---

169. Some exceptional cases are as follows: on the one hand, even though D. H. Mellor maintains the tenseless theory of time, he rejects the idea of persisting objects which have temporal parts. Cf. idem, *Real Time*, Chap. 8. On the other hand, while holding the tensed theory of time, S. McCall accepts the idea of temporal parts of persisting objects. Cf. idem, *Model of the Universe*, chapter 2 and 7. However, many philosophers argue that there is a concrete correspondence between the tenseless theory with the perdurancism and the tensed theory with the endurancism. See Holt, "Timelessness and the Metaphysics of Temporal Existence," 149–56; Carter and Hestevold, "On Passage and Persistence," 269–83; and Lowe, *Possibility of Metaphysics*, especially, chapter 4, "Time and Persistence."

170. Lewis, "Persons, Morality, and Tenselessness," 309.

171. Cf. Helm, *Eternal God*.

172. Cf. Lewis, "God and Time"; Padgett, *God, Eternity and the Nature of Time*; and Craig, *Time and Eternity*.

namic conception of time is correct, God is most plausibly understood to be temporal."[173]

However, we must ask, if the tensed theory of time is correct, then must God be temporal as we are? Herein lies my central issue for the proceeding study in which I will reconcile a biblical and theological understanding of God's eternity and the dynamic temporal world. In other words, more specifically, if the tensed (dynamic) theory of time is correct, how can we conceive God's eternity and its relation to time? Indeed, this is a key issue in this study. However, before addressing this, we must show how the philosophical and scientific understandings of time affect theological understandings of God's eternity and its relation to time in the following chapter 5.

173. Craig, *Time and Eternity*, 115.

5

Contemporary Theological Debates on God's Eternity and Its Relation to Time

Introduction

CURRENTLY, IN PHILOSOPHICAL THEOLOGY, THE DEBATE ON THE NATURE of time is very significant for our understanding of God's eternity and its relation to time. As we have seen in chapter 4, there are two competing theories of time, the tenseless (static, B-series) and the tensed (dynamic, A-series) theory. In addition, for understanding divine eternity, there are basically two alternative conceptions, timeless and everlasting eternity. Therefore, concerning the problem of God's eternity and its relation to time, in a logical sense, we can think about the following four basic possible options: (1) "timeless eternity—tenseless time"; (2) "timeless eternity—tensed time"; (3) "everlasting eternity—tenseless time"; and finally, (4) "everlasting eternity—tensed time."[1]

Among these possibilities, probably option (3) "everlasting eternity–tenseless time" is the most implausible possibility. Accordingly, no one actually takes this option in debates on God's eternity and its relation to time. As we have seen in chapter 3, classical theologians maintained the view of option (2) "timeless eternity—tensed time" (cf. E. Stump and N. Kretzmann), but recently many philosophers and theologians assert that such a timeless eternity can be properly understood only in tenseless theory of time. Therefore, option (1) "timeless eternity—tenseless time" is held by some theologians regarding God's eternity and its relation to

---

1. However, Leftow presents that God's eternity is timeless regardless the problem of the nature of time, tenseless or tensed theory of time. Cf. Leftow, *Time and Eternity*, 17–18.

time (cf. P. Helm). In this view, God is timelessly eternal which means that He exists absolutely "outside" of tenseless (static) time. Recently, however, option (4) "everlasting eternity—tensed time" is raised as an alternative conception in conceiving divine eternity and its relation to human time, though, as we shall see, there are many variations of this option.

In regard to the two options (1) and (4) one must ask, are these two the only alternative possibilities? Are there not any other possibilities? In this thesis, in contrast to those two main options, I shall endeavor to set up another alternative understanding of God's eternity and its relation to time based on the tensed (dynamic) understanding of time. The reason is that, as we have seen in chapter 4, if we take a tenseless (static, A-series) view of time, then there are no serious problems with the classical view of divine timeless eternity, however, in current times many theologians have asserted that God is temporal because the tensed (dynamic, A-series) theory of time is correct. Thus, if time is tensed, then should we discard the classical conception of God's eternity? For this problem, in this thesis, I will propose a Trinitarian analogical understanding of God's eternity and its relation to time.

Before doing so, in this chapter, concerning recent theological discussions on the issue, I will deal with four possible options concerning the relationship between God's eternity and human time: "absolute timelessness" (P. Helm), "everlastingness" (N. Wolterstorff), "relative timelessness" (A. G. Padgett), and "accidental temporalism (timelessness and omni-temporalism)" (W. L. Craig).[2] As previously mentioned, the timeless understanding of God's eternity with tensed (dynamic) theory of time was the conception of classical theism.[3] Recently, however, such an idea of atemporality of divine eternity has been widely criticized and rejected by many theologians and philosophers for various reasons.[4]

2. For this discussion, I will basically use the following work, Ganssle, *God and Time: Four Views*. In this collective work of four evangelical theologians, P. Helm, N. Wolterstorff, A. G. Padgett, and W. L. Craig, we can grasp the importance of the issue, the gist of debates and various possible options in thinking about God's eternity and its relation to time and its significance for evangelical theology.

3. For a reformulation of Boethius' definition, see Stump and Kretzmann "Eternity," 429–58. However, according to Craig's analysis, some classical theologians' view of time can be interpreted as a tenseless theory of time. Idem, "Was Thomas Aquinas a B-Theorist of Time?," 475–83.

4. For example, B. Davies summaries several major objections to God's timelessness as follows: "1. If God is timeless, he cannot be a person. 2. If God is timeless, his

First of all, according to biblical teaching, God is a personal Being who really acts and works in this temporal world and directly communicates with His creatures. However, many theologians assert that this essential biblical tenet cannot be compatible with the idea of the timeless eternity of God. Secondly, according to temporalists, a timeless God cannot be omniscient because He cannot know the tensed affairs in this temporal world. In addition, the doctrines of divine impassibility and immutability, too, do not fit with the biblical God who really interacts with His creatures in time, for change must be in time. However, today, in philosophical perspective, one of the most powerful reasons for criticism rests in the views of the nature of time. The absolute timeless eternity of God coincides with the tenseless (static) theory of time without any serious problems. In contrast to this, however, the tensed (dynamic) theorists of time assert that God must be a temporal being because the nature of time is tensed, though there are many other theological reasons. In recent debates, according to J. Simons, this temporalist's assertion seems to make a consensus among many theologians and philosophers.[5] Accordingly, the main purpose of this chapter is to analyze correctly various understandings of God's eternity and its relation to time according to their particular views of the nature of time.

An Absolute Timeless Eternity of God: Paul Helm

In recent debates, P. Helm is probably one of the most vigorous advocates of the "absolute timeless" eternity of God on the philosophical basis of the tenseless view of time with other theological reasons. Helm clearly argues the absolute timeless view of divine eternity in his *Eternal God* and "Divine Timeless Eternity."[6] Against "temporalism," Helm defines "eternalism" as follows, "God exists timelessly eternally," and therefore "God does not exists in time, He exists 'outside' time."[7]

---

knowledge entails absurd consequences or is restricted. 3. If God is timeless, he cannot act. 4. If God is timeless, he cannot command our admiration or love. 5. There is Biblical precedent for rejecting the view that God is timeless. 6. There is no good reason for supposing that if there is a God, then he is timeless." Idem, "Timeless God?," 215. For a good counter argument against timeless eternity, see also Feinberg, "Arguments Against Timeless Eternity," in *No One Like Him*, 395–427.

5. Cf. Simons, "Eternity, Omniscience and Temporal Passage," 554.
6. Helm, *Eternal God*, and "Divine Timeless Eternity," 28–60.
7. Helm, "Divine Timeless Eternity," 28–29.

According to him, this absolute timeless view of God's eternity is the "mainstream" view in classical theism, e.g., St. Augustine, Boethius, St. Anselm, Thomas Aquinas, John Calvin, and many others (cf. most of classical theologians maintained the tensed view of time). However, concerning recent debates on the issue, Helm rightly points out that the biblical data do not directly support either eternalism or temporalism, because the Bible was not concerned with this issue. Therefore, if we attempt to find a definite answer for the problem in Scripture, it may be an anachronistic question. Accordingly, as expected, Helm says that, "there is no real evidence" in Scripture for eternalism, nor for temporalism. In this sense, we can say that the biblical data are underdetermined in this controversial problem (cf. chapter 2 in this study).[8] As Helm says,

> [I]n my view God's timeless eternity is consistent with the teaching of Scripture. That teaching is, with respect to our particular question, somewhat underdetermined; that is, the language of Scripture about God and time is not sufficiently precise so as to provide a definitive resolution of the issue one way or the other. So it would be unwise for the eternalist to claim that divine timeless eternity is *entailed* by the language of Scripture. But a lack of entailment need not alarm us, because such situations quite commonly arise in connection with the careful, reflective construction of Christian doctrines.[9]

According to Helm, therefore, it is true that the timeless conception of God's eternity in classical theism is basically owed to the conceptual apparatus of Neo-Platonism, like the conceptual languages of Greek metaphysics in the doctrine of the Trinity, e.g., person (*persona*), essence (*essentia*), or substance (*substantia*).[10] However, this does not mean that timeless eternalism is incompatible with biblical teaching about God. He says that, "the [biblical] data are compatible with eternalism but do not require it."[11] For this reason, Helm asserts that we need "a second order reflection" for a profound understanding of the problem of God's eternity and its relation to time.[12]

---

8. Ibid., 31–32.
9. Ibid., 31 (italics original).
10. Cf. ibid., 32.
11. Ibid.
12. Cf. Helm, *Eternal God*, 5.

The Foundations for the Conception of God's Absolute Timeless Eternity

If we cannot clearly find the idea of absolute timeless divine eternity in Scripture, then, for Helm, what is the basis for the conception? According to him, God's timeless eternity comes from the following three basic theological arguments: (1) the idea of the divine fullness or self-sufficiency (aseity); (2) the Creator-creature distinction; and (3) the conclusion of cosmological argument for God's existence.[13] Of course, as we shall see, these arguments are closely inter-related.

First, while appealing to Augustine, Boethius, and Anselm, Helm asserts that the concept of the absolute timeless eternity of God is based on God's self-sufficiency (i.e., aseity) and perfection in His nature.[14] He insists that if God is in time as we are, then He must undergo the passage of time, the flow of time from the past through the present to the future. However, God is the Perfect Being, so He cannot be subject to transitory temporal passage. That is, God does not have memory of the past in the same way we do. Furthermore, since God is a simple Being (i.e., divine simplicity), He cannot have temporal parts as we have. As Boethius defined, according to His fullness and perfection, God possesses the whole of His life together in His eternity. Therefore, the temporalists' assertion is totally incompatible with the nature of God's perfect Being, divine fullness and self-sufficiency, and divine simplicity.

Secondly, the idea of divine timelessness is an obvious articulation of the distinction between the Creator and the creature. Helm states that, "divine creation is a unique metaphysical action, the bringing into being of the whole temporal order, not a creation of the universe by One who is already subject to time."[15] That is to say, while God is a self-existent Being, the universe is "metaphysically contingent" and has its source only in God, the Creator.[16] Therefore, there is an absolute difference between the Creator and His creatures, and thus between God's eternity and the world's time. This is clear in the teaching of the doctrine of *Creation ex nihilo*. Time was created with the creation of the world, and thus God lacks time and exists outside of time. As we shall

---

13. Cf. Helm, "Divine Timeless Eternity," 34.
14. Cf. ibid., 33–34.
15. Ibid., 33.
16. Ibid., 47.

see, this distinction between the Creator and His creatures is connected to Helm's "two standpoints theory."

Finally, according to Helm, we need a cosmological argument for the idea of divine timeless eternity and God's contingent creation. Recently, against "absolute" timeless eternity, W. L. Craig proposed a "modified understanding of divine timeless eternity." By this, Craig asserts that, "God is timelessly eternal but only until the moment of creation; at this point he becomes temporal."[17] Concerning Craig's proposal of such an "accidental temporalism," however, Helm asserts that God exists "timelessly before" and "after" the creation of the universe. In saying that, for Helm, "before" means an ontological priority, not in the temporal sense. As he states,

> For the eternalist, temporality is an essential feature of creatureliness; the universe is created by God with time, not in time— "all at once" only in the sense that the creation is the product of a divine timeless decree. The universe could not have begun with an event such as the "big bang," since the big bang is itself a physical effect. Thus for the eternalist, God's creation of all that is ("the universe") is not a scientific event, like the exploding of a star or the splitting of an atom, nor a series of such event; nor is it a unique historical event . . . It is the bringing of the universe into being from a standpoint outside it. For this reason the idea that God exists (timelessly) "before" the universe cannot mean that God exists temporally before it . . . rather in the way . . . another kind of priority, betokening a constitutional or hierarchical or normative arrangement. There was no time the Creator was not, any more than there was a time when the creation was not.[18]

However, concerning W. L. Craig's assertion, a significant question must be raised: How can Helm explain God's action in the temporal world after the first moment of the creation of time and the universe? That is to say, as Craig asserts, does God necessarily need to change in His mode of existence from timeless to temporal because of His creation of the temporal world? Does God acquire "a new relation" at the mo-

---

17. Ibid., 47. As we shall see, Craig asserts that God is timeless before creation of the universe, but "God acquires a new relation at the moment of creation. At the moment of creation, God comes into the relation of sustaining the universe or at the very least that of coexisting with the universe, relations which he did not before have." Idem, "Tensed vs. Tenseless," 222, as cited in Helm, "Divine Timeless Eternity," 49.

18. Helm, "Divine Timeless Eternity," 51–52.

ment of creation? For this problem, at first, Helm asserts that, because of divine perfection, simplicity, and immutability, God cannot change and be changed in His mode of existence by His creation. In a very strong sense, Helm asserts that, "it is impossible for the Changeless One to change."[19] Furthermore, while appealing to the tenseless view of time, Helm even states that, "there need be no temporal first moment of creation, and so the universe need not have begun (temporally) to exist, for from the divine standpoint the universe is eternal, even though it exists contingently."[20] In other words, God's creation of the universe is not a temporal event, nor was there a temporal beginning-point for the universe to exist because it is co-eternal with God. Thus, for him, "God has a timelessly eternal relation with the temporal world, but a relation that is nevertheless contingent."[21] In philosophical theory of time, as he himself asserts, Helm's position can be properly understood as based on the tenseless theory of time or a deterministic understanding of four-dimensional space-time. However, Helm seems to expose a difficulty in that while clearly insisting on the biblical teaching of *creatio ex nihilo*, which means that the world and time have an absolute beginning, he also asserts that the temporal world is co-eternal with God based on the tenseless view of time.

Then, after creation, how can God relate to the universe or act in His created temporal world? For this question, while accepting Aquinas' classical position, Helm asserts the view of "God's eternal will and its temporal effects." In Helm's view, "to act is to bring about something as the result of intending or desiring or willing that thing, and to do so for a purpose."[22] In this sense, the events, which occur in various points of time-sequence, are exactly the scattered temporal effects of God's one eternal will or God's action at once for them in His timeless eternity. Helm explains this as follows,

> The correct way to think of God's eternally willing something in time is to think of one eternal act of will with numerous temporally scattered effects. As an analogy, we may think of a per-

---

19. Ibid., 34. That is to say, for Helm, it means that "It is not that God is immutable because he is unwilling to change, but because his perfect nature is such that he need not and cannot change" (p. 35).

20. Ibid., 49.

21. Ibid.

22. Ibid., 53.

> son's action in setting the timer on her central heating system. This is (we may suppose) one action, analogous to God's eternal willing. But this one action has numerous temporally scattered effects, analogous to the effects in time of God's one eternal act of willing; as a result of the one act, the system fires at 7:00 a.m., goes off at 12:00, fires again at 2:00 p.m., goes off again at 10:30 p.m. day after day. The basic point is: there can be one decision to bring about different effects at different times.[23]

Accordingly, in Helm's view, God's one eternal will, like setting a timer, brings about all series of temporal events in this world. However, can we really think of such a timer-effects analogy as God's real action and re-action with His creatures in the temporal world? It seems to be a deistic description of God's action in that God sets the timer in His eternity which can only result in its effects in the time sequence. However, in Scripture, there are various descriptions of divine direct and real actions and re-actions with God's creatures in time, real divine-human dialogues with His peoples, or even changes in the divine mind (e.g., "divine repentance"). How can Helm explain such biblical descriptions of God's direct actions in the temporal world? For this controversial problem, Helm appeals to Calvin's theory of divine accommodation. That is to say, according to Helm, we cannot take the biblical statements such as "God repented" in their literal sense, because God does not literally repent and cannot do so in virtue of His wholly immutable nature. However, although they are false in the literal sense, they can convey some truth about God. That is, some expressions of divine repentance were taken to record the appearance of things and events "in an unpedantic and vivid way."[24] In this sense, it is just a metaphorical expression of God's truth in our human language. It is none other than God's accommodation for recording His eternal truth in our human language. In the case of divine-human dialogue, it is also understood in this way. If we take the dialogue between God and man as a real dialogue, then the absolutely immutable God cannot represent Himself as a dialogue partner. Thus, in Helm's view, it is just a "make-believe," not a "real," dialogue for us. At any rate, for Helm, the eternal God is immutable and thus necessarily timeless in the absolute sense.

23. Ibid.
24. Ibid., 46.

A Counter Argument to Some Objections

Today, the idea of divine absolute timelessness is rejected by many theologians and philosophers for various reasons. First, one of the main reasons for objecting to the timeless eternity is its inner incoherence regarding the problem of "simultaneity" (e.g., R. Swinburne and A. Kenny). For example, A. Kenny says that, "On St. Thomas' view, my typing of this paper is simultaneous with the whole of eternity. Again, on this view, the great fire of Rome is simultaneous with the whole of eternity. Therefore, while I type these very words, Nero fiddles heartlessly on."[25] For the problem of simultaneity, as we well knew, the classical conception of divine timelessness and simultaneity is represented by Boethius' famous definition: God's timeless eternity is "the complete, *simultaneous* and perfect possession of everlasting life."[26]

In using Boethius' definition, there have been some recent fresh attempts to defend the classical conception of divine timelessness in revised forms according to recent advanced theories of time; for instance, E. Stump and N. Kretzmann's "ET-simultaneity,"[27] and B. Leftow's "quasi-temporal eternity (QTE)."[28] However, according to Helm's judgment, these attempts are not successful because the idea of "timeless duration" is a "puzzling concept" and "self-contradictory."[29] Helm says that divine timeless eternity is a part of negative theology and therefore it just denotes divine imcomprehensibilty. As he says,

> [I]t is perhaps wiser ... to think of the assertion of divine timeless eternity as a piece of negative thinking about the divine essence, a fragment of negative theology. For divine eternity is time*less*ness, and it cannot be expected that human analogies and models will throw much light on what more positively it is or is like. . . . Part of what it means to say that God is incomprehensible is to say that though we believe that God is timeless

---

25. Kenny, *God of the Philosophers*, 38–39, as cited in Helm, "Divine Timeless Eternity," 35.

26. As cited in Helm, "Divine Timeless Eternity," 35–36.

27. Cf. Stump and Kretzmann, "Eternity," 429–58, and "Eternity, Awareness, and Action," 463–82.

28. Cf. Leftow, "Eternity and Simultaneity," 148–79.

29. Helm, "Divine Timeless Eternity," 37.

we do not and cannot have a straightforward understanding of what his timeless life is. We cannot echo God's self-knowledge.[30]

Although it is true that God is incomprehensible, the finite cannot comprehend the infinite. However, in my view, it is not a satisfying answer to the question to simply say God is incomprehensible, as Helm did, for God reveals Himself to us in His words and actions, and finally in the Word of God, Jesus Christ. As "faith seeking understanding," Christian theology must provide a more proper answer to such a question about God's eternity and its relation to time.

Secondly, according to temporalists, the idea of divine timeless eternity cannot be accepted because it directly implies God's immutability and impassibility. That is to say, in the view of timeless eternity, God does not have any feelings; for example, emotion, affection, anger, pleasure, and so forth. In addition, by virtue of God's perfect Being and His timelessness, God cannot change or be changed by his creatures because change occurs only in time, or is in time. By definition, a timeless God is not in time, but "outside" of time. Therefore, God's action cannot take time, nor can He change in His mind. Then, temporalists ask "how could such an impassible God be a personal God," and "how can we relate to or dialogue with the impassible God?" For these questions, Helm replies that, on the one hand, "the idea of timeless eternity is based on the idea that God has fullness of being, that he is 'pure act,' and not that he is like a withdrawn, sadly incapacitated human being. Impassibility is not a defect but a perfection; it signals fullness, not deficiency."[31] On the other hand, according to Helm, in a more positive sense, even a timelessly eternal God has joy, care, pleasure and love. As he says, "They are fundamental states of mind, part of the divine fullness and glory, and of the engagement of that divine fullness with his creation. These permanent states of the divine being are differently experienced by God's human creatures according to their various situations and conditions."[32]

Finally, between atemporalists and temporalists, one of the most important and controversial point is the problem of omniscience. That is to say, many temporalists assert that a timelessly eternal God cannot be omniscient. In other words, a timeless God cannot know what

30. Ibid., 37–38.
31. Ibid., 39.
32. Ibid., 39–40.

time it is "now" or which event is occurring now, for He is not in time and everything is present *all at once* for a timelessly eternal God. In this sense, "God cannot know what we know [i.e., the temporal facts]. So God cannot be omniscient."[33] Furthermore, temporalists insist that God's omniscience of the future is not compatible with human free action. Against such temporlists' claim, Helm asserts that God knows "all the times when each of us make true utterances such as 'It is now . . .' . . . when it is uttered, for he knows that it is uttered at some particular time."[34] In addition, according to Helm, if God is temporal, then He cannot have knowledge about timeless eternal propositions. Therefore, the temporalists' position, too, has the same dilemma as the atemporlists'. However, as such, Helm's view can be defended only in the tenseless view of time, as he clearly states that, "if the tensed theory of time is correct, it may be that fullness of God's life will require his temporality."[35]

Tenseless Time and God's Timeless Eternity

For his defense of the absolute timeless eternity of God, Helm mainly appeals to the tenseless (static, B-series) theory of time (i.e., philosophical perspective) and "the two standpoints theory"—the divine and human standpoint (i.e., theological perspective). At first, concerning his two standpoints theory.[36] That is to say, according to Helm, the temporal order or sequence in the created universe can be understood in two very different ways, either from God's timeless standpoint or from our temporal standpoint. Accordingly, from our temporal standpoint, God's timeless creation as a whole, which is extended or ordered in time, looks like a continuously unfolding temporal series, as a *Creation*

33. Ibid., 40.
34. Ibid., 41
35. Ibid., 23.
36. Helm says, "There is an inclination to confuse the standpoint of the Creator with that of the creature. From the Creator's standpoint his creation is a timeless whole, including, as it does, the incarnation. However, from the standpoint of an intelligent creature the universe may be thought to be coeternal with God, for there may be no time when the universe is not. For such a creature the universe unfolds as a temporal sequence and because such an agent is in time, he is able to represent the universe as having a past, a present and a future . . . As paleographers and geologists and cosmologists investigate the past, they investigate past phases of what is (from the Creator's standpoint) the one creation. But from the divine standpoint the universe is one whole that exists by the eternal will of God." Ibid., 55.

continua. However, "it is necessarily the case that God, if he is timelessly eternal, cannot translate his eternal standpoint into ours, nor can we, creatures of time, translate our various successive temporal standpoints into his."[37] While criticizing Thomas Nagel's view from nowhere, Helm says that God has His own unique where and when of timeless (and spaceless) eternity. God stands outside space and time, and therefore He has a unique perspective on the universe, which is free from either temporal or spatial indexicals. Therefore, we must not confuse the unique standpoint of the timeless God and that of our transient temporal succession.

Finally, as a philosophical basis, we must point out that Helm's understanding of the absolute timeless eternity of God can be properly understood in the tenseless (static, B-series) theory of time. As we have seen in chapter 4, according to the tenseless view of time, all temporal events have ontologically the same position, not before or after in temporal sequence, but they are only in a relation of earlier than, simultaneous with, or later than. Therefore, the expressions of temporal passage, past, present, and future are not the objective feature of reality. They are merely mind-depended states of affairs, not real ontological objectivity. In this sense, Helm asserts that,

> If God had created the temporal order as an A-series from his standpoint, then God would himself be in time. So it makes better sense for the eternalist to suppose that God created the temporal order as a B-series. From the divine standpoint no one moment of the series would be privileged by being present, but as regards presentness, pastness or futurity, all moments would be in exactly the same position, even though some moments would be earlier in relation to others in the series, some later. It is a temporal order, in which causal powers operate. And yet it is a B-series of a rather special kind, whose every moment is also eternally present to God.[38]

Conclusively, according to Helm, we must not abandon the absolute timeless eternity of God in classical theism, for it is the very essence of God as the perfect Being. In addition, the tenseless theory of time strongly supports the "absolute timeless" eternity of God.

---

37. Ibid., 56.
38. Ibid., 58.

In critical observation, along with other theological reasons, the philosophical bases of P. Helm's absolute timeless eternity of God are the perfect being theory and the tenseless view of time. However, concerning the tenseless view of time, in my view, one of the most implausible thoughts is that, as Helm says, the temporal word itself is co-eternal with the eternal God in tenseless sense. If it is true that the biblical teaching of creation that God created the world *ex nihilo*, how then can the world be co-eternal with the Creator? How about its eschaton, the end? Scripture clearly teaches that the world and thus time itself have an end. Furthermore, there are not sufficient reasons for the tenseless view of time to be the only correct view. In addition, Helm's analogy of a timer and its series of effects cannot properly explain God's direct acts and His interventions in the temporal world, nor can it explain God's direct and real dialogue with His peoples in Scripture. That is to say, while too much emphasis is given to the absolute transcendence of God the Creator beyond the world and to God's absolute timelessness over time, Helm does not properly explain a positive and real relationship of God with His creature, and thus neglects God's positive relation to time, which is most clearly revealed in the Incarnation of the eternal Word of God, the Son, in time.

An Everlasting God: Nicholas Wolterstorff

Among many others, N. Wolterstorff obviously asserts the temporality of God (i.e., everlasting divine eternity). We can see his view of God's everlasting eternity in his well-known article, "God Everlasting," and more recently in, "Unqualified Divine Temporality."[39] In these works, Wolterstorff clearly asserts that the biblical God is not eternal in the timeless sense, but temporal, and therefore everlasting. The following statements most clearly present Wolterstorff's view of God's everlasting eternity:

> It might seem obvious that God, as described by the biblical writers, is a being who changes, and who accordingly is fundamentally noneternal. For God is described as a being who *acts*—in creation, in providence, and for the renewal of mankind. He is an agent, not an impassive factor in reality. And from the

---

39. Wolterstorff, "God Everlasting," 181–203, and "Unqualified Divine Temporality," 187–213.

> manner in which his acts are described, it seems obvious that many of them have beginnings and endings, that accordingly they stand in succession relations to each other, and that these successive acts are of such a sort that their presence and absence on God's time-strand constitutes changes thereon. Thus it seems that God is fundamentally noneternal.[40]

And again,

> [T]he biblical presentation of God presupposes that God is everlasting rather than eternal. God is indeed without beginning and without end. But at least some of his aspects stand in temporal order-relations to each other. Thus God, too, has a time-strand. His life and existence is itself temporal. . . . Further, the events to be found on God's time-strand belong within the same temporal array as that which contains our time-strands. God's aspects do not only bear temporal order-relations to each other but to the aspects of created entities as well. And the aspects and succession of aspects to be found on God's time-strand are such that they constitute *changes* thereon. God's life and existence incorporates changeful succession.[41]

First of all, according to Wolterstorff, the biblical God is not timelessly eternal, but fundamentally temporal. Typically, in the Scriptures, God is presented as "a redeeming God." For example, while mentioning the story of God's calling of Moses in its real-dialogue and the deliverance of Israelites from Egypt in a temporal succession, Wolterstorff says that "God as conceived and presented by the biblical writers is a being whose own life and existence is temporal."[42] Moreover, God the Redeemer cannot be a timelessly eternal God, because He is "a God who changes" in time.[43] God's temporality is essentially and decisively manifested in the life, death, and resurrection of Jesus Christ.[44] Therefore, he asserts that, it is an obvious fact that God, who is presented in the Bible as God the Redeemer, is temporal, and therefore "a theology which opts for God as eternal cannot be a theology faithful to the biblical witness."[45]

40. Wolterstorff, "God Everlasting," 192–93.
41. Ibid., 202.
42. Ibid., 181.
43. Cf. ibid., 182.
44. Cf. ibid., 181.
45. Ibid., 182.

In his argument, one of Wolterstorff's main points is in that Scripture God has His own history, and thus He is temporal. In his view, the biblical God is not a static being, but always an acting God as an agent within history. As he says, "God is represented in Scripture as One who has a history of acting and responding."[46] That is to say, God always acts within time-strands. He says that,

> [I]t seems evident that the biblical writers regard God as having a time-strand of his own on which actions on his part are to be found, and that some at least of these actions vary in such a way that there are changes along the strand. It seems evident that they do not regard changes on time-strands as confined to entities in God's creation. The God who acts, in the way in which the biblical writers speak of God as acting, seems clearly to change.[47]

Thus, the biblical God is fundamentally temporal and everlasting, not timelessly eternal, since "if something has a history, then perforce that being is in time."[48]

Finally, in classical theism, the conception of divine immutability and divine timeless eternity are inseparably interconnected with each other. That is to say, according to atemporalists, changes can be possible only in time. However, God is ontologically immutable because of His aseity, simplicity and perfection, and thus God is timelessly eternal. However, based on his own understanding of the biblical God who is an acting God within history, Wolterstorff rejects the classical conception of divine ontological immutability. That is, in his view, God is mutable in His life, and there is a change in divine knowledge.

> [The biblical] representation of God as having a history, which then can be narrated, is not exceptional but typical of Scripture's representation of God: God responds to what transpires in human affairs by performing a succession of actions, including actions of speaking. An implication of this representation of God is that there's change in God's life; if a person does one thing at one time and a different thing at a later time, then there's change in that person's life. Behind the change in action there is, in turn, a change in knowledge . . . These, I say, are implications of how

---

46. Wolterstorff, "Unqualified Divine Temporality," 187.
47. Wolterstorff, "God Everlasting," 193.
48. Wolterstorff, "Unqualified Divine Temporality," 188.

Scripture represents God: God has a history, and in this history there are changes in God's actions, responses and knowledge.[49]

In this sense, Wolterstorff re-interprets some of the biblical passages which are generally used as proof texts for divine ontological immutability in classical theism (e.g., Mal 3:6, Ps 102:27, and Jas 1:17). Then, Wolterstorff asserts that the biblical writers are just commenting about "God's unswerving fidelity" and His everlastingness in covenant, not about ontological immutability. Therefore, he concludes: "God's ontological immutability is not a part of the explicit teaching of the biblical writers. What the biblical writers teach is that God is faithful and without beginning or end, not that none of his aspects is temporal. The theological tradition of God's ontological immutability has no explicit biblical foundation."[50]

A Counter Argument to God's Timeless Eternity

First of all, according to Wolterstorff, the conception of God's timeless eternity is not at all compatible with the biblical God. As we have seen, Wolterstorff believes that the biblical God is fundamentally temporal, and thus the everlasting God. The biblical God really acts within human affairs and has His own history. And thus He is a mutable God within His personal life and in His knowledge. If Wolterstorff's understanding of the biblical God is correct, then where did the ideas of timelessness and immutability of God in classical theism come from? According to him, "the most important factor accounting for the tradition of God eternal within Christian theology was the influence of the classical Greek philosophers on the early theologians;" e.g., Parmenides and Plato.[51] That is to say, Wolterstorff believes that the conception of God's timelessness is none other than a result of the hellenization of Christian theology in classical theism. Accordingly, it cannot be compatible with the biblical understanding of God. It is a Babylonian captivity for the biblical God in the Greek philosophies. Thus, we need a "dehellenization" of Christian theology, and the starting point is to recover the biblical understanding

---

49. Ibid.
50. Wolterstorff, "God Everlasting," 202.
51. Ibid., 182–83.

of the "God everlasting." For Wolterstorff, it is an urgent and necessary task for Christian theology. As he asserts:

> What is the case, though, is that the patterns of classical Greek thought are incompatible with the pattern of biblical thought. And in facing the issue of God everlasting versus God eternal we are dealing with the fundamental pattern of biblical thought. Indeed, I am persuaded that unless the tradition of God eternal is renounced, fundamental dehellenizing will perpetually occupy itself in the suburbs, never advancing to the city center. Every attempt to purge Christian theology of the traces of incompatible Hellenic patterns of thought must fail unless it removes the roadblock of the God eternal tradition. Around this barricade there are no detours.[52]

Furthermore, he believes that if God does not have a history, and is therefore timelessly eternal, God's knowledge about human affairs must be extremely confined. As he states, "Were God eternal, God's knowledge would be extremely constricted in scope. Of no tensed fact would God have any knowledge; God would not have knowledge of any A-series facts, only B-series facts. As a consequence, God could neither respond to what transpires in the world nor enact the decision to act at a certain time. If God were eternal, God's action would have to be entirely noninterventionist."[53] In addition, according to Wolterstorff, if the conception of God's timeless eternity is correct, then it cannot be compatible with human free action. He states that "if we are capable of free action, then there must be facts of the matters as to what we would do in various situations, and God must know those facts. There must be 'counterfactuals of freedom.' Suppose we were capable of free action, but there were no facts as to what we would freely do in all the various situations in which we would find ourselves. Then God would simply have to take a risk. Hence it is that those who hold to God's eternity either deny human freedom or embrace the thesis that there are counterfactuals of freedom."[54]

Finally, as we have seen in Helm's case, concerning God's action in the temporal world, the atemporalist strategy is "God's one eternal will and its temporal effects." However, according to Wolterstorff, such an

---

52. Ibid., 183.
53. Wolterstorff, "Unqualified Divine Temporality," 206–7.
54. Ibid., 208.

eternalist view fails to give a proper understanding of the most decisive action of God in Jesus Christ, His incarnation, life, death, and resurrection. As he asserts, "The actions of Jesus were not simply human actions brought about by God, plus human actions freely performed by Jesus in situations brought about by God; they were God's actions. In the life and deeds of Jesus it was God who dwelt among us. The narrative of the history of Jesus is not just a narrative concerning events in the history of the relationship of a human being to God; it's a narrative about God. God does have a history; the doctrine of the incarnation implies that the history of Jesus is the history of God."[55]

Tensed Time and God's Everlasting Eternity

Alongside his plain literal interpretation of Scripture, is his appeal to the tensed (dynamic, A-series) theory of time as a philosophical basis. For the problem of the nature of time, while briefly introducing J. M. E. McTaggart's distinction between A-series and B-series of time, he rightly points out the key issue in recent debates: "whether the A-series is an objective feature of time [or not]."[56] In other words, the problem of whether or not the passage of time is the objective reality of the world. Based on the presentism of the tensed theory of time, Wolterstorff asserts that various tenseless theories of time (e.g., date-reference theory, indexical theory, token-reflexive truth condition theory) are untenable altogether. The tenseless sentences cannot translate the unique meaning of the tensed sentences without losing their tensed meaning. Against the tenseless view of time, therefore, he summarizes his tensed view of time as follows:

> What's wrong with this picture, as the tense theorist sees things, is that it [cf. the tenseless theory of time] treats past, present and future as properties of events and regards the three properties as equal in status. In fact the present is basic, in the following way. What's fundamental in time is the *occurrence* of events—this for the most part having nothing to do with your and my temporal relationship to those events. When an event occurs, that's when it's present; being present at *t* and occurring at *t* come to

---

55. Ibid., 209–10.

56. He continues, "No one disputes that the ordering of events in the B-series is objectively real; the issue under discussion is whether the distinction between past, present and future marks a difference in ontological status of events." Ibid., 195.

> the same thing. It's only because an event occurs—and it can't occur without occurring at some time—that it has a location anywhere in the B-series. If it's now past, that's because its occurring is now sometime in the past. There's no other way for it to get into the past than that way. Its occurring is now over. What remains now is the *fact that it did occur*. But the *fact that it did occur* is very different from *its occurring*. The distinction between present, past and future marks a difference in the ontological status of events; and of these, the status of the present is basic. . . . What about the future? Are future events likewise components of facts, and can refer to them? . . . My own view . . . is that only when an event is occurring or has occurred can it be a component of facts and can it be referred to. There are lots of general facts about the future, but no facts having particular events as constituents.[57]

According to Wolterstorff, even though events are obviously within time, there are also nonevents (e.g., things, substances–human beings, animal and plants, properties, numbers, and so on). However, many nonevents (things) have their own history or biography which is a complex of events within time-strands. But numbers are different in that "numbers have no history. They neither come into existence nor go out; nor do they change."[58] Therefore, numbers are not in time, since they do not have history. For Wolterstorff, therefore, the key point is, "whether or not something has history as the determinant of whether or not it is in time."[59] Then, how about God? Does God have a history? If so, in following Wolterstorff's criterion, God must be in time, not outside of time. In Wolterstroff's view, the acting God has a history. In this way, according to the biblical representation of God and the tensed theory of time, Wolterstorff confirms that God is fundamentally temporal and therefore everlasting.

> But if God has no history, then God lacks tensed knowledge. For one can know that something is presently happening only when it is; the knowledge that some event is occurring can occur only when that event itself is occurring. The endurance of the knowledge exactly tracks the endurance of the event. So if God has knowledge of present-tensed facts, then there's change

57. Ibid., 196–97. For Wolterstorff's criticism of the tenseless theories of time, see pp. 197–202.

58. Ibid., 202.

59. Ibid., 203.

in God's knowledge—as indeed there is if God has knowledge of past-tensed facts and future-tensed facts. Since those facts come and go, God's knowledge of them comes and goes. That's why, if God has knowledge of tensed facts, God has a history; there's a story to be told about God's knowledge.[60]

However, for Wolterstorff, the temporal God does not have the defect of contingent and transitory time as we have because God is the everlasting God and the Lord of time. As he says, "Though God is within time, yet he is Lord of time. The whole array of contingent temporal events is within his power. He is Lord of what occurs. And that, along with the specific pattern of what he does, grounds all authentically biblical worship of, and obedience to, God. It is not because he is outside of time—eternal, immutable, impassive—that we are to worship and obey God. It is because of what he can and does bring about within time that we mortals are to render him praise and obedience."[61]

In critical observation, Wolterstorff's understanding of God's everlasting eternity essentially depends on a straightforward literal interpretation of Scripture and the tensed view of time. In doing so, Wolterstorff rightly points out God's positive relation to time, and thus His real acts in the temporal worlds and His real dialogue with His peoples. However, we must be careful in interpreting biblical texts, especially concerning God's repentance, changing His mind, and so forth. That is to say, as P. Helm and others point out, these can be interpreted as anthropomorphic or figurative expressions, which are God's accommodation to human language. In addition, although we must give attention to the essential literal meaning of the biblical texts, at the same time, we must also give attention to its genres which are included in the biblical texts. In Scripture, there are various literary genres, for example, narratives, poets, and prophets, and so on. Therefore, a poetic text must be interpreted in a different way from narrative texts. In this sense, it cannot be acceptable that the literal interpretation directly supports God's ontological mutability in Scripture. Furthermore, concerning his everlasting interpretation of God's eternity, according to the biblical doctrine of *creatio ex nihilo et cum tempus*, time has its absolute beginning and thus its end too. In this sense, there must be a qualitative and ontological difference, not a quantitative one, between God's eternity and human

60. Ibid., 206.
61. Wolterstorff, "God Everlasting," 203.

time. This means that God's eternity is not a mere infinity of time (i.e., everlasting time) without beginning and end. Finally, the tensed view of time is still being debated and is not yet a proved theory.

God's Eternity as Relative Timelessness: Alan G. Padgett

We have previously seen two extremely different views of God's eternity: P. Helm's view of absolute timeless eternity and N. Wolterstorff's view of everlasting eternity. However, in recent debates on the issue, there are also various modified views. In the following sections, I will deal with the following two interesting *via media*: A. G. Padgett's "relatively timeless eternity of God" and W. L. Craig's "accidental temporalism: timeless and omnitemporal eternity of God." As we shall see, even though both accept the tensed theory of time and thus propose that God is essentially temporal, their strategies and detail contents differ. At first, while criticizing the two extreme views, A. G. Padgett tries to suggest an alternate understanding of God's eternity: "Eternity as Relative Timelessness."[62] In the following statement, while distinguishing some conceptual frames of time and eternity, Padgett presents the nugget of his argument as follows:

> It has become commonplace, since Beothius, to distinguish between eternal as timeless, and eternal as everlasting. An eternal being is "everlasting" if it has beginningless and endless existence in time. An eternal being is "timeless" if it has a mode of existence that is somehow beyond or above time. Further, two senses of "timeless" can be distinguished. When "time" means duration in the abstract, "timeless" will mean that no duration ever occurs in the life of that which is timeless. Something "timeless" in this sense would lack any extension or location in *any* time whatsoever. On the other hand, by "time" we may mean our own system of Measured Time, and/or the time of our space-time continuum. In this case, something will be "timeless" if it does not exist within any Measured Time, nor within our space-time continuum. Our Measured Time Words, then, like "day" or "one thousand years ago" could not truly apply to that which is timeless in this weaker sense. We can distinguish between these two

---

62. We can find Padgett's view of divine eternity in his following works, "God and Time," 209–15; *God, Eternity and the Nature of Time*; and "Eternity as Relative Timelessness," 92–110.

senses by calling the former an "absolute" timelessness, and the latter a "relative" timelessness. I will argue that God is timeless in a relative sense, and not in an absolute sense. The concept of God's being in time and yet timeless obviously needs fuller development. God is eternal, we will argue, because (i) he is not in any Measured Time, (ii) his life need not occur within the time of our space-time universe, and (iii) he is not "subject" to the negative aspects of the passage of time.[63]

With such a proposal of Padgett's view, a relatively timeless God's eternity, lets begin our investigation for a more delicate conception of God's eternity and its relation to time.

A Critique of Everlasting and Absolute Timeless Eternity

First, according to Padgett, the everlasting view of God's eternity is clearly consistent with a straightforward literal interpretation of Scripture. However, as he correctly points out, "The main problem with the everlasting model is not logical consistency but theological inadequacy."[64] That is to say, God as "an infinite, personal Creator" transcends any merely created categories, e.g., gender, space, and so on. St. Augustine (cf. his doctrine of *creatio cum tempore*) and some recent physicists (cf. Stephen W. Hawking, the big-bang cosmology) agree with each other in insisting that time is also a created category which has a beginning with the physical universe. In this sense, God as the Creator must transcend time in some sense. Therefore, a mere everlasting conception of God's eternity cannot conceive the transcendence of God beyond created time. According to Padgett, this may be a most serious objection to the everlasting view of God's eternity.

Then, what about the absolute timeless conception of God's eternity? This traditional view rightly pays attention to God's transcendence over time. However, it is incompatible with other truths; for example, a libertarian understanding of human free will. More significantly, according to Padgett, it is true only in the case that the stasis (tenseless, B-series) theory of time is correct (cf. Stump and Kretzmann maintains timeless eternity based on tensed theory of time). But, for Padgett, since the stasis theory of time is false, we must reject the timeless conception

---

63. Padgett, "God and Time," 210.
64. Padgett, "Eternity as Relative Timelessness," 93.

of divine eternity too. Therefore, Padgett adopts the process (dynamic, tensed, A-series) theory of time, which affirms the reality of temporal passage of the past, present and future. According to him, the understanding of God's eternity depends on the theories of time as follows:

1. On the timeless view, God cannot have any real change. This follows from the very idea of a timeless being.
2. Since God sustains all things, God is responsible directly for the being of all things, at all times.
3. On the process theory of time, things come into and pass out of existence with the passage of time.
4. On the stasis theory of time, nothing that ever has existed or will exist passes out of existence from a timeless perspective. God creates/sustains the whole of the universe "tenselessly" or timelessly.
5. On the process theory, bringing something into existence, or ceasing to sustain something, is a real change in the Creator, not the creature.[65]

In Padgett's view, however, the process theory of time is true for this temporal world. If the process theory of time is correct, then at least the future does not yet exist. Therefore, "when God creates something, that can be a change only in God, not in the creature, for the creature does not yet exist."[66] This means that "God undergoes real change."[67] Accordingly, if the process theory of time is true, then God is not timeless, but temporal.

Against B. Leftow and E. Stump, therefore, Padgett asserts the idea that a timeless God cannot be compatible with the process (tensed) theory of time. He says that,

> The definition of something's being timeless is (a) that it exists, (b) that it does not exist at any time and (c) that its existence has no extension in time. God can be all these things and still have to wait for a temporal world to pass by. What follows from God's timelessness is that God never changes, but it does not mean that all times can now be "present" to God. All times' being present to God, while a traditional idea, is incoherent. Being past,

65. Ibid., 97.
66. Ibid.
67. Ibid.

being present and being future are temporal properties that God cannot partake of, if God is absolutely timeless. What we might say is that God *coexists* with every moment in time. This is true, but only in one sense. We might mean that God coexists with every moment of time, in the sense that for each present moment, however long time lasts, God coexists (timelessly) at that moment. There should be no problem with this meaning. On the other hand, we might mean that all times coexist timelessly with God (or in eternity). This second sense is incoherent. First of all, things that exist in time cannot coexist timelessly. Nothing that is temporal can also be timeless. In the second place, all times cannot and do not coexist in any sense—and certainly not "timelessly" or "in eternity." Different times are not all present, and only present things are fully real (on the process view). Things have happened in the past, and things will happen in the future, but those things are not real. Therefore they cannot coexist with present things.[68]

According to Padgett, against Leftow and Stump, the use of the STR does not change this logical fact, for God does not have a "frame of reference." Furthermore, "Since timeless existence is so very different from temporal being, even if every event existed in God's timeless 'frame of reference' then God would have to re-create all events within the flow of temporal passage—which is absurd."[69] Conclusively, only if the stasis theory of time is true, is the traditional conception of God's timelessness compatible with God's sustaining acts for the temporal universe and God's omniscience of concrete physical states of affairs (not a mere abstract or prepositional knowledge) concerning an indeterminate future. However, in Padgett's view, the stasis theory does not fit with our ordinary daily experience of time and our common sense or wisdom on the temporal passage of past, present and future. It is heavily reliant on metaphysical abstraction, symbolic logic or theoretical physics, not the real world. Therefore, he concludes that the concept of God's absolute timelessness, which is based on the tenseless (static or B-series) theory of time, must be rejected.[70]

---

68. Ibid., 98.
69. Ibid., 99–100.
70. Cf. ibid., 104.

A Via Media: *Eternity as Relative Timelessness*

While rejecting a mere everlasting and absolute timeless view of God's eternity, Padgett suggests an alternate theory of divine eternity, "relative timelessness," which theologically means that "God is the Lord of time."[71] For his relatively timeless view of God's eternity, Padgett begins his argument with the following two presuppositions:

1. The process (tensed, A-series) theory of time is true.
2. God is the Creator and Sustainer of everything within the temporal universe.

Then, his argument continues as follows:

3. God is not only temporal for sustaining the temporal world, but also, as the Creator, transcends the created (physical, measured) time in some sense.
4. Therefore, God as the Lord of time is "relatively timeless."

As we have seen, Padgett adopts the process (dynamic, tensed, or A-series) theory of time as a correct one. Then, Padgett distinguishes "time as a pure duration, which can flow without any changes taking place in the world, and time understood as the measure of change."[72] However, as Aristotle defined time as "the numbering of change according to before and after," measured time alone fits with our ordinary experience and common sense. Furthermore, according to modern physical science, measured time is not absolute and it is dependent on the laws of nature. And therefore it clearly shows that physical, measured time is a created time.

On the other hand, according to Padgett, if God really sustains the temporal world, then He must be temporal in some sense.[73] However,

---

71. Ibid.
72. Ibid., 105.
73. Padgett explains this as follows: "God sustains the universe, which means in part that he is responsible for the fundamental ontological status of things. Because the universe is an ever-changing reality, things do change in their fundamental ontological status at different times—a change we must ascribe to God, and cannot ascribe to the objects themselves, since this has to do with their very existence. God himself, therefore, does different things at different times. This implies change in God. Whenever a change occurs, a duration occurs. Therefore, God is in time." And, thus, "God's time cannot be unrelated in this way to our time, if God sustains our universe. For sustaining

God's own time is different from our created measured-time, because it is not created. Rather, God's being is the metaphysical precondition for God's time, which can be understood as "pure duration" that is relatively timeless, not vice versa. That is to say, in Padgett's own word, "God's time exists because God exists (not the other way around)."[74] Concerning this point, Padgett states as follows,

> God is not contained within time, not even God's own time. Rather, God's Being is *conceptually prior* (in terms of ontological dependence) to eternity, even though God's life is not temporally prior to God's time. God's eternity is thus similar to other divine attributes that are always part of God's existence but are not logically essential to the divine Being. Thus, God remains the Lord of time and the Creator of our (measured) time.[75]

Then, for him, what is exactly God's time? According to Padgett, in contrast to our physical (i.e., measured) time, God's time is infinite, and it is also immeasurable by any created metric system. That is to say, "God is not in any Measured Time (and therefore not in ours) based on two considerations: (i) God is not subject to the laws of nature, as anything in Measured Time must be; and (ii) any Measured Time is relative to a particular frame of reference, which need not apply to God."[76] This is the essential difference between God's time and our God-created measured time. Therefore, Padgett concludes as follows:

> God is relatively timeless—that is, timeless relative to our created, measured time. This means, first, that God is the Creator of our time (space-time universe). Our time takes place within (and only because of the prior existence of) God's own time. Second, even God's own time, eternity, exists only because God exists (and not the other way around). Even eternity is dependent, ontologically, on God's very Life and Being. The Being of God is thus rightly at the heart of the whole of reality in history

---

is a causal relation. If both cause and effect are temporal, a cause must be either before or simultaneous with its effect (those who believe in retrocausation may add 'after'; it does not affect the argument). Since both God and the world are temporal, and since God effects the world, the world must be in the same time as God. We are in God's time. God is in himself temporal in some ways, because of his relationship with the world." Idem, "God and Time," 209 and 210–11.

74. Padgett, "Eternity as Relative Timelessness," 106.

75. Ibid., 107.

76. Padgett, "God and Time," 211.

or eternity, in heaven and on earth. Third, God's own time is infinite and cannot be measured by our time. Eternity is infinite and immeasurable.[77]

Finally, according to Padgett, in a theological sense, God's relatively timeless eternity means that God is the Lord of time. That is to say, it means, first, that God is the master of time, He is not limited by time. Second, God's life is infinite from eternity to eternity, and thus it is not limited by time. God is the ever-living fountain of being itself, and He is immutable in His fundamental nature and power. In this sense, God is the Lord of time because God has an entire plan for all possibilities and eventualities from eternity by providence. Padgett summarized his view in the following statement:

> The fact God is the Lord of time I have interpreted to mean that he has a plan or design for history, that nothing takes place outside of the divine will; that he is not limited or changed in any fundamental way by the passage of time, and that God is a metaphysically necessary Being who lives forever and ever. To this I would add the metaphysical properties of relative timelessness. By "relative timelessness" I mean that God is the Creator of our (physical, measured) time; that in contrast to our time, God's eternity is infinite and immeasurable; and finally that God's time is dependent on God's Being, not the other way around.[78]

In critical observation, as we have seen, while rejecting the absolute timeless and the plain everlasting view of God's eternity, Padgett suggests his own view of a "relatively timeless" God's eternity. For this view, on the one hand, Padgett rightly rejected the everlasting view because it does not properly denote the qualitative difference (i.e., the transcendence) between God's eternity and time, which is clearly revealed in *creatio cum tempore* (i.e., the measured world time is created and thus has its absolute beginning and end). On the other hand, for him, the timeless view, too, cannot be acceptable because the process (tensed) theory of time is correct. In this way, in a sense, even though Padgett rightly conceived the qualitative difference between God's eternity and time, he does not properly deal with God's real communicative actions in the temporal world and thus His real engagement in time, which is most definitely revealed in the person and life of Jesus Christ in whom

77. Padgett, "Eternity as Relative Timelessness," 107.
78. Ibid., 108.

eternity became time without ceasing to be eternal being. Therefore, although he states that God is the Creator as well as the Sustainer of the world time, it appears to be a superficial allusion. The reason is that, according to Padgett's view, even though God's temporality is an intrinsic nature, it is always transcendent beyond measured time, and thus eventually it does not actually engage in the world's time.

Furthermore, his arguments are at times inconsistent. That is to say, Padgett says that there is a "real change" in God because of His creation of the temporal world and just for this reason He is temporal, but at the same time he also says that it is "pure duration." For Padgett, the difference between God's time and created (measured) world time is that it is not created and thus infinite and immeasurable time without beginning and end. As he says, God's time is relatively timeless in the sense that it is not contained within the world time. God's time only exists because God's Being exists, not vice versa. Accordingly, in my judgment, Padgett's view is very similar to Newtonian "absolute time," which is God's time as pure duration without reference to anything external. One more problem in Padgett's argument is that, according to him, even though eternity as God's time is similar to the other divine attributes, it is a "part of God's existence," and thus not logically essential to the divine Being.[79] However, according to the doctrine of divine simplicity, all divine attributes are exactly the same as God's essence, and thus essential to the divine Being (i.e., God = eternity, and all of his attributes, not a "part" of God's existence). At any rate, in this way, Padgett asserts the intrinsic temporality of God, but at the same time his concept of God's relatively timeless eternity (i.e., God's time) differs from the plain everlasting view (e.g., Wolterstorff's). More significantly, for his relatively timeless view of God's eternity, Padgett depends on the philosophical concept of time, the process (tensed) view of time. However, for Padgett's view, what is deficient is its theological foundation. That is, Padgett does not give us a proper and sufficient theological exposition of God's real relation to human time.

---

79. As Padgett says, "God's eternity is thus similar to other divine attributes that are always part of God's existence but are not logically essential to the divine Being." Ibid., 107.

A Timeless and Accidental Omnitemporalism: William L. Craig

Probably, W. L. Craig is one of the most vigorous debaters on the issue. He has focused on the issue and published many articles and monographs concerning this topic.[80] The following statement briefly and clearly shows Craig's view of God's eternity and its relation to time: "Accidental omnitemporalism."

> It seems to me, therefore, that it is not only coherent but also plausible that God existing changelessly alone without creation is timeless and that He enters time at the moment of creation in virtue of His real relation to the temporal universe. The image of God existing idly before creation is just that: a figment of the imagination. Given that time began to exist, the most plausible view of God's relation to time is that He is timeless without creation and temporal subsequent to creation.[81]

Biblical Data and God's Relation to Time

Concerning the problem of God's eternity and its relation to time, W. L. Craig basically agrees with a consensus that the biblical evidence for the nature of God's eternity is unclear and thus underdetermined.[82] However, for his own view, Craig gives attention to the following two

---

80. Here are only some of them, Craig, *Existence of God and the Beginning of the Universe*; "Was Thomas Aquinas a B-Theorist of Time?," 475–83; "God and Real Time," 335–47; "Timelessness and Creation," 646–56; "New B-Theory's *Tu Quoque* Argument," 249–69; "Tense and the New B-Theory of Language," 5–26; "Tensed vs. Tenseless Theory of Time," 221–50; *Tensed Theory of Time*; *Tenseless Theory of Time*; *Time and Eternity*; and "Timelessness and Omnitemporality," 129–60.

81. Craig, "Timelessness and Omnitemorality," 160.

82. Craig says, "Divine eternity is one of those attributes of God which is underdetermined with respect to the biblical data. A literal reading of the biblical texts gives the overriding impression that God is eternal in the sense of existing at all times, not in the sense of being timeless. But there are passages which point in another direction, especially those suggesting that time had a beginning. More importantly, the fact that the biblical authors did not writes as philosophers should make us wary of pressing their descriptions of God into categories which may not have been germane to their purpose. The Christian who wants to understand more profoundly the nature of divine eternity and God's relationship to time has no recourse but to reflect philosophically on these issues if he is to come to some well-founded views on such questions." Idem, *Time and Eternity*, 239.

essential biblical tenets. That is, on the one hand, according to Scripture, God really interacts with the temporal world. Therefore, "it is indisputable that the biblical writers typically portray God as engaged in temporal activities, including foreknowing the future and remembering the past, and when they speak directly of God's eternal existence they do so in terms of beginningless and endless temporal duration (Ps 90:2; Rev 4:8)."[83] On the other hand, he reveals much biblical data which speak of the absolute beginning of time itself. In Craig's view, Gen 1:1 denotes an absolute beginning of not only the physical universe but also time itself. In the NT, according to Craig, John 1:1 also implies that time begins with creation (cf. Philo's doctrine of the divine Logos). Among many other biblical texts, the following texts evidently speak of the absolute beginning of time; for example, Prov 8:22–23 (*me 'olam*—before time), Jude 1:25 (*pro pantos tou aionos kai nun kai eis pantas tous aionas*—before all time and now and forever), Titus 1:2–3 ("in the hope of eternal life that God, who never lies, promised before age-long time [*pro chronon aionion*] but manifested at the proper time"), 2 Tim 1:2–3 (*pro chronon aionion*—before time began), 1 Cor 2:7 (*pro ton aionon*—before the ages), and so on. Consequently, based on those two essential biblical messages, Craig concludes as follows:

> Evidently it was a common understanding of the creation described in Genesis 1:1 that the beginning of the world was coincident with the beginning of time or the ages; but since God did not begin to exist at the moment of creation, it therefore followed that he existed "before" the beginning of time. God, at least "before" creation, must therefore be atemporal. Thus, although scriptural authors speak of God as temporal and everlasting, there is some evidence, at least, that when God is considered in relation to creation he must be thought of as the transcendent Creator of time and the ages and therefore as existing beyond time.[84]

In saying that, Craig's assertions are the following:

---

83. Craig, "Timelessness and Omnitemporality," 129–30.

84. Ibid., 131–32. In another place, he says, "I argued that the biblical data concerning divine timelessness/temporality are mixed. Usually the Bible speaks of God in temporal terms; but in contemplating God's creation of the world, the biblical authors do state that time had a beginning and thereby imply that God without the universe is timeless" (p. 175).

1. According to Scripture, time began with God's creation of the world (*creatio cum tempore*—creation with time).

2. Therefore, God exists timelessly without creation of the temporal world.

3. After creation of the temporal world, however, God is temporal because He sustains and interacts with the temporal world in a real sense, which is supported by Scriptural evidences.

God's Timelessness

In recent debates, Craig holds that the atemporlists' argument for God's absolute timeless eternity is based mainly on the following two ideas: (1) theologically, they use traditional perfect being theology, and (2) philosophically, they employ the tenseless theory of time, which is dependent on the static interpretation of Einstein's STR. At first, a temporal being is characterized by its transitory and incomplete flow of time's passage, for the past is gone forever and the future is not yet real. As he says, "Time has a savage way of gnawing away at life, leaving it transitory and incomplete, so that life in its fullness can never be enjoyed by any temporal being."[85] However, as we have seen in Boethius, God is the perfect being who "possesses the whole fullness of interminable life at once." Thus, according to classical theism, God is necessarily timeless because "the fleeting nature of temporal life is incompatible with the life of a most perfect being such as God is."[86] Craig summarizes this line of argument in classical theism as follows:

1. God is the most perfect being.
2. The most perfect being has the most perfect mode of existence.
3. Temporal existence is a less perfect mode of existence than timeless existence.
4. Therefore God has the most perfect mode of existence.
5. Therefore God has a timeless mode of existence.[87]

---

85. Craig, *Time and Eternity*, 68.
86. Craig, "Timelessness and Omnitemporality," 132.
87. Ibid., 133.

Recently, therefore, there have been some attempts to defend traditional timeless eternity based on the static interpretation of Einstein's STR, which is the static (or tenseless) view of time (e.g., P. Helm). According to Craig, however, "the flow of time is an ineradicable part of the experience of a temporal being."[88] Thus, in Craig's view, such an escape route is not successful. Moreover, in some contexts, Craig says that temporal incompleteness is not an imperfection for a perfect being, for the consciousness of time's flow can actually be an enriching experience of temporal life to him. Concerning this point, Craig states:

> R. W. Hepburn cautions against downplaying the importance of the flow of consciousness in awareness of music, for example. Music appreciation is not merely a matter of apprehending tenselessly the succession of sounds. Quoting Charles Rosen to the effect that "the movement from past to future is more significant in music than the movement from left to right in picture," Hepburn believes that the phenomenon of music calls into question any claim that a perfect mode of consciousness would be exclusively atemporal. All this goes to call into question premise 3 of the argument for divine timelessness from the incompleteness of temporal life. Timeless life may not be the most perfect mode of existence of a perfect person.[89]

For divine timelessness, on the basis of the doctrines of divine simplicity and immutability, a similar argument has been suggested, as we can see in Aquinas, as follows:

1. God is simple or 1'. God is immutable. Then we add
2. If God is simple or immutable, then He is not temporal, from which we can logically deduce
3. Therefore, God is not temporal. Since temporality and timelessness are, as we have seen, contradictories, it follows that
4. Therefore, God is timeless.[90]

Once again, according to Craig, divine simplicity and immutability are not good reasons for defending God's timelessness. The reason is that the doctrines are not supported by Scripture and not plausible theologically. As he states,

---

88. Ibid., 134.
89. Ibid., 136. For this argument, see also Craig, *Time and Eternity*, 67–74.
90. Craig, *Time and Eternity*, 29–30.

> The doctrines of divine simplicity and immutability are more controverted than the doctrine of divine eternity. To try to prove divine timelessness via divine simplicity or immutability, therefore, takes on the air of trying to prove the obvious via the less obvious. More specifically, the doctrines of divine simplicity and immutability as explained above find absolutely no support in Scripture, which at most speaks of God's immutability in terms of His faithfulness and unchanging character (Mal 3:6; Jas 1:17). Philosophically, there seem to be no good reasons to embrace these radical doctrines, and weighty objections have been lodged against them.[91]

However, concerning God's timelessness, Craig asserts that if there is no temporal universe, then God is timeless, not by any other reasons. That is to say, since God as Spirit is incorporeal, He is spaceless. Likewise, without the temporal world, God is timeless. Craig insists this as follows:

> According to the Christian doctrine of creation, God's decision to create a universe was a freely willed decision from which God could have refrained. We can conceive, then, of a possible world in which God does refrain from creation, a world which is empty except for God. Would time exist in such a world? . . . But suppose God were altogether changeless. Suppose that He did not experience a succession of thoughts but grasped all truth in a single, changeless intuition. Would time exist? A relationalist like Leibniz would say no, for there are no events to generate a relation of *earlier than* or *later than*. There is just a single, timeless state.[92]

God's Omnitemporality

According to Craig, many temporalists maintain the temporality of God because of the impossibility of God's atemporal personhood. That is, in biblical teaching, God is essentially a person, but not a thing, a metaphysical principle, or a mathematical entity. Therefore, "They argue that in order to be a person, one must possess certain properties that inherently involve time. Since God is essentially personal, he cannot be timeless."[93] For example, Daniel Dennett includes some conditions of

---

91. Ibid., 31.
92. Ibid., 78.
93. Craig, "Timelessness and Omnitemporality," 137.

personhood as rationality, consciousness, verbal communication, and so on.[94] Robert Coburn points out the issue as follows:

> Surely it is a necessary condition of anything's being a person that it should be capable (logically) of, among other things, doing at least some of the following: remembering, anticipating, reflecting, deliberating, deciding, intending, and acting intentionally. To see that this is so one need but ask oneself whether anything which necessarily lacked all of the capacities noted would, under any conceivable circumstances, count as a person. But now an eternal being would necessarily lack all of these capacities in as much as their exercise by a being clearly requires that the being exist in time. After all, reflection and deliberation take time, deciding typically occurs at some time—and in any case it always makes sense to ask, "When did you (he, they, etc.) decide?"; remembering is impossible unless the being doing the remembering has a past; and so on. Hence, no eternal being, it would seem, could be a person.[95]

Concerning this problem, Craig rejects Coburn's view since a timeless God can be a person who has such personal properties (e.g., rationality, consciousness, verbal communication, etc.) and can really act and engage in those activities. Therefore, Craig states,

> In conclusion, then, the argument for divine temporality based on God's personhood cannot be deemed a success. Advocates of a temporal God have not been able to show that God cannot possess timelessly the properties essential to personhood. On the contrary, a timeless God can be plausibly said to fulfill the necessary and sufficient conditions of being a person. A timeless, divine person can be a self-conscious, rational individual endowed with freedom of the will.[96]

In Craig's view, however, God is temporal not for any other reason but the fact that God created the temporal world and the tensed theory of time is correct. That is to say, since the tensed view, which believes in the objective reality of temporal becoming and tensed facts, is the correct theory of time, and if God really created the universe and acts in the temporal world, then God must be temporal. For this assertion, Craig

94. Dennett, "Conditions of Personhood," 175–96.
95. Coburn, "Professor Malcolm on God," 155.
96. Craig, "Timelessness and Omnitemporality," 140. For more detail arguments, see pp. 136–40 and his *Time and Eternity*, 77–86.

argues for God's real relation to the temporal world and His knowledge of tensed facts.

In sum, according to Craig, God is timeless without the temporal world. However, He freely willed and created the temporal world. Therefore, at the moment of creation, there is an extrinsic (not intrinsic) change on God's part, for the temporal world comes into existence. That is to say, after creation, since God comes into a real relation with the temporal world, He must be a "temporal" God. Craig explains this as follows:

> For at the first moment of time, God stands in a new relation in which he did not stand before (since there was no "before"). Even if in creating the world God undergoes no *intrinsic* change, he at least undergoes an *extrinsic* change. For at the moment of creation, God comes into the relation of *sustaining* the universe or, at the very least, of *coexisting with* the universe, relations in which he did not stand before. Since he is free to refrain from creation, God could have never stood in those relations, had he so willed. But by virtue of his creating a temporal world, God comes into a relation with that world the moment it springs into being. Thus even if it is not the case that God is temporal prior to his creation of the world, he undergoes an extrinsic change at the moment of creation of the world which draws him into time in virtue of his real relation to the world. The argument of the advocate of divine temporality can be summarized as follows:
>
> 1. God is creatively active in the temporal world.
> 2. If God is creatively active in the temporal world, God is really related to the temporal world.
> 3. If God is really related to the temporal world, God is temporal.
> 4. Therefore God is temporal.
>
> This argument, if successful, does not prove that God is essentially temporal, but that if he is Creator of a temporal world—as he in fact is—then he is temporal.[97]

In Craig's view, the second reason for God's temporality is that the tensed view of time is the correct theory for the temporal world. According to biblical teaching, God must be omniscient, and therefore God must be temporal. That is, a timeless God cannot know the tensed

97. Craig, "Timelessness and Omnitemporality," 140–41 (italics original).

facts about the temporal world because they are relative to the present and therefore change their truth-value.[98] According to the metaphysical principle of *presentism*, the present time ("now") alone is the real fact, for past times no longer exist and future times do not yet exist. Therefore, "if *t* involves presentness, then God, in grasping *t* at present, must be in the present, that is to say, must be temporal."[99] In other words, if God is timeless, then, since He does not know what time it actually is now, He does not know tensed facts. Consequently, if there is a dynamic temporal world, and since God is omniscient, He must be temporal. For this, his argument goes as follows:

> Any being *does* know tensed facts cannot be timeless, for his knowledge must be in constant flux, as the tensed facts known by him change. Thus we can formulate the following argument for divine temporality:
>
> 1. A temporal world exists.
> 2. God is omniscient.
> 3. If a temporal world exists, then if God is omniscient, God knows tensed facts.
> 4. If God is timeless, he does not know tensed facts.
> 5. Therefore God is not timeless.
>
> Again, this argument does not prove that God is essentially temporal, but if successful, it does show that if a temporal world exists, then God is not timeless.[100]

As we have seen, in Craig's view, there are two powerful reasons for thinking that God is temporal with the temporal world: God's real relation to the dynamic temporal world and His changing knowledge of tensed facts. In this sense, regarding the philosophical theory of time, Craig's view is based on the tensed (dynamic, A-series) theory of time.[101] Accordingly, if one adopts the philosophical tenseless theory

---

98. As Craig says that, "Thus what is a fact at one moment may not be a fact at another moment. It is now a fact that I am writing this sentence; in a moment it will no longer be a fact. Thus the body of tensed facts is constantly changing." Ibid., 146.

99. Ibid., 149.

100. Ibid., 146.

101. In his *Time and Eternity*, Craig states that, "I argued that, given the truth of a dynamic or tensed theory of time, God cannot be timeless if a temporal world exists. For if a tensed theory of time is correct, there are tensed facts and temporal becoming. In that case God, in virtue of His omniscience and creative activity, must know tensed facts and be the cause of things' coming to be. But in doing those things, God changes

of time and thus denies the objective reality of temporal becoming and tensed facts, then temporalism is logically meaningless.[102] However, according to Craig, there are no good reasons for accepting the tenseless theory of time.[103] Therefore, he concludes as follows: "Given a dynamic theory of time, it follows from God's creative activity in the temporal world and his complete knowledge of it that God is temporal. God quite literally exists now. Since God never begins to exist nor ever ceases to exist, it follows that God is omnitemporal. He exists at every time that ever exists."[104]

God, Time, and Creation

As we have seen, concerning the problem of the nature of God's eternity and its relation to time, W. L. Craig asserts an alternative view that "God is simply timeless without creation and temporal subsequent to creation." This position, however, raises a serious question as to whether or not there is a beginning of time itself. If time is infinite without a beginning point, then God is simply everlasting. According to Craig, however, time has its absolute beginning with the universe. For this, Craig appeals to the standard cosmological theory of Big-Bang and the metaphysical principle of the impossibility of an actual infinite (cf. the *Kalam* cosmological argument).

---

both extrinsically and intrinsically and therefore must be temporal. The crucial assumption here is that a dynamic theory of time is true." Idem, *Time and Eternity*, 240.

102. We can see this in Craig's following statement, "But there does remain one way of escape still open for defenders of divine timelessness. The argument based on God's real relation to the world assumes the objective reality of temporal becoming, and the argument based on God's knowledge of the temporal world assumes the objective reality of tensed facts. If one denies the objective reality of temporal becoming and tensed facts, then the arguments are undercut. In short, the defender of divine timelessness can escape the arguments by embracing the static or tenseless theory of time.... But this represents a very unpalatable route of escape, for the static theory of time faces formidable philosophical and theological objections, not to mention the arguments that can be offered on behalf of a dynamic theory of time." Idem, "Timelessness and Omnitemporality," 151–52.

103. He says, "The most plausible view of the nature of time, then, is that time involves an objective distinction between past, present, and future, and that temporal becoming is a real, mind-independent feature of the world." Craig, *Time and Eternity*, 240. For Craig's detailed arguments about the tensed and tenseless theory of time, see *Time and Eternity*, 116–216; *Tenseless Theory of Time*; and *Tensed Theory of Time*.

104. Craig, "Timelessness and Omnitemporality," 153.

At first, according to the standard model of the Big-Bang theory, time and space came into existence with the Big-Bang as a initial singularity. This means that time has its beginning, and thus past time is not infinite. Craig cites the British physicist P. C. W. Davies as follows:

> If we extrapolate this prediction to its extreme, we reach a point when all distances in the universe have shrunk to zero. An initial cosmological singularity therefore forms a past temporal extremity to the universe. We cannot continue physical reasoning or even the concept of spacetime, through such an extremity. For this reason most cosmologists think of the initial singularity as the beginning of the universe. On this view the big bang represents the creation event, the creation not only of all the matter and energy in the universe, but also of spacetime itself.[105]

In this sense, Barrow and Tipler also assert that, "At this singularity, space and time came into existence; literally nothing existed before the singularity, so, if the Universe originated at such a singularity, we would truly have a creation *ex nihilo*."[106] Thus, the standard Big-Bang theory, even though there are various modified theories, is considered one of the most powerful scientific theoretical evidence for the beginning of time, which is consistent with the biblical doctrine of *creatio ex nihilo*.

In addition, Craig speaks of a metaphysical principle of the impossibility of an actual infinite. For this, he argues as follows:

1. An actual infinite cannot exist.

2. A beginningless series of equal past intervals of time is an actual infinite.

3. Therefore, a beginningless series of equal past intervals of time cannot exist.[107]

According to Craig, therefore, an actually infinite number of things cannot exist (cf. the *Kalam* cosmological argument).[108] For this, at first,

---

105. Paul Davies, "Spacetime Singularities in Cosmology and Black Hole Evaporations," in *The Study of Time III*, ed. J. T. Fraser, N. Lawrence, and D. Park (Berlin: Springer, 1978) 78–79. As cited in Craig, *Time and Eternity*, 217–18.

106. Barrow and Tipler, *Anthropic Cosmological Principle*, 442. As cited in Craig, *Time and Eternity*, 218.

107. Craig, *Time and Eternity*, 221.

108. Cf. Craig, *KALAM Cosmological Argument*; "*Kalam* Cosmological Argument and the Hypothesis of a Quiescent Universe," 104–8; and "Graham Oppy on the *Kalam* Cosmological Argument," 1–11.

he points out the difference between a potential infinite and an actual infinite as follows:

> A potential infinite is a collection that is increasing toward infinity as a limit but never gets there. Such a collection is really indefinite, not infinite ... By contrast, an actual infinite is a collection in which the number of members really is infinite. The collection is not growing toward infinity; it *is* infinite, it is "complete."
> ... Now the argument is, not that a potentially infinite number of things cannot exist, but that an actually infinite number of things cannot exist. For if an actually infinite number of things could exist, this would spawn all sorts of absurdities.[109]

Craig further believes that, since the direction of time is from past to future, and if the series of past seconds is beginningless, then an actually infinite number of seconds have elapsed. In this sense, a beginningless series of equal past intervals of time cannot exist. "Thus, time must have a beginning."[110] Now, we have arrived at the end point of Craig's argument. As we have seen, according to Craig, time has its absolute beginning, but God does not have a beginning of His existence at all. Therefore, we can say that God alone must exist timelessly beyond the Big-Bang, the creation of time and the temporal universe. In His timeless eternity, God must be changeless; otherwise time would exist. Then, with God's creation of the world, time also began, and God entered into time at the moment of creation in virtue of His real relations with the created temporal world. Craig concludes that, therefore, "God must be timeless without the universe and temporal with the universe."[111]

---

109. Craig, *Time and Eternity*, 221.

110. Ibid., 226.

111. Ibid., 233. Elsewhere, Craig states that, "This remarkable conclusion merits our reflection. Like the incarnation, the creation of the world is an act of condescension on God's part for the sake of His creatures. Alone in the self-sufficiency of His own being, enjoying the timeless fullness of the intra-Trinitarian love relationships, God had no need for the creation of finite persons. His timeless, free decision to create a temporal world with a beginning is a decision on God's part to abandon timelessness and to take on a temporal mode of existence. He did this, not out of any deficit in Himself or His mode of existence, but in order that finite temporal creatures might come to share the joy and blessedness of the inner life of God. ... As a result of God's creation of and entry into time, He is now with us literally moment by moment as we live and breathe, sharing our every second. He is and will be always with us. He remembers all that has transpired, knows all that is happening, and foreknows all that is to come, not only in our individual lives but throughout the entire universe" (p. 241).

In critical observation, first of all, W. L. Craig's view of God's eternity and its relation to time is very simple and clear. As he says, God is timeless by Himself before creation, but He is temporal after the creation of the temporal world. In asserting such an accidental temporality of God's eternity, he appeals to the biblical doctrine of *creatio ex nihilo*, Big-bang cosmology, and the *Kalam* Cosmological Argument for the timelessness of God before the creation, and then, after the moment of creation, God is temporal because of His real engagement in the temporal world and the tensed (dynamic) theory of time. In this way, Craig tries to show the qualitative difference as well as the real relationship between God's eternity and time. In contrast to A. G. Padgett's view of the relative timelessness of God's eternity, Craig does not think of the temporality of God as essential to his nature, but only as an accidental temporality. However, in doing so, this raises a real problem in that God accidentally changes His mode of existence by the creation of the temporal world. Even though Craig says that this is an extrinsic and not an intrinsic change on God's part, it seems to be a real change in His mode of existence in that God, just like us, is in the temporal succession.

However, should we think that God has changed his mode of existence just because of His act of creating the temporal world? Furthermore, even if the tensed theory of time is correct, should God be also subordinated to the succession of temporal sequence as are we? That is to say, in order to insist on God's accidental temporality based on the philosophical tensed theory of time, Craig abandoned many things in biblical theological heritage (cf. divine simplicity, ontological immutability, etc.) Therefore, theologically, a more significant problem for W. L. Craig's theory is that he actually confines God Himself by a philosophical concept in saying that God is temporal because He created the temporal world and the tensed theory of time is correct. Furthermore, any philosophical enterprise or conceptual frame should not set theological agenda or confine theological frame or its content.

Conclusion

Up to now, we have seen some typical understandings in recent debates concerning the problem of God's eternity and its relation to time according to a specific theory of time. Each view has its own strengths and weaknesses in that it is based on a specific metaphysical and scientific theory of time, biblical interpretations, and theological considerations.[112] Here I will mention only a few with a view toward theological aspect. First of all, in the case of P. Helm's view of the absolute timeless eternity of God, he restates the traditional understanding of God's timeless eternity theologically based on divine aseity, and philosophically on perfect being theory of Greek ontology and the tenseless theory of time. Thus, he emphasizes the aspect of God's absolute transcendence beyond the temporal world. But, according to some theologians, if the tensed (dynamic) theory of time is correct, then the conception of divine timeless eternity is implausible. As we have seen in chapter 4, however, the views of philosophers and scientists are divided on the problem of the nature of time. Thus, at this point, we cannot simply determine whether it is right or wrong.

However, I want to point out a significant problem for God's eternity and its relation to time within the tenseless theory of time. That is, as P. Helm states, even if the tenseless theory of time is correct, then the world in the tenseless space-time continuum, which eternally exists as it is, is co-eternal with God. Even though the eternal God and temporal creatures are not ontologically identical, but they are co-eternal (i.e., the creatures are in tenseless time and God is outside of the tenseless time continuum). Then, theologically, there is no place for the doctrine of *creatio ex nihilo*, which means that God brought about the world into existence out of nothing. If we adopt a relational definition of time, then the tenseless theory of time is not plausible. In addition, as many theologians point out, a crucial problem is God's communicative action within on-going human history and God's real relation with the creatures. In my view, Helm's explanation of "one eternal divine will and its temporal effects" (cf. a mechanical timer model) cannot properly describe dynamic divine-human communicative actions and God's "real" relation to the temporal world, which are described in the normal sense of scriptural language. In my view, the "right time" effects in tenseless time continuum are not "real" and "direct" communicative actions. Thus, eventually, this emasculates God's real sustaining acts (i.e., providence) for the world at every moment. Furthermore, if God and

---

112. See mutual critiques and responses of the authors for each article in Ganssle, ed., *God and Time: Four Views*, 61–91; 111–28; 161–86; and 214–38.

the world tenselessly coexist eternally, it cannot adequately explain the incarnation, crucifixion, and resurrection of Jesus Christ, God's renewal of human beings from sin and His triumph over evil, the consummation and renewal of the whole world, and so on. But, there can be other approaches in order to solve this problem.

In contrast to P. Helm, the others (N. Wolterstorff, A. G. Padgett, and W. L. Craig) adopt the tensed (dynamic or A-series) theory of time. However, as we have seen, their understandings of God's eternity and its relation to time differ from one another. At first, N. Wolterstorff's view is very clear in that God is not timelessly eternal, but fundamentally everlasting within time. Insisting on the everlastingness of God's eternity, Wolterstorff appeals to a consistent literal interpretation of biblical descriptions about God and His actions within history. In doing so, Wolterstorff's essential claim is that God has a history in His own life, and thus He is essentially a temporal being. While insisting on God's temporality in plain sense, Wolterstorff emphasizes the aspect of God's immanence within the temporal world on the basis of the tensed theory of time. However, as he says, he is not yet confident in the problem of whether or not temporality is an intrinsic nature of God's life.[113]

Concerning this point, if we take seriously the doctrine of *creatio ex nihilo*, world time must have a beginning and is a created category for the existence of creatures. Accordingly, we cannot simply say that God is everlasting within time. Furthermore, God cannot be subjected to world time (i.e., measured time), for He is the Creator of it. Thus, even though God really acts within our world time, God also transcends it. In this sense, a simple and plain everlasting view cannot adequately explain the qualitative, not mere quantitative, difference between God's eternity and time. Conclusively, we cannot accept the two extremely radical views, absolute timeless eternity and plain everlasting eternity. There may be a *via media*, by which we can more properly describe the biblical God, His transcendence and immanence, and His eternity and its relation to time. Finally, therefore, in this chapter, we also found two alternative understandings: W. L. Craig's accidental temporalism and A. G. Padgett's relative timelessness eternity of God. However, as already mentioned, their views also have difficulties and limitations.

Accordingly, we must to find a theological way in which we can more properly conceive God's eternity and its relation to time. As we

---

113. See Wolterstorff's own argument in Ganssle, *God and Time: Four Views*, 238.

shall see, one of the more proper options is a Trinitarian analogical view. For this, I will define "time" as "a mode or a form of existence." That is to say, physical time exists because of the physical world as its form. According to the doctrine of *creatio ex nihilo*, God created everything, which is visible and invisible, out of nothing. In this sense, physical (measured) time is a created category for the existence of the universe, and therefore it is the form of the existence of creatures. Thus, physical time has its beginning with the creation of the universe, and there was no time before creation. According to the biblical teaching, God is the necessary, self-existent, and perfect Being in His own nature. Accordingly, it must be emphasized that God's mode of existence is qualitatively different from our own finite existence.

In this sense, on the one hand, we can say that God, as the Creator, transcends physical time because He is not subject to the natural laws or to any other created categories. However, on the other hand, God really engages in the temporal world in His creation, providence, and redemption of the world. Therefore, in my view, we can more properly conceive God's eternity and its relation to time in an "analogical way," which can simultaneously grasp the qualitatively difference and the positive relationship between God's eternity and time. I will deal with this theological approach in the following "Part Two, Toward a Trinitarian Analogical Understanding of Time and Eternity."

PART TWO

Toward a Trinitarian Analogical Understanding of Time and Eternity

6

Time, Eternity, and the Trinity in the Theology of Karl Barth

Introduction

IN THE TWENTIETH CENTURY, IT WAS KARL BARTH WHO PROFOUNDLY and systematically reconceived God's eternity and its relation to time, especially, in a trinitarian analogical way. That is to say, for Barth, his thorough trinitarian thinking opened the possibility for a new dynamic understanding of God's eternity and time as well as their relationship to each other. In fact, his magnum opus, *Church Dogmatics*, as a whole, was written from start to finish in a consistent trinitarian framework. However, we must first understand the reason why the theme of the relation between time and eternity is so important in K. Barth's trinitarian theology. In a sense, as R. H. Roberts rightly points out, "The so-called 'inner logic' of the *Church Dogmatics* is the axis of eternity and time unfolded through the motif of the 'analogy of faith.'"[1] However, it must be added that it was possible and fully developed in the structure of his thoroughly pervasive trinitarian thinking.[2] Generally, the development of K. Barth's theology has been classified in the following three theological stages: (1) liberal theology, (2) dialectical theology (or the theology of crisis), and (3) analogical theology.[3]

---

1. Roberts, "Karl Barth's Doctrine of Time," 88.

2. For this point, see Hunsinger, "*Mysterium Trinitatis*," 165–90.

3. Cf. von Balthasar, *Theology of Karl Barth*, 64–167; and Palakeel, *Use of Analogy*, 13–20.

The Importance of the Theme of Time and Eternity in Karl Barth's Trinitarian Theology

While turning away from the nineteenth century anthropocentric Protestant liberal theology,[4] the early dialectical Barth also vigorously rejected the analogy of being (*analogia entis*) in Roman Catholic theology. His reason for this rejection is that at the basis of natural theology there is an anthropocentric principle, which assumes the human ability to grasp God. In his *The Epistle to the Romans*, therefore, Barth declared as follows:

> [I]f I have a system, it is limited to a recognition of what Kierkegaard called "infinite qualitative distinction" between time and eternity, and to my regarding this as possessing negative as well as positive significance: "God is in heaven, and thou art on earth." The relation between such a God and such a man, and the relation between such a man and such a God, is for me the theme of the Bible and the essence of philosophy. Philosophers name this KRISIS of human perception—the Prime Cause: the Bible beholds at the same cross-roads—the figure of Jesus Christ.[5]

In this statement, Barth wanted to strongly emphasize God's wholly otherness from the world and therefore the infinite qualitative distinction between God and man. According to Barth, there are "the crevasse, the polar zone, [and] the desert barrier" between God and man, and this distance has "its essential, sharp, acid, and disintegrating ultimate significance."[6] For Barth, God is a "wholly Other" Being from us. Therefore, there cannot be any ontological connection (i.e., *analogia entis*) between God and man. There is only an "infinite qualitative distinction." In this way, in order to emphasize the distinction between God and man, Barth intentionally used the dialectics of *eternity* and *time*

---

4. Karl Barth's radical change of his theological thought was brought about by the signing of 93 German Intellectuals (including most of his theological teachers) of a manifesto, which supported the war policy of Kaiser Wilhelm II (1914). In this situation, his seeking of a new theological approach resulted in a form of dialectical theology in *Epistle to the Romans*, 1919. In doing so, Barth "pledged to 'restore God and the Word of God to the right place in theology' by giving theology a 'wholly other foundation.'" Palakeel, *Use of Analogy*, 15–16. See also Busch, *Karl Barth*, 81–83, and Hartwell, *Theology of Karl Barth*, 7.

5. Barth, *Epistle to the Romans*, 10 (italics mine).

6. Ibid., 49.

against Thomistic *analogia entis* as well as an anthropocentric German cultural Protestantism.

However, in his later phase, Barth was not satisfied with a strict dialectical method alone, for it had failed to express both the real and active relationship between God and man. Nor did it properly address God's real communicative action with His people in His word. According to H. U. von Balthasar, therefore, after Barth's study of Anselm,[7] his theological methodology shows a turning point once again. In Barth's theology, this has been considered to be a shift away from a radical dialectical theology to a kind of analogical theology.[8] In this third stage, Barth emphasizes the "fellowship," "relationship," and "covenant partnership" between God and man alongside "distinction" and "distance" as in his early dialectical theology. This was possible through analogical thought, and thus, as Barth himself discerned, a kind of analogical thinking is "unavoidable" for Christian theology.[9]

Recently, however, B. McCormack criticizes the highly influential "von Balthasar thesis," which demonstrates a clear transition from dialectic to analogy in K. Barth's theology, as a misleading view. According to McCormack, Balthasar wrongly granted Barth's work on Anselm as a clear "turning-point," but there is an ongoing continuity in Barth's dialectical theology.[10] In a sense, McCormack's view can be accepted because Barth never accepted Thomistic *analogia entis*. Actually, in

---

7. This was published as Barth, *Fides Quaerens Intellectum. Anselms Beweis der Existenz Gottes im Zusammenhang seines theologischen Programms*, München 1931, and English translation as *Anselm: Fides Quaerens Intellectum*, trans. I. W. Robertson (Cleveland and New York: World Publishing, 1962).

8. Cf. Balthasar, "Conversion to Analogy," in his *Theology of Karl Barth*, 86–113; Palakeel, *Use of Analogy*, 13–66; and Chia, *Revelation and Theology*, 201–25. After Balthasar, most of commentators of Barth followed his interpretation. For example, Jung Young Lee says, "his study on Anselm (*Fides Quaerens Intellectum*) has not only unlocked the door for his *Church Dogmatics* but also marked the beginning of his analogical thinking from his dialectical method." Idem, "Karl Barth's Use of Analogy," 131.

9. See the following Barth's own statement: "In distinction to both likeness and unlikeness 'analogy' means similarity, i.e., a partial correspondence and agreement (and, therefore, one which limits both parity and disparity between two or more different entities). The term is burdened by its use in natural theology, and it needs specific clarification in this respect. But at this point it is as such unavoidable. If in this fellowship there can be no question of their parity or disparity, there remains only what is generally meant by analogy: similarity, partial correspondence and agreement." Karl Barth, *Church Dogmatics* (hereafter cited as *CD* with its volume number), II.1, 225.

10. Cf. McCormack, *Karl Barth's Critically Realistic Dialectical Theology*, 1–28.

his *Church Dogmatics*, Barth condemned the *analogia entis* of Roman Catholicism as "the invention of Antichrist."[11] Therefore, in contrast to *analogia entis*, Barth suggested his own *analogia fidei* (analogy of faith) as a Protestant counter principle.[12] That is to say, for Barth, an analogy between God and man is only possible "from the Creator to the creatures" (i.e., analogy in a *catalogical* sense), not *vice versa*. In this sense, Barth's understanding of analogy is a "dialectical analogy" in that it is not a category of being but only that of faith based on God's self-revelation. Accordingly, Barth insists that an analogy for Christian theology is not a correspondence between the Being of God and that of other entities, but it is given through God's self-revelation, especially, in the Word of God, Jesus Christ, who is the Word made flesh and in whom eternity became time. Here we can find the foundation of Barth's Christocentric Trinitarian theology.

Even after Barth's move toward such an analogical perspective, since he rejected *analogia entis*, he still asserts that the axis of time and eternity functions continually as a very significant theological category as in his early strict dialectical theology.[13] That is to say, in the mode of *analogia fidei*, the axis of time/eternity replaces the traditional category of "being" in *analogia entis*. Because of his rejection of *analogia entis*, for Barth, time, instead of being or substance as such, becomes the medium of differentiation and relation between God and man. In Barth's view, time and eternity have no independent ontological status, and therefore there is a "functional replacement" between being and time. Concerning this fact, R. H. Roberts correctly points out that, for Barth, "time is a surrogate for substance in general. The relation of God's being in eternity to his being in time is understood in a mutual actualism in such a way

---

11. *CD*, I.1, xiii.

12. According to McCormack, "The *analogia fidei* is itself an *inherently dialectical concept*. Far from representing the abandonment of dialectic, the 'analogy of faith' is grounded in . . . the 'dialectic of veiling and unveiling' in revelation." McCormack, *Karl Barth's Critically Realistic Dialectical Theology*, 16 (italics original).

13. Therefore, Roberts observed that, "The most relevant factor in the immediate historical context of Barth's early development and his later, mature work concerns the treatment of the axis of eternity and time, understood as categories of infinite and finite existence, in both the evolution of idealist thought in Germany and in its later dissolution in the face of hostile philosophical criticism." Idem, "Karl Barth's Doctrine of Time," 90.

that ontology and temporality are deeply enmeshed."[14] Conclusively, in Barth's Trinitarian theology, the category of time and eternity, instead of the traditional category of being, functions the medium of a relation and distinction between God and man (the world). In doing so, he creatively reconceived time and eternity as a dynamic relationship in his comprehensive Trinitarian framework. In this way, the importance of the qualitative difference and the positive relationship between time and eternity lies in Barth's whole Trinitarian theology.

Karl Barth's Understanding of Analogia Fidei

In *Church Dogmatics*, as we shall see, *analogia fidei* is a theological and methodological principle for not only Barth's whole theology, but also his constructive and dynamic understanding of time and eternity. Therefore, before turning to his trinitarian analogical conception of time and eternity, we need a brief understanding of Barth's doctrine of the analogy of faith (*analogia fidei*).[15] If we say that, in a sense, all theological discourses are ultimately analogous, the real question then becomes what kind of analogy can more properly describe the biblical understanding of the God-world, eternity-time, and divine transcendence-immanence relationship. That is to say, if there is an analogy, a correspondence in infinite qualitative distinction between God and the world, eternity and time, what is its proper criterion or foundation? Indeed, in the beginning of the twentieth century, the debate on the meaning and use of analogy in theology among E. Przywara, K. Barth, and H. U. von Balthasar was one of the key issues for an ongoing debate between Protestant and Roman Catholic theologies.[16]

---

14. Ibid., 89.

15. According to Morse, "the entire *Church Dogmatics* may be said to be Barth's presentation of what he means by the *analogia fidei*." Idem, "Raising God's Eyebrows," 40. For discussions on Barth's conception of *analogia fidei*, see the following: Balthasar, *Theology of Karl Barth*; Moore, "Analogy and Karl Barth," 175–80; Nielsen, "Debate between Karl Barth and Erich Przywara," 24–46, and "Analogy as a Principle of Theological Method Historically Considered," 197–219; Pöhlmann, *Analogia Entis oder Analogia Fidei?*; Mondin, *Principle of Analogy*; Hammer, "Analogia Relationis gegen Analogia Entis," 288–304; Lee, "Karl Barth's Use of Analogy," 129–51; Wells, "Karl Barth's Doctrine of Analogy," 203–13; Mechels, *Analogie bei Erich Przywara und Karl Barth*; Morse, "Raising God's Eyebrows," 39–49; Chavannes, *Analogy between God and the World*; Palakeel, *Use of Analogy*.

16. Concerning the debates and discussions on analogy in the twentieth century, see the following works: Przywara, *Analogia Entis*; Balthasar, *Theology of Karl Barth*;

In the beginning of the twentieth century, E. Przywara proposed the "analogy of being" (*analogia entis*) as the formal principle of Roman Catholic theology.[17] Accepting the classical Lateran formula of analogy, he defined *analogia entis* as follows: "there is greater similarity between creator and creature only within an ever-greater dissimilarity."[18] By this Thomistic formula of *analogia entis*, Przywara tried to establish a middle ground between the anthropocentrism of nineteenth century liberal theology and the theocentrism of the radical dialectical theology of the early Barth, who emphasized "the infinite qualitative distinction between time and eternity" and thus between God and the world. As we have seen, however, K. Barth strongly denounced the idea of *analogia entis* as "the invention of anti-Christ."[19] The reason is that it assumes our intrinsic possibility of speaking about and knowing about God by the natural order and in virtue of being without God's revelation. And thus it is the very basis of natural and anthropocentric theology. Accordingly, Barth asserted *analogia fidei* against *analogia entis*.[20] As

---

Nielsen, "Debate Between Karl Barth and Erich Przywara," 24–46; Foley, "Catholic Critics of Karl Barth," 136–55; Mondin, *Principle of Analogy*; Pöhlmann, *Analogia entis oder Analogia fidei?*; Lochbrunner, *Analogia Caritatis*; Chavannes, *Analogy between God and the World*; Palakeel, *Use of Analogy*; Chia, *Revelation and Theology*.

17. Cf. Przywara, *Analogia Entis*.
18. As cited in Palakeel, *Use of Analogy*, 128.
19. *CD*, I.1, xiii.
20. According to J. Y. Lee's observation, the main reasons for Barth's rejection of *analogia entis* are as follows: "(1) The *analogia entis* eliminates the qualitative distinction between God and man and reduces them only to a quantitative distinction. Thus man and God belong to the same category of being. (2) The *analogia entis* assumes man's receptiveness to God's revelation apart from God's grace. Thus it conceives that the knowledge of God is capable in natural man *prior to* and *apart from* God's encounter. (3) The *analogia entis* reverses the direction of Divine-human encounter. Instead it starts from God to man, it begins from man to God. Thus it is a counterpole to the grace which moves downward. (4) Finally, the *analogia entis* makes out of the 'He' an 'It' and of the "Becoming' a 'Being.' God, who is static and impersonal, is quite contrary to our God, who is always personal and dynamic in His relation to man." Lee, "Karl Barth's Use of Analogy," 136. Ford also says that, "[Barth's] objection to natural theology and the *analogia entis* is that they try to see God's relationship to the world as structurally fixed and discernible apart from God choosing to speak. The *analogia fidei* points in contrast to the fact that God is always a free personal presence, who is there to be invoked and who uses particular analogies to give knowledge of himself in ever new events (knowledge for which the *analogia entis* searches in the nature of the analogies themselves)." Ford, "Barth's Interpretation of the Bible," 62. According to Palakeel, "Barth's fundamental argument for the rejection of analogy of being is that

Barth says, "There is no *analogia entis* but only an *analogia fidei*."[21] In doing so, Barth criticizes *analogia entis* as follows:

> How can we possibly stand on the same plane as God in His Being? Certainly not in virtue of what God is in Himself apart from His revelation. For as God in Himself He is what He is as God in His revelation—the Lord and Creator and Judge and Redeemer from all eternity and in His essence as the triune God. How can this being, which is the origin and boundary of all being, have only a part as we do in some being in general? How can this being, therefore, come to stand on the same plane as our own being? Certainly God in His being does not come to stand on the same plane as we do in our being merely in virtue of what we are apart from His revelation.... And where then is the comparability between His Creator-being and our creature being, between His holy being and our sinful being, between His eternal being and our temporal being? Where then is the analogy on the basis of which the knowledge of God is possible to us? *If there is a real analogy between God and man—an analogy which is a true analogy of being on both sides, an analogy in and with which the knowledge of God will in fact be given—what other analogy can it be than the analogy of being which is posited and created by the work and action of God Himself, the analogy which has its actuality from God and from God alone, and therefore in faith and in faith alone?*"[22]

What, then, is analogy? According to Barth, analogy is a middle way (*via media*) between parity and disparity, or between univocation and equivocation. For him, therefore, analogy means, in distinction to both likeness and unlikeness, "similarity, i.e., a partial correspondence and agreement (and, therefore, one which limits both parity and dispar-

---

it would amount to the deification of man and the exaltation of the human above the divine possibilities. This is again in danger of absolutising philosophy over revelation." Palakeel, *Use of Analogy*, 51. See also, Mondin, *Principle of Analogy*, 168.

21. *CD*, I.1, 437. See also Lee, "Karl Barth's Use of Analogy," 133–38.

22. *CD*, II.1, 83 (italics mine). However, Barth did not deny analogy itself, as he stated as follows: "Our reply to the Roman Catholic doctrine of the *analogia entis* is not, then, a denial of the concept of analogy. We say rather that the analogy in question is not an *analogia entis* but according to Rom. 12:6 the *analogy of faith*, the likeness of known in the knowing, of the object in thought, of the Word of God in the word that is thought and spoken by man, as this differentiates true Christian prophecy in faith from all false prophesy." *CD*, I.1, 243–44.

ity between two or more different entities),"[23] and that "the same term, applied to two different objects, designates the same thing in both but in different ways."[24]

In Barth's view, however, *analogia fidei* is given by grace and is thoroughly based on the pure act of God's self-revelation in the Word of God. The natural man, in virtue of his being, cannot know and speak about God at all. According to Barth, God is the One who reveals Himself, and thus God can be known only through His revelation. Therefore, a theological analogy can be established only by God's self-revelation in human language. As Barth says,

> [T]he truth is that man with his human word "similarity" participates in the (as such) incomprehensible similarity which is posited in God's true revelation, so that in it God participates in man and his word. . . . if our decision for the concept of analogy is not arbitrary; if it is not self-grounded upon a secret prejudice in favour of an immanent capacity of this concept, but occurs under the compulsion of the object; if it is not, then, a systematic but an exegetical decision.[25]

In this sense, for Barth, *analogia fidei* is *analogia revelationis*.[26] God can only be known through His self-revelation, which comes to man as a free gift in His self-manifestation, finally and fully realized in the incarnation of the Word of God, Jesus Christ. Therefore, it is God's unconditional grace for us, *sola gratia*. Accordingly, *analogia fidei* is also called *analogia gratiae*, for our faith itself is possible only through God's grace. Furthermore, as Barth says, "Man can have this knowledge only in faith and obedience to the revealing God. We know God only because God has chosen to reveal Himself to us. Hence the only analogy capable of understanding and interpreting God and revelation is the analogy of faith (*analogia fidei*)."[27] In this sense, *analogia revelationis* can be said to be an epistemological form of Barth's *analogia fidei*, for man can know

---

23. *CD*, II.1, 225.
24. *CD*, II.1, 237.
25. *CD*, II.1, 227.
26. According to Barth's own words, "it is quite clear that there can self-evidently be no question of anything but the *analogia fidei sive revelationis* even in this description of creaturely occurrence as a mirror and likeness." *CD*, III.3, 51.
27. Palakeel, *Use of Analogy*, 23.

about God only through His revelation and in faith which is given by God Himself in grace.

According to Barth, God is not a static being, but always "the Being-in-action" and *actus purus et singularis*.[28] Concerning the reality of God, Barth says, "God is who He is in the act of His revelation,"[29] and also "God is who He is in His works."[30] Therefore, Barth's concern focuses not on the "being or being only as the being of God," but on the God who revealed Himself as the One who is in His action and works.[31] Barth also emphatically states that, "on the basis of His revelation we always understand God as event, as act and as life."[32] God is always in His act, and is known in His self-revealing action. God is not a static being, but a living and acting God. In this way, according to J. Palakeel's analysis, Barth founded his doctrine of analogy not on a static "being" but on "God's act." In this sense, we can say that his *analogia fidei* is "not an analogy of being but an analogy of act."[33] Accordingly, we can clearly see that the ontological basis of the *analogia fidei* is Barth's dynamic understanding of God as the Being-in-action, not a static being itself or substance. In the same sense, as we shall see, Barth's creative and dynamic understanding of eternity and time, too, is based on this doctrine of God's being-in-action in Trinitarian framework.

Furthermore, according to Barth, an analogy between God and man can be established by the fact that the human being was created according to the image of God. However, Barth does not accept the traditional doctrine of the *imago Dei*, because it was also based on an *analogia entis*. According to his own creative exegesis of Gen 1:26–27, in Trinitarian terms and in accepting Bonhoeffer's idea, Barth asserts *analogia relationis*, instead of *analogia entis*, between God and man. As Barth says, "the 'Let us' as the distinctive form of the creative fiat in v. 26, and therefore the plurality in the divine being is plainly attested in this passage, the differentiation and relationship, the loving co-existence and co-operation, the I and Thou, which first take place in

---

28. Cf. *CD* II.1, 257–72.
29. *CD*, II.1, 257.
30. *CD*, II.1, 260.
31. Ibid.
32. *CD*, II.1, 264.
33. Palakeel, *Use of Analogy*, 139.

God Himself."[34] Then, God created the being of man as male and female in correspondence to the divine I-Thou relationship in the Triune God. In this sense, "Man is the repetition of this divine form of life; its copy and reflection."[35] For Barth, this I-Thou relationship is the image of God in human being as male and female.[36] Therefore, Barth says as follows:

> The relationship between the summoning I in God's being and the summoned divine Thou is reflected both in the relationship of God to the man whom has created, and also in the relationship between I and the Thou, between male and female, in human existence itself. There can be no question of anything more than an analogy.[37]

Barth says that it is "a clear and simple correspondence, an *analogia relationis*."[38] The analogy of relation between God and man, the *tertium comparationis*, is "simply the existence of the I and the Thou in confrontation."[39]

According to Barth, however, the differentiation and relationship between the I and the Thou in the divine being are not identical to the differentiation and relationship between male and female.[40] Thus, he asserts, "analogy, even as the analogy of relation, does not entail likeness but the correspondence of the unlike."[41] It is an analogy, "i.e., similarity

---

34. *CD*, III.1, 196.

35. Ibid., 185.

36. In the text of Gen 1:26–27, while interpreting "image (*tselem*)" and "likeness (*demuth*)" as "original" and "prototype," Barth says that, "Man is not created to be the image of God but ... he is created in correspondence with the image of God. His divine likeness is never his possession, but consists wholly in the intention and deed of his Creator, whose will concerning him is this correspondence.... At any rate, the point of the text is that God willed to create man as a being corresponding to His own being—in such a way that He Himself (even if in His knowledge of Himself) is the original and prototype, and man the copy and imitation." *CD*, III.1, 197.

37. Ibid., 196.

38. Ibid. In another place, Barth says that, "there can be no question of an analogy of being, but of relationship. God is in relationship, and so too is the man created by Him. This is his divine likeness." *CD*, III.2, 324.

39. *CD*, III.1, 185.

40. Barth states, "It also belongs to his creatureliness that the relationship between the I and the Thou in man take place only in the form of the differentiation and relationship between two different individuals, whereas in the case of God they are included in the one individual." Ibid., 196.

41. Ibid., 196.

in dissimilarity."[42] In this sense, *analogia fidei* is not based on a similarity between God and man in the category of "being," but "the similarity of two relations" in a partial correspondence. That is to say, it is a similarity between the I-Thou relationship in the divine being as the Trinity (e.g., Father to Son), and the I-Thou relationship in the human beings as male and female (e.g., husband to wife).[43] Accordingly, it is quite clear that Barth's *analogia fidei* is not based on the static concept of being but the dynamic relationship of persons. In this way, *analogia fidei* is also called *analogia relationis*, analogy of I-Thou relationship, and this is Barth's ontological form of his *analogia fidei*.[44]

As already mentioned, K. Barth's *analogia fidei* is, however, always a "dialectical analogy" in that he never accepted *analogia entis*, and he emphasized again and again the infinite qualitative distinction between God and man. Even if there can be an analogy, in Barth's view, it is possible only in God's self-revelation, grace, and in our faith which is also given by God Himself. In Barth's conception of *analogia fidei*, therefore, "everything comes from above downward, everything is a pure gift and miracle of grace."[45] Therefore, its real, true, and concrete foundation is Jesus Christ, the God-man, who is the only man analogous to God. While appealing to Paul (1 Cor 1: 15; 2 Cor 4:4), Barth insists that the true image of God is Jesus Christ in whom the invisible God Himself has become visible. As he says, "In Him we have *the* image in face [i.e., the concrete visual form] of which the question of the original is finally answered," as Paul declared "the man Jesus as the real image of God, and therefore as the real man created by God."[46]

Therefore, we can find the true *analogia relationis* between God and man through Jesus Christ, the God-man. Then, according to Barth,

---

42. *CD*, III.2, 324.

43. Cf. Mondin, *Principle of Analogy*, 168.

44. However, we must remember that *analogia relationis* is not a natural or intrinsic analogy between God and man, but only a form of the analogy of faith. As J. Palakeel says that, "According to Barth, man is not an image of God by nature; there is no natural analogy between man and God; it is only by grace that man becomes the image of God. The reason is simple. According to him, even the *analogia relationis*—the analogy of human I-Thou and divine I-Thou—is only an analogy of faith, because man can know this analogy only after revelation has manifested the mystery of the Trinity." Idem, *Use of Analogy*, 30.

45. Palakeel, *Use of Analogy*, 65–66.

46. *CD*, III.1, 202 and 203.

centered on Jesus Christ, there is a sequence of analogy of relation: an *analogia relationis* between the perichoretic inner relationship of the Trinitarian persons, between the divinity and the humanity of Jesus Christ, the God-man, between Christ's humanity and the humanity in general man, and finally between man and his fellow-man.[47] For Barth, therefore, there is one true and perfect God-given analogy between God and man.[48] It is Jesus Christ, *vere Deus vere homo*, in whom the Word became flesh.[49] In this sense, as we shall see, the time of Jesus Christ, the God-man, is also the true analogy between God's eternity and human time, for eternity became time in Him without ceasing to be eternal.

K. Barth's Understanding of Time

In his early radical dialectic theology, Barth's understanding of time is characterized by a negation of it as the opposition to eternity. In *The Epistle to the Romans*, therefore, Barth says that "time is nothing when measured by the standard of eternity" (ER, 43). "There is no magnificent temporality of this world which can justify men before God" (ER, 56). And again, "No road to the eternal meaning of the created world has ever existed, save the road of negation" (ER, 87). Accordingly, R. H. Roberts states that, "in the dialectical phase of Barth's development this overcoming of the antithesis [between time and eternity] was by the annihilation of time by eternity."[50] This is a corollary of which Barth strongly emphasized the infinite qualitative distinction between God's eternity and human time. In so doing, Barth desires to emphatically denote the infinite qualitative distinction between God and man as well

---

47. Then, Barth develops step by step *analogia relationis*: between the relations in the Trinity; between God and Jesus Christ; between Jesus Christ's divinity and humanity; between Jesus Christ's humanity and humanity in general; and between man and man the other; and therefore between God and man. Cf. *CD*, III.2, 218–25, and Palakeel, *Use of Analogy*, 26–29.

48. Barth says that, "The humanity of Jesus, His fellow-humanity, His being for man as the direct correlative of His being for God, indicates, attests and reveals this correspondence and similarity." *CD*, III.2, 220.

49. Concerning the Christocenticity of Barth's understanding of analogy, Chia says that, "Barth's Christocentric approach, which applies the Platonic concept of *logos* as the *a priori Uranalogans* resulting in the notion of Christ as the archetype of all analogies, makes his doctrine of analogy not just a new argument against the Catholic notion of the *analogia entis*, but a new creation in theology." Chia, *Revelation and Theology*, 205.

50. Roberts, "Karl Barth's Doctrine of Time," 97.

as between God and the world. For Barth, the wholly otherness of God from the world is expressed typically by the phrase "*God is in heaven, and thou art on earth.*" However, as we shall see, in his later analogical theology, while holding the infinite distinction between God's eternity and time, Barth also speaks of a positive and analogical relationship between them in his comprehensive Trinitarian theology.[51] We can find Barth's mature Trinitarian analogical understanding of time and eternity in his *Church Dogmatics*,[52] and that will be my main emphasis.

Time as the Form of God's Creation

First, concerning the ontological status of time, Barth believes that time is neither an eternal nor an independent thing (or a being) apart from God, but God's creation. Barth declares that, "God is the Creator of time."[53] Time is a created thing, and thus a finite thing, which is under God's rule and control like other created things. In Barth's own words, "It is itself, of course, the creation of God (or more correctly, the creation of His eternity). But it actually begins together with His creation, so that we have to say that His creation is the ground and basis of time."[54] With the doctrine of *creatio ex nihilo*, here Barth accepts Augustine's idea of "creation with time" (*creatio cum tempore*). For Augustine, as we have seen, there cannot be a time prior to creation, thus the world was created *with* time but not *in* time. Concerning this point, Barth further states as follows:

> What is the meaning of *cum tempore* if it does not mean *in tempore*? If there is no creature and therefore no time prior to

---

51. Cf. Hunsinger, "*Mysterium Trinitatis*," 165–90.

52. In his *Church Dogmatics*, we find Barth's main statements concerning time and eternity in the following sections: "God's Time and Our Time," I.2 (pp. 45–70); "The Eternity and the Glory of God," II.1 (pp. 608–40); "Creation, History and Creation History," III.1 (pp. 67–76); "Man in His Time," III.2 (pp. 437–640); "Unique Opportunity," III.4 (pp. 565–94); "Holy Spirit and Christian Hope," IV.3.2 (pp. 902–42), etc. I found only a few previous studies on Barth's understanding of time and eternity, see Jenson, "God's Being in Time," in his *God after God*, 123–35; Guy, "Man and His Time," 199–287; Roberts, "Karl Barth's Doctrine of Time," 88–146; Hunsinger, "*Mysterium Trinitatis*," 165–90, this article was also included in his *Disruptive Grace*, 186–209; and Leftow, "Response to *Mysterium Trinitatis*," 191–201.

53. *CD*, I.2, 47.

54. *CD*, III.1, 68.

creation, it is no less true that there is no creation prior to the creature and time. Prior to the creature there is only God's pure being at rest and at movement in itself; and prior to time there is only His eternity. But His eternity is itself revealed in the act of creation as His readiness for time, as pre-temporal, supra-temporal (or co-temporal) and post-temporal, and therefore as the source of time, of superior and absolute time. And therefore His revelation, the act of creation, is simultaneous with the emergence of the creature and the commencement of time; it does not take place outwith but within the new sphere which is posited by it. In other words, creation no longer takes place in the sphere of God's pure, inner being, where it finds its basis and possibility and (as an *opus ad extra internum*) is willed and planned in the divine decree of salvation and peace. But (as an *opus ad extra externum*) it now takes place outside this sphere, where over against and distinct from it the creature comes into being in the new sphere posited by it and arising from the fact that it takes place.[55]

In classical theism, as we have seen in Chapter 3, God's eternity was conceived as a timeless eternity, for, simply, there was no time before the creation. However, in distinguishing from Augusine, Barth advances one more step to assert "creation in time" (*creatio in tempore*) with "creation with time" (*creatio cum tempore*). As he says, "But we must also say that His creation takes place *in time* and therefore has a genuine history. It is undoubtedly true that God in His eternity is the beginning of time. There is thus no sense in talking of a divine creation which was only eternal, which did not carry with it time, our time, relative time, as the form of existence of the creature, and which to that extent did not already take place in time."[56] Why should Barth assert creation "in time"? We can find Barth's reason for discussing *creatio in tempore* in the following statement:

> The concept of a creation which does not take place in time is one which can be legitimately applied only to God's decree of grace and creation as it was taken in the bosom of His eternity. Our present concern, however, is with its execution and actualization; with creation itself and as such, with which time is at once actualized as well, which with the creature posits time as its form of existence, and which to that extent does not take

---

55. *CD*, III.1, 70–71.
56. Ibid., 68 (italics mine).

place before but in time. For the rest, the concept of a creation not taking place in time can only be used illegitimately to describe God's eternal original relation to an eternal world exactly like Himself.[57]

That is to say, according to Barth, the problem is this: if the creation actually took place in eternity, not in time, the world itself would be co-eternal with God. In addition, for Barth, as the Being-in-action, God's act in relation to creatures is only possible in the mode of time. Time is the field for God's acts and His works. Without creation, there is only God's eternal being and eternity. Therefore, Barth asserts as follows: "His eternity is not merely the negation of time, but an inner readiness to create time, because it is supreme and absolute time, and therefore the source of our time, relative time. But it is true that in this sense, in His pure, divine form of existence, God is not in time but before, above and after all time, so that time is really in Him."[58] This means that God created the world in His own time, and then there is also our time, as a created relative time, with the creation of the world as the form of the creatures' existence. Therefore, elsewhere, Barth clearly says that, "time was created simultaneously with the universe as its form of existence."[59] In this way, Barth conceives God's eternity not as a timeless one but as a "supreme and absolute time" in contrast to the created relative time of creation. However, Barth's position is still unclear in saying that it is "an inner readiness to create time." Even though it can be said so, in my view, it is not just a readiness, but it must be said that God's time itself as such is the form of His own eternal existence. Otherwise, we must posit an ontological change in God's mode of existence from the timeless eternity to a temporal phase as a stage of the preparation of creation, as discussed by J. Moltmann.[60] This cannot be acceptable because of divine ontological immutability.

57. Ibid.
58. Ibid.
59. *CD*, III.2, 521.
60. Moltmann, *God in Creation*, 112–18. For God's preparation of His creation of the temporal world, according to Moltmann, there are two possible models: (1) "The idea of God's creative resolve," and (2) "The idea of God's primordial self-restriction." For a detailed exploration, see also his *Coming of God*, 280–84. Moltmann posits a "time of creation" (i.e., *primordial time* which is God's time) between God's absolute eternity and created time, as he says: "In considering God's creative act, how can we think of God's eternity and the temporality of the creature simultaneously, without the one's canceling

At any rate, for Barth, as we have seen, created time is a creation of God with the creation of the world. However, Barth conceives that it is not just a creature beside other creatures (i.e., things or beings), but the form of God's creation.[61] As Barth asserts, "time is not a something, a creature with other creatures, but a form of all the reality distinct from God, posited with it, and therefore a real form of its being and nature."[62] Therefore, time is the form of the created world for its whole life, and, more positively, it is also ordained to be the field for God's acts and His works for His creatures. In this sense, created time as such differs from God's own time. As Barth continues,

> [T]ime as such, i.e., our time, relative time, itself created, is the form of existence of the creature; it is, in contradiction to eternity, the one-way sequence and therefore the succession and division of past, present and future; of once, now and then; of the beginning, middle and end; of origin, movement and goal. When God creates and therefore gives reality to another alongside and outside Himself, time begins as the form of existence of this other.[63]

Therefore, in Barth's view, world time, our relative time, is in the very beginning of God's creation as the form of creation. According to the narrative of God's creation in Gen 1, "time undoubtedly begins with the first divine 'Let there be' and the first creaturely 'It was.'" Then, God's

---

out the other? There is no transition and no meditation between eternity and time if time and eternity are defined over against one another. We therefore have to proceed from the assumption that it was only a self-alteration of eternity which made created time possible and made room for it. This is what the doctrine of God's essential creative resolves says. The question: what was God doing before he created the world and time? is not a pointless question. It has to be answered by saying that before the creation of the world, God resolved to be its Creator in order to be glorified in his kingdom. The unique transition from eternity to time is to be found in this self-determination of God's. In this essential resolve, God withdrew his eternity into himself in order to take time for his creation and to leave his creation its own particular time. Between God's essential eternity and the time of creation stands *God's time* for creation—the time appointed through his resolve to create." Idem, *God in Creation*, 114. In this way, Moltmann advances Augustine's doctrine of *creatio cum tempore* a further step to his own *creatio cum tempore* and *in tempore*. However, I cannot accept Moltmann's idea of primordial time, for it means an ontological change in God.

61. As Barth says, "time is certainly God's creation or, more correctly, a form of His creation." *CD*, II.1, 608, cf. 465.

62. *CD*, III.2, 438.

63. *CD*, III.1, 67–68.

work on the fourth day, the creation of constellations, gives us only the measure of time for the knowledge of time, not time itself. As he states:

> [I]f it is only God's fourth work—the creation of the constellations (Gen 1:16–18)—that gives us the measure of time which man finds so useful and which forms an objective basis for the knowledge of time (although not, of course, its real basis, not time as such, but the clock and calendar to establish it, not for God the Creator but for man) this does not overthrow the preceding truth that time had actually commenced with the divine creation and the emergence of the creature, time being from the very first the form in which creatures began to exist and even the underlying divine speech and action of the Creator proceeded.[64]

In saying this, what Barth really means is that created time itself is not merely measured time, a clock time, as a measuring form by the heavenly bodies, but it is also and most fundamentally the form of the creatures' existence as a whole and the form for God's creation itself.

Time as the Form of Life

According to Barth, time is the form of God's creation, but it is also the form of life, i.e., human existence.[65] Thus, the nature of man as a created being is characterized by his temporality. As Barth says that, "Humanity is temporality. Temporality, as far as our observation and understanding go, is humanity."[66] "To be man is to live in time. Humanity is in time."[67] According to Barth, therefore, the problem of time is "a problem of all anthropology."[68] Time is the *conditio sine qua non* of human existence. Barth declares that, "If man had no time, if his existence were timeless, he would have no life."[69] Therefore, man lives only in his own time, which is given by God as the form of his life, and he cannot escape from it. In this way, according to Barth, time is a constitution of human life, and therefore they are inseparable from each other. Life presupposes

64. Ibid., 71.
65. Cf. *CD*, III.2, 521.
66. Ibid., 522.
67. Ibid., 521.
68. Ibid., 439.
69. Ibid., 437.

time which is the form of human existence. Furthermore, Barth applies this idea to God Himself. As he says,

> Even the eternal God does not live without time. He is supremely temporal. For His eternity is authentic temporality, and therefore the source of all time. But in His eternity, in the uncreated self-subsistent time which is one of the perfections of His divine nature, present, past and future, yesterday, to-day and to-morrow, are not successive, but simultaneous. It is in this way, in this eternity of His, that God lives to the extent that He lives His own life.[70]

However, human time is different from God's time (i.e., eternity). That is to say, in God's time (i.e., the authentic time, and thus eternity) all time (past, present and future) is "simultaneous" in pure duration, but in human time (i.e., inauthentic time, the created time), these three temporal elements are "successive" in one-way sequence. Barth's distinctive concept of simultaneity in God's time can be understandable only in Trinitarian terms, for God's time is the form of the Triunity (i.e., the Trinity in unity).[71] For Barth, therefore, this is one of the decisive differences between God's time (i.e., eternity) and human time, which is "simultaneity" in the former and "successiveness" in the later. Barth clearly states this point as follows:

> Man lives as he has time and is in his time. It is his time to the extent that it is not God's eternity, not the simultaneity of present, past and future, but their succession. And it is his time to the extent that it is given him in a fixed span when he is created the soul of his body to live before God. It is for the sake of this life willed by God, and as its form, that he has time. He has it, therefore, as his lifetime; as the time for each of his individual life-acts and for their connected sequence, his total lifetime. He is in this time, and this time alone. The constitution of man's being as the soul of his body presupposes his temporality.[72]

For Barth, as we have seen, time is real, not a mere illusion, as far as it was given to us by God as the real form of our life.[73] However, accord-

---

70. Ibid., 437–38.

71. For a fine analysis of Barth's concept of God's time in Trinitarian framework, see Hunsinger, "*Mysterium Trinitatis*," 165–90.

72. *CD*, III.2, 438.

73. Cf. ibid., 521.

ing to Barth, we do not have the power to have control over time. We cannot create it, take it or keep it. We cannot contract out of it, extend it, stop it, or jump over it. Even we cannot accelerate or retard it. Barth says, "Above all, we cannot reverse it, making it move back from the future through the present and into the past."[74] This means that time is our *conditio sine qua non* and at the same time our limitation. We do not have time as our own possession, but only acquire it for our life. Without time, as Barth says, there is no life. Therefore, for Barth, "all this supports the view that time as our form of existence is no less ordained by a higher power than existence itself."[75] Only the eternal God alone has time for us because He is the true Life, and He gives us our time, and therefore He gives us our life. In this sense, time is the gift of God for us, as divinely given space for human life. More significantly, in Barth's view, time is the category of covenant relationship between God and man. As he says, "Time was in fact willed and created in order that there might take place His dealings in the covenant with man, which finds its counterpart in the relationship between man and his fellows. It is for this reason and in this sense that time is the form of our existence."[76]

Time as Lost Time

As Barth clearly shows us, God created time for us as the form of our existence, and gives it to us as a gracious gift for our life. However, for Barth, "our" time is at the same time a "lost time" because of the Fall. Therefore, "Between our time and God-created time as between our existence and the existence created by God there lies the Fall."[77] And thus, our time after the Fall is a very different time from the original God-created time for us. It is a distorted and lost time. Accordingly, we cannot directly identify our lost time with the time originally created by God. In this sense, Barth says that, "Our time, the time we know and possess, is and remains lost time, even when we believe that God is the Creator of time. God-created time remains a time hidden and withdrawn from us."[78] At this point, however, even though Barth dis-

74. Ibid., 524.
75. Ibid., 525.
76. Ibid., 527.
77. *CD*, I.2, 47.
78. Ibid.

tinguishes fallen time (i.e., time after the Fall) from original created time, he does not give us an explanation of what is the actual difference between them. I will argue this problem in chapter 8.

Rather, Barth explains the fallen time from the uncertainty of our time experience. That is to say, according to Barth, the very fact that our time is a lost time is the reason why the nature of time remains perpetually a perplexing problem for us, like an unsolvable problem. The great difficulty in our experience of time lies in the following three questions: What is meant by "the present"? Does time have a beginning and an end? What is the relationship between eternity and time? Because of the difference between our time, "as lost, fallen, condemned time," and the original God-created time, those questions are quietly unanswerable to us, and to this extent God-created time remains hidden and withdrawn apart from God's revelation.[79] For this reason, even though time is a necessary condition of human existence, at the same time, it remains as an absolute uncertainty for our existence. As Barth describes,

> "Our" time [is] . . . the time of man as isolated from God and fallen into sin. It is the time whose flux has become a flight. It is the time in which there is no real present and therefore no real past and future, no centre and therefore no beginning and no end. . . . It is time without any recognizable ground or meaning in eternity. This is how time appears and must appear when it is no longer an order established by God and to be appropriated and acknowledged by man, but a human work and institution. . . . As the time of lost man it can only be lost time. And it is with this lost man, who has only this lost time, who in reality has no time at all.[80]

As beings in the lost time, therefore, we cannot determine what time really is. Apart from God's revelation, the situation is just the same for the human species as a whole, any of its social groups, or any individual man. As fallen time, for Barth, one of the characteristics of our time is its "lostness" and "emptiness." At first, says Barth, "For us the past is the time which we leave and are in no longer."[81] It was once ours, but is no longer ours, and thus it may be a partially or completely forgotten reality. "It has now eluded us and been taken from us. It has remained

---

79. *CD*, I.2, 49.
80. *CD*, III.1, 72.
81. *CD*, III.2, 512.

behind, never to be restored."[82] Although there are some islands of memory in the ocean of oblivion, the past is filled with "a great flood of forgotten reality." Even its limited sphere of memory is not the present reality. It is a mere "subjective accident or skill," and "merely demonstrates the gulf which lies between what was and what is."[83] Accordingly, it is no longer ours, for it has ceased to belong to us.

Similarly, the future is "the time which we do not yet have but perhaps will have."[84] We may anticipate it in expectation, but it is still an uncertain illusion, and thus not yet ours. "We do not even know whether we will have a future. We do not know whether the time to come will be ours at all. But even if it will be, it is not ours now. We are only moving towards it."[85] In this regard, the future is even more obscure and less ours than the past. According to Barth, however, the most obscure of all is the present, right now, the time which seems to be most securely ours. Then, what is the present? The past and the future have at least duration, but the present does not. It is just an instant, a moment between the vanished past and the unknown future. "It is the time between the times, . . . [It] is no time at all, no duration, no series of moments, but only the boundary between past and future, a boundary which is never stationary, but always shifts further ahead. It is the moment we can never prevail upon to stay, for always it has already gone or not yet come."[86] Therefore, in the present we do not have time, for it is an empty moment. As a result, there is no "real time" for the lost man at all.[87] Our time is totally lost and empty. As we have seen, Barth's understanding of the uncertainty of human time experiences as such is similar to that of Augustine. However, Barth does not appeal to human consciousness in order to resolve the riddle of time as did Augustine.[88] Rather, according to Barth, our true knowledge of time can be available

---

82. Ibid.
83. *CD*, III.2, 513.
84. Ibid.
85. Ibid.
86. Ibid., 514.
87. In Barth's own words, "We do not have it at any time; that we no longer have the past, do not yet have the future and certainly do not have the present, because it is only the step from the one darkness to the other." Ibid., 516.
88. For Augustine's understanding of time, see Augustine, *Confessions*, 209–31.

not from our fallen mind or any exploration of our time experience but only through the time of Jesus Christ, the "true man" (*vere homo*).

The Time of Jesus Christ: God's Eternity in Time

K. Barth's conception of time is characteristically a "theological" understanding in that it is essentially focused on the time of revelation in Jesus Christ. This is Barth's "particular standpoint" for the understanding of human time as well as for understanding God's eternity.[89] Apart from God's revelation, as a fallen man, we cannot truly understand the nature of time. Therefore, Barth asserts that, "we must let ourselves be told what time is by revelation itself."[90] Our true knowledge of time is only available in God's revelation, the unique event of Jesus Christ. For Barth, the statement, "God reveals Himself" is equivalent to "God has time for us." As he says, "The time God has for us is just this time of His revelation, the time that is real in His revelation, revelation time."[91] Therefore, in order to understand God's eternity as well as human time, Barth asserts that, "we must take our bearings first and decisively from the man Jesus in His time."[92] In this sense, Barth rejects any metaphysical or scientific conception of time which pursues the nature of time by examining human experience through the phenomenological investigation of human existence (e.g., Augustine and Heidegger).[93] It cannot be a precondition for investigating the concept of revelation time.

According to Barth, God's revelation is the event of Jesus Christ, and this event had its own time.[94] Therefore, the time of revelation is "God's time, the time He has for us, the time of Jesus Christ."[95] In dis-

---

89. *CD*, III.2, 439. For this, Barth says, "in the interpretation of the concept of this time, which is now our task, we shall not have to take as a basis any time concept gained independently of revelation itself. If our consideration of the question as to the time of revelation is serious, we shall at once be aware (1) that we have no other time than the time God has for us, and (2) that God has no other time for us than the time of revelation. Thus we must let ourselves be told what time is by revelation itself, and only then, and with that reference, from our idea of the time of revelation as such." *CD*, I.2, 45.

90. *CD*, I.2, 45.

91. Ibid.

92. *CD*, III.2, 439.

93. Cf. *CD*, I.2, 45–46.

94. Cf. ibid., 49.

95. Ibid.

Time, Eternity, and the Trinity in the Theology of Karl Barth 213

tinguishing both the time of creation and our lost time, Barth called the time of revelation "the third time" and "the real time." In contrast to our lost and empty time, the time of Jesus Christ is "the real" and "the fulfilled" time, which is expected in the Old Testament and fulfilled in the New Testament.[96] For Barth, in John 1:14, "the Word became flesh" also means that "the Word became time."[97] The Word, the eternal Son of God, became flesh, and thus He is with us and among us in our human time. He says, "Becoming flesh, it [i.e., the Word] clothed itself with time, the time of a man's life."[98] Without ceasing to be what He is (i.e., the eternal Word), He also becomes what we are (i.e., the temporal man). Jesus Christ is "very God" (i.e., the true eternal God) and "very man" (i.e., the true and real temporal man).[99] In this sense, the statement, "God has time for us" in His revelation means that God gives Himself to us in time.[100] This is the very meaning of the incarnation of the eternal Son of God in our earthly time. Without ceasing to be the eternal God, He has made Himself a worldly, human, temporal God in the man Jesus, and therefore He is *vere Deus vere homo*.

Therefore, the time of Jesus Christ is constituted by "the lifetime of a man," which is really a section of our "historical time" or "world history." Concerning this point, Barth says, "It does not remain transcendent over time, it does not merely meet it at a point, but it enters time; nay, it assumes time; nay, it creates time for itself."[101] The events in the earthly life of Jesus Christ are genuinely temporal and therefore as temporally determined and limited as any other real events in our temporal space. "Like all men, the man Jesus has His life time: the time bounded at one end by His birth and at the other by His death; a fixed span with a particular duration within the duration of created time as a whole; the time

---

96. Cf. ibid. As Barth says, "If God's revelation has a time also, if God has time for us, if we really (really, in a theologically relevant sense) know and possess time, it must be a different time, a third time, created alongside of our time and the time originally created by God." Ibid., 47.

97. Ibid., 50.

98. *CD*, III.1, 73.

99. *CD*, I.2, 132.

100. Barth explains this as follows, "When I really give anyone my time, I thereby give him the last and most personal thing that I have to give at all, namely myself." Ibid., 55.

101. Ibid., 50.

for His being as the soul of His body."[102] In the early Christian creed, the particular location of Jesus's time is typically expressed by "the *passus sub Pontio Pilato*."[103] Therefore, no one can deny the reality of the time of Jesus Christ. If we deny His real temporality, then we cannot but fall into Docetism.

Jesus Christ, the Lord of Time

As we have seen, the time of revelation, the time of Jesus Christ, is genuine time, an indication that God has real time for us in our lost time. The time of Jesus Christ is the time of the Lord: "Compared with our time it is mastered time and for that very reason real, fulfilled time."[104] Jesus lives in His time "once for all" not only as the Judge for God, but as the Representative for men. Jesus Christ is "Alpha *and* Omega, the beginning *and* the end, the first *and* the last" at the same time.[105] The time of Jesus Christ, as God's time for us, acquires simultaneously the present, the past and the future. He is the One who "was, and is, and is to come" (Rev 4:8). "It makes this life at once the centre and the beginning and end of all the times of all the lifetimes of all men."[106] Even though Jesus lives in His own particular time location in world history, He is the Contemporary of all men because "He lives for God and for them all."[107] Therefore, "He belongs to all times simultaneously. He is the same Christ in all of them. There is no time which does not belong to Him."[108] In this sense, Jesus Christ is really the Lord of time. As Barth says,

> It is because the Word was made flesh, the Eternal entered time, that the man Jesus is the Lord of time, and His time is the fulfillment of time, embracing all time, the first and last time which in every present is His own time. As there can be no repetition of

---

102. *CD*, III.2, 440.

103. *CD*, I.2, 51. Cf. *CD*, III.2, 441.

104. *CD*, I.2, 52.

105. Ibid., 53.

106. *CD*, III.2, 440. For Barth's detailed description of the likeness and difference between our lost time and the time of Jesus Christ, see ibid., 463–64.

107. Ibid., 440.

108. Ibid., 466.

the being of this man, there can be no repetition of this human being in time.[109]

As the Lord of all time, Jesus Christ is the Healer of our lost time, for His time takes "the place of our non-genuine and improper time as genuine, proper time."[110] He re-creates and heals the wounds of our lost time, which is the emptiness and the ever fleetingness of the present, and the deep separation of past and the future from one another and from the present.[111] Therefore, it is the time of grace itself, the time in which God's covenant takes place. Accordingly, "the lifetime of Jesus is this time of salvation," and, it is salvation for our lost time as well.[112] It is the Messianic time of redemption. "With the commencement of this time, our lost time as such is both condemned to perish but also transformed and renewed."[113] With the coming of Jesus as the Bearer of God's good news, our lost time is fulfilled, and the kingdom of God is at hand. And this implies that "the eschatological salvation is no longer just a future expectation, but a present reality."[114] In the time of Jesus Christ, the Son and the Head of all things, "all time is brought to an end and begins afresh as full and proper time."[115] Thus, the time of Jesus Christ as the Lord of time is the time of God's grace for the fulfillment of our lost time. Barth says, "The *raison d'etre* of all time, both past and future, is that there should be this fulfillment at this particular time."[116] With the coming of Jesus Christ, the law, all the promises and prophesies of the Old Testament were fulfilled. For the phrase, "the time is fulfilled" (Mark 1:15), is undoubtedly meant to describe an absolutely unique event marking the ending of the old time and the beginning of the new time.[117] Barth explains this as follows:

> The Son of God "came"; He was sent from God, sent to men. Therefore He was Himself "born of a woman, born under the

---

109. Ibid., 512.
110. *CD*, I.2, 66.
111. Cf. *CD*, II.1, 617.
112. *CD*, III.2, 441.
113. *CD*, III.1, 73.
114. *CD*, III.2, 460.
115. Ibid., 462.
116. Ibid., 459.
117. Cf. ibid., 460.

> law." He entered the temporality which is that of each and every man. . . . The mission of the Son actually brings the fullness of time with it, and not *vice versa*. With the mission of the Son, with His entry into the time process, a new era of time has dawned, so far-reaching in its consequences that it may be justly called the fullness of time. Man has now reached maturity. He has become God's son and heir, the "Lord of all." He has become a free man. This is the event which gives time its fullness. . . . This fulfilled time is before or after all other time. Hence it makes all time, *Chronos* as such, in the sequence and succession of which this fulfillment was achieved, fulfilled time. . . . Henceforth all time can be regarded only as time fulfilled in this particular time.[118]

With Jesus Christ's death on the cross the old (our condemned and lost) time, has passed, and, at the same time, with His resurrection from the dead the new and real time has appeared. In this sense, the real time, the prototype of time, is not the time of creation, but "the lifetime of Jesus Christ, the turning point, the transition, the decision which were accomplished in His death and resurrection."[119] As the Lord of time, He normalizes our lost time, He heals its wounds, and He fulfills and makes it real and proper time. And then, "He returns it to us in order that we might have it again as 'our time.'"[120] Since He invites us to His genuine real time in faith, we, too, can have the real time again in Him and by Him. This real time, which we have in Jesus Christ, is God's time of grace. In Jesus Christ, God creates "His time of grace—the time of His covenant with man" for our lost time, and, in doing so, He exalted our condemned time "as a new and true and fulfilled time, i.e., a time ruled by God."[121] Accordingly, Barth says that, "In this way the time of grace, the time of Jesus Christ, is the clear and perfect counterpart of the time of creation. Like it, and in contrast to 'our' empty time, it is fulfilled time."[122]

---

118. Ibid., 459.
119. *CD*, III.1, 76.
120. Ibid., 74.
121. Ibid., 73.
122. Ibid., 75.

God's Eternity in Human Time

According to Barth, the time of Jesus Christ is not only the time of man, but also the time of God (i.e., eternal time).[123] It is "the time which God has assumed for us, and thus granted to us, the men of all times; the time of His covenant; or, as the Bible sees it, the great Sabbath; the year of salvation; fulfilled time."[124] Therefore, it is the particular time, in which God's eternity dwells in our human time. God is really in our time, but He is also the Lord of time as the Eternal God. That is to say, "He is temporal in unity and correspondence with His eternity."[125] Furthermore, Jesus's lordship over time is clearly manifested in His "second history," the Easter time, of the forty days between His resurrection and ascension. What is the implication of the Easter time of Jesus Christ as the Resurrected? For this, Barth says that,

> Jesus is the Lord of time in the sense expounded because He is the Son of God, and as such the eternal God in person, the Creator of all time and therefore its sovereign Ruler. Either He is this, or He is not the Lord of time at all. But we insist that He is the Lord of time because He has revealed Himself as such, because in the resurrection His appearance has proved to be that of the eternal God. Otherwise we have no grounds for making this claim, and it is better not to pretend that we have.[126]

Particularly enough, therefore, the Easter time of Jesus Christ is the clearest manifestation of God's eternity in human time, for "in this time the *man* Jesus was manifested among them in the mode of *God*. It is essential to a true understanding that both His humanity and His deity should be kept in view."[127] In these forty days, the presence of the man Jesus in the mode of God is "the total, final, irrevocable and eternal

---

123. For this point, Barth says that, "According to Is. 40:8 the Word of our God 'abideth for ever.' And according to Jn. 1:14 this Word became flesh. And according to the entire New Testament witness, it remained flesh even in His resurrection. It is still flesh even in His glory at the right of God the Father. Therefore eternity . . . is not apart from time. So the time God has for us, as distinguished from our time that comes into being and passes away, is to be regarded as eternal time." *CD*, I.2, 50.

124. *CD*, III.2, 462, cf. 464.

125. Ibid., 519.

126. Ibid., 464–65.

127. Ibid., 448 (italics original).

manifestation of God Himself."[128] At the same time, it is "the concrete demonstration of the God who has not only a different time from that of man, but whose will and resolve it is to give man a share in this time of His, in His eternity."[129] Therefore, with His Easter time, in the whole earthly lifetime of the man Jesus, "God was in Christ" (2 Cor 5:19). In this sense, it is "the heart of all other times" because of the clearest appearance and presence of God's eternity in our human time. In other words, God's eternity was really and truly in the time of Jesus Christ for reconciling our lost time to His true and real time, the eternal time.

> It is the Lord of time who became temporal and had time: His own time at the heart of all the times of the being created by Him; and this time in the same way as He had it in Himself before all created being, as He will have it with all created being when the time of this being is over. Here, in this creature, in this man, who had His own time of life and death, and beyond this His time of revelation, God, the Creator and Lord, had already had time before His time, eternal time. It is the time which He took to Himself, thus granting it as a gift to the men of all time. It is the time which He willed to have for us in order to inaugurate and establish His covenant. It is the time which is the time of all times because what God does in it is the goal of all creation and therefore of all created time. Since God in His Word had time for us, and at the heart of all other times there was this particular time, the eternal time of God, all other times are now controlled by this time, i.e., dominated, limited and determined by their proximity to it.[130]

The presence of God's eternity in human time has some significant insights for our understanding of time. On the one hand, it means that, "God Himself once took time and thus treated it as something real."[131] Therefore, the existence of the man Jesus in time is our guarantee that time as the form of our existence is real, not a mere illusion, form, abstraction, or figment of our imagination as assumed by many philosophical theories of time.[132] It is willed and created by God, and is given to us by God. Time is actually "the formal principle of His free activity

---

128. Ibid., 449.
129. Ibid., 450–51.
130. Ibid., 455.
131. Ibid., 456.
132. Cf. ibid., 455–56 and 520.

outwards,"¹³³ and thus it is the field for God's action in His covenant with us and for His works in creation, revelation and salvation for us. Even more, in the fulfilling and surpassing of creation in Jesus Christ, "God actually takes time to Himself and makes it His own. He raises time to a form of His own eternal being."¹³⁴ On the other hand, however, in a critical sense, the presence of God's eternity in human time manifests that "there is no such thing as absolute time, no immutable law of time.... There is no time in itself, rivaling God and imposing conditions on Him. There is no god called Chronos."¹³⁵ Accordingly, time *per se* does not have any "independence or autonomy" over, against and apart from the eternal Creator.¹³⁶ Rather, it demonstrates the fact that God Himself, as the Creator, the Reconciler and the Redeemer, is the Lord of time. God has all power over time because He is God, the Creator and the Ruler over time, in His eternity.¹³⁷ Therefore, our response should be one of praise for His complete lordship over time, and confession that, "My times are in thy hands" (Ps 31:15).

K. Barth's Understanding of God's Eternity: Eternity as the Form of the Triune God's Existence

In *The Epistle to the Romans*, Barth emphasized the absolute difference between God and man by the phrase "the infinite qualitative distinction" between God's eternity and human time. In his *Church Dogmatics*, however, Barth's understanding of God's eternity is modified as a dynamic form according to his Trinitarian dialectic analogical thinking.¹³⁸

133. *CD*, II.1, 609.

134. Ibid., 616.

135. *CD*, III.2, 456.

136. Concerning this point, Barth further states that, "In Jesus Christ it comes about that God takes time to Himself, that He Himself, the eternal One, becomes temporal [without ceasing to be eternity] ... [Therefore,] No contraction or diminution of deity takes place, but the true and fullest power of deity is displayed, in the fact that it has such power over itself and its creatures that it can become one with it without detriment to itself." *CD*, II.1, 616.

137. Cf. ibid., 609.

138. In this sense, Roberts points out that, "The change from a negative to a positive appreciation of the importance of the concept of eternity in relation to time is one gauge of the degree of transformation in Barth's theological thought." Idem, "Karl Barth's Doctrine of Time," 100.

In this case, for Barth, his comprehensive Trinitarian thinking opened a possibility for a dynamic and positive understanding of God's eternity and its relation to time. In this sense, G. Hunsinger rightly points out the following:

> God's time is as ineffable for Barth as the doctrine of the Trinity that gives it form. Barth makes perhaps the first sustained attempt in history to reformulate eternity's mystery in full trinitarian terms. The mystery of eternity becomes in effect a subtopic in the mystery of the Trinity. Eternity holds no perplexities that cannot be stated in trinitarian terms, and the Trinity has no formal aspects irrelevant to the question of eternity, so that the form of the Trinity and the form of eternity coincide. Barth unfolds the mystery of God's eternal time within a fully trinitarian framework.[139]

First of all, as he defined time as the form of human existence and of other creatures,[140] now, Barth defines eternity as the form of the Triune God's existence. That is, as Barth asserts, eternity is "the form of the divine being in its triunity."[141] Without creation, "God's being remains in His eternal triune essence, in His entirely different form of existence, on His own unsearchable way . . . [in] His inner glory."[142] As we have seen, for Barth, life and time are inseparable from one another. Therefore, "God lives eternally," and thus "eternity is the living God Himself."[143] Without creation, God has His own inner life in the *perichoresis*, the mutual inner relationship of the Triune God; the Father, the Son, and the Holy Spirit. However, according to Barth, even the inner life of the eternal Triune God is not timeless, but, essentially, "God has and is Himself time . . . in His essence as the triune God."[144] Barth insists therefore that,

> Eternity is the dimension of God's own life, the life in which He is self-positing, self-existent and self-sufficient as Father, Son and

---

139. Hunsinger, "*Mysterium Trinitatis*," 169.

140. Barth says that, "Time, in contradiction to eternity, is the form of existence of the creature" (*CD*, III.1, 67), and also time is "the form of our existence and our world" (*CD*, II.1, 613). Cf. *CD*, III.2, 558.

141. *CD*, II.1, 615.

142. *CD*, III.1, 69.

143. *CD*, II.1, 639, 640.

144. Ibid., 615.

Holy Ghost. It is this in contrast to time as the dimension of our life—the dimension in which past, present and future follow in succession. Eternity is not created. Eternity is God Himself. For as God is self-existent, He is also His own dimension. But time is willed and created by God as a reality distinct from Himself.[145]

As in classical theism, for Barth, eternity is God's essence, and thus God Himself.[146] Therefore, Barth thinks of God's eternity as a quality of His absolute freedom.[147] Accordingly, Barth deals with this idea of God's eternity in the section on "the Perfections of the Divine Freedom" in his *Doctrine of God*.[148] According to Barth, while time is "the formal principle of His free activity outwards," eternity is "the principle of His freedom inwards."[149] Hence eternity is God's essence, as in Anselm's view, which is the same principle for the other divine attributes: divine unity, uniqueness and simplicity, and so forth.[150] As Barth states,

> [Eternity] is not only a quality which He possesses. It is not only a space in which He dwells. It is not only a form of being in which He shares, so that it could belong, if need be, to other realities as well, or exist apart from Him in itself.... Eternity is the Living God Himself. This radically distinguishes the Christian knowledge of eternity from all religious and philosophical reflection on time and what might exist before and after time.... We have simply to think of God Himself, recognizing and ador-

---

145. *CD*, III.2, 526.

146. As Barth says, "it is the essence of God Himself; in this way God is Himself eternity." *CD*, III.1, 67.

147. Cf. *CD*, II.1, 608. Concerning this point, Barth defines God's eternity as follows, "eternity in itself and as such is to be understood as a determination of the divine freedom. Like the unity and constancy of God, it primarily denotes the absolute sovereignty and majesty of God in itself and as such, as demonstrated in the inward and outward activity of His divine being and operative in His love as His, the eternal love. God's love requires and possesses eternity both inwards and outwards for the sake of its divinity, its freedom. Correspondingly, it requires, creates and therefore possesses in its outward relations what we call time. Time is the form of creation in virtue of which it is definitely fitted to be a theatre for the acts of divine freedom." *CD*, II.1, 464–65.

148. Cf. *CD*, II.1, 608–77.

149. Ibid., 609.

150. Barth also says that, "As the eternal One God is the One who is unique and one with Himself. He is also present to Himself and therefore omnipresent. Again, as the eternal One God is constant, and He is also the One who omnipotently knows and wills." Ibid., 609.

ing and loving the Father, the Son and the Holy Spirit. It is only in this way that we know eternity. For eternity is His essence.[151]

Therefore, Barth says that "to say eternity is to say God."[152] However, more significantly, as he rejected *analogia entis*, Barth rejects the traditional doctrine of God which is based on the concept of being. At this point, Barth replaces the static concept of being or substance by his own concept of God as the Being-in-action. In doing so, Barth makes eternity as the essence of God as the Being-in-action, and thus the source of the deity of God. The following statement clearly demonstrates this:

> Eternity is the source of the deity of God in so far as this consists in His freedom, independence and lordship. At the very place at which later theology fell under the influence of Greek philosophy and made the concept of being predominant, the Bible speaks of the eternal God. According to the Bible it is not being as such, but that which endures, duration itself, which is the divine. It is this which also characterizes and distinguishes the holiness and righteousness and wisdom of God, and also His grace and mercy and patience, or in a word, His love as divine. Eternity is before and after, above and below being. Being does not include eternity, but eternity includes being. The genuineness of being is examined and weighed and measured and tested by eternity. It is being or non-being according to its relation to eternity. God Himself is eternal, and for that reason and in that way He is.[153]

However, for Barth, we cannot properly understand God's eternity apart from His revelation, the time of Jesus Christ, because He is the true manifestation of God and His eternity. Without His revelation, our investigation of God's eternity will be a mere human abstraction. Therefore, as Barth describes the nature of human time from the time of Jesus Christ, he tries to conceive the nature of God's eternity from the time of Jesus Christ, not from any other human metaphysics, sciences, or any other enterprises. According to Barth, in Rev 1:8, "I am the Alpha and the Omega, saith the Lord, which is, and which was, and which is to come, the Almighty," the speaker is God in His identity with the man Jesus, and the context does not speak of a timeless being, but a being in

---

151. Ibid., 638–39.
152. *CD*, III.2, 558.
153. *CD*, II.1, 610.

time who has His own life. That is to say, "Here is no timeless being, but a strictly temporal one, though of course it differs from all other temporal being as that which is divinely temporal."[154] Similarly, the divine formulae in Exod 3:14, "I am that I am," too, speaks of "a being in time, but the reference is to the divine being, the being of Yahweh, in time." In connecting the two passages, according to Barth, this means that,

> I am He who has life in Himself. That is to say, I am sovereign over my being. Even as present I am He who was and will be. All this applied to the being of the man Jesus in time. The all-inclusive "I am" rules out any notion that the three dimensions, present, past and future, simply follow one another in succession.... It means: "I am all this simultaneously. I, the same, am; I was as the same; and I will come again as the same. My time is always simultaneously present, past and future." That is why I am the Alpha and Omega, the beginning and the ending, the first and the last. Since my present includes the past and the future it is both the first and last at all other times. All times have their source and end in my time. Of course, all these other times are real times, for at the heart of them I have time. But other times are previous or subsequent to mine. They are overshadowed, dominated and divided into periods by my time. It is my present that makes them either past or future, for my present includes both. I was, and I am to come, as surely as I am and live. ...As I am in my time, all time is my time, my before or after.[155]

Therefore, as God Himself was manifested in the time of Jesus Christ, eternity is not a mere negation of time, and thus it is not timeless at all. In His revelation, in the time of Jesus Christ, God is the eternal God, but not the absolutely timeless God of the Greeks, rather He also reveals Himself as the temporal God, who is the covenant-partner with Israel and human beings in time.[156] In another place, Barth states, "Eternity in which He Himself is true time and the Creator of all time is revealed in the fact that, although our time is that of sin and death, He can enter it and Himself be temporal in it, yet without ceasing to be eternal, able rather to be the Eternal in time."[157]

154. *CD*, III.2, 465.
155. Ibid., 465–66.
156. Cf. *CD*, I.2, 66.
157. *CD*, IV.1, 187–88.

Eternity as God's Time

According to Barth, as we have seen, only God is eternal, but eternity itself is not any more timeless. For Barth, God is always the Being-in-action. He is in His action and works. The conception of Barth's "the Being-in-action" has "immediate temporal implications."[158] Accordingly, Barth says that, as expected, "God has time because and as He has eternity."[159] However, it is certainly not the same time that we have, the created time, relative time, unauthentic time, and the lost time. Rather, in Barth's view, God's eternity is the true, real, supreme, authentic, and absolute time. As Barth asserts, "He is supremely temporal." In this sense, God's eternity is the authentic temporality, the uncreated self-subsistent time, which is one of the perfections of His divine nature.[160] He asserts that, therefore, eternity is "first and foremost God's time and therefore real time."[161] In saying that, even Barth asserts that, "it is itself temporal, and would be so even if no time existed apart from it."[162] In this way, Barth defines eternity as God's time, which is the form of His existence as the Triune God.[163] We can clearly see Barth's dynamic and constructive understanding of God's eternity in the following statement:

> Eternity is not merely the negation of time. It is not in any way timeless. On the contrary, as the source of time it is supreme and absolute time, i.e., the immediate unity of present, past and future; of now, once and then; of the centre, beginning and end; of movement, origin and goal. In this way it is the essence of God Himself; in this way God is Himself eternity. Thus God Himself is temporal, precisely in so far as He is eternal, and His eternity is the prototype of time, and as the Eternal He is simultaneously before time, above time, and after time.[164]

---

158. Roberts, "Karl Barth's Doctrine of Time," 110.
159. *CD*, II.1, 611.
160. Cf. *CD*, III.2, 437–38.
161. *CD*, II.1, 613.
162. Ibid., 620.

163. In so doing, Barth criticizes the traditional view of eternity as timelessness or non-temporality. Therefore, he insists that, "The theological concept of eternity must be set free from the Babylonian captivity of an abstract opposite to the concept of time." Ibid., 611.

164. *CD*, III.1, 67–68.

Then, what is the nature of eternity as God's time? At first, in Barth's view, the decisive characteristic of eternity as God's time is its "pure duration" and "simultaneity." That is to say, in His eternity, the three occasions of beginning, succession and end (or past, present and future) are not three but one, not separate as a first, a second and a third occasion, but only one simultaneous occasion. Therefore, as Barth summarizes, "Eternity is the simultaneity of beginning, middle and end, and the extent of it is pure duration."[165] Eternity has and is pure duration and simultaneity, which is lacking to human time.[166] In God's time, what Barth emphasized as the simultaneity of the three particularities of the past, the present, and the future in one unity can be fully understood only in trinitarian terms. Accordingly, while Barth accepted Boethius' classical definition of God's eternity, "*tota simul perfecta possessio vitae*,"[167] he reformulated it within his trinitarian framework. That is, for Barth, this par excellent definition of God's eternity can be fully conceived only in the doctrine of the Trinity. In a similar sense, the following observation by G. Hunsinger is equally correct.

> What Barth does with this definition, in effect, is simply to relocate it within an explicit doctrine of the Trinity. Life and simultaneity are, as we have seen, ideas that Barth associates with the Trinitarian *perichoresis*. Totality, perfection, and possession are, in turn, ideas that correlate with the simplicity, singularity, and sovereignty of the Trinitarian *ousia*. From this standpoint the one strikingly new element in the definition is "interminability." The definition states not merely that the divine life is endless or unlimited, but that it cannot possibly terminate, that it knows no possible dissolution, not only no tendency but no possible

---

165. *CD*, II.1, 608.

166. Cf. ibid., 608. In this way, God's time is eternity. There is "no fixed, no margins, no other measure but Himself." *CD*, III.2, 558. In another place, therefore, Barth adds that, "Eternity simply lacks the fleeting nature of the present, the separation between before and after. Eternity is certainly the negation of created time in so far as it has no part in the problematical and questionable nature of our possession of time, our present and our beginning, continuation and ending. But eternity is not the negation of time *simpliciter*. On the contrary, time is absolutely presupposed in it. Eternity is the negation of time only because and to the extent that it is first and foremost God's time and therefore real time, in the same way as God's omnipresence is not simply the negation of our space, but first and foremost is positively God's space and therefore real space." Ibid., 613.

167. Ibid., 614. Here, Barth critically accepts Boethius' definition of God's eternity, "Total, simultaneous and complete possession of unlimited life." Ibid., 611.

tendency toward nonbeing. Therefore the definition of eternity does not depend on the negation of time.[168]

However, even though Hunsinger just says that "Barth . . . *simply* relocate[s] it within an explicit doctrine of the Trinity," in my judgment, this is a very significant contribution to Christian theology by K. Barth. That is, in combining both his dialectic analogical thinking and this Trinitarian thinking, Barth opened a new way toward a Trinitarian analogical understanding of God's eternity and its relation to time. Therefore, this can be considered a "Copernican turning point" in conceiving God's eternity and its relation to time.

In Barth's conception of the Triune God's time, the eternal God Himself, as the true duration, is the beginning, succession and end, all at once in His own essence. In His own time, the Triune God is *tota simul* "between present, past, and future, between 'not yet,' 'now' and 'no more,' between rest and movement, potentiality and actuality, whither and whence, here and there, this and that."[169] Therefore, God is the *nunc*, the pure present.[170] This is Barth's temporal interpretation of the "the one God in threefold repetition" of the Triune God in eternity, who is "[the] One in three distinctive modes of being subsisting in their mutual relationship: Father, Son, Holy Spirit."[171] In His unity, the Triune God; the Father, the Son and the Holy Spirit, "all" is pure duration, undividedly beginning, succession and end, all at once in "the *nunc aeternitatis*." As God's time, therefore, eternity is not static, but dynamic in its perfection, unlike our time. Barth explains this as follows:

> Yet in it there is order and succession. The unity is in movement. There is a before and an after. God is once and again and a third time, without dissolving the once-for-allness, without destroy-

---

168. Hunsinger, "*Mysterium Trinitatis*," 179.

169. *CD*, II.1, 612.

170. Ibid., 611.

171. *CD*, I.1, 348, 350. According to Barth, God is "the one God, i.e., the one Lord, the one personal God." *CD*, I.1, 359. However, God is not just in one mode, "but this one God is God three times in different ways, so different that it is only in this threefold difference that He is God, so different that this difference, this being in these three modes of being, is absolutely essential to Him." *CD*, I.1, 360. "The threeness of the one God," says Barth, "is the threeness of revealer, revelation and being revealed, the threeness of God's holiness, mercy and love, the threeness of the God of Good Friday, Easter and Whitsunday, the threeness of God the Creator, God the Reconciler and God the Redeemer." *CD*, I.1, 361–62.

ing the persons or their special relations to one another, without anything arbitrary in this relationship or the possibility of its reversal. If in this triune being and essence of God there is nothing of what we call time, this does not justify us in saying that time is simply excluded in God, or that His essence is simply a negation of time. On the contrary, the fact that God has and is Himself time, and the extent to which this is so, is necessarily made clear to us in His essence as the triune God. This is His time, the absolutely real time, the form of the divine being in its triunity.[172]

In this sense, we can only properly understand Barth's following statements in trinitarian terms: "Eternity is the living God Himself," and "God's eternity is itself beginning, succession and end."[173] And, in this way, eternity, as God's time which is "the absolutely real time," is "the form of the divine being in its triunity."[174]

Furthermore, concerning its relation to human time, Barth describes eternity in the following three specific terms of "the pre-temporality, supra-temporality and post-temporality of eternity."[175] That is to say, "He, His eternity itself, is able to be before it, above it and after it."[176] For Barth, each of these terms corresponds to the following three distinct stages of the word time: "creation as the basis of man's existence established by God, reconciliation as the renewal of his existence accomplished by God, [and] redemption as the revelation of his existence to be consummated by God."[177] In this way, according to Barth, it is the summary of the whole content of the Gospel and the Christian message, which is revealed in God's eternity and its relation to time.

At first, by the "pre-temporality" of eternity, Barth denotes the eternal God's ontological priority and the absolute divine freedom from ob-

172. CD, II.1, 615.
173. CD, III.2, 526 and CD, II.1, 611.
174. CD, II.1, 615.
175. Ibid., 619. By using these terms, Barth describes the Biblical idea, which is "God as the One who is and rules before time, in time and again after time, the One who is not conditioned by time, but conditions it absolutely in His freedom. He does this in a threefold respect. He precedes its beginning, He accompanies its duration, and He exists after its end. This is the concrete form of eternity as readiness for time. It is God's power, indeed God Himself, who has the power to exist before, above and after time, before its beginning, above its duration and after its end" (ibid).
176. Ibid., 620.
177. Ibid.

ligation to His creatures. It is God's "pre-time," which precedes all other beginnings, and thus it designates the divine "pre-existence," which precedes all other creatures. And also, it is "the pure time of the Father and the Son in the fellowship of the Holy Spirit" without creation.[178] In addition, it is the time, more correctly the "before-time" (i.e., "once" before all time), for God's pre-determination and fore-ordination of everything, including time itself. Only in this sense, it is God's eternity in the aspect of "the absolute readiness for time."[179] That is, for Barth, God's time as eternity is not an accidental temporality, but it in itself is essentially the form of the Triune God's existence from eternity to eternity.

Secondly, the "supra-temporality" of eternity means essentially "the perpendicular relationship" with each present, or each single part of our time. It is the divine "Now," as the *nunc aeternitas*, over the time sequence. According to Barth, however, for the completeness of the idea, this term must be used with "co-temporality," and "in-temporality" because he wants to express with these terms the idea that "eternity is the element which embraces time on all sides."[180] This means God's omnipresence or omni-temporality in our time. That is, God endures in His pure and perpetual duration, which accompanies the fleeting duration of our time. God's eternity is in our time, and also time itself is in His eternity, just like "a child in the arm of its mother."[181] In this sense, according to Barth, "All time is really in His hands."[182] Therefore, all of our actions in each moment of time sequence have a direct meaning and responsibility in relation to God.

Finally, the "post-temporality" of eternity means that God is the "after-time," and that God will exist after all time, each time, and everything. In time, everything will have reached its goal and end, and then there is eternity as the goal and the end, the *eschaton*, beyond which any other goal and end cannot exist.[183] At the end of all time, there is God's eternity and God Himself because He is the Last. There is no life, no history in time, which can end at any other point than in Him as its fulfillment and its judgment. Therefore, God is "the absolute, unsurpass-

---

178. *CD*, II.1, 622. Cf. *CD*, I.1, 426–27.
179. Cf. *CD*, II.1, 618.
180. Ibid., 623.
181. Ibid.
182. Ibid., 625.
183. Cf. ibid., 629.

able future of all time and of all that is in time."[184] In this absolute future of our time, God's revelation will be completed and the kingdom of God will be drawn fully. After all time, and thus in God's post-temporal eternity, there is no veil any more, and thus every eye shall see "the One who is all in all." Then, Barth says, "God is also post-temporal eternity, the eternity to which we move."[185] There is no new horizon, and it is the perfection of God Himself in His post-temporality.

However, for Barth, it must emphasize that these three forms of God's eternity cannot be separate from or opposite to one another. Furthermore, we cannot and must not overemphasize one over the others. If we do so, then we cannot but fall into a dangerous one-sidedness. According to Barth, in church history, many theological mistakes have taken place in this one-sided emphasis. For example, in the sixteenth century, the Reformers' theology overemphasized the pre-temporality of God's eternity, and thus they eventually overemphasized the doctrine of election and divine providence. In doing so, it made God's supra-temporality or co-temporality a kind of appendix. Then, as a partial reaction against the one-sidedness of emphasis a pre-temporality, eighteenth- and nineteenth-century Protestant anthropocentric theology paid too much attention to man in time, and therefore God's supra-temporality. In this case, God's pre-temporality has only a partial significance as a mere introduction, and God's post-temporality, i.e., eschatology, also remained as a mere appendix. Finally, at the end of the nineteenth and the beginning of the twentieth century, as a third reaction, the post-temporality of God was re-discovered, but it also was over-emphasized as eschatological theology. As in Rom 11:36, "God is the One and all, the beginning, the middle and the end, the One who was, and is, and is to come, at perfect peace within Himself. So then, if we are to love Him and know Him, we must give Him equal attention and seriousness in all three dimensions as the source and content of all time and all that is time."[186] Therefore, Barth asserts that, "the post-temporality of God must not become the content of a mere appendix, or the pre-temporality the content of a mere introduction; and a dislike of the truth of God's supra-temporality (which is historically understandable through the misuse of this truth in the past) must not be allowed to

---

184. Ibid., 630.
185. Ibid., 631.
186. Ibid.

dictate what is said."[187] Rather, "always and everywhere and in everyway God exists as the eternal One" in the sense of the pre-temporality, the supra-temporality and the post-temporality.[188] They are "equally, truly and really" God's eternity and therefore the living God Himself.[189]

Therefore, although we cannot but understand God's eternity in each of the three modes in its particularity, God's true eternity is in its unity, a mutual interrelated particularity. However, at the same time, the three forms do not have "uniformity" in them, and thus they cannot be exchanged or confused. According to Barth, in the three distinct forms of God's time, there is really a "direction" which is irreversible, in its order of the beginning, the middle, and the end. Barth explains this point in terms of the doctrine of the Trinity: "a *preichoresis*, a mutual indwelling and interworking of the three forms of eternity."[190] In this distinction in the unity of the three forms of eternity, "God is eternal, and therefore the Creator and Lord of time, the free and sovereign God."[191] In this sense, Barth's dynamic understanding of eternity as God's time and its relation to time can be understood only in his complete Trinitarian framework.

The Relationship between God's Eternity and Human Time

In chapter 5, we saw various contemporary understandings of God's eternity and its relationship to time. Concerning those views, first of all, Barth clearly rejected the absolute timeless view of God's eternity (e.g., P. Helm), in saying that, "Eternity itself is not timeless" at all.[192] According to Barth, the eternal Triune God lives in His own time. In this sense, God is "supremely temporal."[193] In addition, we cannot simply understand God's eternity as pure or absolute timelessness because eternity became time in the true man, Jesus Christ. That is, the eternal God Himself, without ceasing to be the eternal God, took time and made it His own

---

187. Ibid., 637.
188. Ibid., 621, 623, and 631.
189. Ibid., 638, 640
190. Ibid., 640.
191. Ibid.
192. *CD*, III.2, 526. Cf. *CD*, III.1, 67.
193. *CD*, III.2, 437.

in the man Jesus Christ.[194] However, Barth rejected the everlasting view of God's eternity as well (e.g., O. Cullmann, N. Wolterstorff). As Barth clearly states, our "time is not eternity."[195] And thus, "Eternity is not, then, an infinite extension of time both backwards and forwards. Time can have nothing to do with God. The infinity of its extension cannot help it. For even and especially in this extension there is the separation and distance and contradiction which mark it as time and distinguish it from eternity as the creature from the Creator."[196] In this sense, God's time is eternity, which is not just time without beginning and end; rather God Himself is the Alpha and the Omega, the beginning and the end at the same time. Therefore, it would be wrong simply to identify God's eternity with a mere everlasting time (i.e., "time without beginning and end") because this view attributes to it "an idealized form of creaturely existence."[197]

Furthermore, Barth also rejected the accidental temporalism of God's eternity (e.g., W. L. Craig), which is the view that God is absolutely timeless in His eternity without creation, but He is temporal in and with His creation of the world and time. Concerning this view, Barth asserts an intrinsic temporality of God in saying that "God has time because and as He has eternity."[198] And again, "God's eternity is in time. Time itself is in eternity."[199] In this way, time pre-exists in God's eternity.[200] Conclusively, Barth states as follows:

> There is no place here for the reservation or secret complaint or accusation that basically and in Himself God is pure eternity [i.e., absolute timeless eternity] and therefore has no time, or that he has time for us only apparently and figuratively. Those who do not have time are those who do not have eternity either. In fact it is an illegitimate anthropomorphism to think of God as if He did not eternally have time; as if he did not have time, and therefore time for us, in virtue of His eternity.[201]

194. Cf. *CD*, II.1, 617.
195. *CD*, III.2, 526.
196. *CD*, II.1, 608.
197. *CD*, III.2, 558.
198. *CD*, II.1, 611.
199. Ibid., 623.
200. Cf. ibid., 612.
201. Ibid.

For Barth, what, then, is the exact relationship between God's eternity and human time? First, according to Barth, eternity is "the source of time." In His eternity, God has His own time in His mode of the threefold eternal God, the Father, the Son, and the Holy Spirit. In His own inner tri-personal life, the *perichoresis*, the mutual inner relationship of the Triune God, eternity as God's time is the living God Himself. However, of course, it differs from our created time, which is the form of our existence. As a created time, our time is unauthentic and relative. In contrast to our created and fallen time, God's eternity is the supreme, the authentic, and the uncreated self-subsistent time, which is one of the perfections of His divine nature, and thus His very essence, and even God Himself. Therefore, there is an incomparable infinite qualitative (not just quantitative) difference between God's eternity and human time. However, for Barth, even though time itself is God's creation, "it is undoubtedly true that God in eternity is the beginning of time."[202] Therefore, eternity as God's own time is "the source of all time."[203]

According to Barth, in a sense, eternity is also "the readiness for time." Eternity itself as God's time is not created time. It is "the absolute basis of time, and therefore absolute readiness for it."[204] In His eternity, as the perfection of His freedom, God does not need our time, and, as the Creator, does not owe us to give time. As the Reconciler, the eternal God does not need to take our time to Himself as His own. "According to His Word and work," however, "God was not satisfied merely with His pure, divine form of existence. His inner glory overflowed outwards. He speaks His Word and acts in His work with and for 'another' than Himself. This 'other' is His creature."[205] Accordingly, God has time, the true and absolute time, in His eternity. Then, He gives it to us by creating and preserving time. Finally, He takes time to Himself for us by becoming time in Jesus Christ.[206] For Barth, all of this is the grace of God and a readiness for time. In saying that, however, Barth does not mean a transition from an absolute timeless eternity to a supremely temporal eternity in God Himself.

---

202. *CD*, III.1, 68.
203. *CD*, III.2, 437. Cf. *CD*, III.1, 67.
204. *CD*, II.1, 618.
205. *CD*, III.1, 68.
206. Cf. *CD*, II.1, 618.

Time, Eternity, and the Trinity in the Theology of Karl Barth 233

In addition, in Barth's view, eternity is "the prototype of time."[207] That is, as God has His own time as the form of His existence, He gives us time as our form of existence. It means that there is an analogy, a partial correspondence within infinite difference between God's time and our time. However, as we experience it, our time (the created, relative and unauthentic time) always has "the one-way sequence, and therefore the succession and division of past, present and future; of once, now and then; of the beginning, middle and end; of origin, movement and goal."[208] In contrast to our time, God's eternity is simultaneously before time, above time, and after time. It is "pure duration" without any succession and division of past, present, and future. It is simultaneity all at once. This is the infinite qualitative difference between God's time and our time. However, "eternity does not lack absolutely what we know as present, as before and after, and therefore as time. Rather this has its ultimate and real being in the *simul* of eternity."[209] It is simply free from "all the fleetingness and the separation of what we call time."[210] In this sense, eternity as God's time is the "prototype" of our human time, and thus there is an dialectic analogical relationship between them. Barth's states, "God is both the prototype and foreordination of all being, and therefore also the prototype and foreordination of time. God has time because and as He has eternity."[211]

Therefore, according to Barth, there is a partial similarity within an infinite qualitative dissimilarity between God's eternity and human time. On the one hand, there are infinite qualitative differences. Among them, for Barth, a decisive and fundamental difference lies between "simultaneity" as the pure duration in God's time and temporal "successiveness" as ever fleetingness in our human time. On the other hand, there is also a partial similarity in that God's time is the source, the readiness, and the prototype of our time. Yet, according to Barth, "the real fellowship," between God's time and human time, and thus between the eternal God and the temporal man, is revealed and provided only by, in, and with the time of Jesus Christ. In this sense, the time of Jesus

---

207. *CD*, III.1, 67. Cf. *CD*, II.1, 611.
208. *CD*, III.1, 67.
209. *CD*, II.1, 613.
210. Ibid., 617. Cf. 613.
211. Ibid., 611.

Christ is the only true, real, and God-given analogy between God's eternity and human time. As Barth says,

> The fact that the Word became flesh undoubtedly means that, without ceasing to be eternity, in its very power as eternity, eternity became time. Yes, it became time. What happens in Jesus Christ is not simply that God gives us time, our created time, as the form of our own existence and world, as is the case in creation and in the whole ruling of the world by God as its Lord. In Jesus Christ it comes about that God takes time to Himself, that He Himself, the eternal One, becomes temporal, that He is present for us in the form of our own existence and our own world, not simply embracing our time and ruling it, but submitting Himself to it, and permitting created time to become and be the form of His eternity.[212]

However, we must remember Barth's following statement as well: "Yet even in God's fellowship with His creature, this eternity still belongs exclusively to God. In its fellowship with God the creature is permitted to taste it in one way or another, but it does not on that account itself become God and therefore eternal."[213]

At last, in my view, the following statements can be considered as a synopsis of Barth's creative and dynamic Trinitarian analogical understanding of God's eternity and its relation to time:

> We cannot understand God's eternity as pure timelessness. Since it became time, and God Himself, without ceasing to be eternal God, took time and made it His own, we have to confess that He was able to do this. He was not only able to have and give time as Creator, but in Jesus Christ He was able to be temporal. If we say that God's eternity excluded this possibility, we are not speaking of the eternity which He has revealed to us, and therefore not of God's real eternity, the true eternity. We are speaking of a poor, sham eternity. True eternity includes this possibility, the potentiality of time. True eternity has the power to take time to itself, this time, the time of the Word and Son of God. It has the power itself to be temporal in Him. We cannot deny it this power. It has exercised it in Jesus Christ. In Jesus Christ it has been revealed as its power. But this being the case we cannot understand eternity only as the negation of time. It is obvious that we are dealing with the power of the Creator and Lord of

---

212. Ibid., 616.
213. Ibid., 609.

Time, Eternity, and the Trinity in the Theology of Karl Barth

the world. It is pure power. To use it does not burden God with the being of the creature, and to apply it does not lay Him under obligation to the creature. He always maintains His superiority in it. When He subjects Himself to time He does freely what he does not have to do. He masters time.[214]

Barth continues,

> The God who does this and therefore can do it is obviously in Himself both timeless and temporal. He is timeless in that the defects of our time, its fleetingness and its separations, are alien to Him and disappear, and in Him all beginning, continuation and ending from a unique Now, steadfast yet moving, moving yet steadfast. He is temporal in that our time with its defects is not so alien to Him that He cannot take it to Himself in His grace, mercy and patience, Himself rectifying and healing it and lifting it up to the time to eternal life. The power exercised in Jesus Christ consists in His triune being.[215]

However, before closing this chapter, it is worth mentioning the following two criticisms concerning K. Barth's understanding of God's eternity and its relation to time. Barth's conception of time and eternity has been often misunderstood and criticized that it is "inconsistent" in itself and, more significantly, "incoherent" with the philosophical understanding of time. First, concerning the problem of inconsistency, A. G. Padgett writes:

> Karl Barth is passionately involved with theology [for the problem of God's eternity and time]. In a way that is typical of his "dialectical theology," Barth wants to say two things at the same time about divine eternity. On the one hand, Barth wrote: "Time has nothing to do with God" (CD, II/1, p. 608). On the other hand, he also wrote: "Even the eternal God does not live without time. He is supremely temporal" (III/2, p. 437).[216]

In a similar way, G. Hunsinger states that,

> A terminological headache may be noted at the outset. When discussing eternity, Barth's use of the word "time" can be quite ambiguous. The word's meaning sometime shifts, it seems, from one sentence to the next. A more vexing case would be difficult

---

214. Ibid., 617.
215. Ibid., 617–18.
216. Padgett, *God, Eternity and the Nature of Time*, 141.

to recall unless it were Paul's slippery use of the word *nomos* in Romans 7–8. Barth can say in one place, for example, that "Time has nothing to do with God," while also asserting that "God . . . is supremely temporal." (III/2, p.437)[217]

However, in my reading, there does not seem to be such an inconsistency in Barth. That is to say, as already argued, Barth's conception of eternity and time is essentially an analogical (i.e., in a best sense, a dialectical analogy, not just "dialectical" or "analogical") understanding. Therefore, if we neglect this point when we read Barth (at least his *Church Dogmatics*), there seems to be an inconsistency, but the fact is not likely so. That is, when Barth emphasizes an infinite qualitative difference between God's eternity and human time, he says that "Time has nothing to do with God." However, concerning a positive relationship, he says that "God . . . is supremely temporal." For Barth, therefore, there is a partial correspondence within infinite qualitative difference between God's eternity and time. In my view, this is a more proper way to understand K. Barth's conception of God's eternity and its relation to time.

A more significant criticism of K. Barth is his incoherency with the philosophical theory of time. According to Padgett's judgment, Barth's emphasis of "simultaneity" of past, present, and future in God's time (i.e., real time) implies a static (tenseless) theory of time. However, for Padgett, since the dynamic (tensed or process) theory of time is correct, Barth's doctrine of time and eternity is incoherent. Padgett states his judgment as follows:

> [In] "Barth's Doctrine of Time" . . . Real time, time as it was meant to be, excludes process. Thus just as we saw with Aquinas, Barth's doctrine of eternity and time implies the stasis theory of time, at least for "real time." . . . Unfortunately, Barth simply accepted most of the concept of timeless eternity as he found it in the tradition. His only correction is to insist that eternity is not the opposite of time. Barth still accepted the idea that God's eternal Now includes all other human times: past, present and future. And this is what leads Barth's doctrine into contradiction. . . . Barth's doctrine of time and eternity, then, is inconsistent at the very point where he accepts the traditional doctrine of divine non-temporality.[218]

---

217. Hunsinger, "*Mysterium Trinitatis*," 168.
218. Padgett, *God, Eternity and the Nature of Time*, 144–45.

However, according to B. Leftow's philosophical analysis, Barth's conception of God's time (i.e., eternity) is "not obviously inconsistent."[219] First of all, in my view, contrary Padgett's judgment, Barth's doctrine of time is essentially based on the dynamic (tensed) theory time. This is clear in that Barth characterized our time in its successiveness and fleetingness from the past through the present to the future. As Barth states, our time (i.e., the created and the lost time) always has "the one-way sequence, and therefore the succession and division of past, present and future; of once, now and then; of the beginning, middle and end; of origin, movement and goal."[220]

However, the real problem lies in Barth's conception of God's time. As we have seen, on the one hand, for Barth, the qualitative difference between God's time and our time is nothing other than its lack of successiveness of past, present, and future. It is simultaneity all at once. However, on the other hand, even in God's time, there is a succession. As he clearly says, "Yet in it there is order and succession. . . . There is a before and an after."[221] Yet, unlike our time, in God's time, the succession is in one unity, i.e., simultaneity, because it is "the form of the divine being in its triunity."[222] It is none other than the particularity of the mode of Triune God's existence. Therefore, God is essentially temporal in His own time. In my judgment, for Barth, it can be said that the mystery of God's eternity and its relation to time is the mystery of the doctrine of the Trinity, nothing more nothing less. Therefore, Barth's conception of God's eternity and time can be properly understood only in his Trinitarian framework.

Conclusion

In this study, rather than master Karl Barth's doctrine of time and eternity in its full sense and thus its applications to his whole Trinitarian theology, I focused on extracting his main idea from various places in his magnum opus, *Church Dogmatics*, and then organized it in an understandable form. In doing so, the following important points are

---

219. For his detail argument, see Leftow, "*Mysterium Trinitatis*," 198. Especially, see his detail analysis in philosophical perspective, pp. 194–201.

220. *CD*, III.1, 67.

221. *CD*, II.1, 615.

222. Ibid.

necessary for understanding Barth's conception on the theme as well as his whole theology. In Barth's theology, the problem of God's eternity and time is not an isolated doctrine, but it is a framework in order to understand his whole Trinitarian theology, from the doctrine of revelation to eschatology.[223] Also in his investigation of God's eternity and time, Barth does not begin from any abstract, metaphysical or scientific concepts of time, nor from human experience of time or even the time of creation. For Barth, this leads only to a dead end. We cannot know and understand our time as well as God's eternity apart from God's revelation. Therefore, he begins from the unmovable reality of God's self-revelation in Jesus Christ and His unique time, that is to say, "the eternal God became the temporal man in Jesus Christ for us" (i.e., eternity became time in Jesus Christ for us). In a sense, Barth's doctrine of time and eternity as well as his whole Christocentric Trinitarian theology is no more than a comprehensive theological attempt to interpret this reality of God's self-revelation in Jesus Christ.

Then, what is the core of Barth's understanding of God's eternity and its relation to time? As we have seen, Barth defined God's eternity and human time in a trinitarian analogical way. First of all, time (and its counterpart eternity) is the mode or form of existence. That is to say, God's eternity is the form of the Triune God's existence, and time is the form of the human (including all creatures) existence. Accordingly, for Barth, there is "an infinite qualitative difference" between God and man, eternity and time. In holding this, he replaced the concept of being with the concept of time/eternity in order to avoid the analogy of being. Accordingly, Barth says, "Eternity is the living God Himself" and "Time is humanity." In Barth's theology, the category of eternity and time actually replaces the category of being in classical theology since he rejected *analogia entis*. As a result, for Barth, "time, instead of being or substance as such, becomes the medium of relation and disrelation between God and man."[224]

At this point, Barth asserts his own dialectical analogy—*analogia fidei*. According to Barth, for our Christian theological investigation, a proper analogy is not *analogia entis* but only *analogia fidei*. And therefore, the concrete, real, God-given and thus true analogy is Jesus Christ,

---

223. Even though he did not actually write on the doctrine of eschatology, we can find its motive in various places in his *Church Dogmatics*.

224. Roberts, "Karl Barth's Doctrine of Time," 144–45.

vere Deus vere homo. Then, an analogy by definition denotes that there is a partial similarity in dissimilarity between two different entities or objects. Therefore, concerning our issue, there is an analogy, a similarity (i.e., a partial correspondence) within an infinite qualitative difference (dissimilarity) between God's eternity and human time. It is clearly manifested only in the time of Jesus Christ, in which God's eternity became human time. In this sense, therefore, Barth's *analogia fidei* must be a dialectical analogy, which is God-given, the true and real analogy, not ours or something else in virtue of our being.

At first, there is a similarity (i.e., a partial correspondence) between God's time and our human time. For Barth, God's eternity is not an absolute timelessness, but God is supremely temporal. The eternal God lives in His own time as the inner life of the mutual interrelationship of the Triune God. Accordingly, eternity is the Triune God's own time. As such, God's time is the true, authentic, real time. It is characterized by its pure duration in the beginning, the middle, and the end. It is divine simultaneity over past, present and future. By His nature, God is Alpha and Omega, the first and the last, and the beginning and the end. Thus, eternity is pre-, supra-, and post-temporality in its unity. In this sense, God's eternity is the source, the readiness, and the prototype of time. Barth states that, therefore, in the time of Jesus Christ, it is clearly manifested that God's eternity is in time, and thus time is also in His eternity. However, at the same time, there is also an infinite qualitative difference (i.e., dissimilarity) between God's eternity and human time, between God and the world.[225] Our time, created-time itself is not God's eternity. In this sense, "Time can have nothing to do with God."[226] God Himself, as the Creator, created time as the form of finite existence. Therefore, the eternal God alone, as the Creator and Lord of time, has time and thus the power over time. As such, our time is always characterized by succession, fleetingness, separation, and passing away. Our time is a relative, unauthentic time, and even a lost time. In this situation, God did not leave us alone in this lost time. The eternal God, without ceasing to be eternity, took our time as His own in the

---

225. Barth says, "The divine and creaturely subjects are not like or similar, but unlike. They are unlike because their basis and constitution as subjects are quite different and therefore absolutely unlike, that is not even the slightest similarity between them." *CD*, III.3, 103.

226. *CD*, II.1, 608.

God-man, Jesus Christ. Thus, eternity itself became time in the time of Jesus Christ. This is the Gospel, the Good-News for us, for Jesus's time is the time of God's revelation, the time of fulfillment, and therefore the time for the manifestation of God's grace and the time of salvation for our lost and empty time. Then, in Jesus Christ's time of fulfillment, our wounded, fallen, lost, and thus empty time is also healed, saved, fulfilled, and will be glorified in eternity (i.e., God's time). In this sense, the time of Jesus Christ is the only true analogy between God's eternity and human time. The time of Jesus Christ is not only the true eternity of God but also true human time.

Conclusively, for Barth, God's eternity is essentially temporal, but in a more correct sense, supremely temporal as the pre-, the supra- and the post-temporal. Therefore, God's time does not have any of the defects of our time, succession, fleetingness, and separation. In this sense, we can say that Barth's understanding of God's eternity is a "transcendent temporality," which is conceived according to his dialectical analogy, *analogia fidei*. In this way, Karl Barth tried to resolve the problem of God's eternity and its relation to time in his fully Trinitarian theology. In so doing, he made a turning point and set up a new way toward a trinitarian analogical understanding of God's eternity and its relation to time. As Barth believes, "The theological concept of eternity must be set free from the Babylonian captivity of an abstract opposite to the concept of time."[227] In the following chapter, we will see another significant theological achievement, that of Hans Urs von Balthasar, who more concretely paved the way, of which K. Barth began its construction, toward a trinitarian analogical understanding of God's eternity and its relation to time.

---

227. *CD*, II.1, 611.

7

Time, Eternity, and the Trinity in the Theology of Hans Urs von Balthasar

Introduction

HANS URS VON BALTHASAR (1905-1988)[1] WAS BORN IN LUCERNE, Switzerland. He had an excellent musical talent especially for the piano, and did his doctoral study in Vienna, Berlin, and Zürich on the problem of eschatology in German literature, philosophy, and culture (1928).[2] In 1929, he entered the order of the Society of Jesus, studied theology under the influence of Erich Przywara and then Henri de Lubac, and finally was ordained in the priesthood in 1936. After ordination, his first full-time assignment as a priest was to work for the Jesuit periodical, *Stimmen der Zeit* in Munich. However, because of Nazi war policy, he returned to Switzerland to be a student chaplain at the University of Basel (1940-1948). There Balthasar met Karl Barth. He also came in contact with a protestant physician, Adrienne von Speyr, who was converted to Catholicism under his direction. Balthasar, under her encouragement, also left the Society of Jesus (1950), and together they established a "secular institute," the Community of St. John (*Johannes-Gemeinschaft*).

1. For an overall introduction to H. U. von Balthasar's life and theology, see the following: Riches, *Analogy of Beauty*; Roberts, *Theological Aesthetics of Hans Urs von Balthasar*; Schindler, *Hans Urs von Balthasar*; O'Donnell, *Hans Urs von Balthasar*; McGregor and Norris, *Beauty of Christ*; Oakes, *Pattern of Redemption*; Scola, *Hans Urs von Balthasar*; Gawronski, *Word and Silence*; Kehl and Löser, *Von Balthasar Reader*; Gardner et al., *Balthasar at the End of Modernity*; Oakes and Moss, *Cambridge Companion to Hans Urs von Balthasar*.

2. Balthasar's doctoral dissertation was published as *Geschichte des eschatologischen Problems in der modernen deutschen Literatur* (Zürich: Universität Zürich, 1930), which was enlarged to a three volume work, *Apokalypse der deutschen Seele* (1937-1939).

At that time, he founded also a publishing house, *Johannes Verlag* (1947). In later years, he also co-founded a theological journal, *Internationale Katholische Zeitschrift—Communio* (1972) against a rival periodical, *Concilium*, which was under the influence of Karl Rahner.[3] Throughout his whole life, while devoting his energy to the renewal of the church and theology as a theologian, Balthasar actively worked as a secular priest, and also as a writer, translator, editor, lecturer, and publisher. Balthasar died three days before his investiture as a Cardinal by Pope John Paul II in June 1988.[4]

According to Balthasar himself, as a theologian, the central interest of his own life is "the task of renewing the Church through the formation of new communities that unite the radical Christian life of conformity to the evangelical counsels of Jesus with existence in the midst of the world, whether by practicing secular professions or through the ministerial priesthood to give new life to living communities."[5] All other activities are subordinated to this central task. In a sense, Balthasar's theological career was very unusual in that he worked as an isolated theologian. He did not serve as a theological professor in a theological seminary or university, and was not invited to the Second Vatican Council. However, today, his great theological achievement has been gradually acknowledged in the theological world, not only his characteristic theological method but also its creative and profound content.[6] In developing his theology, Balthasar was influenced by a variety of factors, some of which include:[7] (1) his massive and profound understand-

---

3. Concerning conflict and comparison between Balthasar and K. Rahner, see Endean, "Von Balthasar, Rahner, and the Commissar," 33–38, and Rowan Williams, "Bathasar and Rahner," 11–34.

4. For Balthasar's brief biography, see the following: Henrici, "Hans Urs von Balthasar, 7–43; L. Roberts, *Theological Aesthetics*, 6–26; Kehl, "Hans Urs von Balthasar," 3–54; Nichols, "Introduction to Balthasar," 2–10. See also, Balthasar, *My Work*.

5. Balthasar, *My Work*, 95.

6. According to Dennis J. Keefe, Balthasar's work is "the most sustained and comprehensive theological enterprise by a Catholic scholar in this century, and one which must rank with the classic theological achievements of the Catholic past." Idem, "Review of *the Glory of the Lord*, vol.1," *Thomist* 48 (1984) 663.

7. De Lubac once said that, "This man is perhaps the most cultivated of his time. If there is a Christian culture, then here it is! Classical antiquity, the great European literatures, the metaphysical tradition, the history of religions, the diverse exploratory adventures of contemporary man and, above all, the sacred sciences, St. Thomas, St. Bonaventure, patrology (all of it)—not to speak just now of the Bible—none of them

ing of classical and modern culture (including philosophy, literature, art, drama, etc.—e.g., Dante, Pascal, Buber, Romano Guardini, Paul Claudel, Rainer Maria Rilke, and Georges Bernanos);[8] (2) his enthusiastic studies on the patristic heritage under the influence of Henri de Lubac (e.g., Origen, Gregory of Nyssa, Maximus the Confessor);[9] (3) a renewed understanding of *analogia entis* under the influence of Erich Przywara who gave a philosophical foundation for Balthasar's analogical thinking; (4) a creative dialogue with Karl Barth's comprehensive biblical, christocentric, and thus theocentric trinitarian theology;[10] (5) and finally, a mystic theological insight which came from Adrienne von Speyr's spiritual and mystical experience on Christ's descent into hell.[11] Although it cannot be clearly distinguished, the development

---

that is not welcomed and made vital by this great mind. Writers and poets, mystics and philosophers, old and new, Christians of all persuasions—all are called on to make their particular contributions. All these are necessary for his final accomplishment, to a greater glory of God, the Catholic symphony." Idem, "Witness of Christ in the Church: Hans Urs von Balthasar," 272–73. Cf. L. Roberts, *Theological Aesthetics*, 12.

8. According to O'Donovan, "One hears he is a Barthian, a mystic, a papalist. The true Balthasar, however, is not an integrist but a cultural theologian whose work ranges from the ecclesiological to the mystical and whose works are collages of culture and Christianity." Idem, "Evolution under the Sign of the Cross," 602.

9. Balthasar's studies of the Church Fathers were published as *Kosmische Liturgie* and *Die Gnostischen Centurien des Maximus Confessor* on Maximus the Confessor (1941), *Présence et Pensée* on Gregory of Nyssa (1942), and *Parole et Mystère chez Origène* on Origen (1957).

10. Actually, Balthasar was, among Roman Catholic theologians, one of most serious conversation partners concerning Karl Barth's theology. Like K. Barth's theology, in spite of the dissimilarity between them, Balthasar's theology can be highly characterized as a biblical, christocentric, and trinitarian theology. His creative engagement with Barth' theology was published as *Karl Barth: Darstellung und Deutung seiner Theologie* (Köln: Verlag Jakob Hegner, 1951), translated as *The Theology of Karl Barth*. For Balthasar, according to Riches and Quash, Barth's theology remained "one of the fixed points by which he set the course of his own work." Riches and Quash, "Hans Urs von Balthasar," 135. See also, John Thompson, "Barth and Balthasar: An Ecumenical Dialogue," in *The Beauty of Christ*, 171–92; and Quash "Von Balthasar and the Dialogue with Karl Barth," 45–55.

11. The influence of Adrienne von Speyr was the most decisive factor after 1940. Balthasar himself wrote that, "It was Adrienne von Speyr who showed the way in which Ignatius is fulfilled by John and therewith laid the basis for most of what I have published since 1940. Her work and mine are neither psychologically nor philologically to be separated: two halves of a single whole, which has as its center a unique foundation." *My Work: In Retrospect*, 89. For Balthasar's own writing on the mystic vision of von Speyr, see *First Glance at Adrienne von Speyr*, and other transcripts. See also, Kerr, "Adrienne von Speyr and Hans Urs von Balthasar," 26–32.

of Balthasar's theology can be roughly classified by the following two phases: the early Balthasar when he focused on German idealism and patristics, and the later Balthasar period of his monumental trilogy–*Herrlichkeit, Theodramatik,* and *Theologik*.[12] As a whole, Balthasar's theology can be characterized as a biblical, analogical, and Christocentric Trinitarian theology. It is, according to J. R. Scahs, "always the attempt to get to the center, to the indivisible whole or gestalt of the mystery of God's Trinitarian love, revealed in Jesus Christ and communicated in history through the Spirit in the church."[13]

H. U. von Balthasar's Analogical Theology: Analogy as a Central Principle

In order to properly understand Balthasar's highly prolific works and the very diverse aspects of his theology,[14] we must first grasp his concept of analogy and its function in his theology. As Balthasar himself rightly points out, in K. Barth's theology, as it is true in his own theology, the principle of analogy functions as one of "all-determining principles," which is "the fundamental and formal set of theological principles that determine all the individual doctrines" like a strong thread uniting a beautiful pearl necklace.[15] Accordingly, R. Chia rightly observed that, for Balthasar, the concept of analogy is "the governing principle of his thinking and the basic structure of his theology which brings together the various aspects of his theology into a coherent whole."[16] Indeed,

---

12. Cf. Palakeel, *Use of Analogy,* 68–70, see also footnote 6 (p. 68). Especially in his trilogy, Balthasar greatly synthesizes his whole philosophical, literary, exegetical, and theological studies. The trilogy is divided according to the "transcendentals"–beauty, goodness, and truth. It has been translated and published in English as *The Glory of the Lord: A Theological Aesthetics* (7 vols., San Francisco: Ignatius, 1982–1989), *Theo-Drama: Theological Dramatic Theory* (5 vols., San Francisco: Ignatius, 1988–1998), and *Theo-Logic: Theological Logical Theory* (3 vols., San Francisco: Ignatius, 2000–2005).

13. Sachs, *"Deus Semper Major,"* 633.

14. von Balthasar, like K. Barth, was one of the amazingly prolific theological writers in the 20th century. The entire list of Balthasar's works was published as a monograph, see Capol, *Hans Urs von Balthasar: Bibliographie 1925–1990,* and for a list of English translation, see Schindler, ed., *Hans Urs von Balthasar,* 299–305; McGregor and Norris, *Beauty of Christ,* 267–69.

15. von Balthasar, *Theology of Karl Barth,* 24–25.

16. Chia, *Revelation and Theology,* 21. In this sense, Palakeel also says that, "Analogy is the key to interpret both his theology and his theological method." Idem, *Use of Analogy,* 68.

Balthasar's monumental trilogy, *The Glory of the Lord*, *Theo-Drama*, and *Theo-Logic*, is a creative articulation of his quest to express the relation between God and the world in terms of aesthetics, drama and logic, with each of these corresponding to the analogy of the transcendentals, beauty, goodness, and truth respectively.[17] That is to say, Balthasr's entire theology is an analogical mediation "between aesthetic beauty and revealed glory, between human drama and the all-encompassing Theo-drama, or between the enquires of philosophy and the obedient reflection of prayerful faith."[18] According to Balthasar, however, there is always an ever-greater ontological difference between God and the world. Therefore, in his view, analogy is a necessary means to conceive a correspondence within an ever-greater distinction, and a partial similarity within ever-greater dissimilarity between human reason and God's revelation. As we shall see, it is the same for our theme as we grasp Balthasar's Trinitarian analogical understanding of the relation between human time and the ever-greater God's "super-time" (i.e., eternity).

First, as we have seen, Balthasar's fundamental theological concern lies in how to explain the relationship between God and man (the world). In his tireless theological investigation through his whole life, the initial question is "Why is there anything at all and not simply nothing?"[19] How can we properly conceive the relationship between God's transcendence and immanence, and thus between God and the world? Actually, his entire life and theological endeavors are nothing other than an enthusiastic quest for the problem of expressing the relation between God and the world, in which he finally found an answer in the two fundamental Christian doctrines of the Trinity and the Incarnation.[20] So, "His quest finds its goal in the Christic centre, where incarnation and paschal mysteries become the focal point of any contact between God and man. All analogies converge at this point, where Jesus Christ is seen as the concrete *analogia entis*."[21] In this way, for Balthasar, analogy receives a renewed foundation, which is characteristically Christocentric and Trinitarian. As we shall see, Christology is the departing-point and the centre of his analogical theology in that the

17. Cf. Wolfgang Treitler, "True Foundations of Authentic Theology," 169.
18. Riches and Quash, "Hans Urs von Balthasar," 137.
19. Balthasar, *Glory of the Lord*, V, 613.
20. Cf. Balthasar, *My Work*, 118.
21. Palakeel, *Use of Analogy*, 75.

Triune God's supreme act of love is manifested in the person and life of Jesus Christ, the God-man, in a unique way. Therefore, Balthasar's entire theological investigation and method can be summarized in the one word "analogy," since the relationship between God and the world, transcendence and immanence, and eternity and time, can be properly conceived only in an analogical way. Therefore, according to Balthasar, analogy is "necessary" for Christian theology.[22]

The influence of E. Przywara and K. Barth was crucial in Balthasar's development of his own concept of analogy. At first, under the influence of E. Przywara's Thomistic understanding of *anaologia entis*,[23] Balthasar initially accepted the following famous definition from the Fourth Lateran Council (1215): "As great as may be the similarity, so much greater must the dissimilarity between creator and creature be preserved."[24] However, in his later phase, Balthasar had a serious theological dialogue with K. Barth's Christocentric *analogia fidei*.[25] This dialogue was probably the most influential in Balthasar's own theological construction of analogical theology. Finally, he established his own creative concept of analogy on the basis of Chalcedonian Christology and a Trinitarian foundation. In doing so, he provided a third possibility between the alternatives, an *analogia entis* within *analogia fidei*, which is characterized as a Christocentric Trinitarian *catalogical analogy*.[26]

---

22. Elsewhere, Balthasar defines analogy as follows: "analogy is a human mode of judging about the truth, regardless of whether the analogy (as an observed likeness, correspondence, or proportion) is thought to lie in judgments bearing on objective relationships [*Verhältnisse*] or in these relationships themselves." Idem, *Theo-Logic*, II, 311.

23. Cf. Przywara, *Analogia Entis*; Collins, "Przywara's '*Analogia Entis*,'" 265–77; and Zeitz, "Przywara and von Balthasar on Analogy," 473–98. Jean-Marie Faux wrote that, "Przywara was the first contemporary thinker who furnished Balthasar the tools of his reflection." Idem, "Un Theologien: Hans Urs von Balthasar," *Nouvelle Revue Theologique* 10 (1972) 1014. As cited in Zeitz, "Przywara and von Balthasar on Analogy," 476–77.

24. As cited in Riches and Quash, "Hans Urs von Balthasar," 137.

25. Cf. Balthasar, *Theology of Karl Barth*, 64–167.

26. For studies on Balthasar's conception of analogy, see the following: Lochbrunner, *Analogia Caritatis*; Schmid, *Im Ausstrahl der Schönheit Gottes*; De Schrijver, "Die Analogia Entis in der Theologie Hans Urs Balthasars," 249–81, and *Le Merveilleux accord de l'Homme et de Dieu*; Palakeel, *Use of Analogy in Theological Discourse*, 67–124; Dalzell, *Dramatic Encounter of Divine and Human Freedom in the Theology of Hans Urs von Balthasar*, 59–100; and Chia, *Revelation and Theology*, 227–58.

ANALOGIA ENTIS AS A CATHOLIC UNDERSTANDING OF ANALOGY

Balthasar's concept of analogy is essentially an analogy of being (*analogia entis*) which is based on the traditional Catholic understanding of *analogia entis*. Even though Balthasar's focus will be moved to a Christological center, throughout his entire theological life he never abandoned the concept of *analogia entis*.[27] In the early stage, for Balthasar, like Przywara, *analogia entis* is a metaphysical principle in order to conceive the relationship between nature and *Übernature*, the mystery of a similarity within ever-greater dissimilarity between the Creator and the creature in the form of an analogy of creation. While accepting the Thomistic conception of the ontological difference between existence and essence (*esse* and *essentia*, or beings and Being), and between Being (essence) and God, Balthasar tries to conceive *analogia entis* as a partial correspondence within ever-greater difference, a similarity within ever-greater dissimilarity between God and the world. In his trilogy, Balthasar attempted to see Being and God in and through the analogies of transcendentals, beauty, goodness, and truth, which are essentially the properties of being.[28] In the later period, however, "beyond the ontological difference," Balthasar emphasizes that, "God is the sole sufficient ground for both Being and the existent [*esse* and *essentia*]."[29] Furthermore, while accepting Anselmian conception of God, Balthasar conceives "the essence of God is to be ever-greater" (*das*

---

27. According to Palakeel's observation, "This basic Catholic presupposition is visible at all stages of his evolution. What has changed is only the categories and the way of understanding the concept of being and its relation to God and the world.... [Therefore, we can] find a shift from an anthropological to Christological understanding of [analogy of] being." Idem, *Use of Analogy*, 100.

28. As a good example, concerning the truth, Balthasar's argument is as follows: "The truth of the world is grounded in the truth of God that reveals itself in it. But, in the order of creation, this revelation remains indirect; the medium in which God appears is the creature, which as such is not God. Consequently, this creature has a real, creaturely truth of its own that is no more identical to God's truth than creaturely being is identical to the Divine Being. Rather, *there is an analogy between both relations*. Indeed, *because truth is the measure of being, the analogy is perfectly congruent*. The creature's truth is as contingent as is its being. But just as the being of the creature has consistency only in God's being that lives in and above him, so, too, creaturely truth is what it is, namely, truth, only on account of truth of God that sustains and makes it possible." Idem, *Theo-Logic*, I, 244–45 (italics mine).

29. Balthasar, *Glory of the Lord*, V, 624.

Wesen Gottes ist das 'Je-mehr').[30] God is, in His infinite freedom, "to be 'He-who-is-always-greater': we can never catch up with him."[31] In the relationship between the Creator and the creature, for Balthasar, God is neither "the wholly Other," nor "the non-Other," but "the Ever-Greater" God in the sense of Anselm, but originally and biblically in that of the Johannine comparative.[32]

Therefore, in using the Lateran Formula, Balthasar tries to defend "the transcendence of God at the same time overcoming the dialectics involved in the wholly other by insisting on both similarity and dissimilarity."[33] If God, "the absolute Being," is the ultimate ground of Being, then metaphysics completes itself in His revelation, "God's free Word of absolute love," which is "the fundamental metaphysical act . . . within the Ontological Difference."[34] According to Balthasar, therefore, God is, on the one hand, "the Totally-Other, incomprehensible, essentially different from the world, in and of himself most blessed and unspeakably exalted above everything else which can be thought of."[35] However, on the other hand, God is the "Ever-Greater" God, who appears and seizes hold of us in absolute, overwhelming, and ultimately incomprehensible love. Love is, therefore, "the form of revelation (*caritas forma revelationis*)."[36] This God's absolute self-giving love within the God-world distinction is fully manifested in the concrete *analogia entis*, Jesus Christ, the *Verbum Caro*, and thus the God-man, who is the form (*Gestalt*) and content of God's self-manifestation *pro nobis* and *pro mundo*.

---

30. Balthasar, *Theologik*, III, 219. Cf. Palakeel, *Use of Analogy*, 104.
31. Balthasar, *Theo-Drama*, II, 119.
32. Cf. Balthasar, *Theo-Drama*, II, 128–30, 230.
33. Palakeel, *Use of Analogy*, 104. This means that, according to Palakeel, "By virtue of the analogy in creation there is similarity between God and man, but there is always greater dissimilarity, because absolute dissimilarity would rule out revelation. So between God and man there is a greater dissimilarity. In this he is much indebted to Przywara, who relying on the Lateran formula, came up as a champion of *analogia entis* as the place of discourse on God" (ibid).
34. Balthasar, *Glory of the Lord*, V, 637.
35. Balthasar, *Love Alone*, 48.
36. Ibid., 49.

A Christocentric Analogy

Balthasar's serious theological studies and dialogues with the Fathers (e.g., Maximus the Confessor) and K. Barth made a clearly corrective turning point toward a Christological concentration in his theological methodology as well as in its content.[37] Then, God's revelation in Jesus Christ became the departure point for his analogical theology.[38] Accordingly, Christocentrism is to be one of the most important characteristics in Balthasar's understanding of analogy as well as in his entire theology. For Balthasar, as we have seen in K. Barth's theology, Jesus Christ must be "the real theological centre" and "the norm of our concrete history," and thus the heart of all analogical thinking.[39] As Balthasar says,

> Between the divine and the created natures there is an essential abyss. It cannot be circumvented. The fact that the person of Jesus Christ bridges this abyss without harm to his unity should render us speechless in the presence of the mystery of his person.[40]

According to Balthasar, Jesus Christ is the absolute, God-given, and true analogy. And therefore, He is "the concrete analogy of being (*analogia entis*), since he constitutes in himself, in the unity of his divine and human natures, the proportion of every interval between God and man."[41] In the God-man, Jesus Christ's hypostatic union of divinity and humanity, we can see the only proper relationship between

---

37. Cf. Balthasar, "Christocentrism," in his *Theology of Karl Barth*, 326–63.

38. For Balthasar, Christ is the definitive Word of God and the definitive revelation of God. "In Christ, God speaks a final Word (*eschaton logon*), albeit in the midst of the ongoing drama of the world." Idem, *Theo-Drama*, II, 124. Accordingly, for Balthasar, "theology is first and foremost the loving contemplation of faith upon the personal Word which God has spoken to the world in Jesus Christ." Sachs, "*Deus Semper Major*," 631.

39. Balthasar, *My Work*, 60; and his *Theology of History*, 17.

40. Balthasar, *Theo-Drama*, III, 220.

41. Balthasar, *Theology of History*, 69–70. He also says that, "The measure of maximum nearness and of maximum separation between God and man is given its foundation and its roots and altogether surpassed by the real nearness and real distance between Father and Son in the Spirit on the Cross and in the Resurrection. The Son alone knows what it means to live in the Father, to rest in his bosom, to love him, to serve him, and he alone can know the full significance of being abandoned by him" (p. 9).

God and man. As the concrete analogy of being, Jesus Christ is "God's Interpreter," and thus He lets us see the unity of God and human existence in His person and life. As Balthasar says, "if he is the Word of God made flesh (Jn. 1:14), then this Word, this Son must also be God's final interpretation."[42] In the same sense, the decent of Christ is the unique "form" (*Gestalt*) of the glory of God manifest in the world. As the concrete *analogia entis*, Jesus Christ is the *instrumentm conjunctum* between God and man.[43]

> We find the reason for this analogical relation by looking at the center, Jesus Christ himself. By virtue of the hypostatic union, there is nothing in him which does not serve God's revelation. As the center of the world, he is the key to the Interpretation not only of creation, but of God himself.[44]

In saying that Jesus Christ is the concrete *analogia entis*, it means that Christ is the foundation of the all possible theological analogies, and thus an *analogia entis* is possible only within an *analogia fidei*. In this way, through ongoing discussions, Balthasar's *analogia entis*, which came from E. Przywara, and K. Barth's *analogia fidei* met each other at the unique common concrete foundation of analogy, the only true God-given analogy, Jesus Christ. Therefore, Balthasar finally presents his own conception of theological analogy as always an *analogical entis* within *analogia fidei*.

A Catalogical Analogy

It must also be emphasized that Balthasar's concept of analogy is a *catalogical analogy*.[45] For Balthasar, the philosophy of being, *analogia entis*, which is grounded in the Christological and Trinitarian foundation, is essentially *catalogical*.[46] This means that "it is not the ascent of religious man to the absolute One, but rather the descent of the Trinitarian God

---

42. Balthasar, *Does Jesus Knows Us*, 73.
43. Cf. Balthasar, *Theology of History*, 17.
44. Ibid., 20.
45. The Greek preposition "*ana-*" means an upward movement, but "*kata-*" means a downward movement.
46. See Balthasar, "Kata-logical Aspects" in his *Theo-Logic*, II, 173–218. See also, Henrici, "Philosophy of Hans Urs von Balthasar," 165–66.

of love to man that is the departure point of von Balthasar's theology."[47] Balthasar's catalogical understanding of analogy comes from his concentration on the mutual love of the inner-trinitarian persons, and then on the Incarnation, the descent of the Son from the Father. The Word made flesh, Jesus Christ, is the self-manifestation of God and the only concrete analogy of being in this world. That is to say, Bathasar's concept of catalogical analogy is founded upon the threefold *kenosis theory*.[48]

According to Balthsar, in following Bulgakov, there are three forms of kenosis in the Triune God.[49] The first and primary kenosis is the intratrinitarian event, the generation of the consubstantial Son by the eternal Father's expropriating Himself, and then its expansion to the mutual self-expropriation or self-donation of the Son and the Spirit. The second kenosis is seen in the Triune God's self-limitation in endowing His creatures with freedom in creation, and further in making a covenant with Israel. Lastly, the third and final kenosis is the Incarnation of the Son, and His giving Himself to the place of death on the Cross. In this way, for Balthasar, the concept of God's self-*kenosis*, self-humbling, and self-descent, became the key foundation of his catalogical analogy. This Trinitarian and Christocentric catalogical thinking can provide a new framework for understanding *analogia entis*. By giving this catalogical foundation as an analogy of being, Balthasar attempted to mediate between *analogia entis* and *analogia fidei*. W. Treitler gives an excellent explication about Balthasar's idea of catalogical analogy in using the Chalcedonian Christological formula as follows:

> In terms of analogy: in this determinate man, Jesus of Nazareth, in whom God is present in unsurpassable and unique manner as himself (*similitude; indivise, inseparabiliter*—similarity; undividedly, inseparably) God is revealed as the *Deus semper maior*, God who is ever greater (*maior dissimilitude; inconfuse, immutabiliter*—greater dissimilitude; unconfusedly, unalterably). In terms of cataloging: in the Son of God sent from God (true God

---

47. Löser, "Being Interpreted as Love," 475.

48. Wolfgang Treitler points out this perspective as follows: "Cataloging as a theological concept of method formulates thus the awareness of a theological methodology that God's self-expression in the incarnate Son can only be read truly from above downward as a formed process of following the divine *kenosis* in the theological re-flection (*Nach-Denken*)." Idem, "True Foundations of Authentic Theology," in *Hans Urs von Balthasar*, ed. D. L. Schindler, 171.

49. Cf. Balthasar, *Theo-Drama*, IV, 323–32, and his *Mysterium Paschale*, 23–36.

from true God) the truth of free and sinful humanity before God becomes completely manifest (*similitude; indivise, inseparabiliter*), but in such a way that God has nothing in common with sin but, as the one who infinitely towers above sin, he brings sin into an annihilating and saving judgment (*maior dissimilitude; inconfuse, immutabiliter*). Since, however, the definiteness of this catalogical analogy lies in the Son who descended, it remains clear that analogy is really founded in cataloging even here. Analogy, understood in these terms, goes completely through Jesus, the Christ, according to Balthasar, and thus Christ himself is analogy in a catalogically discernible specificity: absolute analogy, thus *analogia entis*, but also *analogia libertatis* and *analogia salutis*, the absolute catalogical analogy.⁵⁰

Analogia Caritatis: An Analogia Entis within Analogia Fidei

As we have seen, Balthasar's concept of analogy is essentially an analogy of being. However, as a theological analogy, it cannot be thinkable apart from the analogy of faith, because without *analogia fidei*, *analogia entis* simply falls into a mere human metaphysical principle. Therefore, while mediating between E. Przywara's *analogia entis* and K. Barth's *analogia fidei*, Balthasar proposed that *anlogia entis* must be placed within *analogia fidei*, and he found their common, concrete foundation in the God-man, Jesus Christ, who is not only the absolute, the God-given, the concrete *analogia entis*, but also the true, real, and concrete foundation of *analogia fidei*. Balthasar succinctly states that the analogy of being must be placed within the analogy of faith, as follows:

> It is not formulas that are battling one another (*analogia fidei* against *analogia entis*) but two ways of understanding the one revelation of God, each taking the measure of the other. And if we simply have to substitute formulas for the kind of hard work set before us, then we can sum up the issue using this formula: (1) Barth's way of understanding God' revelation in Christ includes the analogy of being within the analogy of faith; and (2) the way the Catholic authors we have been citing understand the christocentricity of God's plan for the world allows the analogy of being to gain its density and concreteness only

---

50. W. Treitler, "True Foundations of Authentic Theology," 176.

within the wider analogy of faith (understood in the widest possible sense).[51]

In sum, Balthasar's understanding of analogy is a Christocentric and Trinitarian *catalogical analogy*. After a full-length analysis, M. Lochbrunner rightly characterized Balthasar's distinctive concept of analogy of being as *analogia caritatis* (analogy of love).[52] For Balthasar, Being can be properly interpreted as love, and thus the essence of Being is love.[53] The Bible declares that, "God is Love" (1 John 4:8). Furthermore, according to Balthasar, love is the unity of the three transcendentals; truth, goodness, and beauty.[54] Therefore, in my view, Balthasar's subject matters of his monumental trilogy are nothing other than a threefold musical variation of one beautiful harmony of the Triune God's unconditional love for the world (cf. John 3:16). In the Johannine perspective, God Himself is love (cf. 1 John 4:8), and thus the mystery of Being is a mystery of love. As we have seen, the catalogical aspect of *analogia caritatis* is manifested in the threefold kenosis of the Triune God's love. Love is the form of God's mutual self-donation *in se* and of self-manifestation *pro nobis*. In the God-man, Jesus Christ, we can see the *admirabile commercium* (marvelous exchange) in the relationship of God and man in love. In this sense, the Triune God's absolute love alone, which is most clearly manifested in the incarnate Son and His paschal mystery, is the real foundation of analogy, a similarity within ever-greater dissimilarity between God and man. Therefore, Balthasar believes that Jesus Christ is the concrete love of God *pro nobis* as well as the concrete *analogia caritatis* between God and man.

H. U. von Balthasar's Understanding of Time

Now, we turn to our subject matter, Balthasar's Trinitarian analogical understanding of God's eternity and its relation to time. Unfortunately,

---

51. Balthasar, *Theology of Karl Barth*, 382.

52. See Lochbrunner, *Analogia Caritatis*, 288–306.

53. Balthasar says that, "Being and love are co-extensive." Idem, "Der Zugang aur Wirklichkeit Gottes," in *Mysterium Salutis*, vol. II, ed. J. Feiner and M. Löhrer (Einsiedeln, 1967) 17, as cited in Löser, "Being Interpreted as Love," 475.

54. Cf. Balthasar, *My Work*, 118. He says, "In the trinitarian dogma, God is one, good, true, and beautiful because he is essentially Love, and Love supposes the one, the other and their unity."

however, Balthasar does not give us a systematic exposition of his doctrine of time as well as God's eternity, or their relationship as a monograph.[55] Balthasar's ideas and expositions are pervasively scattered here and there throughout his prolific works. In this sense, it is really true that, as W. Löser rightly points out, "in fact von Balthasar's work is characterized by the impressive variety in themes he takes up and even by his selection of the linguistic and expressive forms which he uses for presenting this variety of content."[56] Hence it is a serious difficulty which arises when one attempts to systematically grasp a specific theological subject-matter in Balthasar's theology. Accordingly, in this study, I will take Balthasar's scattered ideas on time and eternity and sketch them briefly in order to present them in a somewhat understandable systematic form.

The Created Time: The Mode of Existence for the Creature

In understanding the nature of time, Balthasar basically followed St. Augustine's conception of time.[57] First, according to Balthasar, time itself (and its counterpart eternity) is not an independent ontological concept (i.e., being or thing). That is to say, even though it is a fundamental structure of being, time *per se* is not a being, and is not a subject which has a life and personal freedom of its own.[58] Time is an ontological nature or fundamental property of the creatures, and thus of human existence. As Balthasar says that,

> [T]he mysterious nonidentity between essence and existence is intimately related to the phenomenon of time. Indeed, insofar as time is a fundamental structure of being, this nonidentity is even coextensive with it. This does not mean, of course, that being and time are the same thing: even on this understanding of

---

55. I have found only the following two previous studies on Balthasar's understanding of time or eternity: O'Hanlon, *Immutability of God*, 88–109. This is also summarized by the author as an article, "Does God Change?," 161–83; and Thurman, "Time in the Theological Aesthetic of Hans Urs Von Balthasar."

56. Löser, "Being Interpreted as Love," 475. Many others point out the same difficulty in their studying of Balthasar's theology, see Hunt, *Trinity and the Paschal Mystery*, 58–59; O'Hanlon, *Immutability of God*, 5; Donald Mackinnon, "Some Reflections on Hans Urs von Balthasar's Christology," in *Analogy of Beauty*, ed. Riches, 169.

57 For this point, see Balthasar, *Theological Anthropology*, 1–42.

58. Cf. O'Hanlon, *Immutability of God*, 88.

time, time remains a particular, albeit fundamental, property of the creature's being. Our affirmation does mean, however, that the phenomenon of time belongs to the core of the creature's ontological make-up and that the philosophical analysis of time is the most adequate entryway to living, concrete understanding of the real distinction.[59]

Generally, therefore, although time can be considered to be the principle of differentiation between God and man, we must bear in mind that it always has two sides, "positive and negative, likeness and unlikeness, an affinity to eternity and to nothingness," which are inextricably interwoven.[60] That is, in Balthasar's view, analogical thinking alone can properly conceive the difference and positive relationship between eternity and time.

In a positive sense, for Balthasar, as for Augustine, time is the result of God's good creation from the realm of nothingness to being. Hence original created time in itself is neither evil nor sinful. As the creature itself is a good creation of God ("it was very good," Gen 1:31), created time, too, is good in itself. Then, what is time? Where is it from? According to Balthasar, as for Augustine, "time results from the radical not-being-God of the creature," and it is "the distance from Creator to the creature."[61] When the finite being advances from non-being, its duration unfolds and thus, at the same time, its time comes into existence.[62] In this sense, Balthasar states, "Time is the principle of total differentiation from God and all similarity to God."[63] In my view, Balthasar's conception of time as a "distance" between God, the Creator, and the creatures can be considered as a very significant theological insight. As a good creation of God, time is real as the mode of existence of the finite creature. Therefore, for Blathasar, the nature of created time lies in its "givenness" to the creature as "a gift," which is the form of its existence. In the same sense, it clearly shows that the creature's existence itself is a gift of God. As Balthasar says, "Time's givenness is most clearly seen in

59. Balthasar, *Theo-Logic*, I, 195.
60. Ibid., 196.
61. Balthasar, *Theological Anthropology*, 23.
62. Elsewhere, however, Balthasar also says that, "time is from eternity and [goes back] to eternity." See his *Theo-Drama*, V, 100–102. As we shall see, Balthasar's such a statement can be explainable and understandable only in a Trinitarian and Christological perspectives.
63. Balthasar, *Theological Anthropology*, 23.

the fact that man has control neither of its beginning nor of its ending."[64] Time is not produced or controlled by us (i.e., by our consciousness), but is given from "a super-temporal or eternal plane; admitted into biological realm (and hence into the physical realm)."[65] Hence, "my time" is given to me "as my very own mode of existence."[66] Furthermore, Balthasar asserts that, since time is God's good creation, it can be "the medium of the good and beautiful deeds of God."[67] Therefore, history as a totality of time can be the medium, the space, and the theatre for the manifestation of the Triune God's sublime Theo-drama of love, which is centered on the Christ-event.[68]

As to the negative aspect of human time, however, as an individual, I always live in "my own" finite time, but it is not my own possession. Though time is my own mode of existence, at the same time it does not belong to me. Time is always withdrawn from me in that I cannot have control over my entire past and future, except the single, "here-and-now," vantage point of the present.[69] Therefore, "My time is so outside my control that I do not know how long it will be, which means that I cannot envisage my existence in an extended duration like a play with several acts."[70] Time, as the past in memory and the future in expectation, is "the product of a bifurcation of consciousness," and the present as well, is an ever fleeting, transient moment.[71] In contrast to God's ever-present eternity, the creature's time is fragmentary and finite because it always "tends toward non-being" (cf. Augustine, *Confessions*, XI, 14). According to Balthasar, as for Augustine, the future time and the past time do not exist, and the present moment also "flees at such lightning speed from being future to being past, that it has no extent of duration at all [*extenditur*] ... the present has no length" (XI, 15). It shows the paradoxical and fragmentary nature of our finite time.[72] Therefore, ac-

---

64. Balthasar, *Theo-Drama*, IV, 95.

65. Ibid., 98.

66. Ibid., 97.

67. Balthasar, *Theological Anthropology*, 23.

68. Cf. Balthasar, *Theological Anthropology*, 108–20, and *Theo-Drama*, V, 91–95, 100–102.

69. Balthasar, *Theo-Drama*, IV, 97.

70. Ibid.

71. Ibid., 98.

72. Ibid., 97–98, and see also his *Theological Anthropology*, 1–42. We can see Augustine's argument on time in his *Confessions*, "Book 11."

cording to Balthasar, time is not a static, spatial spread, but it is itself in flux, an ever-fleetingness.[73] In this sense, Balthasar accepts the tensed (dynamic/A-series) theory of time.

The Sinful Time: The Mortal Time

According to Balthasar, as for Augustine, to move out from God is creation, and to wander away from God is sin.[74] However, "Sin, which 'I do not want [to do]' (Rom 7:15), stands like a strange power between man and God."[75] As a result of sinful alienation from God, Balthasar states that "sinful time, in contrast to creation time, leads sooner to death."[76] As Augustine shows us, there is always the "immanence of death in every moment of corrupted time."[77] Therefore, sinful time is characterized as "the unreal time" or "the mortal time." "Life in mortal time is altogether 'sickness' and 'corruption' (Ps 102:6); everywhere there is weariness, everywhere weakness, everywhere decay."[78] According to Balthasar, as an individual, my time is a "death-bound time" in that my own existence is always running toward death.[79] God-given finite time as the form of every individual existence has its end in death.[80] In a theological sense, in contrast to the original created time, the problem of death is the nature or destiny of lost, sinful, or corrupted time. As Balthsar says,

> Time, in fact, is either real time, in which man encounters God and accepts his will, or it is unreal time, lost and corrupted:

---

73. In this sense, Balthasar's view of time can be seen as a dynamic (tensed) theory of time (cf. Chapter 4 in this study). It is clear in Balthasar's following statement: "Presence occurs as that which is just arriving at each new moment.... From moment to moment, presence is always just now coming toward us [*zukommt*]. This is its futurity [*Zukünftigkeit*]. The future is not a state of being or time lying alongside, and separate from, the present, but a direction within the present, within existence itself. Because of this immanent futurity, existence is essentially open-end; even more, it is essentially a beginning, a promise, a *hope*, an upspringing." Idem, *Theo-Logic*, I, 196–97, see also his *Theo-Drama*, IV, 98.
74. Cf. Balthasar, *Theological Anthropology*, 5.
75. Ibid., 27.
76. Ibid., 28.
77. Ibid.
78. Ibid., 29.
79. Balthasar, *Theo-Drama*, IV, 101.
80. Cf. Balthasar, *Glory of the Lord*, VII, 164.

time as the finite in self-contradiction, an unredeemed promise, a space full of nothing, duration leading nowhere. That is the time of sin and sinners, the time in which God is not to be found because man flees the encounter; the time that becomes punishment for him.[81]

In the same sense, Balthasar insists that "concrete time" (as the time of mankind consisting of individual mortal human beings) or the stretched span of time of the "macro human being," and thus chronological time is not some indefinite, non-mortal, and hence nonhuman time, but it is also running toward death altogether. As Balthasar says, "Logically speaking, once the succession of generations has come to an end (with the death of the last man), time too is suspended."[82] This means that, therefore, time as a totality (i.e., a neutral, chronological time, history as a whole), too, is a mortal and finite time, and thus a "death-bound time."[83] This mortality and finiteness is the very nature of sinful time as the form of the alienated creature's existence from the eternal God, the Creator. Accordingly, for Balthasar, the problem of time, as a sinful time, is none other than the very problem of death.[84]

The Time of Jesus Christ: The Norm of History

As we have seen, in Balthasar's view, Jesus Christ, the God-man, is the One, the God-given, and hence "the concrete *analogia entis*" between God and man (the world). In the same sense, Jesus Christ alone is "the norm" not only of our being but also of our concrete history as the totality of the creature's time.[85] Undoubtedly, we cannot truly understand our time as well as God's eternity apart from the time of Jesus Christ, for human temporality and divine eternity are uniquely encountered and united in Christ's time because of the hypostatic union of human-

81. Balthasar, *Theology of History*, 41. In theological aspect, Balthasar distinguished between various modes of time, as follows: "the time of Paradise," "the time of sin," "the time of the Redeemer," "the time of Christ," and so on. (Ibid., 41–42).

82. Balthasar, *Theo-Drama*, IV, 102.

83. According to Balthasar, for Augustine, "historical time as human duration represents a homogeneous medium comprehensible by man, while subhuman, animal time (*Confessions*, X, 17) and the time of the angels (*Gen. Lib. Imp.* 8) are also modes of creaturely duration, though measured differently." Idem, *Theological Anthropology*, 7.

84. For this point, see Balthasar's "Time and Death," in *Theo-Drama*, IV, 95–135.

85. Cf. Balthasar, *Theology of History*, 17, 19, and 21.

ity and divinity in His historical existence (i.e., His person and life in time). As the true man and the true God, Jesus Christ's time is the only source for true knowledge about the reality and meaning of human time as well as God's eternity, and the mysterious relationship between the two. Therefore, the time of Jesus Christ alone is the concrete analogy between human time and divine eternity. For this point, Balthasar says as follows:

> We find the reason for this analogical relation by looking at the center, Jesus Christ himself. By virtue of the hypostatic union, there is nothing in him which does not serve God's revelation. As the center of the world, he is the key to the interpretation not only of creation, but of God himself.[86]

Jesus Christ's Mode of Time: Eternity in Time

The Incarnation, *Verbum caro factum est* (John 1:14), means that, "the Word that is God became man, without ceasing to be God. The Word that is infinite became finite, without ceasing to be infinite. The Word that is God took a body of flesh, in order to be man."[87] It also means that God's eternity became human time without ceasing to be eternity in Jesus Christ. The truly temporal man, Jesus, is the same person who is the eternal Word, Christ. Accordingly, for Balthasar, "Just as, within 'the christological analogy of Being,' the humanity of Jesus Christ is the appropriate expression of God's divinity, so too his 'time' expresses (without being identical to) the eternity of God."[88] According to Balthasar, this is the only way for our enquiry into the meaning of time as well as God's eternity. As Balthasar says, therefore, "Only a genuine theology of time, gained from the contemplation of Christ's existence, can provide a sound concept of eternity, consistent with Revelation."[89]

According to Balthasar, first of all, the form of Jesus's existence in time is the receptivity of the Father's will. To do the Father's will is Jesus's mission and the key of His whole existence. In the negative sense, therefore, "the meaning of the Incarnation, of Jesus's manhood, is, first

86. Ibid., 20.
87. Balthasar, *Explorations in Theology*, I, 149. For Balthasar's full exposition on this, see also his *Glory of the Lord*, VII, 33–235; *Theo-Logic*, II, 219–361.
88. O'Hanlon, *Immutability of God*, 90.
89. Balthasar, *Theology of History*, 47.

borne in upon us as a not-doing, a not-fulfilling, a not-carrying-out his own will."[90] But, in a positive sense, "The Son's form of existence, which makes him the Son from all eternity (John 17:5), is the uninterrupted reception of everything that he is, of his very self, from the Father."[91] In eternity, the Father's act of generation is to beget the Son, who receives not something alien but the Father's own Being. Therefore, Jesus Christ's temporal mode of being is the manifestation, the translation into the temporal world of the eternal form of His existence as the perfect receptivity from the Father. In this sense, the Son's existence can be understood "as receiving, as openness to the will of the Father, as subsistent fulfillment of that will in a continuous mission."[92]

In my view, such a conception of Balthasar, time as the Son's receptivity of His being from the Father, is the key point in his Trinitarian analogical understanding of God's eternity and its relation to time. For Balthasar, therefore, in contrast to the perfect receptivity and obedience of the Son to the Father's will, our sin is nothing other than "to break out of time" in order to arrogate to ourselves a sort of eternity. "God intended man to have *all* good, but his, God's, time; and therefore all disobedience, all sin, consists essentially in breaking out of time."[93] Hence, the restoration of the broken order by the Son of God is completed with His perfect reception, obedience and patience to the Father's will. Accordingly, Balthasar says that, "Now it is his receptivity to everything that comes to him from the Father that is the basis of *time* and *temporality* as these terms apply to the Son in his creaturely form of existence."[94] The Son has time for God, and receives it from God. It means also that God has time for the world in Jesus Christ. In the following statements, we can find a kernel of Balthasar's thinking about time:

> Thus the whole basis of time for the Son is his receptivity to God's will. In that receptivity he receives time from the Father, both as form and as content. The time that he receives is the Father's time, qualified moment by moment. For him, there is no such thing as "time in itself"; . . . To have time means, for him, to have time for God, and is identical with receiving time

---

90. Ibid., 29.
91. Ibid., 30.
92. Ibid., 31.
93. Ibid., 36–37.
94. Ibid., 33 (italics original).

from God. Hence the Son, who has time, in the world, for God, is the point at which God has time for the world. Apart from the Son, God has no time for the world, but in him he has *all* time. In him he has time for all men and all creatures: in relation to him it is always Today.[95]

According to Balthasar, as the true man (*vere homo*), the time of Jesus Christ is genuinely human mortal time in that it follows through to death, the Cross. In this sense, Balthasar says that, it is "the time of a single mortal man, a time that unhesitatingly runs towards death—and a death the time of which can be known (if this is genuinely to be the time of a man) only to God, and can be determined only by him (Matt 6:27 following Job 14:5)."[96] However, at the same time, Jesus Christ's temporal mode of existence is also the expression of His very eternal mode of existence, the true God (*vere Deus*). That is to say, the *Verbum Caro*, the descended Son's existence in time is a representation of His eternal life in relationship with the Father. In Jesus Christ, the eternal being presents Himself in the transient moment without ceasing to be eternal.[97] And therefore, we can say that, in Jesus Christ's temporal mode of existence, God's eternity is in human time. More directly, Balthasar says that, "The presence of the Son is the presence of eternity in time. This is a factor that transforms the world: 'Through him, the relationship of the Father to creatures is altogether changed.'"[98] There is not any contradiction between time and eternity in Jesus Christ. It is clear in that, before the Passion, the very structure of Jesus's temporality transfigured on Mount Tabor, which gives a most unmistakable expression to His eternal life.[99] Therefore, the incarnate Son of God, before His Passion and Resurrection, is truly and equally God and man, eternal and at the same time temporal in one person. In this sense, "His

95. Ibid., 40–41.
96. Balthasar, *Glory of the Lord*, VII, 165.
97. Ibid., 167. Cf. *Theo-Drama*, V, 247. He says, "If he is truly in time (so that he must suffer and die), he is still the eternal one, who enters time, and thus brings his eternity with him into time and transience." Idem, *Theological Anthropology*, 35.
98. Balthasar, *Theo-Drama*, V, 250. He continues, "All these reflections on the Christ-event are meant to lead to this realization: If, in Jesus Christ, eternal life has genuinely penetrated the world's temporal sphere, this temporal sphere does not unfold 'outside' eternity but within it. We must not forget, however, that this, just like the Incarnation, remains a mystery" (ibid.).
99. Balthasar, *Theology of History*, 36.

mode of time in his earthly life spanned not only the analogy between body-duration and soul-duration, which we contrast in popular speech as mortal-immortal, but also the unique analogy between existence as it is with the Father and existence as it is in the world."[100] On Mount Tabor, Jesus Christ's divinity and eternity, which are hidden through His earthly life, were clearly and gloriously manifested to the disciples as a constant, ever-accompanying presence. At the same time, significantly enough, Moses and Elijah, who represent the Law and the Prophets respectively, were visibly present and accompanying the Lord. In a theological sense, for Balthasar, this means that, "the time of promise is present and immanent in the time of fulfillment, not as something abstract but in the physical presence of the persons and events which constitute it."[101] Therefore, the time of Jesus Christ, moment by moment and bit by bit, is more than itself; that is, "it is the presence of all things fulfilled: the 'fullness time' in a qualitative sense, of time exalted to the plane of eternity."[102]

Because of this, the time of Jesus Christ transcends all other modes of time (i.e., creation time, sinful time, or redeemed time, etc.) because His humanity (as the Second Adam and the archetype and prototype of man before God) differs from all other human existence, and thus it is "the universal norm of time."[103] This means

> Theologically, then, we may distinguish between various mode of temporality: the time of Paradise when God was open to man, and conversed with him in the breath (= spirit) of the evening breeze (Gen 3:8); the time of sin which as such is lost, flowing toward disaster, since God repents of having made the world (Gen 6:6), and allows what he formed out of the waters of chaos to return into the waters of chaos (2 Pet 3:6); the time of the Redeemer, when God again takes time to himself for the sake of the world; time centered on Christ's time as preparation and realization, the time of the Old and New Covenants; and

---

100. Ibid., 91.
101. Ibid.
102. Ibid., 91–92.
103. According to Blathasar, Jesus Christ "establishes in his earthly life the absolute norm for the world's time. He does this in his relation to the Father (which permits no inner development but is merely taken through the successive situations of a human life, fulfilling them all), and thus to the *kairos* of the Father, to the 'hour' of his death and resurrection, in which the (vertical) time measure is established for all human vertical and horizontal times." Idem, *Theological Anthropology*, 113.

Time, Eternity, and the Trinity in the Theology of Hans Urs von Balthasar

the time of men who, in and through Christ, come to share once again in real time.[104]

Accordingly, for Balthasar, "The whole of human time is thus structured analogically within itself, and the key to the whole of it is Christ's mode of time, in which it culminates."[105]

The Risen Christ's Forty Days: Time in Eternity

According to Balthasar, the unique time of Jesus Christ's forty days between Resurrection and Ascension has a profound significance for understanding time, eternity, and their relationship. That is to say, the resurrected Jesus Christ's forty days reveal the definitive and normative presence of eternity in time and time in eternity.[106] As Balthasar says, "The forty days during which the risen Christ showed himself on earth belong both to his earthly time and to his eternal time."[107] On the one hand, the risen Christ's forty days are surely earthly time like ours, since His natural human relationships with the disciples are continued–they physically hear, see, touch one another and eat together, and its climax is the scene with doubting Thomas (John 20:24–26) and the meal together by the lake of Tiberias (21:8–14). In this sense, the risen Christ's time is not a mere "ghost-time," but a real and genuine time with us in that He is not a spirit but tangible flesh and blood in that He eats the same fish and bread with His disciples. Therefore, according to Balthasar, "The first truth about the risen Christ's time, which no other truth can invalidate, is that his time is not divorced or estranged from our time, but is in an ordinary, straightforward way continuous with it."[108]

However, on the other hand, as we can see in the story of Emmaus, as they were walking and talking together within the alteration, succession and interweaving of words and actions, they did not recognize the risen Christ. This is the difference between before and after the

---

104. Balthasar, *Theology of History*, 42.

105. Ibid., 43.

106. Cf. Byrne, "Hans Urs von Balthasar and the Mystery of the Forty Days after Easter," 34. He says that, for Balthasar, "The forty days disclose the mode of Christ's personal presence which is the foundation for every other mode of his presence in time, in the Church, and in the world" (ibid.).

107. Balthasar, *Theology of History*, 83.

108. Ibid., 85.

Resurrection. According to Balthasar, "What this episode reveals is not the immutable relationship of an eternal present, a *nunc stans*, to the successive moments of mutable time, but the eternal allowing itself to be drawn into time and going along with it in genuine companionship."[109] In other words, the risen Christ's earthly time is "simultaneously his eternal time [and] makes no difference. That would only be a contradiction if one postulated that time and eternity could not be united, and consequently that time could not be redeemed and preserved within eternity; in the most positive sense, taken up into it."[110] The time of the risen Christ, the forty days, reveals the glory of His divinity and all the fullness of God's eternity. It is unique time in that eternity is clearly presented in and accompanied with time. Therefore, the time of the forty days is "genuine time, though indeed no longer time dedicated to death, but resurrection-time; no longer a time for suffering and meriting, no longer time as a burden, but time as a blessed spaciousness, and the possession of that which has been merited, which is sovereignty bestowed by the Father."[111] As Paul declares that, "Death no longer has dominion over him" (Rom 6:9). By the resurrection of the Son from death, mortal time, death-bound-time itself ends.

Furthermore, the forty days of the resurrected Jesus Christ show that His "past," all the temporal and historical course of His earthly life, has not simply passed away, but is "transformed into his Resurrection, taken up into it, eternalized, and thus made into a living possession that he can share, the things of which he is going to build his Church."[112] Accordingly, the risen Christ's Ascension "did not make him a stranger to our world."[113] Unlike the time of Paradise or the time after the Judgment, the time of Jesus Christ's forty days is not "a self-contained time," but it exists to serve as "a bond between his earthly life and the time of the Church" and as the indivisible unity between the Kingdom of God and His Church.[114] Hence, it is also an "anticipation" of the coming event of Pentecost and the foundation of the succeeding period of

109. Ibid.
110. Ibid., 84.
111. Ibid., 86.
112. Ibid.
113. Ibid., 87.
114. Ibid.

the history of His Church. Finally, the time of the forty days clearly shows us "both the end of history and its totality." As Balthasar says,

> [A]s the end of history, the *eschaton*, he is present at its center, revealing in this one particular *kairos, this* historical moment, the meaning of every *kairos* that can ever be. He does not do this from some point outside and above history, he does it in an actual historical moment, in which he is present both prove that he himself is alive and to be the self-utterance of the Kingdom.[115]

According to Balthasar, by His Incarnation and His whole earthly life, Jesus Christ is the eternal being made temporal, and thus now, by His Resurrection and Ascension, He is the temporal being made eternal. By His resurrection and the time of forty days, human time, the lost, sinful, and hence mortal time is fulfilled, redeemed, and finally is taken up into the immortal God's time (i.e., eternity) in Jesus Christ. In this sense, God's time for the world is always the time of His grace, the time of His revelation, the time of His redemption, and thus it is God's vertical "Now" in our horizontal time, the "Today" (Heb 3:7, 4:7), the "acceptable time" (2 Cor 4:2; Isa 49:8) because it is the present vertical time of salvation for us and for the world as a whole.[116]

Therefore, the time of Jesus Christ is the time of *eschaton* in the sense of "already" and "here and now" but "not yet" for us. Balthasar says that, "his going to death must coincide with his going toward the end of 'heaven and earth.'"[117] God's time, the "future of God" (i.e., the last day, the end of time) is not a timeless idea, but an event of divine freedom breaking into our sinful time as His grace, in which He brings His salvation for us.[118] It is God's time for saving us, the time of grace, which is always "today," and thus God has His own time in Jesus Christ.[119] In this sense, the time of Jesus Christ is the universal norm of all time, for everything is "consummated" in Him and in His time. Accordingly, for Balthasar, "He is *universale in re*, the supra-temporal in time, the universally valid *in* the here-and-now, necessary being *in* concrete fact;

---

115. Ibid., 88 (italics original).
116. Cf. Balthasar, *Theological Anthropology*, 35.
117. Balthasar, *Glory of the Lord*, VII, 166.
118. Cf. Balthasar, *Theological Anthropology*, 35.
119. Balthasar, *Prayer*, 115.

in the thirty-three years of his life the accent is on the *res*, and during the forty days on the *universale*."[120]

In this way, the time of Jesus Christ clearly shows us the fact that eternity is in time (Incarnation and the earthly life), eternity accompanies time (the Forty days), and finally time is in eternity (Ascension), but each of them cannot be separated from the others. In the time of Jesus Christ, not only eternity is in time, but also time is in eternity. In this way, eternity and time have embraced the time of Jesus Christ, the true man and the true God. Now, as in eternity, the risen Christ is in time with the power to transform human time and the whole history through the work of the Holy Spirit. The time of the Church, especially through the time of the Eucharist and the sacraments, has an eschatological orientation in common with that of the forty days in the work and the power of the Holy Spirit. Therefore, according to Balthasar, "As the Cross anticipates the Last Judgment, so the forty days are a foretaste of eternal life."[121] Our Lord, the exalted Christ is always with us to be *pro nobis* (Jesus says, "surely I am with you always, to the very end of the age [i.e., the end of world time]," Matt 28:20), and, in His *parousia*, He will return in glory with the power to raise up our sinful time with Him into the glory of God's eternity.[122]

H. U. von Balthasar's Understanding of God's Eternity

Like K. Barth, H. U. von Balthasar's understanding of the biblical God, too, is characteristically the Triune God, who reveals Himself in Jesus Christ. For Balthasar, there is no other God besides the one true God, the Trinity.[123] Therefore, Balthasar's concern is not an abstract *De Deo*

120. Balthasar, *Theology of History*, 92.

121. Ibid., 99.

122. Cf. Balthasar, *Theo-Drama*, V, 53, and see also Byrne, "Hans Urs von Balthasar," 39. R. Byrne says that, "Thus transformed, Christ becomes transforming for us. The Resurrection appearances are transforming encounters in which Jesus is revealed as with us in time and for us (*pro nobis*) in order to draw us beyond time into the eschatological kingdom" (p. 39). Accordingly, "the basic principle which interprets the mystery of the forty days for von Balthasar is that Christ's mode of existence in our lives, in the Church, and in the sacraments is fundamentally no different from that of the forty days themselves. In our lives he is the risen Lord, living in the eternity of the Father, his earthly time transformed into his eternal duration, and precisely as the eternal Christ accompanying his people in and through time" (p. 46).

123. As Balthasar says, "Indeed, from the perspective of the New Covenant we must say that the revelation of God that takes place in Jesus Christ is primarily a Trinitarian

Uno, but *De Deo Trino* (i.e., *Deus Trinitatis*) who is manifested Himself in Jesus Christ's person, life, and extremely in His *mysterium paschale*.[124] According to Balthasar, the doctrine of God in classical theism does not adequately conceive the mystery of the Trinity, which is an intensely dramatic engagement with the world of suffering in the paschal mystery of Jesus Christ's death and resurrection.[125] That is to say, according to Balthasar, the immanent Trinity can be understood only through the economic Trinity, which is revealed specifically through the sheer splendor of the trinitarian event of love in Jesus Christ.[126] The *Verbum Caro*, the form (*Gestalt*) of the Son in time, is "the *revelation of the Trinity*."[127] Therefore, according to Balthasar, a Trinitarian *Theo-Logic* (theology) is possible only through a Trinitarian *Theo-Drama* (economy).

The Economic Trinity: The Triune God in the Temporal "Theo-Drama"

For Christian faith and theology, the genuine knowledge of God, the Trinity, is revealed and made accessible only on the basis of God's self-

---

one: Jesus does not speak about God in general but shows us the Father and gives us the Holy Spirit." Idem, *Theo-Drama*, V, 67.

124. Cf. Balthasar, *Theo-Drama*, V, 66–67. While criticizing the traditional approach to the knowledge of God, which is centered *De Deo Uno*, O'Hanlon points out that, "[the] most important of all is von Balthasar's contribution to *De Deo Uno* is his theology of the love of God as it is revealed above all in Jesus Christ on the Cross. . . . This, von Balthasar is saying, is what God is, the short he is, this is what grounds all else. . . . the Trinity . . . It is at center." Idem, "H. U. von Balthasar and *De Deo Uno*," 126.

125. Cf. Hunt, *What Are They Saying about the Trinity?*, 49.

126. Balthasar says that, "God is trinitarian life; but for us he is life in the incarnation of the Son, . . . If we try to contemplate God's life in the Trinity in itself, we only find a vacuum, unreality, mathematical concepts or vague speculations. We can no more make the Trinity in itself an 'object' of contemplation that the pagan mystics and Christian ascetics of old could 'objectify' the super-essential unity of God by abstraction from all created multiplicity." Idem, *Prayer*, 154.

127. Balthasar, *Theo-Drama*, V, 121 (italics original). In citing from Adrienne von Speyr's works, Balthasar states as follows: "His life on earth is an image and an expression of the divided triune life in heaven. In his individual being he manifests the uniqueness of the Father, and of the Son, and of the Spirit. . . . There will never, then, be two possibilities of seeing God: one through the Father, and the other through the Son. Rather, the Son is the revelation of God the Father . . . entire openness to the eternal Evermore of the Father. And this takes place, according to his own words, through the Holy Spirit, who is the bond of both" (ibid.).

revelation in Jesus Christ. The following statement by Balthasar clearly shows this:

> We know about the Father, Son and Spirit as divine "Persons" only through the figure and disposition of Jesus Christ. Thus we can agree with the principle, open by enunciated today, that it is only on the basis of the economic Trinity that we can have knowledge of the immanent Trinity and dare to make statement about it.[128]

According to Balthasar, there is "no Trinitarian doctrine without Christology," and at the same time there is "no Christology without Trinitarian doctrine."[129] In conceiving a Christocentric doctrine of the Trinity, unlike others, Balthasar distinctively emphasized Jesus Christ's paschal mystery, the events of the three days of the *Sacrum Triduum*, especially the descent into hell on the Holy Saturday.[130] For him, "all that is christological and soteriological by rooting it in the mystery of the Trinity."[131] And thus, "What is revealed in the Son 'is not a human ideal, but divine, eternal life.'"[132] Jesus Christ's paschal mystery is a trinitarian soteriological event *pro nobis* and *pro mundo*, but at the same time it is a theological event *in se* in that it essentially discloses God's own Being, as the Trinity.[133]

---

128. Balthasar, *Theo-Drama*, III, 508.

129. Cited in Saward, *Mysteries of March*, 10.

130. For example, Barth's trinitarian understanding focused upon the Incarnation as the event of God's self-revelation in Jesus Christ, and thus Rahner's too, but Moltmann emphasized the event of the Cross, which clearly reveals the Triune God. Distinctively, Balthasar's profound theologizing of *Mysterium Paschale* is an influence of Adrienne von Speyr's spiritual experience on the Holy Saturday, "the mystery of Christ's Descent into Hell, which Balthasar explicitly calls the center of all Christology." *Mysterium Paschale*, 7. This work was first published in *Mysterium Salutis* (1969) as a contributing chapter. Cf. Hunt, *Trinity and the Paschal Mystery*, 58–59.

131. Balthasar, *Mysterium Paschale*, 140, and see also 174–76. In another place, Balthasar says, "For it is precisely in the Kenosis of Christ (and nowhere else) that the *inner* majesty of God's love appears, of God who 'is love' (1 John 4:8) and therefore a trinity." Idem, *Love Alone*, 71.

132. Balthasar, *Theo-Drama*, V, 247. Thus, according to Balthasar, "we must see the doctrine of the Trinity as the ever-present, inner presupposition of the doctrine of the Cross." Idem, *Theo-Drama*, IV, 319.

133. Cf. Balthasar, *Mysterium Paschale*, 29.

However, according to Balthasar, the economic Trinity is essentially grounded in and presupposes the immanent Trinity.[134] For this conception, as we have seen, Balthasar describes the threefold *kenosis* of the Triune God. The first and primary *kenosis ad intra* is the inner-trinitarian drama of God's love, the generation of the Son from the Father in the very same essence.[135] This primal "self-emptying" and "self-giving" divine action of the eternal *kenosis ad intra*, which is the "eternal exteriorization" or "distinction" of God from God in the immanent Trinity, gives the "space," the ground and the ontological condition of the pos-

---

134 Balthasar explicitly says that "the economic Trinity . . . always presupposes the immanent [Trinity]." *Theo-Drama*, IV, 362. Concerning the problem of the relationship between the immanent Trinity and the economic Trinity, Balthasar rightly points out a theological danger within the simple identification between them, like so-called K. Rahner's axiom, "The economic Trinity *is* the immanent Trinity, and vice versa," and J. Moltmann's direct identification of the crucifixion of the Son to the trinitarian event with the Father. According to Balthasar, therefore, it is essential that we must distinguish between the internal divine processions in the eternal God's Being (*ad intra*, the immanent Trinity) and the process of saving history outside of himself (*ad extra*, the economic Trinity). Without this essential distinction, as Balthasar says, "God is entangled in the world process and becomes a tragic, mythological God. A way must be found to see the immanent Trinity as the ground of the world process (including the crucifixion) in such a way that it is neither a formal process of self-communication in God, as in Rahner, nor entangled in the world process, as in Moltmann. The immanent Trinity must be understood to be that eternal, absolute self-surrender whereby God is seen to be, in himself, absolute love; this in turn explains his free self-giving to the world as love, without suggesting that God's 'needed' the world process and the Cross in order to become himself (to 'mediate himself')." Idem, *Theo-Drama*, IV, 322–23.

135. Balthasar gives a deeper explanation on the primal self-kenotic divine drama *ad intra*, as follows: "The Father, in uttering and surrendering himself without reserve, does not lose himself. He does not extinguish himself by self-giving, just as he does not keep back anything of himself either. For, in this self-surrender, he *is* the whole divine essence. Here we see both God's infinite power and his powerlessness; he cannot be God in any other way but in this 'kenosis' within the Godhead itself. (Yet what omnipotence is revealed here! He brings forth a God who is of equal substance and therefore uncreated, even if, in this self-surrender, he must go to the very extreme of self-lessness.) It follows that the Son, for his part, cannot *be* and *possess* the absolute nature of God except in the mode of receptivity: he receives this unity of omnipotence and powerlessness from the Father. This receptivity simultaneously includes the Son's self-givenness (which is the absolute presupposition for all the different ways in which he is delivered up to the world) and his filial thanksgiving (Eucharist) for the gift of consubstantial divinity. The world can only be created within the Son's 'generation'; the world belongs to him and has him as its goal; only in the Son can the world be 'recapitulated'. Accordingly, in whatever way the Son is sent into the world (*precession* here is seen to be *mission*, up to and including the Cross), it is an integral part of 'co-original' thanksgiving for the world." Idem, *Theo-Drama*, IV, 325–26.

sibility of all other subsequent relationships of God to the world in His temporal *kenosis ad extra*: creation and all the contingencies of human freedom, the Incarnation, and the unique "separation" in the paschal mystery (i.e., abandonment, suffering, death, and finally descent into hell).[136] As Balthasar says,

> God the Father can give his divinity away in such a manner that it is not merely "lent" to the Son: the Son's possession of it is "equally substantial." This implies such an incomprehensible and unique "separation" of God from himself that it *includes* and grounds every other separation—be it never so dark and bitter.[137]

Accordingly, for Balthasar, all other possible drama between God and the world in the temporal economy of creation, providence, and salvation (*kenosis ad extra*) is already contained in the eternal, primal Theo-drama (*Urdrama*) of the inner-trinitarian love (*kenosis ad intra*). In this sense, "It is a case of the play within the play: our play 'plays' in his play."[138] The following statement succinctly explains this:

> [I]t is the drama of the "emptying" of the Father's heart, in the generation of the Son, that contains and surpasses all possible between God and a world. For any world only has its place within that distinction between Father and Son that is maintained and bridged by the Holy Spirit. The drama of the Trinity lasts forever: the Father was never without the Son, nor were Father and Son ever without Spirit. Everything temporal takes place within the embraces of the eternal action and as its consequence (hence *opera trinitas ad extra communia*).[139]

According to Balthasar, therefore, the immanent Trinity is uniquely and explicitly manifested in Jesus Christ's paschal mystery of *Sacrum Triduum Mortis*: Good Friday, Holy Saturday, and Easter Sunday. In this grandest drama in world history, the Triune God has actually appeared and acted, and therefore it is truly His own drama, *Theo-Drama*:[140] In

---

136. Cf. Balthasar, *Mysterium Paschale*, 28; and also see, Hunt, *Trinity and the Paschal Mystery*, 61; and his *What Are They Saying about the Trinity?*, 52.

137. Balthasar, *Theo-Drama*, IV, 325.

138. Balthasar, *Theo-Drama*, I, 20. Cf. Hunt, *Trinity and the Paschal Mystery*, 60–61.

139. Balthasar, *Theo-Drama*, IV, 327.

140. Balthasar says that God really appears in the economic Theo-drama in this world stage and history: "Can God appear in the play? Or is the play 'theodramatic' only insofar as it is organized *by* God and produced *for* him and *in his presence*? The

this marvelous Theo-Drama, God the Father is its Author, the Son is the central Actor, and the Holy Spirit is its Director.[141] Now, let's see the climax of the unique and once for all *Theo-Drama* of Love in world history *pro nobis*.

Going to the Cross (the Death): Good Friday

Even though the Incarnation of the Son in human flesh is the first action of self-revelation of the Triune God, for Balthasar, the paschal mystery of Jesus Christ is its climax, the final act of the Trinitarian Theo-drama of love.[142] Indeed, according to Balthasar, "It is the hour of the Father when the triune eternal divine plan is executed to clean away the whole terrible mess of the world's sin and consume it in the fire of suffering love."[143] Concerning Jesus Christ's obedience in His self-giving love to the Father's will even to death on the Cross, Balthasar says that, in this remarkable and unique manner, "his obedience presents the kenotic translation of the eternal love of the Son for the 'ever-greater' Father."[144] Accordingly, in Balthasaar's view, it is a dramatic manifestation of the "selflessness" of the three Persons' inner-trinitarian reality, which is the mutual self-giving and self-kenotic event of love. Therefore, "the redemptive Kenosis is itself indivisibly trinitarian."[145]

On the Cross, the Son experiences absolute abandonment from the Father. That is to say, "in this ending life that gives the Son this feeling, but much deeper, his inner bearing of the irreconcilable contradiction between the sin he has within him and the salvific will of the loving Father. As the embodiment of sin he can no longer find any support in God; he has identified himself with that which God must eternally turn away from himself."[146] At this moment, however, the Holy Spirit unites the abyss, the difference, and this absolute estrangement between

---

Christian answer is that God has actually appeared in the play: in Jesus Christ, the Son of the Father, who possesses the Spirit 'without measure.' . . . He is able to become immanent in the world drama without surrendering his transcendence above and beyond it." Idem, *Theo-Drama*, III, 506 (italics original).

141. Cf. Dalzell, *Dramatic Encounter of Divine and Human Freedom*, 118.
142. Cf. Balthasar, *Theo-Drama*, V, 247, and *Mysterium Paschale*, 35.
143. Kehl and Löser, *Von Balthasar Reader*, 148.
144. Balthasar, *Mysterium Paschale*, 91.
145. Ibid., 35.
146. Kehl and Löser, *Von Balthasar Reader*, 148–49.

the Father and the Son by stretching their mutual love to the point of unbearability. In this way, "the infinite difference within God which is the presupposition of eternal love and gets bridged by the Holy Spirit; and the salvation-historical difference in which the alienated world is reconciled with God."[147] According to Balthasar, therefore, in this most sublime Trinitarian drama of chrisotological-soterological event, the mystery of Jesus Christ's death on the Cross is "the highest revelation of the Trinity."[148]

Going to the Dead (the Descent into Hell): Holy Saturday

Probably, one of the most creative and controversial contributions of Balthasar's theology lies in his emphatic theologizing of Holy Saturday (i.e., Jesus Christ's descent into hell). Balthasar says that, "the theology of Holy Saturday . . . stands as the mysterious middle between cross and resurrection, and consequently properly in the center of all revelation and theology."[149] The Father's sublime love for the Son in the eternal immanent Trinity as well as for us (the world) in the economic salvation is most clearly and dramatically manifested in the Son, Jesus Christ's descent into hell. According to Balthasar, "Christ's experience of hell on Holy Saturday is a trinitarian as well as a soteriological experience that forms the necessary conclusion to the cross as well as the necessary presupposition of the resurrection."[150] Even though "hell" is the place of absolute desolation, God-forsakenness, and godlessness, it is always still "a christological place."[151] In Christ's descent into hell, in Balthasar's view, two things are clearly manifested. On the one hand, it reveals the incarnate Son's deeper solidarity with humanity not just in its fleshness, but even in its sinfulness, loneliness,

---

147. Ibid., 149.

148. Ibid., 148.

149. Ibid., 404. Concerning this, A. Hunt states that, "Von Balthasar's treatment of the descent into hell is one of the most striking features of his whole theology. The portrayal of the descent into hell is like the magnificent centerpiece of the breathtaking triptych that is von Balthasar's trinitarian theology. It is also highly controversial, for there is little direct biblical warrant for his extraordinary emphasis on this aspect of the paschal mystery." Idem, *What Are They Saying about the Trinity?*, 55.

150. Kehl and Löser, *Von Balthasar Reader*, 404.

151. Ibid., 422.

alienation, suffering, and finally death of sinners in hell–the absolute God-forsakenness. As Balthasar says,

> Into this finality (of death) the dead Son descends, no longer acting in any way, but stripped by the cross of every power and initiative of his own, as one purely to be used, debased to mere matter, with a fully indifferent (corpse) obedience, incapable of any active act of solidarity—only thus is he right for any "sermon" to the dead. He is (out of an ultimate love however) dead together with them. And exactly in that way he disturbs the absolute loneliness striven for by the sinner: the sinner, who wants to be "damned" apart from God, finds God again in his loneliness, but God in the absolute weakness of love who unfathomably in the period of noontime enters into solidarity with those damning themselves.[152]

In this absolute self-kenotic weakness of God, within Christ's solidarity with the dead, the freedom of the creature (even to the point of rejection of God's absolute love) is respected, but it is retrieved at the end of the passion by God and seized again in its very foundation through His solidarity with those who reject all solidarity with God (i.e., the condemned peoples).[153] On Good Friday, "the economic Trinity objectively acts out the drama of the world's alienation."[154] In Jesus Christ's decent into hell, on the other hand, what is revealed is this: "God is love; the immanent Trinity is revealed in the economic, and precisely as God's 'orthopraxis' in the giving of his Son to divine abandonment and hell, which is the greatest possible conception of God [as Triune Love]."[155] Balthasar explains this as follows:

> This opposition between God, the creative origin (the "Father"), and man who, faithful to the mission of the origin, ventures on into ultimate perdition (the "Son"), this bond stretched to the breaking point does not break because the same Spirit of absolute love (the "Spirit") informs both the one who sends and the one sent. God causes God to go into abandonment by God while accompanying him on the way with his Spirit. The Son can go into the estrangement from God of hell, because he understands his way as an expression of his love for the Father, and he can

---

152. Ibid., 153.
153. Cf. ibid.
154. Balthasar, *Theo-Drama*, IV, 362.
155. Kehl and Löser, *Von Balthasar Reader*, 114.

give to his love the character of obedience to such a degree that in it he experiences the complete godlessness of lost man.[156]

Going to the Father (the Resurrection): Easter Sunday

Now, according to Balthasar, the sublime Trinitarian Theo-drama of love runs toward its final climax, the last act on the last day of *Sacrum Triduum Mortis*, Easter Sunday, the resurrection of the dead Son of God. Without the resurrection, the whole Trinitarian salvific plan; the whole life, the passion, and the death of the Son would be incomprehensible and meaningless. The resurrection, too, for Balthasar, is an explicit Trinitarian event.

> With his death on the cross the Son of God fulfilled his mandate to return to the Father with his human spirit, the Holy Spirit of his mission. As a human being he himself cannot rise from the dead; it is the Father who, as "the God of the living" (Rom 4:17), raises the Son from the dead so that he, as newly united with the Father, might send the Spirit of God into the church.[157]

In the Trinitarian event of the resurrection of the dead Son, the Father, as the Creator, initiates and brings His creative action to its completion in the Triune Drama of love *pro nobis* and *pro mundo*.[158] But, at the same time, the resurrection of the dead Son is actually accomplished in the transfiguring action of the Spirit of God, His *pneuma*.[159] The reunion of the Father and the Son takes place in the powerful action of the Holy Spirit in their inseparable mutual love. In this way, for Balthasar, the Spirit is the "instrument" of the resurrection as well as the "milieu" in which it takes place. Therefore, "the Father raises the Son by his Spirit."[160] Indeed, it is the Holy Spirit who overcomes, bridges and re-unites the abyss, the distance, and the separation between the Father and the Son in the Cross and descent into hell. At this moment,

---

156. Balthasar, *Elucidations*, 82.
157. Kehl and Löser, *Von Balthasar Reader*, 154.
158. Cf. Balthasar, *Mysterium Paschale*, 203–4.
159. Cf. ibid., 204.
160. Ibid., 211.

Balthasar declares, "This economic form of the Trinity comes to an end with the Resurrection."[161]

The Immanent Trinity: The Triune God in Eternity as "Super-Time"

Now, we can turn to the immanent Trinity only through the analogical way of the economic Trinity in world time, which is the unfolding of the eternal Trinitarian Theo-drama *ad extra* in its centerpoint of Jesus Christ's *mysterium paschale*. According to Balthasar, Christ's separation from the Father in paschal mystery is already contained in the supra-temporal processions of the inner-trinitarian event of love. Therefore, we know about God only through Jesus Christ: "the eternal Word expresses the Father."[162] However, at the same time, for Balthasar, "the essence of God is to be ever-greater" (*das Wesen Gottes ist das 'Je-mehr'*), and thus we cannot grasp God even in the eternal bliss state of heaven (i.e., God's incomprehensibility).[163] Moreover, in the immanent Trinity, God is always the "ever-greater God" (*Deus Semper Major*) even to Himself by the Holy Spirit, who is the ever-greater love between the Father and the Son.[164] First of all, therefore, in his understanding of the Triune God, Balthasar emphasizes a dynamic and dramatic characteristic of the divine three personal Being in terms of interpersonal processions, relations, communications, and missions in incommensurable love. All of this is converged into and grounded upon the unique and glorious event of love in the three personal God within their "ever-greater" unity.[165]

---

161. Balthasar, *Theo-Drama*, IV, 364.

162. Balthasar, *Explorations in Theology*, III, 105.

163. Balthasar, *Theologik*, III, 219; Cf. *Theo-Drama*, V, 396. For a full exposition of Balthasar's concept "ever-greater God" in Christological perspective, see Heinz, *Der Gott des Je-mehr*.

164. Balthasar says that, "*Deus semper major* nicht für uns, sondern für Gott selbst (God is ever-greater God not only for us, but also for God himself)." *Theologik*, III, 416. Cf. *Theo-Drama*, V, 78. For a full exposition of Balthasar's concept of the "ever-greater God" in Pneumatological perspective, see Sachs, "Spirit and Life," and this is summarized as "Deus Semper Major," 631–57.

165. According to Balthasar, "God must be eternally in himself 'I' and 'Thou' and the loving unity of both: the mystery of the Trinity becomes the inalienable presupposition of the existence of the world and of the fact that the drama of love is played out between

According to Balthasar, essentially, "God is Love" (1 John 4:8), and "the doctrine of the Trinity is the only doctrine to assert this."[166] For him, the biblical declaration of "God is love" means that therefore God is the Trinity.[167] In this sense, Balthasar's Trinitarian ontology is not the classical static ontology of substance, but it is a dynamic ontology of love. As Balthasar states, "God's inner life is not merely ontological and objective, but spiritual and personal" in mutual love within the three personal God.[168] A. Hunt properly points out that, therefore, in Balthasar's Trinitarian theology, there is a shift from "being" to "love." That is to say, from a "metaphysically-conceived absolute being, *Actus Purus, Ipsum Esse*" to an "intrinsically dynamic *Actus Purus, Ipsum Amare*."[169] As such, Balthasar's dynamic Trinitarian ontology of love made a "decisive turnabout in the way of seeing God," namely, his understanding of divine perfections. For example, God is not "absolute power" in omnipotence, but "absolute love," in which His sovereignty itself manifests not in its own possession, but in its self-abandonment.[170] Likewise, divine absolute freedom, too, is conceived of as the self-giving, self-surrendering in His own nature of Being as love. This is clear in the following statement by Balthasar:

> God is not only by nature free in his self-possession, in his ability to do what he will with himself; for that very reason, he is also free to do what he will with his own nature. That is, he can surrender himself; as Father, he can share the same Godhead with the Spirit. Here too, we are already placed beyond necessity and chance. The fact that the absolute freedom of self-possession can understand itself, according to its absolute nature, as limitless self-giving—this is not the result of anything external to itself; yet it is the result of its own nature, so much so that, apart from this self-giving, it would not be itself. In generating

---

God and the world and that this drama fulfills the world in its interior dimension as the encounter of 'I' and 'Thou.'" Balthasar, *Explorations in Theology*, III, 310–11.

166. Balthasar, *Love Alone*, 71–72. Cf. *Theo-Drama*, V, 122.

167. Balthasar says that, "The kingship of God, who reveals himself as love, is shown to us in the humble obedience of the Son to the Father, and so we are shown that this obedience is essentially love.... For it is precisely in the Kenosis of Christ (and nowhere else) that the inner majesty of God's love appears, of God who 'is love' (1 John 4:8) and therefore a trinity." Idem, *Love Alone*, 71.

168. Balthasar, *Prayer*, 142.

169. Hunt, *What Are They Saying about the Trinity?*, 59–60.

170. Balthasar, *Mysterium Paschale*, 28.

the Son, the Father does not "lose" himself to someone else in order thereby to "regain" himself; for he is always himself by giving himself. The Son, too, is always himself by allowing himself to be generated and by allowing the Father to do with him as he pleases. The Spirit is always himself by understanding his "I" as the "We" of Father and Son, by being "expropriated" for the sake of what is most proper to them.[171]

In the very same sense, for Balthasar, the Triune God is analogously conceived as an eternal "event" of love in His essence, which is constituted by an eternal relational process of reciprocal self-surrendering, and unceasing giving and receiving between the Triune persons in one unity.[172] It can be said that, with the concept of the eternal Being (essence), there is equally an eternal (not temporal) "happening" in God's Being. Expressions such as "beget," "give birth," "proceed" and "breathe forth" in the immanent Trinity are not a mere motionless order or sequence, but "eternal acts in which God genuinely 'takes place.'"[173] Therefore, there is a unity within two contradictory concepts: God's eternal or absolute Being (*Sein*) and the dynamic eventful life of the Trinity as event and "happening" (*Geschehen*).[174] Furthermore, Balthasar finds a concrete ground for the union of the two contradictory notions in the ontology of love, the absolute Being as love, who is the Trinity. However, Balthasar clearly rejects any idea of creaturely "becoming" in the sense of Whiteheadian Process theology. That is to say, according to Balthasar, God does not "become" love, but God "is" essentially and eternally love as the Triune God.[175] God, as the Trinity, is always "ever-greater" love, which accepts even the world's "ever-greater" (i.e., ever-increasing) re-

171. Balthasar, *Theo-Drama*, II, 256.
172. Cf. Hunt, *Trinity and the Paschal Mystery*, 62–63.
173. Balthasar explains this as follows: "This 'happening' is not a becoming in the earthly sense: it is the coming-to-be, not of something that once was not (that would be Arianism), but, evidently, of something that grounds the idea, the inner possibility and reality of a becoming. All earthly becoming is a reflection of the eternal 'happening' in God, which, we repeat, is per se identical with the eternal Being or essence." Idem, *Theo-Drama*, V, 67.
174. Balthasar, *Theo-Drama*, V, 67.
175. Cf. Hunt, *Trinity and the Paschal Mystery*, 80. For Balthasar's own exposition on this problem of being and becoming, see "Being-Event-Becoming" in *Theo-Drama*, V, 66–81; *Theo-Drama*, III, 157, 190–91, 506–9; and *Theo-Drama*, IV, 319–32. In this sense, Balthasar says, "Thus God remains eternal event, yet without temporal becoming." Idem, *Theo-Drama*, V, 459.

sistance to His love.[176] Balthasar insists that, therefore, as it is revealed through the Incarnation, God's Being is "Super-Becoming" in the immense movement of love inside the Triune God.[177] Indeed, for Balthasar, the *Verbum Caro*, Jesus Christ's whole earthly life in His flesh, the natural succession of moments and seasons, the growth—childhood, youth, and man—throughout His life is analogously a full expression of the "ever-newer," "super-becoming" aspect in the eternal life of the Triune God. In this sense, Balthasar says that, "The Word of God passed through time. Everything in his passage was the word and revelation of the Father, but also revelation of the truth of human existence. God wished to show himself in this life, but God wanted to manifest himself as the eternal Word to men and in this way."[178] Therefore, God is Life and the living God, not a mere static substance, and thus "the Ocean of Being" in which our thought would never be in a position to capture.[179] Accordingly, for Balthasar, "The God who is 'above God' thus remains the God who is *semper maior* (always greater)."[180]

As a consequence, in order to convey such a dynamic vitality of the inner-trinitarian eventful life of love, Balthasar uses the term "supra-temporality" for the mode of existence of the "ever-greater" God rather than the concept of absolute "timeless" eternity in classical theism. For Balthasar's understanding of God, in must be emphasized that God is always an infinite comparative: God is "ever-greater-Being" (*Je-Mehr-Sein*) and thus "He-who-is-always-greater."[181] Accordingly, God's eternity, too, means not an absolute superlative form (i.e., "non-time" or "timelessness"), but a comparative in an analogical sense: "ever-greater" temporality—i.e., "super-time." It is clear in the following statement of Balthasar:

---

176. Cf. Balthasar, *Theo-Drama*, V, 55. It is clear in Balthasar's statement: "Since there is no 'development' in the eternal life of God, and yet that there *is* love's 'ever-greater,' love's constant element of surprise, its inexhaustible manifestation of unity (seen from whatever angle), the development that characterizes the creature is the highest possible approximation to such unattainable vitality." *Theo-Drama*, V, 90.

177. Blathasar, *Presence and Thought*, 153.

178. Balthasar, *Theological Anthropology*, 243–44, for Balthasar's full exposition on this, see also pp. 239–74.

179. Ibid.

180. Ibid., 161.

181. Balthasar, *Theologik*, III, 146 and *Theo-Drama*, II, 119.

"Eternal" here also means infinite, which cannot be expressed by an ultimate superlative (like "highest good") but only by a comparative that is open to the "ever-greater." It is true that God is "ever-greater" than man can grasp, even when the latter has reached eternal bliss; yet, though God himself is perfectly "light," he is also "ever-greater" even to himself: he is that "exuberance" which is most vividly expressed in personal terms by the Holy Spirit.[182]

In the immanent Trinity, according to Balthasar, the Father's act of surrender requires its own area of freedom not only for the Son's act of reception from the Father, but also for the Spirit's act of proceeding and illuminating the most intimate love of Father and Son.[183] Therefore, the "area" for divine action in infinite freedom can develop something like infinite "duration" and infinite "space" in the three personal acts of reciprocal love, the life of the *communio*, of fellowship in the immanent Trinity.[184] For Balthasar, this is the very mode of existence of the immanent Trinity in the *perichoresis* mutual love. Therefore, the immanent Trinity, the Triune God's mode of existence in eternity is not "non-time" or "timeless," but, as we have seen, "ever-greater temporality" or "super-time."[185] As Balthasar says,

> God's "abiding forever" must not be seen as a "non-time" but as a super-time that is unique to him; and this is illustrated in the fact that Christ's time mediates between God's "time" and world-time. Christ's time recapitulates and comprehends world-time, while it also reveals God's super-time.[186]

Indeed, particularly enough, according to Balthasar, the concept of timelessness as "an endless end" characterizes "the non-time of the Cross and Hell."[187] While distinguishing three kinds of "timelessness"– the time in heaven, in hell, and of the Cross, Balthasar says the following, "Nonetheless the timelessness of the cross is not mere negation of

---

182. Balthasar, *Theo-Drama*, V, 78.
183. Cf. Balthasar, *Theo-Drama*, II, 257.
184. Ibid.
185. Balthasar, *Theo-Drama*, V, 32.
186. Ibid., 30.
187. Balthasar, *Glory of the Lord*, VII, 172–73, and see also his full exposition on this issue in "Analogies of Timelessness" in *Theo-Drama*, V, 305–11.

time that characterizes hell, but a 'super-time.'"[188] The blessed in heaven, too, will participate in eternal life (i.e., the supra-temporality, the immortal time) of God, given to us through Jesus Christ.[189] Therefore, the time of Hell alone is "eternal timelessness" and "non-time" which means the time of God-forsakenness as an absolute separation from God's "super-time," and therefore the time of "the limitless, eternal death."[190] However, at the same time, for Balthasar, God's "super-time" does not mean a simple infinite extension of time, which means an everlasting duration without beginning and end.[191] Balthasar uses the term, "super-time," only to denote a dynamic liveliness and vitality of the inner-trinitarian life in eternal love without any defections of fleetingness or consecutive extension of the creature's time. Actually, in comparison to the world time of extension, God's super-time is an ultimately intensive "perfect simultaneity" of their reciprocal inter-relationship in the incommensurable state of unity.[192] Therefore, he says that, "Everything eternal taking place in time is itself beyond time and before all time."[193] Accordingly, God's time is always present and suspended as a vertical "Today" of salvation time in the ever fleeting horizontal "now" of the world time.[194]

God's "Super-Time" and Its Relation to Human Time

Finally, concerning the relationship between God's eternity and human time, Balthasar first describes "the primal idea of time" (with "space")

---

188. Balthasar, *Theo-Drama*, V, 310.

189. Cf. ibid., 305. Elsewhere, Balthasar explains the difference between eternal life and eternal damnation as follows: "Eternal life is a life whose present contains an eternal future but no past. Eternal damnation, on the other hand, would be a life whose present is turned entirely toward the past. It would thus be pure hopelessness. Eternal life would be the perfect fulfillment of the eternal intensification within being itself; it would be what the comparative of life looks like when it has become a state. By contrast, eternal damnation would be the total evacuation of this ever greater plentitude from existence. It would be the futility and absurdity of being become a state." Idem, *Theo-Logic*, I, 198–99.

190. Balthasar, *Glory of the Lord*, VII, 172–73, and *Theo-Drama*, V, 305–6, and 310–11.

191. Cf. O'Hanlon, *Immutability of God*, 92.

192. Balthasar, *Theo-Drama*, V, 93.

193. Ibid., 116–17.

194. Balthasar, *Theological Anthropology*, 35.

in "the coming-to-be of the divine processions" in the inner-trinitarian event of love.[195] The eternal Triune Being in terms of the eternal "event" of love cannot be "the form of its duration as a mere *nunc stans*," in which "everything would contract to a single unmoving point."[196] In that case, it abolishes not only the very space and time for the divine action which makes possible the sublime Trinitarian Theo-drama of love, but also deprives everything which makes world-time exciting and delightful even in a tiny transient moment. Therefore, Balthasar asserts that "time 'makes room' for existent being, indeed, it creates an acting area in which it can realize itself as event. In turn, space requires time so that it may be mapped, investigated and conquered."[197] We can find such a positive aspect of time not in a mere "substance," but in the eternal trinitarian processions of "begetting" and "being begotten," "giving" and "receiving" the event of love, which are always taking place in the divine eternal "Now." However, according to Balthasar, the eternal trinitarian processions are taking place "in the perpetual immediacy of this sudden moment, without limits of time, without sequence in their reciprocal vision, both of them know in perfect simultaneity of their reciprocal love. In their communion, which was from eternity and yet is created afresh at every instant, they know of their ineffable, expectant love for the Spirit, who at this precise moment is proceeding from them both as the expression of their common purpose and expectation."[198] Accordingly, for Balthasar, God's eternity is not a mere absolute timelessness *nunc stans* or "non-time" in classical theism, but "ever-greater" temporality or "super-time" for the ever-greater fullness of the inner-trinitarian life in mutual relationship of love. At the same time, according to Balthasar, God's super-time has a positive aspect for the eventful and delightful liveliness of human time, but only in the analogical sense of "ever-greater," "ever-newer," or "ever-richer," and therefore it is a "super-time."

In this sense, Balthasar says that "there is a deep analogy," a likeness within ever-greater unlikeness, between God's eternity (i.e., super-time) and human time.[199] There are always two sides of time in relation to

195. Balthasar, *Theo-Drama*, V, 91.
196. Ibid.
197. Ibid., 92.
198. Ibid., 93.
199. Ibid., 101.

eternity, a positive and negative, an affinity to eternity and to nothingness, which are inextricably interwoven.[200] For Balthasar, an analogy (i.e., a similarity within ever-greater difference) between them can be properly characterized as an infinite "intensity" for God's super-time and an endless consecutive "extension" for human time.[201] That is, for human time, as Augustine clearly showed us, it is always experienced as a sequence of transient moments and an extended duration or extension (*distentio*).[202] Therefore, for Balthasar, as for Augustine, time is conceived as a "distance" from the Creator to the creature, in both senses of vertical and horizontal.[203] Only in this sense, the following wandering image of time can be understandable: "Time and history come from God and are on the way back to him, in a necessary *recirculatio* from God to God, and God, abandoned and spurned by the world, must be revealed in his wrath at all secular history (Rom 1:18)."[204] The farthest form of its extension (or distance) from God is the time of Hell, the time of God-forsakenness, and thus the time of eternal damnation, which is an "endless" time or "timeless duration" of death.[205]

However, in comparison to human time, God's super-time can be conceived of as a single, perfect moment without any distance or limit as such within human time. As we have seen, therefore, it is a perfect simultaneity in every instant of the eternal Now.[206] It is always occurring "Now," the ever-newer "happening" in the tri-personal inter-relationship of love. In this sense, God's eternity is "not simply timeless but a present that always was and is always coming."[207] Therefore, in Balthasar's view, the divine "Super-time" is the mode of existence of the three personal God in the perfect unity of their reciprocal relationship. As Balthasar says, "In God, distance and nearness exist in a unity that exhibits their constantly intensifying relationship: 'The more the Persons in God differentiate themselves, the greater is their unity.'"[208] Actually, we can see

200. Cf. Balthasar, *Theo-Logic*, I, 196.
201. Cf. O'Hanlon, *Immutability of God*, 93.
202. Cf. Balthasar, *Theological Anthropology*, 6–7.
203. Ibid., 22–23.
204. Ibid., 116.
205. Balthasar, *Theo-Drama*, V, 306.
206. Cf. ibid., 91–93.
207. Ibid., 27, footnote 7.
208. Ibid., 94.

the perfection and completeness of human time with God's eternity in the time of Jesus Christ: "Jesus gathers together the intrinsically transitory, fragmentary nature of time by living every moment of his life in a love of his Father which is shown in his obedience to the latter's will."[209] Throughout His whole earthly life in human time, Jesus Christ lived the "Now" of God from moment to moment by His perfect receptivity and obedience to the Father's will, which is an explicit presentation of the "ever-now" (*je-jetzt*), the fullness, the simultaneity of eternity within His relationship to the Father in the Holy Spirit, which is the mode of Being as the Trinity, i.e., "the Super-time."

Therefore, according to Balthasar, the relationship between God's "super-time" and human time is mediated by the time of Jesus Christ, who is the concrete analogy between God and man. In other words, it reflects the relationship between the economic Trinity in salvation history and the immanent Trinity in eternal love. As we have seen in the threefold *kenotic* event of the triune God, the divine "super-time" of the economic Trinity centered in the Christ-event with creation, sending the Son and the Holy Spirit (i.e., the "*horizontal* Theo-drama," divine action *ad extra*) reflects and is subordinated to the "super-time" of the immanent Trinity with its order of processions (i.e., the "*vertical* Theo-drama," divine action *ad intra*).[210] That is to say, "God's internal processes were 'translated from eternity to time and spread out' in the sequential interplay of work and rest, 'so that we may understand something of God and his eternal life, and of the unity of intention and realization which exists there.'"[211] In this primary schema, "the drama of Christ remains the direct fulfillment of Yahweh's covenant drama with Israel, which has been going on throughout the whole history [through the Holy Spirit]"[212] At the same time, the future of the "realized" *eschaton* in the risen Christ's time, the whole of the Church's time is also the time of the Holy Spirit through the risen Christ's breathing of the Spirit upon the Church.[213] In this way, the whole history of the world is subordinated to Trinitarian "super-time" of salvation history, which is the unfolding of the sublime Theo-drama in the inner-trinitarian life of

209. O'Hanlon, *Immutability of God*, 94.
210. Cf. Balthasar, *Theo-Drama*, V, 29 and 32.
211. Ibid., 91.
212. Ibid., 32.
213. Cf. ibid., 31, and *Theology of History*, 99–100.

love. Therefore, for Balthasar, "eternity can always be inside time, just as time can participate in eternity."[214] Balthasar explains this as follows:

> In the perspective of Father and Son, of creation and redemption, the work and position of the Spirit is revealed to us as the centerpoint of reference where all perspectives meet. For it is the Spirit who makes history into history of salvation, which is to say prophetically oriented toward the Son; and it is he who places the Son in those situations which fulfill the Promise. Because he is the Spirit of the Father and the Spirit of the Son in personal unity, he can, at the same time, be the heart of the Father's command and the heart of the Son's obedience, of the Father's promise in history pointing toward the Son and of the Son's fulfillment of history pointing toward the Father.[215]

Finally, according to Balthasar, time is from God's eternity (i.e., super-time,) and thus it will be taken back up into eternity again. That is to say, for him, as the world (the whole non-divine reality) is from God and in God, so transitory world time as its mode of existence comes from God and goes back to eternity. As Balthasar says, "The world unfolds as the reflection of the eternal self-realization of the Divine Being; it cannot avoid being oriented to the latter. Thus, 'the whole of transitory time acquires a meaning once man learns that both its 'ends' are hooked up to eternity: the very duration of transitory time is an analogy of the eternal.'"[216] Therefore, for Balthasar, world time, sinful time, will not be destroyed or pass away as a "non-time," but is able to flow into eternity because it is ultimately consummated and filled with God's super-time in His eternal love *pro nobis* and *pro mundo* through Jesus Christ's time.[217] He explains this as follows:

> The Son's love is no dead image of the Father's love, but is alive and leads us into the Father's living love. And where these two interpenetrate, there issues forth the Holy Spirit to reign totally in the spirit of man. In this participation in eternal love, time, as the creature's form of being, is not annihilated but consummated and filled to overflowing with the eternal dimensions of divine life. Freed from the modalities imposed upon it by the "first Adam," by the Fall and by the reparation of the Cross,

214. Balthasar, *Theo-Drama*, V, 101.
215. Balthasar, *Theology of History*, 62.
216. Balthasar, *Theo-Drama*, V, 100.
217. Balthasar, *Theological Anthropology*, 38.

man's time attains to its intended perfection in God through Christ's time.[218]

It is analogously, but explicitly, manifested in the life of Jesus Christ, who is the concrete analogy. That is to say, as His temporal existence comes from and goes back to the Father, so His time derives from God's eternity and goes back to eternity again. Indeed, as we have seen, the risen Christ's forty days clearly show this fact that time is transformed and integrated into eternity. Especially, the mark of the resurrected Christ's glorified wounds indicate "the presence of Christ's past in eternity not just as a memory but as a present reality—albeit, since they exist now in the resurrected, victorious Christ, as the presence of a transformed past which is part of that intensity of divine life whose perfection admits of differences which are real and are reconciled."[219] In this way, through the mediation of Christ's time, just as time comes from eternity, so our time will be taken back up into God's eternity, as Balthasar states, "time finds its real home there, in its origin."[220]

> In this light, our life and death seem an episode on the way to eternal life. Thus, the more convinced we are of God's eternal life, the more we bear it within us. So, "the concepts of our daily life are immeasureably expanded." We must not just use our time as a measuring rod: we must "use it as an instrument of our obedience to the triune God. In this way Christians can "make each hour God's hour; if they do this, they will be living more in eternity than in time. Time is no longer a closed system: in the very midst of time they can step over the boundary to eternity."[221]

Conclusion

Even though H. U. von Balthasar does not give us an entirely comprehensive exposition of the doctrine of God's eternity and time as a specific monograph, his creative rethinking of the nature of time and God's eternity pervasively spreads into all aspects of his theological thought and almost all of his works. Indeed, as we have seen, for Balthasar, it

218. Balthasar, *Theology of History*, 46.
219. O'Hanlon, *Immutability of God*, 100.
220. Balthasar, *Theo-Drama*, V, 102.
221. Ibid.

is the foundation of the grand schema, in which the "ever-greater" Theo-drama of the immanent Trinity in love is unfolded through the sublime temporal Theo-drama of the economic Trinity, centered in Jesus Christ's *mysterium paschale*. Here are some important aspects of Balthasar's Trinitarian analogical understanding of God's eternity and its relation to time. As such, in my view, it is a significant contribution to Christian theology.

First of all, in Balthasar's view, time itself is not an independent ontological being (or thing), which has its own life and history. Therefore, we cannot think about a neutral time apart from our existence, for it is the very form of our being or the mode of our existence. That is to say, my time is given to me as my own form of existence. It is an ontological property of being accompanied with its existence. In the same sense, chronological time, history as the totality of the creature's time, too, is not in itself an independent neutral time or everlasting duration without beginning and end. However, for Balthasar, the origin of time is in God Himself, the Triune God in eternal love. In other words, Balthasar defines the most "primal origin" (*Uridee*) of time (and space) in the generation of the Son from the Father in eternity. Accordingly, for him, the nature of time is the "receptivity" of the Son for His existence from the Father's self-expropriation action, and therefore there is a "time" as the mode of Being of the Trinity in the tri-personal mutual love. However, in contrast to ever-transient world time, Balthasar calls it God's "super-time" in order to denote the "ever-greater" God's mode of existence in the perfectly reciprocal inner-trinitarian relationship of love. In my view, Balthasar's understanding of the primal idea of time as the Son's receptivity from the Father in the relationship of love in the immanent Trinity is an excellent theological view to conceive properly in an analogical way the relationship between God's eternity and human time. Thus it can be one of the most significant contributions to the contemporary debates on the understanding of God's eternity and its relation to time.

In so doing, while rejecting both the classical ontology of substance and the process ontology of becoming, Balthasar suggests a dynamic and dramatic ontology of love to convey the fullness of vitality, the eventful life of the Trinitarian love in eternity. Therefore, God's eternity is neither "timeless" eternity nor "everlasting" time, but "Super-time." It can be conceived only as an analogical comparative, not superlative, form with human time. That is, God's eternity is always the "ever-greater" temporality or "super-time." In other words, for Blathasar, there is a similarity within ever-greater dissimilarity between God's super-time and human time. In order to properly explain their analogical relationship, Balthasar admitted the concepts of "intensity" and "extensity." While human time is always experienced as a consecutive extension or endless transient and extended duration, God's super-time can be conceived as a perfect simultaneity, figuratively, as a single point of instant, eternal Now, in the sense of ever-greater intensity. "Here and elsewhere," therefore, Balthasar speaks of "the extended, horizontal, latitudinal aspects of time being found preserved but transformed into the intensive, vertical, longitudinal nature of eternity."[222]

However, such a nature of God's eternity as "super-time" is revealed only in the time of Jesus Christ, who is the only concrete *analogia entis* between God and man. For Balthasar, like K. Barth, there is no other way to know the Triune God and His mode of existence, the supra-temporality. Jesus Christ's temporal mode of existence as a perfect receptivity of His being and mission, and as a perfect obedience to the Father's will is, in an analogical way, a kenotic form *ad extra* of the eternal relationship of receptivity from the Father as the "supra-temporal" mode of existence of the immanent Trinity *ad intra*. While making Jesus Christ's paschal mystery the theological center, Balthasar posits "a real kenosis in God which is not merely functional but ontological."[223] Therefore, as we have seen, Balthasar cannot simply repeat a traditional strict concept of divine timelessness, immutability, or impassibility, and so forth but he also explicitly rejects any univocal attribution of temporality, mutability, or passibility, and any process notions of the creaturely becoming of God. Then, with his creative theologizing of Jesus Christ's *mysterium paschale*, which is essentially a translating or unfolding of the glorious Theo-drama in the supra-temporal inner-trinitarian event of love into this temporal world, Balthasar proposes an analogical way of conceiving and explaining the divine as "supra-temporality," "supra-kenosis," "supra-becoming," "supra-mutability," and so on.

In conclusion, Balthasar's conception of God's eternity is neither an absolute timelessness nor a mere univocal everlasting temporality, but an ever-greater intensive "supra-temporality," which is the Triune

---

222. O'Hanlon, *Immutability of God*, 93.
223. Hunt, *What Are They Saying about the Trinity?*, 53.

God's eternal mode of existence in Love. In this way, based on the concrete analogical foundation of the time of Jesus Christ, Balthasar par excellently presented a Trinitarian analogical understanding of God's eternity (i.e., "supra-temporality") and its relation to human time. That is to say, it is very creative and helpful that Balthasar attempted to conceive God's eternity as "supra-time" in an analogical way through the concept of the receptivity of the Son from the Father in the immanent Trinity, which is manifested in the economic Theo-drama. In doing so, Balthasar gives us a sufficient theological explanation of the "ever-greater" difference of God's eternity from our human time as well as its real and positive relationship with our time. Therefore, in my view, Balthasar has paved a more concrete path, of which K. Barth began its construction, toward a further advance step. Thus, his theology strongly stimulates our theological imagination to renew our understanding of not only God's eternity but also its relation to our time. However, we must remember what Balthasar says that, "It is true that God is [always] 'ever-greater' than man can grasp, even when the latter has reached eternal bliss; yet, though God himself is perfectly 'light,' he is also 'ever-greater' even to himself."[224] While remembering this, in the next Chapter, I will try to present my own view which is an alternative Trinitarian analogical understanding of God's eternity and its relation to time.

---

224. Balthasar, *Theo-Drama*, V, 78.

8

Toward an Alternative Trinitarian Analogical Understanding of Time and God's Eternity

Introduction

UP TO NOW, WE HAVE MADE A LONG JOURNEY FROM BIBLICAL PERSPECtives, and Greek metaphysics to recent Trinitarian understandings, in order to figure out how we can more properly think about God's eternity and its relation to time. Accordingly, this can be considered as a brief history of understandings of God's eternity and time. In so doing, my main purpose has been to observe correctly how one's understanding of time and eternity affects his understanding of God as well as man (and the world), or vice versa. As a result, as we have seen, it is clear that the understanding of God and human being and that of eternity and time are inseparably interrelated. Through our analysis and observation, we discovered very significant and helpful insights for our own understanding of human being and God as well as time and God's eternity. In this final chapter, therefore, while taking the advantages from the theologies discussed, I will present an alternative Trinitarian analogical understanding of God's eternity and its relation to time as my own view.

In classical theism, first of all, one of the most characteristic methodologies in conceiving and describing the nature and the attributes of God is *via negativa* (or *via negationis*, the way of negation). This is "a method of defining or identifying the attributes by negating the attributes of the finite order."[1] According to this method, in contrast to a composite, finite, measurable, passible, mutable, temporal, and thus

---

1. Muller, *Dictionary of Latin and Greek Theological Terms*, 326.

imperfect being of creatures, God is conceived as simple, infinite, immeasurable, impassible, immutable, and timelessly eternal for He is the perfect Being. However, this is not the only option, for such a *via negativa* alone does not properly describe God as a whole. Therefore, there is another methodology, *via eminentiae* (or *via positiva*, the way of eminence). It is "the method for the positive derivation of divine attributes by raising attributes of things in the finite order, particularly spiritual attributes of human beings, to the order of the infinite."[2] In this method, God's attributes are conceived as the highest; for example, omniscience, omnipotence, omnipresence, and the highest in His love, righteousness, and goodness, and so forth.

In addition, there is a third way, *via analogia* (the way of analogy). Such a third method was systematically developed in Thomistic theology as *analogia entis* (analogy of being).[3] Analogy means, by definition, a partial similarity (correspondence) of relations between two different entities. That is, it means that there is a kind of "relationship" between God and man, neither totally alike nor totally unlike, but they share a partial similarity in dissimilarity. However, in its essence, the real problem of such an ontological methodology of these three is that God is essentially conceived according to the metaphysics of being, not God's revelation.[4] As K. Barth vigorously criticized, therefore, it is an anthropocentric natural theology to make God in the image of man, not the biblical God who reveals Himself to us.[5]

Rather, in borrowing K. Barth's terminology, in spite of "the infinite qualitative distinction" between God and the world, the biblical God gives His revelation for us. In His revelation, God reveals not something mysterious, but reveals Himself. It is God's self-revelation in that God gives Himself to us in His communicative actions in this temporal world, especially in Jesus Christ through the Holy Spirit. In such a self-disclosure and His accommodation to us, we are permitted to know and

2. Ibid.

3. Concerning recent arguments on analogy, see the following: Klubertanz, *St. Thomas Aquinas on Analogy*; McInerny, *Logic of Analogy*; Mondin, *Principle of Analogy*; Burrell, *Analogy and Philosophical Language*; Ross, *Portraying Analogy*; Chavannes, *Analogy between God and the World*; Palakeel, *Use of Analogy*.

4. In this case, the Bible was used as a "proof-text" in proving of doctrinal propositions from the Scripture. Concerning this problem, see Kelsey, *Proving Doctrine*.

5. Especially, concerning Barth's and Balthasar's conception of analogy, see chapter 6 and 7 in this study.

to speak about Him. Indeed, this is the very possibility of Christian theology. As J. Palakeel states, "God comes to the world in human form, and makes use of all human means to communicate himself. So theological discourse must follow this logic of God (*theo*-logic)."[6] In God's communicative action, God creates a covenant relationship with His creatures. Such a God-created relationship is the true basis of theological analogy (i.e., a partial correspondence within ever-greater difference) between God and man, not any other our intrinsic natures in us as *analogia entis*. Actually, for Christian theology as "faith seeking understanding" (*fides quaerens intellectum*), there is always only a kind of *analogia fidei*. Such an analogy of faith based on God's communicative action opens a possibility to know about God and to talk about God. In this sense, we can even say that there is "no theology without analogy."[7]

Therefore, the real problem is not the possibility of analogy, but "what, then, is a proper analogy" in order to understand properly the relationship between God and man, and God's eternity and time. In the biblical and theological perspective, the only perfect God-given analogy of being is Jesus Christ, the God-man, in whom the eternal Word of God became flesh and thus eternity became time. Jesus Christ is "the image of the invisible God" (Col 1:15; cf. 2 Cor 4:4). In this sense, Jesus Christ is the center of Christian theology. As we have seen, one of the most important features in the theologies of Barth and Balthasar is Christocentrism. According to Barth, christology has a central place in theology, and determines theology as a whole in all parts. In similar sense, for Balthasar, Christ is the starting point, the norm, the highest standard, and the measure of all things.[8] If we must understand God's revelation and God's time (i.e., eternity) according to a kind of analogical thinking, then the God-given analogy between God and man is Jesus Christ, *vere Deus vere homo*. God gives Himself for us in Jesus Christ through the Holy Spirit. Therefore, according to Barth, the God-man, Jesus Christ is "the archetype of all analogies," and thus the "*a priori Uranalogans*."[9] Accordingly, the time of Jesus Christ is the only true analogy between God's eternity and human time.

6. Palakeel, *Use of Analogy*, 334.
7. Ibid., 338.
8. Cf. Balthasar, *Theology of Karl Barth*, 326–63.
9. Lee, "Karl Barth's Use of Analogy," 131. Cf. Pöhlmann, *Analogia entis oder Analogia fidei*, 111.

Concerning our subject matter, in my view, if we attempt to properly understand not only the qualitative difference between God's eternity and time but also God's real and positive relation to time, a more proper method is *via analogia*. That is to say, analogical thinking is necessary and unavoidable in Christian theology, which attempts to speak about God's transcendence over the world as well as his positive relationship to the creatures (i.e., God's immanence in the world). Therefore, in this concluding chapter, I will propose an alternative trinitarian understanding of God's eternity and its relation to time using the *via analogia*. In such an analogical way, we can avoid a mere negation of time (i.e., the timeless view of God's eternity—*via negativa*) as well as a mere eminence of time (i.e., the temporal infinity, everlasting, or omnitemporal views of God's eternity—*via eminentiae*) in conceiving God's eternity and its relation to time. In this Trinitarian analogical way, therefore, we can more properly conceive not only an infinite qualitative difference, but also a real and positive relationship between God's eternity and human time.

This final chapter will be constituted in the following three successive parts. First, while re-thinking the nature of time as the form of life according to *analogia vitae* (analogy of life), I will strive to re-conceive the nature of God's eternity in Trinitarian terms, especially in the perspective of the economic Trinity. Concerning the so-called K. Rahner's rule, in my view, the economic Trinity has epistemological priority. But, at the same time, the immanent Trinity has ontological priority. That is to say, if we try to conceive the doctrine of the Trinity according to biblical revelation, not speculation based on ontological metaphysics, the proper way is from the economic Trinity to the immanent Trinity, not vice versa. Epistemologically, we cannot but take this order from the economic Trinity to the immanent Trinity. Through salvation history, from creation through redemption in Jesus Christ to its eschatological consummation in the Holy Spirit, God reveals Himself as the Triune God: the Father, the Son, and the Holy Spirit. Therefore, the only true biblical God is the Trinity, who is definitely revealed in the person and life of Jesus Christ through the Holy Spirit. And, then, we immediately and retroactively recognize that there is no other God besides the Living God, who is the Trinity from eternity to eternity (i.e., the immanent Trinity). Ontologically, therefore, the immanent Trinity has the priority over the economic Trinity. This means that the immanent Trinity is the presupposition of the economic Trinity. In this sense, we can say that the economic Trinity is the exact self-revelation or self-translation of the eternal immanent Trinity in time. Therefore, in the second section, according to *analogia relationis* (analogy of relation), I will describe the nature of eternity as the mode of the Triune God's existence in the perspective of the immanent Trinity. Following this, in the third section, I will try to re-state the nature of God's eternity and its relation to time according to *analogia communicationis* (analogy of communication).

Time, Eternity and *Analogia Vitae*

Time is an all embracing reality in this world. Nothing happens outside of time. Objective time can be observed in various forms, metaphysical, physical, biological, psychological, and social context.[10] However, time itself is not an independent being or thing as a substance, but "a form of existence."[11] That is to say, our time is the form of our existence in this world. For instance, in his *Sein und Zeit*, M. Heidegger grasped the nature of human being as "*Dasein*," which means "being-in-the-world" (*In-der-Welt-Sein*). However, according to Heidegger, being and time are inseparable, so it is at the same time "being-in-time" (*In-der-Zeit-Sein*).[12] Secondly, since ancient Greek philosophy, time has been generally conceived by the concept of moving, changing, or becoming. Accordingly, in classical theism, since God is "the perfect Being," God's eternity must be understood as a timeless eternity because God cannot change and cannot be changed in His nature (cf. divine immutability and impassibility). In my view, the current debates and confusions on the understanding of God's eternity among theologians and philosophers are due to such an understanding of the nature of time as *change*.

Time as the Form of Life

In ancient Greek philosophy, even though time is inseparably interrelated to the phenomena of change in the world, time is not change

---

10. Concerning the manifold aspects of time, see Fraser, *Voices of Time*; Hall, *Dance of Life*; Harris, *Reality of Time*; Lippincott et al., *Story of Time*; Baert, *Time in Contemporary Intellectual Thought*.
11. Askin, "Philosophic Concept of Time," 128.
12. Martin Heidegger, *Being and Time*.

itself.[13] For Plato, time is the mode of being for the world of appearance. But, at the same time, time itself encompasses the whole process of succession in becoming. Hence, time as a whole does not change. Because of this, Plato says that time is "a moving image of eternity."[14] Even in the case of Aristotle, time is not change or movement itself. As he says, "time is neither movement nor independent of movement."[15] Rather, for Aristotle, "time is a measure of motion and of being moved, and it measures the motion by determining a motion which will measure the whole motion."[16] Then, Plotinus defines time as "the form of life of the soul." According to Plotinus, time as the image of eternity is the life of the world soul. As he says, time is "a certain expanse (a quantitative phase) of the Life of the Soul."[17] For him, therefore, the activity of the soul, its life, is time itself.[18] Pannenberg's following interpretation is helpful at this point:

> Like Aristotle, Plotinus distinguished time from motion, because that which is not moved or remains stationary still remains within time. Yet time and motion, according to Plotinus, cannot be determined by one another in a fully reciprocal fashion, as Aristotle thought, because all measuring already presupposes time. From what source, then, should the essence of time be determined? Following Plato, Plotinus sought to conceive time as the image [*Abbild*] of eternity. Yet he could not begin, as Plato had done, with any particular form of motion, including circular motion, for time has to be conceived as prior to all motion whatsoever. This is why Plotinus had to develop his theory

---

13. Some philosophers argue about time without change, for instance, see Shoemaker, "Time without Change," 363–81.

14. Plato, *Timaeus*, 37d. in *Plato: Complete Works*, 1241. According to Turetzky, for Plato, "While time is closely connected with the motion of the sphere, it cannot simply be identified with that motion. As an image of eternity, time links the order of the eternal world of forms and unchanging reality with the order of the natural world of changing things. This link makes the created universe into a rational, intelligible harmony that exemplifies the purpose of the Demiurge to make it as beautiful and good as possible.... Time is the moving image of eternity that imparts intelligibility to the celestial motions. These motions are parts of time which, by dividing it, measure it. Plato thus identifies time with the duration of the whole, and the motions of the heavens are literally parts of time." Turetzky, *Time*, 15–16.

15. Aristotle, *Physics*, IV.11.219a1, in *Complete Works of Aristotle*, vol. 1, 371.

16. Aristotle, *Physics*, IV.11.221a1 (p. 374).

17. Plotinus, *Enneads*, III.7.12 (p. 266).

18. Cf. Turetzky, *Time*, 51.

of time as image by relating it to the totality of the eternal itself. He appealed to the soul for mediation, for while the soul is tied to the eternal, it is also the principle that brings about the moving apart of the various moments of life (the *diastasis . . . zoes* or "spreading out of life") within the flow of time.[19]

In biblical perspective, as we have seen in Augustine, Barth, Balthasar and many other theologians, time was created by God as the form of the creature's existence. This is what the biblical doctrine of *creatio ex nihilo et cum tempore* means. Our time itself is not eternal, for it is created with the other creatures. Even it is not an independent being (or thing), but when the world was created from nothing (*ex nihilo*) to being, time simultaneously emerged as the form of existence of the created world. Actually, according to Barth, time is the form of God's creation as well as the form of human existence, including other creatures. As Barth says, "time is not a something, a creature with other creatures, but a form of all the reality distinct from God, posited with it, and therefore a real form of its being and nature."[20] Therefore, time is the form of the created world for its whole life, and it is also ordained to be the field for the Living God's communicative actions and His works for His creatures. That is to say, time as *kairos* and its extended form, history as *chronos*, are the arena for the Living God's communicative actions for creation, providence, and redemption. At the same time, in more proper and positive sense, time can be defined as "the form of existence," and thus "the form of life" for creatures. Time is given by God to us as the form or mode of our life. Accordingly, in borrowing Plotinus' idea, as Pannenberg says, time is "*diastasis zoes* (the spreading out of life),"[21] or as Robert Jenson defines it "the inner horizon of the life of that one in whom all things live and move and have their being."[22]

Therefore, in contrast to the definition of the nature of time as *change* in analytical philosophy, here, I want to propose a biblical and thus a theological conception of the nature of time as *life*. That is, in my view, the nature of time is not *change* but *life*. In saying this, it means that change or movement is just an occasion for perceiving time or a measurement of time's flow in our eventful life. In other words, *change*

19. Pannenberg, *Metaphysics and the Idea of God*, 76.
20. Barth, *CD*, III.2, 438.
21. Pannenberg, *Metaphysics and the Idea of God*, 76–77 and 81.
22. Jenson, *Unbaptized God*, 144.

is a description of the phenomena of time's flow, but not the nature or the content of time. Rather, it is *life* as being in time. Accordingly, in my view, while pursuing the phenomena of time, *change*, philosophers neglect its content, *life*. That is to say, everything, which exists, has its own life, and thus has its own time as the form of its life. Even though being and time are not the same ontological category, they are inseparably interrelated in that the latter is given to us as the form or arena of our life. In this sense, the following statement by Balthasar is acceptable: "time 'makes room' for existent being, indeed, it creates an acting area in which it can realize itself as event."[23] I have my time as the form of my own life, which is given by the Living God to me.[24] Therefore, as the Bible declares, He is "the God of my life" (Ps 42:8) and "the Lord of life" (cf. Deut 30:19–20, 32:39). For example, when God gives an extended life to Hezekiah, the king of Israel, God says that, "I will add fifteen years to your life" (2 Kgs 20:6; cf. Gen 25:7, 47:28; Deut 32:39; Ps 39:4). In this sense, time can be define as the form of our life and thus it is "the home of being" in which we live.

In this perspective, as we have seen, K. Barth rightly points out that the problem of time is "a problem of all anthropology."[25] Time is the form of human existence, and thus it is the essential condition of human life. As Barth says, "If man had no time, if his existence were timeless, he would have no life. . . . [Therefore,] time is the *conditio sine qua non* of his life. If he is to fulfill his being and nature as the soul of his body, he cannot do [so] without time. He must acquire time and possess it."[26] Thus, man lives in his own time which is given by God as the form of his life, and he cannot escape from it. According to Barth, time is a constitution of the life of a living being. Therefore, they are inseparable. Life presupposes time: "Man lives in his time. This simple statement denotes . . . the constitution of human existence."[27] All individuals have

23. Balthasar, *Theo-Drama*, vol. 5, 92.

24. In this sense, Link points out that, "The Israelites thought of life not as a natural or scientific phenomenon, but primarily as duration, the days of a man's life which are granted him by Yahweh, the Lord of life." Idem, "Life," 478.

25. Barth, *CD*, III.2, 439.

26. Ibid., 437.

27. Ibid., 437. Barth continues, "If he lives at all, he lives in his time. His life is a series of the acts of his own movement, enterprise and activity. The fact that this is possible both as a whole and in detail presumes that man has the necessary time to accomplish these acts, i.e., that he is in a position to move in a definite way from his own past

their own time, and therefore the totality of the creature's time constitutes chronological time, history as a whole. Then, this concept can be extended to the whole lifespan of the created world, the universe as a whole.

As we well know, however, even though time is the form of our existence, we do not possess it as ours. This is clear in that we cannot control time. We cannot extend or compress it, nor can we escape from it. Therefore, in positive sense, it is God's gift for our life. Accordingly, the Living God, the Lord of life, is the Lord of time. God gives us time in order to give us our life. But, in negative sense, our life is finite and conditional in that it is essentially dependent on God, the Creator, who is the Lord of life. Just so, our time itself is neither eternal nor everlasting in itself, but finite and conditional. Even before the fall by sin and after eschatological redemption, our eternal life is essentially dependent on God, not eternal life in itself. In Scripture, the dependence is symbolized by "the tree of life" (cf. Gen 2:9). To eat the fruit of the tree of life means to live forever (i.e., an eternal life). According to L. L. Walker, in the biblical context, the tree of life means a "fullness life," not an eternal life as ours.[28] After the fall, God says, "He must not be allowed to reach out his hand and take also from the tree of life and eat, and live forever" (Gen 3:22). However, the tree of life will be given us again after the eschatological consummation in the new heaven and the new earth. In Rev 22:2, we read that, "On each side of the river stood the tree of life, bearing twelve crops of fruit, yielding its fruit every month. And the leaves of the tree are for the healing of the nations." Therefore, after eschatological judgment, even though "there will be no more death" (Rev 21:4)—death is the end of time—our eternal life is still dependent on God, not our own intrinsic nature. Indeed, "the river of the water of life" is flowing from "the throne of God and of the Lamb" (Rev 22:1). In this sense, our eternal life is relative and conditional in that it depends on God's absolute eternal life. The tree of life denotes the formal condition of our relative eternal life. The redeemed people of God "may have the right to the tree of life" (Rev 22:14), but others are not allowed (cf. Rev 22:18). As the Spirit says, "To him who overcomes, I will give the right

---

through his own present to his own future; to be engaged in the fulfillment of these acts and therefore in change, and yet always to retain his own individual identity" (ibid.).

28. Cf. Walker, "Tree of Life," 1260.

to eat from the tree of life, which is in the paradise of God" (Rev 2:7). Robert H. Mounce interprets these passages as follows:

> John has been using the imagery of the magnificent city to describe the people of God in the glorious and eternal age to come. ... [The verses] also portray the eternal state as Eden restored, thus "book-ending" the Christian Bible. In Genesis we were introduced to the tree of life planted in the middle of the garden (Gen 2:9). To eat its fruit was to live forever (Gen 3:22); as a consequence of Adam's sin, therefore, the first couple were banished from the garden to work the ground cursed with thorn and thistles (Gen 3:17–18). Now in Revelation we see redeemed humanity back in the garden, able to eat the bountiful fruit of the tree of life (22:1–2). The curse has been removed (cf. 22:3 with Gen 3:14–24), and God's people are again privileged to "see his face" (cf. 22:4 with Gen 3:8) and serve him. No greater good or more joyous truth could be imagined than eternal fellowship with God and the Lamb! Truly, the unimaginable blessings of Eden have been restored.[29]

After the fall, our time is characterized as mortal time. Even though Barth and Balthasar made a distinction between original created time and sinful time (or lost time), they did not define that difference. As we have seen, in my view, the formal difference is the tree of life. However, the material difference is the Spirit of life. That is to say, the Spirit's withdrawal from us results in our death: "My Spirit will not contended with man forever, for he is mortal" (Gen 6:3; cf. Job 34:14–15). As Scripture declares, "the wages of sin is death" (Rom 6:23; cf. Ezek 18:20—"the soul who sins is the one who will die"). Indeed, death is the end of time as the form of our sinful life. As Heidegger clearly shows us, the human being, Dasein, the being-in-the-world-and-time is always a "being-towards-death" or "being-towards-the-end." Therefore, "death is something that stands before us—something impending."[30] However, the sin of man affects not only his own destiny but also the whole created world (cf. Gen 3:17–19; Rom 8:22). After the fall, therefore, even the totality of creature's time, chronological time, is not infinite, but a death-bound time and thus a mortal time altogether. As a matter of fact, according to a theory of the Big-Bang cosmology, the universe as the totality of the created world has its own mortal time as its own lifespan from the

---

29. Mounce, *Book of Revelation*, 398.
30. Heidegger, *Being and Time*, 294, cf. 274–311.

Toward an Alternative Trinitarian Analogical Understanding 299

beginning of "the big-bang" to the end of "the big-crunch."[31] That is to say, universal time, too, is a death-bound time. Since time is the form of life for delightful and vital events, as Balthasar insists, Hell, the place for the dead and absolute God-forsakenness, is the "timeless" place of eternal death. According to Balthasar, the time of Hell is distinctively conceived as an "eternal timelessness" and "non-time," which means the time of God-forsakenness as an absolute separation from God's eternal life, and thus the eternal death. Therefore, as Balthasar says, it is the time of "the limitless, eternal death."[32] However, as the Bible declares, God is "not the God of the dead but of the living" (Matt 22:32). According to the Gospel of Mark, to enter the kingdom of God is to enter the life of God, and it stands in exact contrast to Hell.[33]

> If your hand causes you to sin, cut it off. It is better for you to enter *life* maimed than with two hands to go into *hell*, where the fire never goes out. And if your foot causes you to sin, cut it off. It is better for you to enter *life* crippled than to have two feet and be thrown into *hell*. And if your eye causes you to sin, pluck it out. It is better for you to enter *the kingdom of God* with one eye than to have two eyes and be thrown into *hell*. (Mark 9:43–47)

Metaphorically, in the sense of natural science, the Black Hole can be considered as a timeless place. In that place, beyond the event horizon which is the boundary of the region of space-time, nothing can escape from it, even light itself, because of infinite gravity. Therefore, S. W. Hawking says, "One could well say of the event horizon what the poet Dante said of the entrance to Hell: 'All hope abandon, ye who enter here.' Anything or anyone who falls through the event horizon will soon reach the region of infinite density and the end of time."[34] According to P. Davies, "the center of the black hole is a spacetime singularity.... If the singularity exists, then it will be a boundary to time itself, an edge of infinity where time ceases to exist and there is no beyond."[35]

---

31. Cf. Hawking, *Brief History of Time*; Davies, *About Time*. In this theory, "the big-bang" is the singularity at the beginning of the universe, and "the big-crunch" is the singularity at the end of the universe. However, for a theological criticism of the big-bang cosmology, see Drees, *Beyond the Big-Bang*.

32. Balthasar, *Glory of the Lord*, VII, 172–73; and his *Theo-Drama*, V, 305–6 and 310–11.

33. Cf. Gutiérrez, *God of Life*, 14.

34. Hawking, *Brief History of Time*, 89.

35. Davies, *About Time*, 121.

Eternity as the Form of the Triune God's Life

One of the most essential characteristics of the biblical identification of God is that the only true God is "the Living God," who distinguishes Himself from the other gods, for example, the idols which do not live (cf. Ps 115:4–8; Jer 10:3–16). In Jer 10:10, we read that, "The Lord is the true God; he is the living God, the eternal King." God reveals Himself as the Living God in His creation, redemptive history, and especially in covenant relationship with His people. Especially, on Mount Sinai, God distinctively reveals Himself as YHWH (Yahweh): "God said to Moses, 'I AM WHO I AM (YHWH). This is what you are to say to the Israelites: I AM has sent me to you'" (Exod 3:14). However, the God who reveals Himself to Moses as YHWH, is none other than the God of the fathers—"the God of Abraham, the God of Isaac and the God of Jacob" (Exod 3:15; cf. 6:2–3). According to Scripture, Yahweh is God's proper name: "Yahweh . . . this is my name forever, the name by which I am to be remembered from generation to generation" (Exod 3:15; cf. Isa 42:8, "I am Yahweh; that is my name!"). Accordingly, God declares again and again, "I am Yahweh, and there is no other; apart from me there is no God" (Isa 45:5, cf. 46:9–10).

Therefore, this proper name par excellence, YHWH, is God's self-identification as the true and living God for Israel in the OT. In contemporary biblical theology, the tetragrammaton, YHWH (Exod 3:14) can be translated in various ways: "I am who I am," "I am he who is," "I will be who I am / I am who I will be," or even "I will be who I will be."[36] It can mean the aseity of God, the absolutely unconditional self-existent Being, "I AM," the One who eternally exists and possesses His own essential life without beginning and end (cf. Ps 102:27).[37] And it also means God's presence in His mighty acts of covenant relationship with His people in redemptive history, "I am / I will be with you" (Exod 3:12) or "I will be present (to bring you out from under the yoke of the Egyptians)" (cf. Exod 6:6–8).[38] The covenant formula of Yahweh with His people is as follows: "I will take you as my people, and I will be your

---

36. Cf. Fretheim, "Yahweh," 1296; Frame, *Doctrine of God*, 36–46.

37. Cf. Grudem, *Systematic Theology*, 169; Eichrodt, *Theology of Old Testament*, vol. 1, 190–92.

38. Cf. Frame, *Doctrine of God*, 39–40 and 95; Weber, *Foundations of Dogmatics*, vol. 1, 417–18.

God. Then you will know that I am Yahweh your God" (Exod 6:7). And it is continued in the prophets, for example, "Yahweh your God is with you, he is mighty to save" (Zeph 3:17). In this sense, clearly, "Yahweh is the redemptive name of God. Yahweh is the Savior, the Redeemer (Isa 43:3, 11, 44:6, 24, 48:17, 49:7, 26)."[39]

However, in my view, an essential meaning of YHWH is that God is *the Living God*, who is eternally YHWH, "I AM," and at the same time always "I am / I will be with you" in redemptive history.[40] Accordingly, the only true biblical God is the Living God, Yahweh—"the God of Life" (*chai elohim, theo zontos*, cf. 1 Sam 17:26; Ps 42:2; Matt 16:16). God Himself is Life, the true and eternal Life (cf. Jer 10:10; 1 Thess 1:9; Heb 12:22; Rev 7:2). And therefore, Yahweh, who is the God of life and the Lord of life, is "the Creator of life" (cf. Gen 1:1; John 1:1-4) and "the Savior of life."

> It is very probable that the much discussed name Yahweh is to be interpreted along these lines and that it means: "I am he who is with you; I am life." The divine presence is at once creative and liberating. "I am life" ("I am who I am"): such is Yahweh. We are faced here once again with the idea of the origin or source of life.[41]

> God's being is intrinsically characterized by life, by being alive. ... It cannot be properly conceived that God could die, because life is intrinsic to God, an attribute of the divine essence. Even when we despair of life (Job 9:21; 2 Cor 1:8), God continues to give us life. ... It is God's very nature to be alive, so much so that God is properly known as the life of all that lives. ... John's Gospel proclaimed that God the Father "has life-giving power in himself" (John 5:26). ... God's life is eternal life. God's life is not only without end but without beginning. For before anything was alive, God was alive (Gen 1:1ff). When this world is gone, God remains alive (Luke 1:33; Heb 7:3).[42]

Such an understanding of God as the Living God or the God of Life, YHWH ("I AM"), is affirmed in Jesus Christ's self-identification in

---

39. Frame, *Doctrine of God*, 40.

40. According to Oden, "This tetragrammaton (YHWH) points awesomely to God's incomparable aliveness.... Not only is God living, but also the source of our life—active and tireless (Isa 40:28; Ps 121:4)." Idem, *Living God*, 65.

41. Gutiérrez, *God of Life*, 12.

42. Oden, *Living God*, 64–65.

the New Testament: "I AM the Life" (John 14:6) and "I AM the Living One" (Rev 1:18). In John's Gospel, Jesus Christ's "I AM" (*ego eimi*) formula reflects YHWH ("I AM") in the OT (e.g., John 6:48—"I AM the bread of life"; 8:12, 9:5—"I AM the light of the world"; cf. 10:7, 14, 11:25, 14:6, 15:1, 5, etc.). Jesus Christ, the Son, is "the Word of Life" (1 John 1:1–2; cf. John 1:1–4), and therefore He is "the author of life" (Acts 3:15). Indeed, Jesus says that, "before Abraham was born, I AM" (John 8:58). In this sense, "He is true God and eternal Life" (1 John 5:20, which is the same formula of Jer 10:10, "Yahweh is the true God; he is the Living God, the eternal King"). Accordingly, J. M. Frame rightly points out that, "Christ is not just God in some general sense, but actually the covenant Lord, Yahweh."[43] It is clear in that Jesus Christ, the Son, declares that "I and the Father are One" (John 10:30). Exactly, as Scripture defines, "the Son is the radiance of God's glory and the exact representation of his being [as the Living God, YHWH]" (Heb 1:3; cf. Col 1:15–17).

Therefore, as the Bible says, "the Father has life in himself, so he has granted the Son to have life in himself" (John 5:26). However, the eternal Word of God became flesh (John 1:14; cf. Phil 2:6–8). This means that eternal life (i.e., eternity) became earthly life (i.e., human time). He is called "Jesus (cf. Joshua)," which is the echo of the name YHWH, the God of redemption "because he will save his people from their sins" (Matt 1:21).[44] At Caesarea Philippi, therefore, Simon Peter confessed that, "You are the Christ, the Son of *the Living God* [i.e., Yahweh]" (Matt 16:16). This confession is the quintessence and the cornerstone of Christology. Jesus is the Christ, the Messiah, and thus Immanuel, "God with us" (Matt 1:23, cf. Isa 7:14; i.e., Yahweh, "I AM with you") in order to give us eternal life in Himself. Accordingly, all biblical messages, the gospel of the Living God for us, can be concentrated in and summarized by the following one verse:

> For God so loved the world that he gave his one and only Son, that whoever believes in him shall not perish but have *eternal life*. (John 3:16)

Since the Son, Jesus Christ, is "the true God and eternal Life" (1 John 5:20), He is "the path of life" (Acts 2:28). In order to give us His eternal life, the Son not only died the death of death on the Cross, but

---

43. Frame, *Doctrine of God*, 42.
44. Cf. Martens, "Names of God," 298.

also was raised from the dead to life by the Living God in the power of the Holy Spirit (cf. Acts 2:32–33, 3:15; Rom 1:4, 8:11, 34). Indeed, Jesus Christ's death on the Cross and resurrection is "the death of death" in that "the last enemy to be destroyed is death" (1 Cor 15:26). In this way, Jesus Christ became the firstfruits of resurrection for us: "Christ has indeed been raised from the dead, the firstfruits of . . . the resurrection of the dead" (1 Cor 15:20–21, cf. 15:22–26). Therefore, Jesus Christ declares that,

> I AM the way and the truth and the life. No one comes to the Father except through me. If you really knew me, you would know my Father as well. From now on, you do know him and have seen him (John 14:6–7). I AM the resurrection and the life. He who believes in me will live, even though he dies; and whoever lives and believes in me will never die (John 11:25–26). [Therefore] now this is the eternal life: that they may know you, the only true God, and Jesus Christ, whom you have sent. (John 17:3)

In Jesus Christ, "death has been swallowed up in victory" (1 Cor 15:54). Accordingly, "the wages of sin is death, but the gift of God is eternal life in Christ Jesus our Lord" (Rom 6:23). In addition, the Son is "the last Adam, a life-giving spirit" (1 Cor 15:45). In this sense, "God has given us eternal life, and this life is in his Son. He who has the Son has life; he who does not have the Son of God does not have life" (1 John 5:11–12). Paul also says that, "Since, then, you have been raised with Christ . . . your life is now hidden with Christ in God. When Christ, who is your life, appears, then you also will appear with him in glory" (Col 3:1–4; cf. Gal 2:20). This is just our ultimate hope for eternal life in Jesus Christ (the Word of life) through the Holy Spirit (the Spirit of life) from the Father (the Living God) who is the Lord of life.

Finally, Scripture defines that "God is Spirit" (John 4:24; 2 Cor 3:17, 18) and the Holy Spirit is characteristically identified as "the Spirit of Life" (Rom 8:2). First of all, in the OT, the Spirit is "Yahweh's *ruach* (breath),"[45] which distinguishes the true Living God from idols (cf. Hab 2:19). In this sense, He is called "the Spirit of *the Living God* [i.e., Yahweh]" (2 Cor 3:3). According to Moltmann, *ruach*, "the word always

---

45. For some detail studies on the Holy Spirit in the OT, see Schweizer, *Holy Spirit*, 10–28; Congar, *I Believe in the Holy Spirit*, vol. 1, 3–14; Moltmann, *Spirit of Life*, 40–57; Montague, *Holy Spirit*, 3–124; and Ferguson, *Holy Spirit*, 15–33.

means something living compared with something dead, something moving, over against what is rigid and petrified."[46] Therefore, Yahweh's *ruach* is the third person of the Trinity in whom the Living God gives us life and "the created ability to live enjoyed by all the living."[47] Indeed, in God's creation of the world, Yahweh's *ruach* worked with Yahweh's *dabar*—His Word, the second person of the Trinity (cf. Gen 1:2, and 3–30; Ps 33:6; Col 1:16–17). Especially, according to the story of God's creation of man, the dust-man became "a living being" ("a living person" or "a being-as-life") by Yahweh's *ruach*, "the breath of life" (Gen 2:7; cf. 1 Cor 15:45). In the sense of biochemistry, the dust-man is literally a body of some chemical elements (i.e., the dusts), hydrogen, carbon, oxygen, nitrogen, phosphorus, and so on. But, when Yahweh breathed His *ruach* in it, the dust-man became "a living being," which can also mean "a being of life" or "a being-as-life"(Gen 2:7). It denotes at least the following two significant facts for human being: (1) man as "the living being" or "a living person" is a special creature in the *imago Dei*, the image of the Living Triune God; but, at the same time, (2) his life is "a gift of God," not his own possession.[48]

The Spirit of God is the agent of creation and the Lord of life who is the giver of life (cf. Gen 1:2; Job 33:4). Therefore, "if it were his intention and he withdrew His Spirit and breath, all mankind would perish together and man would return to the dust" (Job 34:14–15). Indeed, the Living God's withdrawal of His Spirit from us results in our spiritual death. As the Scripture says, "My Spirit will not contended with man forever, for he is mortal" (Gen 6:3). This was the fulfillment of the word of God's condemnation, "for you are dust, you will return to dust" (Gen 3:19). In this sense, for God's peoples, if the tree of life is a formal condition for our eternal life, the Spirit of life, Yahweh's *ruach*, is the essential condition for our eternal life (cf. Gen 3:22–24; Ps 104: 29–30; Isa 32:15). Therefore, in Joel 2:28–32, the Living God, Yahweh promised that, in the last days, "I will pour out my Spirit on all people" again. Such a promise of Yahweh, the pouring out of His Spirit on all people, is the Messianic hope for regenerating our death-bound life, the ultimate redemption for us.

---

46. Moltmann, *Spirit of Life*, 41.
47. Ibid.
48. Cf. Wenham, *Genesis 1–15*, 60–61.

In the NT, "the Spirit of God" (Gen 1:2) dwells in Jesus Christ (cf. Matt 1:18, 3:16). The Spirit of God is inseparably connected with the Messianic mission of Jesus Christ, the Word of God. In fact, it was just the God-given witness to the coming of the Messiah, who is the bearer and the giver of the Spirit of God. Now, Jesus Christ promised to send another Comforter, "the Spirit of truth" (John 14:16, 15:26), and He himself breathed out "the Holy Spirit" (John 20:22). Therefore, "the Spirit of God," Yaheweh's *ruach*, is now called "the Spirit of Jesus" (Acts 16:7), "the Spirit of Christ" (Rom 8:9; 1 Pet 1:11, cf. "the Spirit of Jesus Christ," Phil 1:19), and "the Spirit of His Son" (Gal 4:6). At the day of Pentecost, finally, the Holy Spirit was poured out on all people (cf. Acts 2:1–4), which is the fulfillment of God's promise (cf. Joel 2:28–32; John 15:26; and Acts 2:16–21). Scripture says that, "Exalted to the right hand of God, he has received from the Father the promised Holy Spirit and has poured out what you now see and hear" (Acts 2:33). God the Father, the Living God, gives us the same Spirit of life who raised the Son from the dead to Life as the guarantee of "what is mortal may be swallowed up by life" (2 Cor 5:4–5). In this sense, the Holy Spirit, the Spirit of life, is *the Bond of Life* not only between the Father and the Son, but also between the Living Triune God and us. Therefore, Paul says as follows:

> If the Spirit of him who raised Jesus from the dead is living in you, he who raised Christ from the dead will also give life to your mortal bodies through his Spirit, who lives in you. (Rom 8:11)

According to Robert Jenson, "Time is what happens when the Holy Spirit comes from the Father to the Son,"[49] and then to us because He as Yahweh's *ruach*, the Spirit of life, created and is re-creating our life as well as the world in Jesus Christ, who is the Life and the Resurrection (cf. Ps 104:30). Therefore, the Living God's redemptive action for us is nothing other than the redemption of our fallen time as the form of our death-bound life to the eternal life which is given in the Son, (the true Life) through giving his Holy Spirit (the Spirit of life) to us. In this sense, after the eschaton, in contrast to R. Jenson's idea of the deification of our time, in my view, the Living Triune God will give us a "new time" as the form of our new life (i.e., the eternal life) in the new heaven and the new earth, and the Holy City of God, the new Jerusalem which is

---

49. Jenson, *Unbaptized God*, 144.

"the home of righteousness" (Rev 21:1–2; 2 Pet 3:13; cf. Isa 65:17, 19). And therefore, "there will be no more *death* or mourning or crying or pain, for the old order of things has passed away" (Rev 21:4). The Living God declares, "I am making everything new!" (Rev 21:5).

In this way, the only true biblical God is the Living God, the Trinity as the Lord of life: the Father, the Son and the Holy Spirit. In the traditional conception of the Trinity, the Father, the Living God, "begets" the Son, the Word of Life, and both "breath" the same Spirit of life. Indeed, the actions of "begetting" and "breathing" are the essential factors of life, the Living Being. However, the Living Triune God mutually shares the one and the same eternal Life one with the other. And therefore, the three distinct persons of the Trinity are one unity in His own Life. That is to say, the Triune God of Scripture is the living and acting God as *vita pura et actus purus*, and thus He has His own eternal life in Himself. Actually, as we have seen, the biblical God, the Trinity Himself is the true and eternal Life, *vita vera et aeterna*. Therefore, we can conceive the biblical Living Triune God not as a static and abstract Being of *Actus Purus, Ipsum Esse*, but as an active and Living God of *Actus Purus, Ipsum Vita*.

And therefore, the Living Triune God has His own time as the form of His own eternal life. Accordingly, God's time (i.e., eternity) is the "absolute" and "eternal" time, which is the form of the absolute and eternal life of the Triune God. Here, I define the self-existence of God by the words, "absolute and eternal." In another way, God's absolute time can be thought as the true time, *tempus verus*, or the pure time, *tempus purus*, in contrast to our created relative and then fallen (lost) time by sin. In this sense, K. Barth's following statement is understandable:

> Even the eternal God does not live without time. He is supremely temporal. For His eternity is authentic temporality, and therefore the source of all time. But in His eternity, in the uncreated self-subsistent time which is one of the perfections of His divine nature, present, past and future, yesterday, to-day and to-morrow, are not successive, but simultaneous. It is in this way, in this eternity of His, that God lives to the extent that He lives His own life.[50]

However, our created relative time is qualitatively, not quantitatively, different from God's absolute time (i.e., eternity). In God's time as

---

50. Barth, *CD*, III.2, 437–38.

the form of His own eternal life, there is not beginning and end because He Himself is the beginning and the end at the same time. As God says, "I AM the Alpha and the Omega, the First and the Last, the Beginning and the End" (Rev 22:13; cf. Rev 1:17, 2:8, 21:6; Isa 44:6). This means that the Living Triune God simultaneously possesses the totality and the wholeness of His own life at once. Only in this Trinitarian term, Boethius' following definition of God's eternity can be affirmed in its full sense: "Eternity, then, is the whole, simultaneous and perfect possession of boundless life (*Aeternitas igitur est interminabilis vitae tota simul et perfecta possessio*)."[51] That is to say, in God's time (i.e., the absolute and eternal time), all time (past, present and future) is "simultaneous" in its pure duration. It is clear in that the Living God, the Lord of time, is "who is, and who was, and who is to come" at the same time (cf. Rev 1:4, 8). In Trinitarian terms again, "Holy, holy, holy is the Lord Almighty, who was, and is, and is to come," and "who lives for ever and ever" (Rev 4:8–9, cf. Isa 6:3). The Triune God in eternal praise and worship is the only true Living God, Yahweh, "I AM WHO I AM" from eternity to eternity (Exod 3:14).[52] In connecting the two passages of Rev 1:8 and Exod 3:14, Barth interprets them as follows:

> I am He who has life in Himself. That is to say, I am sovereign over my being. Even as present I am He who was and will be. All this applied to the being of the man Jesus in time. The all-inclusive "I am" rules out any notion that the three dimensions, present, past and future, simply follow one another in succession.... It means: "I am all this simultaneously. I, the same, am; I was as the same; and I will come again as the same. My time is always simultaneously present, past and future." That is why I am the Alpha and Omega, the beginning and the ending, the first and the last. Since my present includes the past and the future it is both the first and last at all other times. All times have their source and end in my time. Of course, all these other times are real times, for at the heart of them I have time. But other times are previous or subsequent to mine. They are overshadowed, dominated and divided into periods by my time. It is my present that makes them either past or future, for my present includes both. I was, and I am to come, as surely as I am and live ... As I am in my time, all time is my time, my before or after ... He belongs to all times simultaneously. He is the same Christ.

51. Boethius, *Consolation of Philosophy* in *Boethius*, 5.6 (p. 423).
52. Cf. Mounce, *Book of Revelation*, 126.

> There is no time which does not belong to Him. He is really the Lord of time.[53]

Furthermore, in my view, in Rev 4:8–9, the "holiness" of the Lord Almighty clearly denotes not only the uttermost "difference" from His creatures but also the "absoluteness" of His eternal time (i.e., eternity) which differs from our created relative time.[54] Therefore, in contrast to Pannenberg, God's time is not merely the wholeness or the totality of life including our created life, but there is an infinite qualitative difference between God's absolute time and our relative time. That is to say, in our created finite time (i.e., the relative time), those three elements of time (past, present, and future) are always "successive" in an ever-transitory sequence of moments. The past is no longer, the future is not yet, and the present always passes away to the past, toward non-being. Therefore, if the Living Triune God, the Lord of time, does not sustain our time, which is created and fallen time towards death, it will pass away to nothing, timelessness as the time of death. Just so, without the Living Triune God, the Lord of life, our life will perish into the eternal death altogether. Accordingly, in conclusion, if we take the definition of time as "the mode or the form of life," the debate between timeless and everlasting eternity can be overcome. Therefore as well, the dilemma of God's eternity and its relation to human time, whether God is timeless or not, appears to be a mere pseudo-problem. That is to say, there is an *analogia vitae* (analogy of life), a partial correspondence within infinite qualitative difference, between God's eternal life and our conditional and finite life, and thus between God's absolute time and our relative time.

Time, Eternity and *Analogia Relationis*

In the previous section, as we have seen, time is "the form of life." Everything, which exists, has it own life. To be "a living being" (or "a being-as-life") means that it has its own life and thus has its own time as the form of existence. In addition, however, one's life is always in relation to others. Traditionally, in Greek ontological metaphysics, "being"

---

53. Barth, *CD*, III.2, 465–66.
54. Cf. Lewis, *Message of the Living God*, 318.

has been understood as a "substance" (*ousia, substantia*, or *essentia*).⁵⁵ In this case, God is conceived as the "Supreme Substance."⁵⁶ In modern philosophies, with René Descartes' *cogito ergo sum* and Immanuel Kant's subjectivism, the understanding of human being is characterized by the "turn to the self" or the "turn to the subject."⁵⁷ In this case, God was understood as the "Absolute Subject."⁵⁸ Recently, however, there are vigorous interests in understanding human being as well as the Being of God in relational terms.⁵⁹ In contrast to the modern "turn to the self," such a current vital understanding of human persons in relation can be called the postmodern "turn to relationality."⁶⁰

Time as the Form of Being-as-Life-in-Relation

According to a relational understanding of being, human being itself is not a monadic substance or an isolated self, but it is essentially related to others. This is one of the very reasons for the recent renaissance of Trinitarian theology. That is to say, a being-as-life cannot exist by itself but in relation to the others. In this sense, I want to define human being as follows: *being-as-life-in-relation*. For instance, W. Pannenberg characterizes a human being as a being of "openness to God" and "openness to the world."⁶¹ In more specific sense, however, human being, a being-as-life-in-relation, can be considered in spiritual, social, and behavioral (biophysical) aspects, and each of them corresponds to the spirit, the soul, and the body of the holistic human person (cf. 1 Thess 5:23).⁶² That is to say, it means respectively the spiritual relation to God, the social relation to the other human beings, and the bio-physical relation to his environmental world. In a proper sense, a human being must be

---

55. Cf. Christopher Stead, *Divine Substance*.
56. Moltmann, *Trinity and the Kingdom*, 10–12.
57. Vanhoozer, "Human Being, Individual and Social," 159.
58. Moltmann, *Trinity and the Kingdom*, 13–15.
59. See the following: Macmurray, *Persons in Relation*; Zizioulas, *Being as Communion*, and "Human Capacity and Human Incapacity," 401–48; McFadyen, *Call to Personhood*; Schwöbel and Gunton, *Persons, Divine and Human*; Torrance, *Persons in Communion*, and "What Is Person?," 199–222; Grenz, *Social God and the Relational Self*; and Shults, *Reforming Theological Anthropology*.
60. Cf. Shults, *Reforming Theological Anthropology*, 11–36.
61. Pannenberg, *What Is Man?*, 1–13.
62. Cf. Cornelis A. van Peursen, *Body, Soul, Spirit*.

conceived as a relational being, not a closed monadic substance or an isolated self at all. Therefore, in this section, I will present that time is the form of the existence of the relational being as life.

First of all, in order to understand human being, the doctrine of the *imago Dei* is the essential foundation for theological anthropology. As A. A. Hoekema says, the creation of human beings in the image of God is "the most distinctive feature of the biblical understanding of man" (cf. Gen 1:26-27).[63] Historically, there have been various interpretations of the *imago Dei*. It was often understood as human reason (rationality), free will, moral capacities, religious responsibility, or lordship over creation as God's agent. However, K. Barth rejects such an attempt to define the image of God in any kind of man's structure, disposition, capacities, and so forth. Rather, Barth understands the "I-Thou relationship" as a key idea of the image of God. According to Barth, there is an I-Thou relationship between man and woman (i.e., other human beings), and this confrontational relationship is the image of God in human being. That is to say, for Barth, in Gen 1:26, "Let us" means "the intra-divine unanimity" of the Triune God in creation of human beings according to "our image and our likeness."[64] Then, Barth gives attention to the fact that God created man as "male and female" in His own image, which means "I-Thou relationship to one another."[65] It is "His own divine form of life" as the Triune God.[66] In this sense, as he says, "Man is the repetition of this divine form of life; its copy and reflection. . . . Thus, the *tertium comparationis*, the analogy between God and man, is simply the existence of the I and the Thou in confrontation."[67] In other words, it does not entail likeness but a correspondence of the unlikeness, an "*analogia relationis*" (analogy of relation). In this way, Barth replaces Thomistic *analogia entis* by his own *analogia relationis*. However, according to Barth and Balthasar, Jesus Christ, the God-man, who is the true image of God (cf. 2 Cor 4:4; Col 1:15) and the only true concrete

---

63. Hoekema, *Created in God's Image*, 11.

64. Barth, *CD*, III.1, 183. According to Barth's interpretation, "in our image" and "in our likeness" are none other than a repetition, so it means "in the likeness of this image" (Ibid., 184).

65. Ibid., 184. For a similar interpretation of the *imago Dei* as a relational being, see Sherlock, *Doctrine of Humanity*, 34-42. Jewett applies this relationship to the relational sexuality of 'male and female,' see his *Who We Are*, 131-83.

66. Barth, *CD*, III.1, 185.

67. Ibid.

analogia entis, is the foundation of all relationship between God and man.

In philosophical arena, an influential criticism of the traditional understanding of human being as a monadic substance or an isolated self came from John Macmurray.[68] In his *The Self as Agent*, Macmurray rejects the Self-as-subject, the "isolated individual," which was understood as a "thinking subject" in the assumption of mind-body dualism. In so doing, he substitutes for it the Self-as-*person*, which is "constituted by the relation of persons."[69] That is to say, according to Macmurray, the traditional concept of the Self as a thinking subject could not resolve the dichotomy between the thinking (theoretical) world and the acting (practical) world. Therefore, first of all, he grasps the Self as an "agent" in the priority of the practical standpoint over the purely theoretical standpoint. He says that, "the Self is agent and exists only as agent," i.e., the bodily agent.[70] In other words, as Macmurray states, "The Self is subject in and for the Self as agent," and "The Self can be agent only by being also subject."[71] Such a view of "the Self-as-*agent*" can properly conceive the human person in both aspects of "doer (action)" as well as "thinker (thinking)" at the same time. Then, in his *Persons in Relation*, Macmurray grasps human being as the Self-as-*person*, who can exist only in personal dynamic relations with the Other. He says, therefore, "there can be no man until there are at least two men in communication."[72]

Indeed, according to Macmurray, "the Self is constituted by its relation to the Other." This means that "it has its being in its relationship; and that this relationship is necessarily personal."[73] For example, all personal actions like love or fear are in reference to other persons, which is constitutive for all personal existence. Therefore, "I," the Self-as-person, always needs "you," the Other, in order to be myself.[74] In Macmurray's view, the relation of the Self (the I) and the Other (the Thou) as persons is a fundamental ontological essence of human being, not an ad-

---

68. Cf. Macmurray, *Self as Agent*, and *Persons in Relation*. The two volumes are the published works of Macmurray's Gifford lectures delivered in 1953–1954.
69. Macmurray, *Self as Agent*, 12.
70. Ibid., 100, cf. 91.
71. Ibid., 101 and 102.
72. Macmurray, *Persons in Relation*, 12.
73. Ibid., 17.
74. Cf. ibid., 69.

ditional aspect. In my view, Macmurray's philosophical understanding of the Self-as-person in relation to the Other corresponds exactly to Barth's theological interpretation of the *imago Dei* in human being as "I-Thou relationship." We can find similar understandings of human beings as persons-in-relation in Alistair I. McFadyen, John D. Zizioulas, Christoph Schwöbel, Colin E. Gunton, Alan J. Torrance, F. LeRon Shults, and Kevin J. Vanhoozer among many others. Accordingly, T. Peters concludes that, "the idea of person-in-relation seems to be nearly universally assumed."[75]

While conceiving human beings in relation to the Other, Emmanuel Levinas defined time as follows: "Time is not the achievement of an isolated and lone subject, but it is *the very relationship of the subject with the Other.*"[76] According to Levinas, first philosophy is not the traditional ontology of the substance or the self, but the problem of the Other, which is the problem of responsibility in the relation to the Other, i.e., ethics. Therefore, Levinas says that "time is the moral being's mode of being," i.e., human being who is responsible for the Other's death.[77] This means that "one becomes oneself through this untransferable, undelegatable responsibility" for the Other's death, and time is the basis of this relationship.[78] Such a relationship with the Other is a relationship with "a Mystery," which is experienced as the exteriority or the alterity. Therefore, for Levinas, the Other is conceived as "the future," which is "what is in no way grasped."[79] In this sense, Levinas states as follows:

> The very relationship with the other is the relationship with the future. It seems to me impossible to speak of time in a subject alone, or to speak of a purely personal duration.[80] Relationship with the future, the presence of the future in the present, seems all the same accomplished in the face-to-face with the Other. The situation of the face-to-face would be the very accomplishment of time; the encroachment of the present on the future is not feat of the subject alone, but the intersubjective relationship. *The condition of time lies in the relationship between humans.*[81]

75. Peters, *God as Trinity*, 37.
76. Levinas, *Time and the Other*, 39 (italics mine).
77. Levinas, *God, Death, and Time*, 43.
78. Ibid.
79. Levinas, *Time and the Other*, 76–77.
80. Ibid., 77.
81. Ibid., 79 (italics mine).

In addition, according to Eberhard Jüngel, death is nothing other than "the event of relationlessness," and therefore, "the essential nature of death is relationlessness."[82] The mystery of our life lies in the fact that we are finite and mortal beings: "human life stands in a relationship with death."[83] However, in Jüngel's view, at the same time, our life is also determined in relation to others. As he says in borrowing Fichte's words, "Man is man ... only among men."[84] In combining those two essential factors of our being-as-life-in-relation, Jüngel states,

> If a man's life is always determined by the relation in which it stands to death, then the other person is also to be understood as always having a relationship to my death, and correspondingly, my life also will always be bound up with the death of the other. From the human point of view then, death is just as much a social fact as life itself. "Vita communis" thus corresponds to "mors publica." ... The time which I no longer have for myself is time which I no longer have for others. In life therefore, we are bound up with one another.[85]

Therefore, for Jüngel, death is nothing other than the end of our time as the form of our life in relation with others. And at the same time it is the event of which "the relationships in which man's life is lived are completely broken off."[86] This means in other words, a human being is a personal being as life in relation with the Other, and time is the form of his existence as such. Therefore, conclusively, time is the form of our life as an individual as well as the form of relation to the Other. That is to say, we can conceive not only of our human being as a being-as-life-in-relation but also of time as the form of the personal existence of the being-as-life-in-relation. In this way, time as the form of our life as an individual being can extend to chronological time, history as a whole, in relation to other human beings and the world. In order to understand this point, T. Horvath's following statement is helpful:

> [H]uman time is both a balance of the multiplicities of subtimes, and a sub-time in another balance of many "other"

---

82. Jüngel, *Death*, 115 and 135.

83. Ibid., 13.

84. Ibid., 30.

85. Ibid., 30–31. Jüngel defines time as follows, "Time is the formal ontological structure of the historicity of human existence" (ibid., 118).

86. Ibid., 113.

multiplicities of sub-times. In addition to non-human times, history implies the times of all individual human beings who form the total human time. Each person has his/her time, his/her history. Yet personal time includes also the time of other peoples. No one's time can be achieved without the other's time. The totality of people's time is history and history is the fulfillment of one's time.[87]

God's Time as the Form of the Triune God's Inter-Relationship

In the previous section, we clearly see that there are three distinct persons (or identities) of the Living Triune God: the Father, the Son, and the Holy Spirit. For Christian theology and faith, there is no other God besides the Living Triune God, who reveals Himself as the Trinity in Scripture, His redemptive actions, and finally in His own Word, the Son, Jesus Christ through the Holy Spirit. However, if the true biblical God is the Trinity and the doctrine of the Trinity is not a mere abstract speculation or a mystery of faith, where is the most proper locus, a concrete place, for perceiving the Living Triune God? In my view, it is the life of Jesus Christ as a whole, His unique person and works, and thus it can be defined as a Christocentric Trinitarianism. As we have seen, even though we focus on Jesus Christ's life, other theologians' emphases are slightly different: for instance, the Incarnation (K. Barth), the Cross (J. Moltmann), Holy Saturday (H. U. von Balthasar), or the Resurrection (W. Pannenberg and R. W. Jenson). Each of the emphases reflects their own specific theological methodology and main theological concern and therefore has its own merit. However, in my view, concerning the problem of the unity of the immanent Trinity and the economic Trinity, we cannot emphasize any one of the moments in Jesus Christ's earthly life. Rather we must consider Jesus's whole earthly life as a trinitarian life, which reveals the immanent trinitarian life in earthly time.

First of all, the Incarnation of the Son, the eternal Word of God in the flesh is the unique revelation of the Living Triune God in visible form (cf. Matt 1: 20; John 1:1, 14, 18; Heb 1:3). As Balthasar points out, "The Incarnation is not the nth performance of a tragedy lying in the archives of eternity. It is an event of total originality, as unique and untarnished as the eternally here-and-now birth of the Son from

---

87. Horvath, "New Notion of Time," 44.

the Father."[88] This means that the Father begets the Son in the Holy Spirit from eternity to eternity. Thus, it reflects and reveals the eternal interrelationship of the three personal inner-trinitarian life (i.e., the immanent Trinity) in visible form, since the pre-existence of the Son, the Word of God, is clear in Scripture.[89] In the baptism of Jesus Christ, God the Father declares through the Holy Spirit, "This is my Son, whom I love" (Matt 3:17; cf. Mark 1:11; Luke 3:22). This echoes "You are my Son; today I have become your Father" (Ps 2:7). In this phrase, "today" can be considered as the divine "Today," the divine eternal Now. In conceiving the Trinity, therefore, the meaning of such an understanding of the Father's begetting of the Son in the Holy Spirit is well pointed out by T. G. Weinandy as follows,

> The Son is begotten by the Father in the Spirit and thus the Spirit simultaneously proceeds from the Father as the one in whom the Son is begotten. The Son, being begotten in the Spirit, simultaneously loves the Father in the same Spirit by which he himself is begotten (is Loved). The Spirit (of Love) then, who proceeds from the Father as the one in whom the Father begets the Son, both conforms of defines (persons) the Son to be the Son and simultaneously conforms or defines (persons) the Father to be the Father. The Holy Spirit, in proceeding from the Father as the one in whom the Father begets the Son, conforms the Father to be Father for the Son and conforms the Son to be Son for (of) the Father.[90]

In this statement, we can clearly see the perichoretic mutual interrelationship in the three persons of the Trinity in His eternity.

Secondly, the works of Jesus Christ as a whole through His earthly life are also the mutual works of the Living Triune God. In His Messianic works, as the Son, Jesus Christ did everything according to the will of the Father, who had sent Him (cf. John 4:34, 5:30; Matt 26:39). As Jesus Christ says, "I have brought you glory on earth by completing the work you gave me to do" (John 17:4). In order to do so, the Father gives "all things" and "all power" to the Son (Luke 10:22; Matt 28:18; John 3:35). Therefore, indeed, the Father is living and doing His work in the Son (John 14:10–11; cf. Acts 10:38). All of the speeches and works of the Son

88. Balthasar, *Theology of History*, 39–40.
89. Cf. Macleod, *Person of Christ*, 45–70.
90. Weinandy, *Father's Spirit of Sonship*, 17.

are nothing other than to glorify the Father in His perfect obedience (cf. John 14:13; Rom 5:19).

Furthermore, the Father loves the Son and thus gives the Holy Spirit "without limit" (John 3:34). The Holy Spirit inseparably dwells in the Son and is always in His works as the empowering authority from the Father (Matt 3:16; Luke 3:22, 4:1, 14–18, etc.) Thus, we read in Acts 10:37–38, "You know . . . how God anointed Jesus of Nazareth with the Holy Spirit and power, and how he went around doing good and healing all who were under the power of the devil, because God was with him." Then, the Holy Spirit glorifies the Son who glorifies the Father (John 16:14) by speaking about not what is His own but what is the Son's (John 16:13, 14), testifying about the Son (John 15:26), and teaching and reminding us of everything said by the Son (John 14:26). Accordingly, all glory belongs to the Living Triune God: "For *from* him and *through* him and *to* him are all things. To him be the glory forever! Amen" (Rom 11:36). In this way, we can clearly perceive the mutual self-distinctions in the three persons of the Trinity and the mutual self-submission to one another in one unity, which is the concrete form of the Trinitarian reciprocal relations.[91]

Thirdly, the event of the Cross and the Resurrection of Jesus Christ is the unique Trinitarian event, and thus it is, as Moltmann says, "the history of history."[92] That is, even though the Incarnation and life before the passion of the Son are the revelation of the Triune God, the event of the Cross and the Resurrection are the unique moments, which reveals not only the distinction, but also the inseparable perichoretic mutual relation of the tri-persons in one unity. As Moltmann rightly points out, "What happened on the cross was an event between God and God. It was a deep division in God himself, in so far as God abandoned God and contradicted himself, and at the same time a unity in God, in so far as God was at one with God and corresponded to himself."[93] The total alienation of the Son from the Father is most clearly stated in Jesus Christ's miserable exclamation from the deep abyss of His being: "*Eloi, Eloi, lama sabachthani?*, My God, My God, why have you forsaken me?" (Matt 27:46). At the same time, however, it is also the clearest manifestation of the perfect union between the Father and the Son in that it is the

---

91. Cf. Pannenberg, *Systematic Theology*, vol. 1, 300–327.
92. Moltmann, *Crucified God*, 247.
93. Ibid., 244.

Son's perfect obedience to the Father's will in His self-surrendering love, so "He humbled himself and became obedient to death—even death on a cross!" (Phil 2:8, cf. Matt 26:39). In this sense, Jesus can finally declare that, "It is finished" (John 19:30). The Son fully accomplished the work that the Father had given Him to do, the Messianic mission (cf. John 17:4).

However, this is not the end of the Theo-story and the final-act of Theo-Drama of the Living Triune God. The Living God, the Father, raised the Son from the dead to Life in the Holy Spirit of life. Then, the Father glorifies the Son by sitting Him down at the right hand of His throne and gives Him "all authority in heaven and on earth" (Matt 26:64, 28:18; Heb 8:1, 12:2). The Resurrection of the Son from the dead to Life is the death of death: "Death has been swallowed up in victory" (1 Cor 15:54). In this sense, this is the definite turning point of history as a whole from death-bound life toward new eternal life. At the same time, it anticipates the Living Triune God's final triumph over the death for us in saying that "the last enemy to be destroyed is death" (1 Cor 15:26; Rev 20:14). In the event of the resurrection, the Spirit of life, the Holy Spirit who is the third person of the Trinity, works as *the Bond of Life* between the Father and the Son. As Pannenberg states, "All three persons of the Trinity are at work in this event. Decisive significance attaches, however, to the work of the Spirit as the creative origin of all life. To that extent we may say that the Father and the Son are referred to the working of the Spirit."[94] In the events of the Cross and the Resurrection, therefore, we can see not only a clear mutual self-distinction of the three persons but also their indissoluble fellowship and mutual perichoretic relationship in the inner-trinitarian life of the one unity. In this way, the whole earthly life of Jesus Christ manifested the eternal Trinitarian life that the Triune God is the only true Living God, the perfect Being-as-life-in-relation.

As we have seen, in the Triune God, the three personal mutual perichoretic inter-relationship is a perfect one which constitutes the unity of the Trinity, and just so the Living Triune God is the perfect Being-as-life-in-relation. Accordingly, the Living Triune God has His own time as the form of His existence as the perfect Being-as-life-in-relation. That is to say, in His own inner life, the *perichoresis*, the mutual inner relationship of the Triune God, eternity as God's time is the Living

---

94. Pannenberg, *Systematic Theology*, vol.1, 315.

Triune God himself. However, where does time come from? First of all, time emerges in the inner Trinitarian relationship as its form. For such a view of God's time as the form of the inter-personal relation of the Trinity, Balthasar's and Jenson's contribution can be considered as very significant insights.

According to Balthasar, time is essentially the form of the Son's receptivity of His being from the Father in eternity. That is to say, the One (the Father as the Living God) is essentially in relation with the Other (the Son), and thus when the Father eternally begets the Son, God's time simultaneously emerged as the form of relation between them. As Balthasar says, "The Son's form of existence, which makes him the Son from all eternity (John 17:5), is the uninterrupted reception of everything that he is, of his very self, from the Father."[95] Therefore, "it is his receptivity to everything that comes to him from the Father that is the basis of *time* and *temporality*."[96] In eternity, the Father's act of generation is to beget the Son, who receives not something alien but the Father's own being. That is to say, in my words, the Living God, YHWH, the Father ("I AM") begets the Son ("WHO I AM"), who is distinct but the same being with the Father. And, at the same time, while receiving Himself as the Son, He simultaneously gives fathership to the Father in the reciprocal relationship of His sonship. Therefore, time can be regard as the form of the reciprocal relation between the Father and the Son ("I AM, WHO I AM"). In this sense, we can properly understand the mysterious proper name of the Living God, YHWH, to the Israelites in the OT only in Trinitarian terms. Hence Jesus Christ's temporal mode of being in the flesh is the clearest manifestation, the exact translation into the temporal world of the eternal form of His existence as the perfect receptivity of His being-as-life-in-relation from the Father: the Son's existence "as receiving, as openness to the will of the Father, as subsistent fulfillment of that will in a continuous mission."[97] Concerning this point Balthasar says as follows:

> Thus the whole basis of time for the Son is his receptivity to God's will. In that receptivity he receives time from the Father, both as form and as content. The time that he receives is the Father's time, qualified moment by moment. For him, there is

---

95. Balthasar, *Theology of History*, 30.
96. Ibid., 33.
97. Ibid., 31.

Toward an Alternative Trinitarian Analogical Understanding 319

> no such thing as "time in itself"; . . . To have time means, for him, to have time for God, and is identical with receiving time from God. Hence the Son, who has time, in the world, for God, is the point at which God has time for the world. Apart from the Son, God has no time for the world, but in him he has *all* time. In him he has time for all men and all creatures: in relation to him it is always Today.[98]

Then, Jenson rightly conceives the nature of time as "the inner horizon of the life of that one in whom all things live and move and have their being," which means that time is the form of life.[99] Therefore, the Living Triune God has His own time as the form of His own Triune life. Then, "Time is what happens when the Holy Spirit comes from the Father to the Son."[100] Jenson explains this as follows,

> Time *is* because the Spirit is not the Father, and because both meet in the Son. Time *is* because God is his own origin and *as* such is *not* his goal; because God is his own goal and *as* such is *not* the "natural" result of his own being as origin; because origin and goal in God are an irreversibly ordered pair; and because Father and Spirit meet and are reconciled in the Son. Time is what happens when the Holy Spirit comes, from the Father and to the Son.[101]

That is to say, according to Jenson, "the life of God is constituted in a structure of relations."[102] Thus, in my words, time is constituted in the three personal inter-relations of the Triune Life. When the Living God, the Father ("WHO WAS") begets the Son ("WHO IS"), simultaneously the Holy Spirit ("WHO IS TO COME") proceeds as the third person, who is the Bond of Life in mutual relation between them. That is to say, the Father as Life begets the Son as His own same Life in mutually breathing the same Spirit of Life. God's time is the form of such a three personal subsisting mutual relationship in the immanent Trinity. Then, as Jenson continues, "God takes time in His time for us. That is His act of creation."[103] In other words, God's creation according to His own

---

98. Ibid., 40–41.
99. Jenson, *Unbaptized God*, 144.
100. Ibid., 144, cf. 111.
101. Ibid., 144 (italics mine).
102. Jenson, *Systematic Theology*, vol. 1, 218.
103. Jenson, *Systematic Theology*, vol. 2, 35.

good will means that He opens a "place" for the other than Himself in His own inner Triune life.[104] This place is the created "time," which is "room" for creation in God's own life. In this sense, "Our time, we may even say, is the accommodation God makes for us in his own triune life."[105] Therefore, when the Living Triune God created the world as other than Himself, there simultaneously emerged created time as the form of relation between the Living Triune God and the world. However, of course, there is an infinite qualitative difference between God's time as the form of the inner-trinitarian relationship and created time in which the Triune God has a relationship with His creatures.

In this sense, God's time is not the same as created time, which is the form of the finite existence of creatures. Even, in contrast to Jenson, I want to say that God's time is not "temporal infinity," as an infinite temporal extension. Rather, we must conceive it as an "infinite intensity," for there is not any tiny crack or gap in the perichoretic inter-relationship of the Triune God, which is the perfect one unity, who "WAS," "IS," and "IS TO COME" at the same time. Metaphorically, therefore, God's time as infinite intensity can be thought of as a single point. In this sense, what Balthasar thought of time as "the distance of the Creator to the creature" can be considered as a significant insight. That is to say, there is not any distance in the three personal perichoretic relation of the Living Triune God. It is perfect like a single point, thus the Living Triune God is *tempus purus* as the form of *ipsum vita*. Therefore, God's time (i.e., eternity) as the form of the perfect interpersonal relations in the Living Triune God is true and pure time, and thus the perfect time. Then, the farthest form from the Living God, who is the true Life, is thus death, timelessness. Accordingly, Hell is the farthest place of relationlessness with the Living God, and thus the place of timelessness, the place for the dead.

In contrast to God's perfect time, after the fall, for our broken time, there is always a broken-relation not only between man and the God of Life, but also between man and other men. In Genesis 3, the immediate results of sin are the brokenness of relationship not only between man and man but also between man and God. That is to say, when man was created in the image of God, before the fall, the relationship of human beings was also relatively perfect because they were created according

---

104. Cf. Jenson, "Aspects of a Doctrine of Creation," 24.
105. Jenson, *Unbaptized God*, 144.

to the image of God, *analogia relationis*. As Adam says to Eve, "this is now bone of my bones and flesh of my flesh" (Gen 2:23). Indeed, they are united as "one flesh" in a perfect relationship, so even they were naked, "they felt no shame" (Gen 2:24, 25). However, after the fall, they immediately felt shame with each other (Gen 3:7), condemned each other (Gen 3:12–13), and finally man killed another man (Gen 4:8). This means none other than a total brokenness of the living relation, which is the essence of the result of the original sin, the disobedience to the Living God. Thus, the living relationship and fellowship between the Living God and man was also totally broken. After the fall, man was afraid of God and hid from His face (Gen 3:8, 10). Then, the Lord of life condemned and drove him out from the Garden of Eden and thus from the tree of life (Gen 3:16–19, 3:24). Man eventually died as condemned by God because of his sin (Gen 3:19, 5:5). Therefore, the result of sin is the brokenness of the living relation between the Living God and man as well as the relation between human beings, and the wages of sin is death (Rom 6:23). In similar sense, as Jüngel rightly says that, death is "the event of relationlessness."

All sin as the disobedience to God is the breaking out of time, which is the form of our living relation with the Living God, and then with other men.[106] Therefore, the redemptive works of the Son in the Holy Spirit are, at first, reconciliation between the Living God and man in order to regenerate the living relationship and fellowship again, and then between man and men in His love which is the *koinonia* (the communion and fellowship, the church) of the Son in the Holy Spirit (Rom 5:10; 2 Cor 5:18–19; Col 1:20; Eph 4:1–6; 1 John 4:7–12). He himself is "the atoning sacrifice" and "the ransom" for our sins as well as that of the whole world (1 John 2:2; Rom 3:25; 1 Tim 2:2) in order to give us eternal life, which is the living relation with the Living God (Rom 6:23; 1 John 5:11–13, 20). Therefore, conclusively, after the fall, our fallen time as the form of our being-as-life-in-[broken]-relation is always a mortal time, death-bound time. In spite of the infinite qualitative difference, however, there is a partial correspondence, an *alanlogia relationis* (analogy of relation) between the Living Triune God and human being as being-as-life-in-relation, and thus between God's perfect time and human broken time as its forms.

---

106. Cf. Balthasar, *Theology of History*, 36–37.

Time, Eternity and *Analogia Communicationis*

The nature of being-as-life-in-relation lies in a mutual sharing of its own life with others. As we have seen, a being-as-life (i.e., a living being) can exist only in relation with others. Therefore, when we grasp human being as a being-as-life-in-relation, the nature of life lies in its communication of life with others. Such a communication of life includes not only a spiritual and verbal aspect, but also a material aspect. For the latter we see, for example, the ecological life-network of the food-chain. That is to say, we can sustain our biological or physical life only by eating other lives, e.g., vegetables, fruits, meats, or even minerals. In biological sense, the actions of eating, digesting, and evacuating can be considered as a communicative action of life, i.e., biological metabolism. In addition, in our body, there are many parasites and viruses with some of them being necessary for maintaining our everyday life cycle and metabolism. Therefore, without such a biological and physical communication of life with our environmental world (eating the other lives, drinking water, and breathing air) we cannot maintain our biological life at all.

In addition, our labor for cultivating and taking care of other lives in love is a positive communicative action of life to make a state of the "fullness of life" in God's created world. This is *economy* (i.e., taking care of the house in which we live), a communicative action of life, as a blessing of God for us as well as our mission to the environmental world. It is our cultural mandate given from the Living God, who is Life and the Creator of life (cf. Gen 1:26–28): "Be fruitful and increase in number; fill the earth and subdue it" (Gen 1:28). However, our cultural mission must be accomplished not in destructive power but in cultivating love and peace. Indeed, in a biological and ecological perspective, life on earth as a whole is a grand symbiotic network, which is a system of sharing or communication of life in mutual relation. As C. Sherlock points out, according to Scripture, "land, people and all living things are thus bound together" (cf. Hos 1:2).[107] That is to say, human beings and their environmental world as a whole constitute a network of communication of life in reciprocal relation. And thus it can be extended to the whole universe. It is true that not only without the communicative relation of life with the Living God (i.e., the spiritual relationship), we

---

107. Sherlock, *Doctrine of Humanity*, 116.

are dead men, but also without the communicative relation of life with the other human beings (i.e., the social relationship) and the environmental world (i.e., the bio-physical relationship), we cannot exist. We are created as such "a living being," a life in relation. However, in this section, I want to narrow down our scope to verbal communication alone, which means a communication of life between personal beings in distinguishing from the other forms of life on the earth.

Time as the Form of Communication of Life in Relation

One of the most essential characteristics of the human being as a living person is his ability to communicate with others. D. Braine rightly points out that, what differentiates human beings from other animals is language, verbal communication. As he states:

> We have seen how the human being is an animal, and seen what human beings have in common with the higher animals—perception, imagination, emotion, and perceptually directed action from emotion. What we have now to identify is the key peculiarity which differentiates the human being from the other animals, and this, I shall says, is *language*—language in that primary sense of the word whose structure, each inseparable from the other, . . . *the mode of linguistic communication*.[108]

Accordingly, E. Cassirer also says that, "whenever we find man we find him in possession of the faculty of speech," i.e., linguistic capacity.[109] In addition, W. Pannenberg, too, states that, "Language and reason are specific to human being as a biological entity. . . . In any case, language is fundamental in all areas of cultural life."[110] In the same sense, in his social theory, J. Habermas shows that communicative action is an essential feature for our social world, which is a "lifeworld," not a mechanical system.[111] That is to say, according to Habermas, communicative action is a form of social interaction, which constitutes the lifeworld of human beings. Then, as K. J. Vanhoozer points out, essentially "language exists for the sake of communication, and signs are to be used for this purpose."[112]

---

108. Braine, *Human Person*, 351–52 (italics mine).
109. Cassirer, *Essay on Man*, 109.
110. Pannenberg, *Anthropology in Theological Perspective*, 339–40.
111. Cf. Jürgen Habermas, *Theory of Communicative Action*.
112. Vanhoozer, *Is There a Meaning in This Text?*, 202.

In this sense, language is "the medium" in which we relate to others and to the world.[113] Therefore, we can say that, the ability of communication in language, the verbal communicative action of human beings is one of the most essential features to being a being-as-life-in-relation. In this sense, we can define man as *homo communicans* (man the communicator) or "*homo loquens*" (man the speaker),[114] alongside *homo sapiens* (man the thinker), *homo faber* (man the maker), or "*homo ludens*" (man the player).[115] Without his ability of communication in language, man cannot be a thinker, a maker, or a player.[116]

Human beings can exist as a being-as-life-in-relation only through inter-human communicative action, that is, through language—the word. In other words, human being can exist as a being-as-life-in-relation only in the inter-human living dialogue, not autistic monologue, with his fellow men. In this sense, language, the communicative action, is our medium and *conditio sine qua non* to exist as a being-as-life-in-relation. In sum, we can exist as a life, a living person, only in relation with the Other. And such a relation is mainly constituted only through our communicative action in language. Therefore, the communication in language for our social life, the "lifeworld," is the mode of our existence as a being-as-life-in-relation. Accordingly, M. Heidegger once rightly called language "the home of being."[117] As such we can say that the communicative action of life is the home of being-as-life-in-relation. In a more broad sense, such a communicative action actually constitutes the relation with the Other, which includes the Living God, fellow human beings, and the environmental world. In this sense, the communicative action of life and a relational being as a living person are inseparable.

However, even though language is the essential feature of our existence as a being-as-life-in-relation, we are not the creator or the master of it.[118] Actually, from a theological perspective, it is not "the chance

---

113. Ibid., 206.

114. Ibid., 201.

115. Johan Huizinga, *Homo Ludens*.

116. Pannenberg points this out as follows, "now it is language that makes thinking possible. Human beings are 'admitted to the essence of language.' Language 'signals' to us 'the essence of a thing.'" Idem, *Anthropology in Theological Perspective*, 341.

117. Heidegger, *On the Way to Language*, 135.

118. For a brief description of the controversy on the origin of language, see Pannenberg, *Anthropology in Theological Perspective*, 341–46.

product of nature," but "a gift of God" as a capacity to communicate with the Living God, "the ultimate communicative agent," with fellow human beings, and with the world.[119] While positing a divine "design plan" for language, K. J. Vanhoozer well explains this point as follows:

> Language is a God-given capacity that enables human beings to relate to God, the world, and to one another. Specifically, language involves a kind of relating with God, the world, and others that yields personal knowledge. Language, that is, should be seen as the most important means and medium of communication and communion. In Genesis 2, for example, God and Adam relate by means of language. Adam also relates to his world by using language to name the animals (Gen 2:19-20), an extraordinary scene that shows humans make the distinctions and connections that both invent and discover the world. Given the centrality in Scripture not only of naming, but of other uses of language (e.g., praising, prophesying, promising, preaching, etc.), and given the many biblical passages on the correct use of the tongue (e.g., James 3), it is clear that God holds speakers accountable for what they say. More importantly, the Bible represents God as the preeminent speaker. Much of what he does takes the form of speech: promising, forgiving, commanding, and so on. The God of the Christian Scriptures is a God who relates to human beings largely through verbal communication. Of course, God can embody his Word with a completeness that human cannot: God's Word was made flesh. *God's Word is thus something that God says, something that God does, and something that God is.*[120]

In connection with this, therefore, Vanhoozer seeks the *imago Dei* of human being in "humanity's unique capacity for communion with

---

119. Vanhoozer, *Is There a Meaning in This Text?*, 205–6, and his *Drama of Doctrine*, 177.

120. Vanhoozer, *Is There a Meaning in This Text?*, 205 (italics original). Concerning the "design plan" for language, which corresponds to A. Plantinga's conception of "the design plan of the human mind," Vanhoozer states that, "Language, like the mind, another divine endowment, was designed by God to be used in certain ways. The design plan specifies when our communicative faculties are functioning properly. Proper function is a matter of accomplishing the purpose for which one's faculties were designed. The proper function of our cognitive faculties, for instance, is to produce true belief. The proper function of our communicative faculties, I contend, is to produce true interpretation—understanding" (ibid.). Accordingly, "the design plan of language is to serve as the medium of covenantal relations with God, with others, with world" (ibid., 206).

God."[121] That is to say, according to Vanhoozer, in the biblical perspective, God is first of all the self-revealing God, the self-communicative Agent. If we accept his Trinitarian ontology of communicative-act, "God's being is a being-in-communicative-act," then, we can conceive that human being was created as a communicative agent in the *imago Dei* as such.[122] For this reason, man can communicate with God and with other human beings. In this sense, we can say that to be a being-as-life-in-relation, a living person is "to be a communicative agent in a web of communicative relationships with others."[123] In using *analogia communicationis*, therefore, we can grasp the traditional and the renewed relational understandings of the image of God together. That is, a human being-as-life-in-relation, as an individual, has two aspects in the image of God—the structural and functional aspects in traditional understandings, but he, as a social being, has also a relational aspect in the image of God. In this way, by the conception of communicative-agent, as Vanhoozer suggests, we can more properly conceive the *imago Dei* as a holistic aspect of human nature—a being-as-life-in-relation, individual and social at the same time. Therefore, there is an analogy, *analogia communicationis*, between the Living God and man, "a living being."

As we have seen, human beings, a being-as-life-in-relation, are essentially communicative agents, and language is the essential feature of their existence as a communicative agents. However, language is inseparably interrelated with time. First of all, all of our speaking of language, the verbal communication, takes place in time. As Balthsar says,

> Even more important is the observation that language, which is the self-revelation of a person, is committed, like music, to this medium of nothingness. It must flow away, syllable by syllable, until the meaning of what is said, distilled like an essence out of what has vanished, can be understood by the listener. With language, however, as the free communication of persons, when and as they like, the temporal moment acquires an historical character. Something unique in time—the person—expresses itself uniquely through language as word or as deed, and creates

---

121. Vanhoozer, "Human Being, Individual and Social," 163.

122. Ibid., 176–77. In another place, Vanhoozer says that, "God communicates with others ('In the beginning was the Word') and that humans, created in God's image, are likewise communicative agents." Idem, *Is There a Meaning in This Text?*, 199.

123. Vanhoozer, "Human Being, Individual and Social," 176.

something unique in time. Thus time, even as a void, not created or controlled by the creature, offers the necessary "space" in which mind can clearly reveal, express, and perfect itself.[124]

In addition, as we experience it in everyday life, our communicative action in language is thoroughly tensed like "was," "is," "will be," and so forth. In this sense, "the tense-structure of a language reflects the time-awareness of its speaker."[125] Accordingly, Gerhard Ebeling says that, "language and the experience of time originate together."[126] Ebeling further explains this point as follows:

> Only through language do the past and future become present and the present gain the depth-dimension of past and future. Language's relation to time is rooted much more deeply than in the fact that we can fill out or even kill time with talking. Language always comes from linguistically experienced time and is challenged to fulfill the claim of time, but also to resist the claim of time. For abstract time is time made speechless. Concrete time, as time *for* something, is time which is meaningful, taken cognizance of in the context of language, though again and again bursting that context; it is time which cannot be mastered linguistically, and makes us speechless. The dimensions of linguistically experienced time pull man *in infinitum* and make the finite inexhaustible and limitless.[127]

Therefore, language is ineliminabilly saturated by time, and thus, as W. L. Craig states, "there is no tenseless language in the world."[128] As we have seen in chapter 4, even though there are vigorous debates between the tensed (dynamic) and the tenseless (static) theorists of time, Q. Smith shows that tensed sentences cannot be translated into tenseless ones without losing their unique tensed meaning.[129] In this sense, generally, the tensed theorists of time (cf. A. N. Prior, R. M. Gale, Q. Smith, R. Swinburne, W. L. Crag, etc.) have a consensus that the pervasive tensed system of all languages and the ineliminability of tense from our ordinary use of language reflect the fact that "tense" is the

124. Balthasar, *Theological Anthropology*, 24
125. Horvath, "New Notion of Time," 46.
126. Ebeling, "Time and Word," 263.
127. Ibid., 264.
128. Craig, *Time and Eternity*, 115.
129. Cf. Quentin Smith, *Language and Time*, 1993). See also my chapter 4 in this study, for the debates between the tensed vs. the tenseless theory of time.

objective feature of reality in the world. W. L. Craig well explains this point view as follows:

> This is doubtlessly due to the fact that language reflects our experience of the world as being tensed, as having a past, present, and future. Some philosophers, however, see an even deeper significance to linguistic tense. They argue that linguistic tense is, as it were, a window on the world: Our language is tensed because reality is tensed. That is to say, there really are tensed facts which are objective features of the world.... Linguistic tense merely exhibits the tense that is a feature of time itself.[130]

Furthermore, according to the Speech act theory of language (cf. J. L. Austin and John Searle), people do many things in speaking, and thus "to speak" something is "to do" something.[131] J. L. Austin believes that, in many cases, our utterances are performative in that a speaker performs some act in saying something.[132] In speech acts theory, our various speech acts are classified as locutionary, illocutionary, and perlocutionary. The following K. J. Vanhoozer's statement is very helpful to understand this:

> Austin distinguishes three different things we do with words, three kinds of linguistic acts: (1) the locutionary act: uttering words (e.g., saying the word "Hello"); (2) the illocutionary act: what we do in saying something (e.g., greeting, promising, commanding, etc.); (3) the perlocutionary act: what we bring about by saying something (e.g., persuading, surprising). Whereas locution has to do with a sign system or *langue*, illocutions and perlocutions have to do with sentences, with language in action or *parole*. The notion of the illocutionary act enables Austin to distinguish between the content of what we say (e.g., the sense and reference of our sentence) and its force (i.e., what we are using the content of our sentence to do). Austin's all-important notion of illocution requires us, I believe, to bring to the fore the speaker's (or auther's) role as agent. The speaker is a *doer*.[133]

---

130. Craig, *Time and Eternity*, 115–16.

131. For the Speech acts theory, see the following: Austin, *How to Do Things with Words*, and *Philosophical Papers*; Fann, *Symposium on J. L. Austin*; Warnock, *J. L. Austin*; Searle, *Speech Acts*, *Expression and Meaning*, and *Mind, Language and Society*; Lepore and Van Gulick, *John Searle and His Critics*; Tsohatzidis, *Foundations of Speech Act Theory*; and William P. Alston, *Illocutionary Acts and Sentence Meaning*.

132. Cf. Austin, "Performative Utterances," in his *Philosophical Papers*, 233–52.

133. Vanhoozer, *Is There a Meaning in This Text?*, 209. Cf. Searle, "How Language

At first, in the concepts of illocutionary and perlocutionary speech-acts, through our utterance of something, there is a sequence of actions in time, saying, hearing, and bringing about something as their effect. For instance, when I enter a room, I say, "This room is so hot!" Then, the host may turn on an air conditioner, and then the room will be cooled as its effect. In this sense, "Language here is the means of transmitting messages through space and time to others" and bringing about some actions and something as its effect.[134] In addition, communicative action in language is a dialogue between the one and the other, and thus it is always an event or an action in the relation of speaking and hearing. In this relation of speaking-hearing, time is the medium of communicative action. Therefore, time is the form of the communicative action of the personal being-as-life-in-relation with others. Living communicative action with the Living God, with other human beings, and with the environmental world is essential for our life to be a being-as-life-in-relation. In this sense, even though Heidegger said that language is "the home of being," I want to modify this idea to that of time is "the home of language" as the form of our speech acts. As a speech act, actually, language creates time as its form to accomplish its original role, the performative action in and through time. In this sense, time is created by the locutionary act, and functions as the medium of the illocutionary acts, and finally ends its role with the perlocutionary act. Accordingly, we can say that time is the home of language in which our communicative action of life is accomplished. Therefore, at the same time, it is the form of our being-as-life-in-relation, which is constituted through our living communicative action of life with the Other.

After the fall, however, for man, there is only totally broken communion and communication with the Living God as well as with other human beings. As Vanhoozer points out, "Hell is [none other than]... the inability to relate to others." He explains this point further as follows:

> The attempt to be without God and others (sinful autonomy) leads to autism, that shriveling of the self to the point of total self-absorption. Spiritual autism thus characterizes a kind of

---

Works," in *Mind, Language and Society*, 135–61; Alston, *Illocutionary Acts and Sentence Meaning*, 11–32.

134. Vanhoozer, *Is There a Meaning in This Text?*, 222.

solitary self-confinement that stems from the inability, or the unwillingness, to communicate with others.[135]

In addition, even though our material living communication of life with the Living God and fellow human beings was totally broken in the Garden of Eden as the result of original sin, this is manifested at the event of Babel in that "the Lord confused the language of the whole world" (Gen 11:9).

God's Time as the Form of the Triune God's Communicative Action

Originally, as K. J. Vanhoozer points out, the biblical God is a supremely communicative Agent. The Living God, YHWH, is the speaking and communicative God. In the very beginning of creation, as Scripture describes, "God *said*, 'Let there be light,' . . ." (Gen 1:3). Then, in other places, the Bible says that, "the Lord *called* to the man, 'Where are you?'" (Gen 1:9), "'Come now, let us reason together,' says the Lord" (Isa 1:18; cf. 41:1), and so on. Indeed, in most cases, the Living God does everything by His saying, i.e., creation, command, promise, forgiveness, and so forth. However, first of all, we must pay attention to the facts that there is an inner communicative action in the tri-personal God (i.e., the immanent Trinity). For instance, "*Let us* make man in *our* image . . ." (Gen 1:26); "the Lord said, 'the man has now become like *one of us* . . .'" (Gen 3:22); "Come, *let us* go down and confuse their language . . ." (Gen 11:7). Concerning these passages, even though the texts do not explicitly say it, in the light of the NT, these God's communicative acts can be considered to be inner-communicative actions among the three persons of the Trinity. The reason is that, as we have seen, the creation of the world is a co-work of the Trinity, the Living God Yahweh (the Father), and His *dabar* (the Word, the Son) and His *ruach* (the Holy Spirit). In John 1:1, we read that, "In the beginning was the Word, and the Word was with God, and the Word was God." Furthermore, the Son Jesus Christ's speech and prayer reveal the perfect eternal communion and communicative relation of the Triune God (cf. John 14:6–21 and 17:1–26).

---

135. Vanhoozer, "Human Being, Individual and Social," 177.

Toward an Alternative Trinitarian Analogical Understanding 331

Accordingly, the biblical God, who is revealed as the Living Triune God in Jesus Christ, is "the ultimate communicative agent" to other beings, the creation, too (i.e., the economic Trinity). As the traditional teaching, therefore, *opera trinitatis ad intra et opera trinitatis ad extra sunt indivisa*. In this sense, while modifying Barth's conception of the Trinity in the scheme of God's self-revelation—revealer (the Father), revelation (the Son), and revealedness (the Holy Spirit), K. J. Vanhoozer applied it to the speech act theory as follows: "The Triune God is communicative agent (Father/author), action (Word/text), and result (Spirit/power of reception)" or "speaker (Father), Word (Son), and reception (Spirit)."[136] Vanhoozer's following statement is a fuller explanation of the Trinity, especially for the economic Trinity, in "the analogy of speech-acts."

> The Father's activity is locution. God the father is the utterer, the begetter, the sustainer of words. He is the agent who *locutus est per prophetas* in former times, and who now speaks through the Son (Heb 1;1–2). God the Father's locution is the result of his providential involvement in the lives of the human authors of Scripture. God works in and through human intelligence and human imagination to produce a literary account that renders him a mighty speech agent. The Logos corresponds to the speaker's act or illocution, to what one *does* in saying. The illocution has content (reference and predication) and a particular intent (a force) that shows how proposition is to be taken. It is illocutionary force that makes a speech act *count* as, say, a promise. What illocutionary act is performed is determined by the speaker; its meaning is therefore objective. The third aspect of a speech act is perlocutionary. This refers to the effect an illocutionary act has on the actions or beliefs of the hearer. For example, by "arguing" (illocution) I may "persuade" (perlocution) someone.[137]

The Living God has communicated Himself in the words of Scripture, but finally in the Word, the Son, who is none other than the Word through whom He made the universe (cf. Heb 1:3). We can find the perfect identity of word and existence in Jesus Christ, in whom the

---

136. Vanhoozer, *Is There a Meaning in This Text?*, 199 and 456.

137. Vanhoozer, *First Theology*, 155. In another place, he states this as follows, [In the triune God's communicative action], "the Father initiates communication; the Son is the content of the communication; the Spirit is the efficacy of the communication. The triune God is the paradigmatic communicative agent: only God can communicate so as always to accomplish his purpose (Isa 55:11)." Idem, *Drama of Doctrine*, 65.

Word was made flesh (John 1:14). Then, as Balthasar says, "The Word of God passed through time. Everything in his passage was the word and revelation of the Father, but also revelation of the truth of human existence."[138] In this way, the Living God, the *Ur*-speaker (the locution), is exactly His own Word in Jesus Christ (the illocution). In the incarnate Word, the Living God perfectly communicates Himself to us. However, we cannot do so. Even though we often say that, "I am the man of my word," we cannot identify our word and our existence. Since the first man's disobedience and distortion of communication, we always deceive not only the Living God but also ourselves. In contrast to this, through His perfect obedience to the Father's will up to His death on the Cross, the Son is the Father's own Word (i.e., *homoousios*), and thus perfectly fulfilled the Father's words of promise (Phil 2:8) in the Holy Spirit. In this way, Jesus Christ is the unique and perfect communication of life *pro nobis*, and thus the Communication between God and man, as He himself is God-and-man, *vere Deus vere homo*. Therefore, without the communion and fellowship with the Word of Life, the Son, there is no life for us, since "God was reconciling the world to himself in Christ" (2 Cor 5:20; cf. 1 Cor 1:9; 1 John 1:2). Accordingly, Jesus Christ declares that, "I am the way and the truth and the life. No one comes to the Father except through me" (John 14:6).

Then, in order to give us the true life, eternal life, the Holy Spirit (the perlocution), who is "the Spirit of truth," leads us to the Word of truth and persuades us in teaching and witnessing the Word of God to us (John 14:17, 26; John 15:26), for "this is eternal life: that they may know you, the only true God, and Jesus Christ, whom you have sent" (John 17:3). Furthermore, when the Holy Spirit comes to us, the confused language of the world is also healed (Acts 2:4; cf. Gen 11:7-9). In this way, the Holy Spirit heals our deadly broken communication to the living one, the communication of life, which is the fellowship of life with the God of Life and among us again. Indeed, the Holy Spirit is the Spirit of communication and communion, the Spirit of tongues, and the Spirit of understanding. The Holy Spirit is the agent of not only the inspiration of the Living God's words but also the incarnation of the Word of Life. Accordingly, He is the unique and the true interpreter of the Word and the words of the Living God, for "God has revealed it to

---

138. Balthasar, *Theological Anthropology*, 243

us by his Spirit. The Spirit searches all things, even the deep things of God" (1 Cor 2:10, cf. 11-14).

Therefore, in these three distinct forms of Triune God's communicative action, the Trinity is perfectly one unity in His communicative action, as the locution (the Father/speaker), the illocution (the Son/Word), and the perlocution (the Holy Spirit/reception). Then, God's time is the form of the Living Triune God's perfect communicative action, and therefore time is the medium for the accomplishment of His Word. As Scripture says, "My Word that goes out from my mouth: It will not return to me empty, but will accomplish what I desire and achieve the purpose for which I sent it" (Isa 55:11; cf. Matt 24:35). Actually, the Living God created time in His speech acts, and then makes it as the medium to fulfill His will (cf. the promise-fulfillment structure in the Bible). In this sense, even though our communicative action in language is a broken one, there is an analogy, *analogia communicationis*, a partial correspondence within infinite qualitative difference between the Living Triune God, the ultimate communicative Agent, and human beings, and thus between God's perfect time and our broken time as its forms.

Conclusion

So far, in order to properly conceive the nature of God's eternity and its relation to time, I propose an alternative Trinitarian analogical understanding of time and eternity. In chapter 5, we saw various contemporary theological understandings of God's eternity and its relation to time. Concerning those views, first of all, God's eternity is not absolute timelessness (e.g., P. Helm) as a negation of time (*via negativa*). If we define time/eternity as the mode or form of life, the eternal God has His own time as the form of His own eternal life. Likewise, we have our time as the form of our conditional and finite life. However, at the same time, the everlasting view of God's eternity too (e.g., O. Cullmann, N. Wolterstorff, and Robert Jenson) cannot be acceptable. God's eternity is not a mere infinite extension of time both backwards and forwards. In this case, God's time is conceived as a mere temporal infinity without beginning and end. According to Scripture, however, God Himself is the Alpha and the Omega, the beginning and the end at the same time, and this is God and His eternity. Therefore, it would be wrong simply to identify God's eternity with the everlasting time (i.e., "time without beginning and end") because this view is a deification of the form of creaturely existence as the eminence of our finite time to God's everlasting time (*via eminentiae*, a temporal panentheism). There must be a qualitative, not a mere quantitative, difference between God's mode of existence, the Creator, and the human mode of existence, the creature.

Furthermore, we cannot also accept the accidental temporalism of God's eternity (e.g., W. L. Craig, and a little different form of J. Moltmann), which is the view that God is absolutely timeless in His eternity, but He is temporal with His creation of the temporal world. That is, we need not think that the self-existent Living God accidentally changed His mode of existence because of His creation of the temporal world. Concerning the problem of change and God, the conception of Cambridge change is helpful. In contrast to real change, a Cambridge change means a relative change in relation. That is to say, in this created world, everything undergoes real, genuine, or ontological qualitative change. However, for God, there is only a Cambridge change in the relational sense, but not a real change in His Being nor in His intrinsic attributes. In the same sense, while asserting God's ontological and ethical immutability, J. S. Feinberg and B. A. Ware recently well argued God's "relational mutability."[139]

It is worth mentioning that, while proposing a Trinitarian analogical understanding of time and eternity, I intentionally presupposed the dynamic (tensed) theory of time for this study. The reason is that if the static (tenseless) theory is correct, even though God cannot be confined by created world orders, we can conceive that God's eternity is timeless without any serious problem. However, the purpose of my study was to answer the following question: if the dynamic (tensed) theory of time is correct, then how can we properly conceive God's eternity and its relation to time? According to the tensed theory of time, our time is always successive from the past through the present into the future. However, in my view, the particularity of God's time is its simultaneity which can be properly understood in Trinitarian terms, and it is the infinite qualitative difference from our ever-transient and successive time.

However, how can God be simultaneous in temporal succession? To answer the question, in my view, the distinction and unity of the

---

139. Cf. Feinberg, *No One Like Him*, 427–36; and Ware, "Evangelical Reformulation of the Doctrine of the Immutability of God," 434–40.

immanent Trinity and the economic trinity is a key point. That is to say, in the immanent Trinity, even though there are successions, like the Father's begetting the Son and breathing out the Holy Spirit, the Triune God is in the perfect one unity. In other words, metaphorically, the three properties of time, the past, the present, and the future are in one unity (i.e., simultaneity). In this sense, God's eternity is qualitatively different from our time. This means that, in Trinitarian terms, the three distinctive persons are one unity. The Trinity is the only true Living God. Therefore, eternity (i.e., God's time) is the form of the inner-trinitarian Life in Himself. Then, after the creation of the temporal world, our created time is always in succession of past, present, and future. In His creation and redemption of our ever-fleeting time, the created and fallen time, the Triune God gives Himself to such a temporal sequence. That is the salvation history in which the Triune God reveals Himself as the Creator, the Reconciler, and the Redeemer, and works *pro nobis* and *pro mundo* in His passionate love. That is the economic Trinity in salvation history. However, the infinite qualitative difference between God's time and our sinful time as death-bound time is this: even though we are subordinated to the fleetingness of time, God is not so because He is the Creator and thus the Lord of time. This is clearly manifested in the time of Jesus Christ. That is, God himself, the Son, handed Himself over to the power of fallen time (i.e., death), but the God of Life (the Father) raised the Son from the dead to Life in the Spirit of Life (the Holy Spirit).

In this way, the Living Triune God conquered and redeemed our fallen time, and will give us a new time as the form of our new eternal life. More significantly, in the unity and distinction of the economic Trinity and the immanent Trinity, the Living Triune God always presents Himself simultaneously in our time sequence. He is the Alpha and the Omega, the Beginning and the End, who Was, Is, and Is to Come at the same time. Therefore, we can say that the mystery of God's eternity and its relation to time is the mystery of the Trinity in the distinction and unity between the immanent Trinity and the economic Trinity. In my view, the two conceptions of the Trinity can be properly conceived in an analogical relationship of distinction in unity (contra. K. Rahner's Rule).[140] In the biblical and theological perspective, for the proper under-

---

140. K. Rahner's rule is as follows, "The 'economic' Trinity is the 'immanent' Trinity and the 'immanent' Trinity is the 'economic' Trinity." Rahner, *Trinity*, 22. However, in

standing of God's eternity and its relation time, the ultimate criterion is the Living Triune God's Being-as-Life-in-relation and His communicative action in eternity (the immanent Trinity) and time (the economic Trinity).

Conclusively, in my view, God's eternity is not an absolutely timeless eternity and also not a mere everlasting time (i.e., the temporal infinity), but in a proper sense it can be understood as a kind of "supratemporality." In contrast to our human time as finite and mortal time as the form of our created and sinful life, God's eternity must also be understood as the "true time" as the form of the true and eternal Life of the Living Triune God. In this study, I attempted to show the difficulties and limitations of various contemporary understandings of God's eternity and its relation to time, and suggested one of more theologically reasonable understandings in *via analogia*. That is to say, while reconceiving time as the form of life, not a static and monadic being (substance) or an ever-fleeting becoming (change), I have proposed that we have our time, which is created and given by God, as the form of our being-as-life-in-relation. Therefore, rather than timeless eternity (*via negativa*) and everlasting time (*via eminentiae*), we have a more proper understanding that God's eternity is His own time as the form of the Living Triune God's perfect Being-as-life-in-relation in *via analogia* according to the following triple analogy, *analogia vitae*, *analogia relationis*, and *analogia communicationis*.

In fact, here I want to suggest implicitly that the triple analogy itself can be considered as a Trinitarian analogy: *analogia vitae* (the Father, the source and the giver of the Life as *Ipsum Vita*), *analogia relationis* (the Son, the relation of life between God and man as the God-and-man), and *analogia communicationis* (the Holy Spirit, the communication of life between the Father and the Son as the Bond of Life as well as between the Living Triune God and the human being-as-life-in-relation).

---

spite of its positive meaning, we cannot simply identify the two concepts of Trinity as a "tautological formula A=A." Cf. Kasper, *God of Jesus Christ*, 273–77. Balthasar also criticizes Rahner's dictum, see his *Theo-Drama: Theological Dramatic Theory*, vol. IV, 273–84 and 319–28. In identifying the two concepts of the Trinity, however, there are some alternative options, e.g., a correspondence model (E. Jüngel), a doxological (and eschatological) model (J. Moltmann, C. M. LaCugna), an eschatological model (W. Pannenberg, Robert W. Jenson), and an analogical model (H. U. von Balthasar). I prefer a kind of analogical model, the distinction in unity of the two concepts of the Trinity.

Therefore, the Living Triune God can really relate to our time without any change in His ontological mode of Being. Indeed, the Living Triune God is the perfect Being-as-life-in-relation *ad intra* as well as *ad extra*. In this way, the only true biblical God, YHWH, is the Living God, the God of Life, as the Trinity: the Father, the Son, and the Holy Spirit. At the same time, the Trinity as the Lord of life is the Lord of time. Therefore, the essential task of Christian theology and faith as a communicative action of life is none other than encountering the Living Triune God who is always with His people in His *Ur*-communicative action of life, witnessing Him to the ends of earth, and praising and worshiping Him forever and ever.

Finally, W. L. Craig summarized absolute timeless eternity of God in classical theism, which is based on the ontology of the perfect being, as follows:

1. God is the most perfect being.
2. The most perfect being has the most perfect mode of existence.
3. Temporal existence is a less perfect mode of existence than timeless existence.
4. Therefore God has the most perfect mode of existence.
5. Therefore God has a timeless mode of existence.[141]

As a conclusion, on the basis of the biblical understanding of the Living Triune God, I want to modify the lines of the above argument:

1. According to the Bible, the only true God is uniquely the Living Triune God; the Father, the Son, and the Holy Spirit.
2. The Living Triune God has His own mode of existence as the perfect Being-as-life-in-relation. He is the true Life, and thus He has His own time (i.e., the Triune God's original time, *Ur*-time, eternity) as the form of His own Triune Life in *perichoresis*, the mutual communicative inner-relationship of the three persons in one unity. Therefore, the Living Triune God reveals Himself as the Creator, the Reconciler, and the Redeemer, who created and sustains the whole world through His communicative action with His creatures.

---

141. Craig, "Timelessness and Omnitemporality," 133.

3. Man, who is created as "a living being" (or "a being-as-life") in the *imago Dei*, has also his own finite mode of existence as a communicative being-as-life-in-relation. His conditional and finite time is the form of his finite life, which is created and given by the Living Triune God as a gift. In this sense, as Plato defined time as "the moving image of eternity," we can say that human time is created in the *imago Dei*, as the form of human existence, including the whole created world.

4. Therefore, there is an analogical relationship between the Living Triune God's perfect Being-as-life-in-relation and the conditional and finite human being-as-life-in-relation. That is to say, according to *analogia vitae, analogia relationis,* and *analogia communicationis*, there is a partial similarity or correspondence within "the infinite qualitative difference" (K. Barth) or "the ever-greater ontological difference" (H. U. von Balthsar) between God and man.

5. Therefore, there is also an analogical relationship between God's time (i.e., eternity) and human time: God's time as the form of the Trinitarian Life and created and fallen human time as the form of created life. In this sense, we can call God's eternity (i.e., God's time) the "true time" as the form of the true Life of the Living Triune God.

9

Conclusion

IN THIS STUDY, CONSIDERING THE DEBATE ON GOD'S ETERNITY AND ITS relation to time, I presented, as an alternative option to classical theism and contemporary panentheism, an analogical understanding (a partial correspondence in ever-greater difference) of the particular problem of eternity-time in the horizon of the God-world relationship. In doing so, the ultimate criterion is the Living Triune God's communicative action in eternity (the immanent Trinity) and time (the economic Trinity), which are essentially in an analogical relationship of distinction in unity (contra. a "tautological formula A=A" of K. Rahner's Rule).

Therefore, I have strived to present a Trinitarian analogical understanding of God's eternity and its relation to time, as well as to show that it is an alternative way to the absolute timeless view in classical theism or the everlasting view in contemporary panentheism. That is, first of all, a kind of *via analogia* can more properly conceive the God-world relation, divine transcendence and immanence, and God's eternity and its relation time than *via negationis* (i.e., the absolute timelessness) and *via eminentiae* (i.e., the everlasting duration). In this Trinitarian analogical way, we can properly conceive not only the infinite qualitative difference but also the real and positive relationship between God's eternity and time. Therefore, this study has examined a trinitarian and a dialectic-analogical understanding, based on the triune God's communicative action, of the twin problems of eternity-time and the God-world relationship, which come from a critical reflection on the views of K. Barth and H. U. von Balthasar. The ultimate criterion for doing so is God's self-communicative action in eternity (the immanent Trinity) and in time (the economic Trinity).

In critically following K. Barth's and H. U. von Balthasar's trinitarian-Christocentric analogical paradigm, I especially focused on the communicative action of the Triune God. In my view, for both theologians, the doctrine of analogy is a formal (methodological) principle, and the concept of God's action is a material skeleton in constructing their whole theological edifice. That is to say, to dissolve the problem of eternity-time, God-world, and divine transcendence-immanence relationship, the purpose of the study was to suggest that a trinitarian analogical paradigm (i.e., in Chalcedonian terms, neither "separated/divided" nor "confused/mixed," but "distinct" in relationship), which is based on the communicative action of the Triune God, could be one of a more proper paradigm than classical theism (which is based on the Greek ontology) and a contemporary panentheistic paradigm.

According to the Bible, God is the "God above us" as the Creator of the world, and, at the same time, He is the "God with us" (i.e., Immanuel) as the Reconciler and our Redeemer. The God of creation is the God of providence, redemption, and consummation at the same time. That is, God is not only transcendent but also immanent. In trinitarian terms, God *in se* (i.e., *opera trinitatis ad intra*, the immanent Trinity in eternity) and God *pro me/nobis/mundo* (i.e., *opera trinitatis ad extra*, the economic Trinity in time) cannot be separated. In other words, God is eternal as the Lord of time, which means that He exists "over" time and really acts "in" time. In this way, by concentrating on God's communicative action in Jesus Christ—the true God and the true man, I proposed a dialectic-analogical middle way (*via analogia*), through the following Trinitarian triple analogy, *analogia vitae*, *analogia relationis*, and *analogia communicationis*, between extreme *via negativa* and *via eminentiae* to conceive God's eternity and its relation to time. That is to say, if there is a partial correspondence in infinite qualitative difference in the relationship between God's eternity and time, the impasse between timeless eternity and everlasting duration can be dissolved in proposing a new Trinitarian ontology, the Being-as-life-in-relation. It could be a Trinitarian ontology of Communion which is based on God's communicative act (cf. K. J. Vanhoozer), not the abstract ontology of Being (classical theism) or the ontology of Becoming or Not-yet-Being (panentheism). The trinitarian ontology of Being-as-life-in-relation (or Being-in-communicative-action) can grasp the aspects of "Being" and "Relation" together at the same time. By this Trinitarian ontology and analogical way, we can continue our navigation of "faith seeking understanding" without abandoning the ship (Being/eternity) and falling into a dangerous ocean (Becoming/time's stream).

In order to fully accomplish this study, however, it needs a further study in the following three perspectives: a more comprehensive study of the biblical conception of time and God's eternity, a thorough Trinitarian systematic theology, and a very diverse interdisciplinary dialogue on the subject matter. That is to say, first of all, in the perspective of biblical theology, I briefly suggested a canonical approach, which is constituted by the time of creation, the time of providence (and redemption), and the time of eschatology. Such a canonical approach alone can discern the whole structure of the qualitative difference of God's eternity and its real and positive relation to time. Then, such a comprehensive biblical study must be connected and applied to a comprehensive Trinitarian systematic theology. The problem of God's eternity and its relation to time is a kernel axis, which constitutes our understanding of God, human beings, and the world. Indeed, it is the problem of theological paradigms between classical theism and contemporary panentheism. Therefore, it is the problem of the total constitution of our world-view and world-history in Theo-Dramatic History (i.e., the redemptive history).

In this connection, it needs also an on-going vigorous interdisciplinary dialogue with philosophy and natural science. For example, in this study, I suggested a biblical and theological conception of the nature of time as *life* against the philosophical conception of the nature of time as *change*. In addition, I prefer and suppose that the tensed (dynamic) theory of time is a more plausible conception than the tenseless (static) theory, but it is not yet proved. However, while realizing the fact that God's eternity cannot be deduced from our conception or experience of world's time and confined in any philosophical framework, we know only in part what God's time (i.e., eternity) really is through the concrete God-given analogy, Jesus Christ who is the Revealer of God's eternity and the Redeemer of our lost time. Therefore, since our theology is always *theologia viatorum* (theology of pilgrims), our voyage in faith seeking understand can never end until "when we shall see face to face, and then we shall know fully" (cf. 1 Cor 13:12) who God is and who we are and about what God's eternity is and what our time is. However, we cannot deny the fact that, at this very moment, we live in our time which is given by God, the Lord of time, who created, sustains, and will consummate it. Accordingly, from moment to moment, we cannot but praise the only true Living Triune God, the God of life and thus the Lord of time, who gives us time in order to give us our life and who will give us a new time in order to give us the eternal life in Himself. *Oh, my Lord, all of my life and my times in this age and the age to come are only in your hand!* (cf. Ps 31:15). "To the only wise God be glory forever through Jesus Christ! Amen" (Rom 16:27).

"Lord, You have been our dwelling place throughout all generations.
Before the mountains were born or you brought forth the earth
    and the world,
From everlasting to everlasting you are God." (Ps 90:2)

"Holy, holy, holy
is the Lord God Almighty,
who Was, and Is, and is to Come." (Rev 4:8)

Soli Deo Gloria!!

Bibliography

Achtner, Wolfgang, Stefan Kunz, and Thomas Walter. *Dimensions of Time: The Structure of the Time of Humans, of the World, and of God*. Grand Rapids: Eerdmans, 1998.

Adam, Barbara. *Time and Social Theory*. Philadelphia: Temple University Press, 1990.

Albright, Carol R., and Joel Haugen, editors. *Beginning with the End: God, Science, and Wolfhart Pannenberg*. Chicago: Open Court, 1997.

Alston, William P. *Divine Nature and Human Language*. Ithaca: Cornell University Press, 1989.

———. *Illocutionary Acts and Sentence Meaning*. Ithaca: Cornell University Press, 2000.

Anselm, *Proslogion, Monologion,* and *De Concordia*. In *Anselm of Canterbury: The Major Works*. Edited by Brian Davies and G. R. Evans. Oxford: Oxford University Press, 1998.

Aquinas, Thomas. *Compendium of Theology*. Translated by Cyril Vollert. St. Louis: Herder, 1949.

———. *Summa Contra Gentiles*. Book One: *God*. Translated by Anton C. Pegis. Notre Dame: University of Notre Dame Press, 1975.

———. *Summa Theologiae*, Vol. 2, 1a.2-11. Translated by Timothy Mcdermott. New York: Blackfriars, 1964.

———. *Summa Theologica*. Vol. 1. Translated by Fathers of the English Dominican Province. Westminster: Christian Classics, 1981.

Ariotti, Piero E. "The Conception of Time in Late Antiquity." *International Philosophical Quarterly* 12 (1972) 526-52.

Aristotle, *The Complete Works of Aristotle*. 2 Vols. Edited by J. Barnes. Princeton: Princeton University Press, 1984.

Askin, Yakov F. "The Philosophic Concept of Time." In *Time and the Philosophies*, edited by H. Aguessy et al., 127-39. Paris: Unesco, 1977.

Augustine. *The City of God against the Pagans*. Edited and translated by R. W. Dyson. Cambridge: Cambridge University Press, 1998.

———. *Confessions*. Translated by F. J. Sheed. Indianapolis: Hackett, 1993.

Austin, J. L. *How to Do Things with Words*. Oxford: Oxford University Press, 1962.

———. *Philosophical Papers*. Oxford: Oxford University Press, 1970.

Azkoul, Michael. "On Time and Eternity: The Nature of History according to the Greek Fathers." *St. Vladimir's Seminary Quarterly* 12 (1968) 56-77.

Baert, Patrick, editor. *Time in Contemporary Intellectual Thought*. Amsterdam: Elsevier, 2000.

Baker, Lynne R. "On the Mind-Dependence of Temporal Becoming." *Philosophy and Phenomenological Research* 39 (1978-1979) 341-57.

———. "Temporal Becoming: The Argument from Physics." *Philosophical Forum* 6 (1974–1975) 218–36.

Balashov, Y. "Persistence and Space-Time: Philosophical Lessons of the Pole and Barn." *Monist* 83 (2000) 321–40.

Balslev, Anindita Niyogi, and J. N. Mohanty, editors. *Religion and Time*. Leiden: Brill, 1993.

Balthasar, Hans Urs von. *Does Jesus Knows Us—Do We Know Him?* Translated by G. Harrison. San Francisco: Ignatius, 1983.

———. *Explorations in Theology*. Vol. 1: *The Word Made Flesh*. Translated by A. V. Littledale and Alexander Dru. San Francisco: Ignatius, 1989.

———. *Explorations in Theology*. Vol. 3: *Creator Spirit*. Translated by B. McNeil. San Francisco: Ignatius, 1993.

———. *First Glance at Adrienne von Speyr*. Translated by A. Lawry and S. Englund. San Francisco: Ignatius, 1981.

———. *The Glory of the Lord: A Theological Aesthetics*. Vol. 5: *The Realm of Metaphysics in the Modern Age*. Translated by Oliver Davies et al. San Francisco: Ignatius, 1991.

———. *The Glory of the Lord: A Theological Aesthetics*. Vol. 7: *Theology: The New Covenant*. Translated by Brian McNeil. San Francisco: Ignatius, 1989.

———. *Love Alone*. Translated by Alexander Dru. New York: Herder & Herder, 1969.

———. *My Work: In Retrospect*. San Francisco: Ignatius, 1993.

———. *Mysterium Paschale: The Mystery of Easter*. Translated by A. Nichols. Grand Rapids: Eerdmans, 1993.

———. *Prayer*. Translated by A. V. Littledale. New York: Sheed & Ward, 1961.

———. *Presence and Thought: Essay on the Religious Philosophy of Gregory of Nyssa*. Translated by Mark Sebanc. San Francisco: Ignatius, 1995.

———. *Theo-Drama: Theological Dramatic Theory*. Vol. 1: *Prolegomena*. Translated by Graham Harrison. San Francisco: Ignatius, 1988.

———. *Theo-Drama: Theological Dramatic Theory*. Vol. 2: *The Dramatis Personae: Man in God*. Translated by Graham Harrison. San Francisco: Ignatius, 1990.

———. *Theo-Drama: Theological Dramatic Theory*. Vol. 3: *The Dramatis Personae: The Person in Christ*. Translated by Graham Harrison. San Francisco: Ignatius, 1992.

———. *Theo-Drama: Theological Dramatic Theory*. Vol. 4: *The Action*. Translated by Graham Harrison. San Francisco: Ignatius, 1994.

———. *Theo-Drama: Theological Dramatic Theory*. Vol. 5: *The Last Act*. Translated by Graham Harrison. San Francisco: Ignatius, 1998.

———. *Theo-Logic: Theological Logical Theory*. Vol. 1: *Truth of the World*. Translated by Adrian J. Walker. San Francisco: Ignatius, 2000.

———. *Theo-Logic: Theological Logical Theory*. Vol. 2: *Truth of God*. Translated by Adrian J. Walker. San Francisco: Ignatius, 2004.

———. *A Theological Anthropology*. New York: Sheed & Ward, 1967.

———. *Theologik*. Vol. 3: *Der Geist der Wahrheit*. Einsiedeln: Johannes, 1987.

———. *A Theology of History*. San Francisco: Ignatius, 1994.

———. *The Theology of Karl Barth*. Translated by Edward T. Oakes. San Francisco: Ignatius, 1992.

Barbour, Ian G. *Issues in Science and Religion*. New York: Harper & Row, 1966.

―――. *Religion in an Age of Science*. San Francisco: Harper & Row, 1990.

―――. *Religion and Science: Historical and Contemporary Issues*. San Francisco: Harper, 1997.

Barr, James. *Biblical Words for Time*. 2nd ed. London: SCM, 1969.

―――. *Semantics of Biblical Language*. Oxford: Oxford University Press, 1961.

Barrow, John, and Frank Tipler. *The Anthropic Cosmological Principle*. Oxford: Oxford University Press, 1986.

Barth, Karl. *Anselm: Fides Quaerens Intellectum (Faith in Search of Understanding)*. Translated by I. W. Robertson. Cleveland and New York: World, 1962.

―――. *Church Dogmatics*. Vol. I.1: *The Doctrine of the Word of God*, 2nd ed. Translated by G. W. Bromiley. Edinburgh: T. & T. Clark, 1975.

―――. *Church Dogmatics*. Vol. I.2: *The Doctrine of the Word of God*. Translated G. T. Thomson and Harold Knight. Edinburgh: T. & T. Clark, 1956.

―――. *Church Dogmatics*. Vol. II.1: *The Doctrine of God*. Translated by T. H. L. Parker et al. Edinburgh: T. & T. Clark, 1957.

―――. *Church Dogmatics*. Vol. III.1: *The Doctrine of Creation*. Translated by J. W. Edwards et al. Edinburgh: T. & T. Clark, 1958.

―――. *Church Dogmatics*. Vol. III.2: *The Doctrine of Creation*. Translated by H. Knight et al. Edinburgh: T. & T. Clark, 1960.

―――. *Church Dogmatics*. Vol. III.3: *The Doctrine of Creation*. Translated by G. W. Bromiley and R. J. Ehrich. Edinburgh: T. & T. Clark, 1960.

―――. *Church Dogmatics*. Vol. III.4: *The Doctrine of Creation*. Translated by A. T. Mackay et al. Edinburgh: T. & T. Clark, 1961.

―――. *Church Dogmatics*. Vol. IV.3.2: *The Doctrine of Reconciliation*. Translated by G. W. Bromiley. Edinburgh: T. & T. Clark, 1962.

―――. *The Epistle to the Romans*. Translated by E. C. Hoskyns. Oxford: Oxford University Press, 1968.

Basinger, David. *The Case for Freewill Theism: A Philosophical Assessment*. Downers Grove, IL: InterVarsity, 1996.

Benjamin, A. Cornelius. "Ideas of Time in the History of Philosophy." In *The Voices of Time*, 2nd ed., edited by J. T. Fraser, 3–30. Amherst: University of Massachusetts Press, 1981.

Bennett, Jonathan. "Counterfactuals and Temporal Direction." *The Philosophical Review* 93 (1984) 57–91.

Berkhof, Louis. *Systematic Theology*. Grand Rapids: Eerdmans, 1988.

Boethius. *The Consolation of Philosophy*. In *Boethius*. Translated by S. J. Tester. Loeb Classical Library 74. Cambridge: Harvard University Press, 1973.

Boslough, John. "The Enigma of Time." *National Geographic* 177 (1990) 109–32.

Boman, Thorleif. *Hebrew Thought Compared with Greek*. Philadelphia: Westminster, 1960.

Brabant, Frank H. *Time and Eternity in Christian Thought*. London: Longmans, 1937.

Bracken, Joseph A. "Panentheism from Trinitarian Perspective." *Horizons* 22 (1995) 7–28.

―――. *Society and Spirit: A Trinitarian Cosmology*. London and Toronto: Associated University Presses, 1991.

Bradshaw, Timothy. *Trinity and Ontology: A Comparative Study of the Theologies of Karl Barth and Wolfhart Pannenberg*. Edinburgh: Rutherford, 1988.

Braine, David J. *The Human Person: Animal and Spirit*. London: Duckworth, 1993.

———. *The Reality of Time and The Existence of God: The Project of Proving God's Existence*. Oxford: Clarendon, 1988.

Broad, C. D. *An Examination of McTaggart's Philosophy*. 2 vols. Cambridge: Cambridge University Press, 1938.

———. *The Nature of Existence*. Vol. 2. Cambridge: Cambridge University Press, 1927. Reprinted, 1968.

———, editor. *Scientific Thought*. London: Routledge & Kegan Paul, 1923. Reprint, Paterson, NJ: Littlefield, 1959.

Brogaard, B. "Presentist Four-Dimensionalism." *Monist* 83 (2000) 341–56.

Broussard, Joseph D. "Eternity in Greek and Scholastic Philosophy." PhD diss., Catholic University of America, 1963.

Buckwalter, H. Douglas. "Time." In *Baker Theological Dictionary of the Bible*, edited by W. A. Elwell, 774–75. Grand Rapids: Baker, 1996.

Bunge, M. "Physical Time: The Objective and Relational Theory." *Philosophy of Science* 35 (1968) 355–88.

Burns, Robert M. "The Divine Simplicity in St. Thomas." *Religious Studies* 25 (1989) 271–93.

Burrell, David. *Analogy and Philosophical Language*. New Haven: Yale University Press, 1973.

———. "God's Eternity." *Faith and Philosophy* 1 (1984) 389–406.

Busch, Eberhard. *The Great Passion: An Introduction to Karl Barth's Theology*. Translated by Geoffrey W. Bromiley. Grand Rapids: Eerdmans, 2004.

———. *Karl Barth: His Life from Letters and Autobiographical Texts*. Translated by John Bowden. Grand Rapids: Eerdmans, 1994.

Byrne, Richard. "Hans Urs von Balthasar and the Mystery of the Forty Days after Easter." *Communio* 14 (1987) 34–48.

Callahan, John F. *Four Views of Time in Ancient Philosophy*. New York: Greenwood, 1968.

Campbell, Cynthia McCall. *Imago Trinitatis: An Appraisal of Karl Barth's Doctrine of the Imago Dei in the Light of His Doctrine of the Trinity*. Ann Arbor: UMI, 1981.

Capek, Milic, editor. *The Concepts of Space and Time: Their Structure and Their Development*. Dordrecht: Reisel, 1976.

———. "The Inclusion of Becoming in the Physical World." In *The Concepts of Space and Time*, edited by M. Capek, 501–24; Dordrecht: Reisel, 1976.

———. *The Philosophical Impact of Contemporary Physics*. New York: Nostrand, 1961.

———. "Relativity and the Status of Becoming." *Foundations of Physics* 5 (1975) 607–17.

———. "Time." In *Dictionary of the History of Ideas*, vol. 4, edited by P. P. Wiener, 389–98. New York: Scribner's, 1973.

Capol, Cornelia. *Hans Urs von Balthasar: Bibliographie 1925–1990*. Freiberg: Johannes Verlag Einsiedeln, 1990.

Carter, W. R., and H. S. Hestevold, "On Passage and Persistence." *American Philosophical Quarterly* 31 (1994) 269–83.

Cassirer, Ernst. *An Essay on Man: An Introduction to a Philosophy of Human Culture*. New Haven: Yale University Press, 1944.

Chadwick, Henry. *The Cambridge History of Later Greek and Early Medieval Philosophy*. Edited by A. H. Amstrong. Cambridge: Cambridge University Press, 1967.

Chavannes, Henry. *The Analogy between God and the World in Saint Thomas Aquinas and Karl Barth*. Translated by W. Lumley. New York: Vantage, 1992.

Chia, Roland. *Revelation and Theology: The Knowledge of God in Balthasar and Barth*. New York: Peter Lang, 1999.

Chisholm, R. M. "Identity Through Time." In *Language, Belief, and Metaphysics*, edited by H. E. Kiefer and M. K. Munitz, 163–82. Albany: SUNY, 1970.

Clarke, Bowman L., and Eugene T. Long, editors. *God and Temporality*. New York: Paragon, 1984.

Clayton, Philip. "The Case for Christian Panentheism." *Dialog* 37 (1998) 201–8.

———. *God and Contemporary Science*. Grand Rapids: Eerdmans, 1997.

———. "The God of History and the Presence of the Future." *Journal of Religion* 65 (1985) 98–108.

Clayton, Philip, and Arthur Peacocke, editors. *In Whom We Live and Move and Have Our Being: Panentheistic Reflections on God's Presence in a Scientific World*. Grand Rapids: Eerdmans, 2004.

Cobb, John B. Jr. *God and World*. Philadelphia: Westminster, 1969.

Cobb, John B. Jr., and David R. Griffin. *Process Theology: An Introduction Exposition*. Philadelphia: Westminster, 1976.

Cobb, John B. Jr., and Clark H. Pinnock, editors. *Searching for an Adequate God: A Dialogue between Process and Free Will Theists*. Grand Rapids: Eerdmans, 2000.

Coburn, Robert C. "Professor Malcolm on God." *Australian Journal of Philosophy* 41 (1963) 143–62.

Collins, James. "Przywara's '*Analogia Entis*.'" *Thought* 65 (1990) 265–77.

Congar, Yves. *I Believe in the Holy Spirit*. Vol. 1: *The Experience of the Spirit*. Translated by David Smith. New York: Seabury, 1983.

Cooper, John W. *Panentheism: The Other God of the Philosophers—From Plato to the Present*. Grand Rapids: Baker, 2006.

Copan, Paul. "Is *Creatio Ex Nihilo* a Post-Biblical Invention? An Examination of Gerhard May's Proposal." *Trinity Journal*, n.s., 17 (1996) 77–93.

Copan, Paul, and William L. Craig. *Creation Out of Nothing: A Biblical, Philosophical, and Scientific Exploration*. Grand Rapids: Baker, 2004.

Copleston, Frederick. *A History of Philosophy*. Vol. 1: *Greece and Rome*. New York: Doubleday, 1993.

Cornford, F. M. "The Elimination of Time by Parmenides." In *The Concepts of Space and Time: Their Structure and Their Development*, edited by M. Capek, 137–42. Dordrecht, Holland: Reidel, 1976.

Coveney, Peter, and Roger Highfield. *The Arrow of Time: A Voyage through Science to Solve Time's Greatest Mystery*. New York: Fawcett Columbine, 1990.

Craig, William L. *The Existence of God and the Beginning of the Universe*. San Bernardino: Here's Life, 1979.

———. "God and Real Time." *Religious Studies* 26 (1990) 335–47.

———. "God, Time, and Eternity." *Religious Studies* 14 (1978) 497–503.

———. *God, Time, and Eternity—The Coherence of Theism II: Eternity*. Dordrecht: Kluwer, 2001.

———. "The New B-Theory's *Tu Quoque* Argument." *Synthese* 107 (1996) 249–69.

---. *The Problem of Divine Foreknowledge and Future Contingents from Aristotle to Suarez.* Leiden: E. J. Brill, 1988.

---. "Tense and the New B-Theory of Language." *Philosophy* 71 (1996) 5-26.

---. *The Tensed Theory of Time: A Critical Examination.* Dordrecht: Kluwer, 2000.

---. "The Tensed vs. Tenseless Theory of Time: A Watershed for the Conception of Divine Eternity." In *Questions of Time and Tense,* edited by R. Le Poidevin, 221-50. Oxford: Clarendon, 1998.

---. *The Tenseless Theory of Time: A Critical Examination.* Dordrecht: Kluwer, 2000.

---. *Time and Eternity: Exploring God's Relationship to Time.* Wheaton, IL: Crossway, 2001.

---. "Timelessness and Creation." *Australasian Journal of Philosophy* 74 (1996) 646-56.

---. "Timelessness and Omnitemporality." In *God and Time: Four Views,* edited by G. E. Ganssle, 129-60. Downers Grove, IL: InterVarsity, 2001.

---. "Was Thomas Aquinas a B-Theorist of Time?" *New Scholasticism* 59 (1985) 475-83.

Craig, William L., and Quentin Smith. *Theism, Atheism, and Big Bang Cosmology.* Oxford: Clarendon, 1993.

Cullmann, Oscar. *Christ and Time: The Primitive Christian Conception of Time and History.* Translated by F. V. Filson. Philadelphia: Westminster, 1950.

Cunningham, E. *The Principle of Relativity.* Cambridge: Cambridge University Press, 1914.

Currid, John D. "An Examination of the Egyptian Background of the Genesis Cosmogony." *Biblische Zeitschrift* 35 (1991) 18-40.

Cushman, Robert E. "Greek and Christian Views of Time." *Journal of Religion* 33 (1953) 254-65.

Dales, Richard C. "Time and Eternity in the Thirteenth Century." *Journal of the History of Ideas* 49 (1988) 27-45.

Dalzell, Thomas G. *The Dramatic Encounter of Divine and Human Freedom in the Theology of Hans Urs von Balthasar.* Bern: Peter Lang, 1997.

Davies, Brian. *The Thought of Thomas Aquinas.* Oxford: Clarendon, 1992.

---. "A Timeless God?" *New Blackfriars* 64 (1983) 215-24.

Davies, Paul C. W. *About Time: Einstein's Unfinished Revolution.* New York: Simon & Schuster, 1995.

---. *God and the New Physics.* New York: Simon & Schuster, 1983.

---. *Other Worlds.* New York: Simon & Schuster, 1982.

---. *Space and Time in the Modern Universe.* Cambridge: Cambridge University Press, 1977.

Davis, Stephen T., Daniel Kendall, and Gerald O'Collins, editors. *The Trinity: An Interdisciplinary Symposium on the Trinity.* Oxford: Oxford University Press, 1999.

Delling, G. "*chronos.*" In *Theological Dictionary of the New Testament,* vol.9, edited by G. Kittel and translated by G. W. Bromiley, 581-93. Grand Rapids: Eerdmans, 1964.

---------. "kairos." In *Theological Dictionary of the New Testament*, vol.3, edited by G. Kittel and translated by G. W. Bromiley, 455-64. Grand Rapids: Eerdmans, 1964.

Deltete, R. J. "Hawking on God and Creation." *Zygon* 28 (1993) 485-506.

Denbigh, Kenneth G. *Three Concepts of Time*. Berlin: Springer-Verlag, 1981.

Dennett, Daniel. "Conditions of Personhood." In *Identities of Persons*, edited by Amelie Oksenberg Rotty, 175-96. Berkeley: University of California Press, 1976.

De Schrijver, Georges. "Die Analogia Entis in der Theologie Hans Urs Balthasars." *Bijdragen* 38 (1977) 249-81.

---------. *Le Merveilleux accord de l'Homme et de Dieu: Etude de l'Analogie de l'Etre chez Hans Urs Von Balthasar*. Belgium: Leuven University Press, 1983.

DeVries, Simon J. "Meaning of Time." In *Holman Bible Dictionary*, edited by T. C. Butler, 1347-49. Nashville: Holman Bible, 1991.

---------. *Yesterday, Today, and Tomorrow: Time and History in the Old Testament*. Grand Rapids: Eerdmans, 1975.

DeWeese, Garrett J. "God and the Nature of Time." PhD diss., University of Colorado, 1994.

Dieks, D. "Special Relativity and the Flow of Time." *Philosophy of Science* 55 (1988) 456-60.

Donnelly, John. "Creation *Ex Nihilo*." In *Logical Analysis and Contemporary Theism*, edited by J. Donnelly, 200-17. New York: Fordham University Press, 1972.

Drees, Willem B. *Beyond the Big-Bang: Quantum Cosmologies and God*. La Salle, IL: Open Court, 1990.

---------. "Quantum Cosmologies and the 'Beginning.'" *Zygon* 26 (1991) 373-96.

Earman, John. "Causation: A Matter of Life and Death." *Journal of Philosophy* 73 (1976) 5-25.

Earman, John, C. Glymour, and J. Stachel, editors. *Foundations of Space-Time Theories*. Minneapolis: University of Minnesota Press, 1977.

Ebeling, Gerhard. "Time and Word." In *The Future of Our Religious Past: Essays in Honour of Rudolf Bultmann*, edited by J. M. Robinson, 247-66. New York: Harper & Row, 1971.

Eddinton, Arthur S. *The Nature of the Physical World*. Cambridge: Cambridge University Press, 1928.

Eichrodt, Walther. *Theology of the Old Testament*. 2 Vols. Translated by J. A. Baker. Philadelphia: Westminster, 1961 and 1967.

Einstein, Albert. "Elektrodynamik bewegter Körper." *Annalen der Physik* 17 (1905) 891-921.

---------. *The Meaning of Relativity*, 5th ed. London: Methuen, 1922. Reprint, Princeton: Princeton University Press, 1974.

---------. "On the Electrodynamics of Moving Bodies." In *The Collected Papers of Albert Einstein*. Vol. 2: *The Swiss Years: Writings, 1900-1909*. Translated by A. Beck, 140-71. Princeton: Princeton University Press, 1989.

Eliade, Mircea. *Cosmos and History: The Myth of Eternal Return*. Translated by W. R. Trask. New York: Harper Torchbooks, 1954.

Ellingworth, P. *The Epistle to the Hebrews*. Grand Rapids: Eerdmans, 1993.

Endean, Philip. "Von Balthasar, Rahner, and the Commissar." *New Blackfriars* 79 (1998) 33-38.

Everitt, Nicholas. "Interpretations of God's Eternity." *Religious Studies* 34 (1998) 25–32.

Fagg, Lawrence W. *The Becoming of Time: Integrating Physical and Religious Time.* Atlanta: Scholars, 1995.

Fann, K. T., editor. *Symposium on J. L. Austin.* London: Routlesge & Kegan Paul, 1969.

Farmer, D. J. *Being in Time: The Nature of Time in the Light of McTaggart's Paradox.* Lanham: University of America Press, 1990.

Faye, Jan, Uwe Scheffler, and Max Urchs, editors. *Perspectives on Time.* Dordrecht: Kluwer, 1997.

Feinberg, John S. "New Dimensions in the Doctrine of God." In *New Dimensions in Evangelical Thought,* ed. David S. Dockery, 235–69. Downers Grove, IL: InterVarsity, 1998.

———. *No One Like Him: The Doctrine of God.* Wheaton, IL: Crossway, 2001.

———. "Process Theology." *Evangelical Review of Theology* 14 (1990) 291–334.

Ferguson, Sinclair B. *The Holy Spirit.* Downers Grove, IL: InterVarsity, 1996.

Fergusson, David, and Marcel Sarot, editors. *The Future as God's Gift: Explorations in Christian Eschatology.* Edinburgh: T. & T. Clark, 2000.

Ferré, Frederick. "Grünbaum on Temporal Becoming: A Critique." *International Philosophical Quarterly* 12 (1972) 426–45.

Findlay, J. N. "Time and Eternity." *Review of Metaphysics* 32 (1978) 3–14.

Fitzgeald, Paul. "Stump and Kretzmann on Time and Eternity." *Journal of Philosophy* 82 (1985) 260–69.

Flood, R., and M. Lockwood, editors. *The Nature of Time.* Oxford: Basil Blackwell, 1986.

Foley, G. "The Catholic Critics of Karl Barth." *Scottish Journal of Theology* 14 (1961) 136–55.

Ford, D. F. "Barth's Interpretation of the Bible." In *Karl Barth: Studies of His Theological Method,* edited by S. W. Sykes, 55–87. Oxford: Clarendon, 1979.

Ford, Lewis S. "Boethius and Whitehead on Time and Eternity." *International Philosophy Quarterly* 8 (1968) 38–67.

Frame, John M. *The Doctrine of God.* Phillipsburg, NJ: P & R, 2002.

———. *No Other God: A Response to Open Theism.* Phillipsburg, NJ: P & R, 2001.

Fraser, Julius T., editor. *Of Time, Passion, and Knowledge: Reflections on the Strategy of Existence,* 2nd ed. Princeton: Princeton University Press, 1990.

———. *Time: The Familiar Stranger.* Amherst: University of Massachusetts Press, 1987.

———. *The Voices of Time: A Cooperative Survey of Man's Views of Time as Expressed by the Sciences and by the Humanities,* 2nd ed. Amherst: The University of Massachusetts Press, 1981.

Fraser, Julius T., and M. P. Soulsby, editors. *Dimensions of Time and Life: The Study of Time VIII.* Madison, CT: International Universities Press, 1996.

French, Anthony P. *Special Relativity.* New York: Norton, 1968.

Fretheim, Terence. "Yahweh." In *New International Dictionary of Old Testament Theology and Exegesis,* vol. 4, edited by Willem A. VanGemeren, 1295–1300. Grand Rapids: Zondervan, 1997.

Friedman, Michael. *Foundations of Space-Time Theories: Relativistic Physics and Philosophy of Science.* Princeton: Princeton University Press, 1983.

Gale, Richard M. *The Language of Time*. London: Routledge and Kegan Paul, 1968.
———, editor. *The Philosophy of Time: A Collection of Essays*. Garden City, NY: Doubleday, 1967.
Ganssle, Gregory E., editor. *God and Time: Four Views*. Downers Grove, IL: InterVarsity, 2001.
Ganssle Gregory E., and David M. Woodruff, editors. *God and Time: Essays on the Divine Nature*. Oxford: Oxford University Press, 2002.
Gardner, Lucy, David Moss, Ben Quash, and Graham Ward, editors. *Balthasar at the End of Modernity*. Edinburgh: T. & T. Clark, 1999.
Gardet, L., et al. *Cultures and Time*. Paris: Unesco, 1976.
Gawronski, Raymond. *Word and Silence: Hans Urs von Balthasar and the Spiritual Encounter between East and West*. Grand Rapids: Eerdmans, 1995.
Geach, Peter T. *God and the Soul*. New York: Schocken, 1969.
Geisler, Norman L. *Creating God in the Image of Man? The New "Open" View of God – Neotheism's Dangerous Drift*. Minneapolis: Bethany, 1997.
Gilkey, Langdon. *Maker of Heaven and Earth*. Garden City, NY: Doubleday, 1959.
Gödel, Kurt. "A Remark about the Relationship between Relativity Theory and Idealistic Philosophy." In *Albert Einstein: Philosopher-Scientist*, edited by P. A. Schilpp, 557–62. Evanston, IL: Library of Living Philosophers, 1949.
Goldman, Alan H. "Reverse Discrimination and the Future: A Reply to Irving Thalberg." *Philosophical Forum* 6 (1974–75) 321–26.
Goldstein, Jonathan A. "The Origins of the Doctrine of Creation *Ex Nihilo*." *Journal of Jewish Studies* 35 (1984) 127–35.
Goodman, Nelson. *The Structure of Appearance*, 2nd ed. Indianapolis: Bobbs-Merrill, 1966.
Gowen, Jule. "God and Timelessness: Everlasting or Eternal?" *Sophia* 26 (1987) 15–29.
Grenz, Stanley J. *Rediscovering the Triune God: The Trinity in Contemporary Theology*. Minneapolis: Fortress, 2004.
———. *The Social God and the Relational Self: A Trinitarian Theology of the Imago Dei*. Louisville: Westminster, 2001.
Gribbin, John. *The Birth of Time: How Astronomers Measured the Age of the Universe*. New Haven: Yale University Press, 1999.
Griffin, David R. *God, Power, and Evil: A Process Theodicy*. Philadelphia: Westminster, 1976.
———. "Green Spirituality: A Postmodern Convergence of Science and Religion." *Journal of Theology* 91 (1992) 5–20.
Grudem, Wayne. *Systematic Theology: An Introduction to Biblical Doctrine*. Grand Rapids: Zondervan, 1994.
Grünbaum, Adolf. "The Exclusion of Becoming from the Physical World." In *The Concepts of Space and Time*, edited by M. Capek, 471–500. Dordrecht: Reidel, 1976.
———. "The Meaning of Time." In *Basic Issues in the Philosophy of Time*, edited by E. Freeman and W. Sellars, 195–228. La Salle, IL: Open Court, 1971.
———. *Philosophical Problems of Space and Time*, 2nd ed. Dordrecht-Holland: Reidel, 1973.
———. "The Status of Temporal Becoming." In *The Philosophy of Time*, edited by R. Gale, 322–53. Garden City, NY: Doubleday, 1967.

Grünbaum, Adolf, and Allen I. Janis. "Is There Backward Causation in Classical Electrodynamics?" *Journal of Philosophy* 74 (1997) 475–82.

Guhrt, J., and H.-C. Hahn. "Time." In *New International Dictionary of New Testament Theology*, vol. 3, edited by Colin Brown, 826–50. Grand Rapids: Zondervan, 1986.

Gunton, Colin E. "Time, Eternity and the Doctrine of the Incarnation." *Dialog* 21 (1982) 263–68.

———. *The Triune Creator: A Historical and Systematic Study*. Grand Rapids: Eerdmans, 1998.

Guthrie, W. K. C. *A History of Greek Philosophy*. Vol. 1: *The Earlier Presocratics and the Pythagoreans*. Cambridge: Cambridge University Press, 1962.

———. *A History of Greek Philosophy*. Vol. 2: *The Presocratic Tradition from Parmenides to Democritus*. Cambridge: Cambridge University Press, 1965.

Gutiérrez, Gustavo. *The God of Life*. Translated by Matthew J. O'Connell. Maryknoll, NY: Orbis, 1991.

Guy, Fritz. "Man and His Time: Three Contemporary Theological Interpretations." PhD diss., University of Chicago, 1971.

Habermas, Jürgen. *The Theory of Communicative Action*. 2 Vols. Translated by Thomas McCarthy. Boston: Beacon, 1984.

Hall, Edward T. *The Dance of Life: The Other Dimension of Time*. New York: Anchor, 1984.

Hammer, K. "Analogia Relationis gegen Analogia Entis." In *Parrhesia*, 288–304. Zürich: Evy-Verlag, 1966.

Harris, Errol E. *The Reality of Time*. Albany: State University of New York Press, 1988.

———. "Time and Eternity." *Review of Metaphysics* 29 (1975) 464–82.

Hartshorne, Charles. *The Divine Relativity: A Social Conception of God*. New Haven: Yale University Press, 1976.

———. "Introduction: The Standpoint of Panentheism." In *Philosophers Speak of God*, edited by C. Hartshorne and W. L. Reese, 1–25. Chicago: University of Chicago Press, 1953.

———. *Omnipotence and Other Theological Mistakes*. New York: State University of New York Press, 1984.

Hartwell, Herbert. *The Theology of Karl Barth*. Philadelphia: Westminster, 1964.

Hasker, William. "Concerning the Intelligibillity of 'God is Timeless.'" *New Scholasticism* 7 (1983) 170–95.

———. *God, Time, and Knowledge*. Ithaca: Cornell University Press, 1989.

Hawking, Stephen W. *A Brief History of Time: From the Big Bang to Black Holes*. London: Bantam, 1988.

Heidegger, Martin. *Being and Time*. Translated by John Macquarrie and Edward Robinson. San Francisco: Harper San Francisco, 1962.

———. *On the Way to Language*. New York: Harper & Row, 1971.

Heinz, Hanspeter. *Der Gott des Je-mehr: Der christologische Ansatz Hans Urs von Balthasar*. Fankfurt: Peter Lang, 1975.

Helm, Paul. "Divine Timeless Eternity." In *God and Time: Four Views*, edited by G. E. Ganssle, 28–60. Downers Grove, IL: InterVarsity, 2001.

———. *Eternal God: A Study of God without Time*. Oxford: Clarendon, 1988.

———. "God and Spacelessness." *Philosophy* 55 (1980) 211–21.

Henrici, Peter. "Hans Urs von Balthasar: A Sketch of His Life." In *Hans Urs von Balthasar: His Life and Work*, edited by David L. Schindler, 7–43. San Francisco: Ignatius, 1991.

———. "The Philosophy of Hans Urs von Balthasar." In *Hans Urs von Balthasar: His Life and Work*, edited by D. L. Schindler, 149–68. San Francisco: Ignatius, 1991.

Henry, C. F. H. "Eternity." In *Evangelical Dictionary of Theology*, edited by W. A. Elwell, 370–72. Grand Rapids: Baker, 1984.

———. "Time." In *Evangelical Dictionary of Theology*, edited by W. A. Elwell, 1094–96. Grand Rapids: Baker, 1984.

Hill, W. J. "Does the World Make a Difference to God?" *Thomist* 38 (1974) 146–64.

Hirsch, Eli. *The Concept of Identity*. New York: Oxford University Press, 1982.

Hoekema, Anthony A. *Created in God's Image*. Grand Rapids: Eerdmans, 1986.

Holt, Dennis C. "Timelessness and the Metaphysics of Temporal Existence." *American Philosophical Quarterly* 18 (1981) 149–56.

Hopkins, Jasper. *A Companion to the Study of St. Anselm*. Minneapolis: University of Minnesota Press, 1972.

Horton, Michael S. *Covenant and Eschatology: The Divine Drama*. Louisville: Westminster, 2002.

Horvath, Tibor. "Jesus Christ, the Eschatological Union of Time and Eternity." *Science et Esprit* 40 (1988) 179–92.

———. "A New Notion of Time." *Science et Esprit* 40 (1988) 35–55.

Hoy, R. C. "Becoming and Persons." *Philosophical Studies* 34 (1978) 269–80.

Hughes, Christopher. *On a Complex Theory of a Simple God*. Ithaca: Cornell University Press, 1989.

Huizinga, Johan. *Homo Ludens: A Study of the Play Element in Culture*. Boston: Beacon, 1955.

Hunsinger, George. *Disruptive Grace: Studies in the Theology of Karl Barth*. Grand Rapids: Eerdmans, 2000.

———. "*Mysterium Trinitatis*: Barth's Conception of Eternity." In *For the Sake of the World: Karl Barth and the Future of Ecclesial Theology*, edited by G. Hunsinger, 165–90. Grand Rapids: Eerdmans, 2004.

Hunt, Anne. *The Trinity and the Paschal Mystery: A Development in Recent Catholic Theology*. Collegeville, MN: Liturgical, 1997.

———. *What Are They Saying about the Trinity?* New York: Paulist, 1998.

Jenni, E. "Time." In *The Interpreter's Dictionary of the Bible*. Vol. 4, edited by G. A. Buttrick, 642–49. Nashville: Abingdon, 1962.

———. "Das Wort 'olam im Alten Testament." *Zeitschrift für die alttestamentliche Wissenschaft* 64 (1952) 197–248 and 65 (1953) 1–35.

Jenson. Robert W. "Aspects of a Doctrine of Creation." In *The Doctrine of Creation: Essays in Dogmatics, History and Philosophy*, edited by Colin E. Gunton, 17–28. Edinburgh: T. & T. Clark, 1997.

———. *God after God*. Indianapolis: Bobbs-Merrill, 1969.

———. *Systematic Theology: The Triune God*. Vol. 1. New York: Oxford University Press, 1997.

———. *Systematic Theology: The Works of God*. Vol. 2. New York: Oxford University Press, 1999.

———. *The Triune Identity: God According to the Gospel*. Philadelphia: Fortress, 1982.

———. "What Is the Point of Trinitarian Theology." In *Trinitarian Theology Today*, edited by Christoph Schwöbel, 31–43. Edinburgh: T. & T. Clark, 1995.

Jess, W. G. von. "Divine Eternity in the Doctrine of St. Augustine." *Augustinian Studies* 6 (1975) 75–96.

Jewett, Paul K. *Who We Are: Our Dignity as Human: A Neo-Evangelical Theology*. Grand Rapids: Eerdmans, 1996.

Jüngel, Eberhard. *Death: The Riddle and the Mystery*. Translated by Iain and Ute Nicol. Philadelphia: Westminster, 1975.

Kaiser, Walter C. *Toward an Old Testament Theology*. Grand Rapids: Zondervan, 1978.

———. *Toward Rediscovering the Old Testament*. Grand Rapids: Zondervan, 1991.

Kant, Immanuel. *Critique of Pure Reason*. Translated by N. K. Smith. London: Macmillan, 1968.

Kärkkäinen, Veli-Matti. *The Doctrine of God: A Biblical, Historical, and Contemporary Survey*. Grand Rapids: Baker, 2004.

Kasper, Walter. *The God of Jesus Christ*. Translated by Matthew J. O'Connell. New York: Crossroad, 1984.

Keeling, S. V., editor. *Philosophical Studies*. Freeport, NY: Books for Libraries, 1966.

Kehl, Medard, and Werner Löser, editors. *The Von Balthasar Reader*. Translated by Robert J. Daly and Fred Lawrence. New York: Crossroad, 1997.

Kelsey, David H. *Proving Doctrine: The Uses of Scripture in Modern Theology*. Harrisburg, PA: Trinity, 1995.

Kenny, Anthony. *The God of the Philosophers*. Oxford: Clarendon, 1979.

Kerr, Fergus. "Adrienne von Speyr and Hans urs von Balthasar." *New Blackfriars* 79 (1998) 26–32.

Kiernan-Lewis, D. "Not Over Yet: Prior's 'Thank Goodness' Argument." *Philosophy* 66 (1991) 241–43.

King-Farlow, J. "The Positive McTaggart on Time," *Philosophy* 169–78.

Kirk, G. S. *Heraclitus: The Cosmic Fragments*. Cambridge: Cambridge University Press, 1954.

Klubertanz, George P. *St. Thomas Aquinas on Analogy: A Textual Analysis and Systematic Synthesis*. Chicago: Loyola University Press, 1960.

Kneale, M. "Eternity and Sempiternity." *Proceedings of Aristotelian Society* 61 (1969) 223–38.

Kneale, William. "Time and Eternity in Theology." *Proceedings of Aristotelian Society* 61 (1961) 87–108.

Knuuttila, Simo. "Time and Creation in Augustine." In *The Cambridge Companion to Augustine*, edited by Eleonore Stump and Norman Kretzmann, 103–15. Cambridge: Cambridge University Press, 2001.

Kronholm, T. "'e4t." In *Theological Dictionary of the Old Testament*. Vol. 11, edited by G. J. Botterweck et al., 434–51. Grand Rapids: Eerdmans, 1999.

Lacey, Hugh M. "The Causal Theory of Time: A Critique of Grünbaum's Version." *Philosophy of Science* 35 (1968) 332–54.

La Croix, R. R. "Aquinas on God's Omnipresence and Timelessness." *Philosophy and Phenomenological Research* 42 (1981–1982) 391–99.

Lafont, Ghislain. *God, Time, and Being*. Translated by Leonard Maluf. Petersham, MA: Saint Bede's, 1986.

Larson, Duane H. *Times of the Trinity: A Proposal for Theistic Cosmology.* New York: Peter Lang, 1995.
Lee, Jung Young. "Karl Barth's Use of Analogy in His *Church Dogmatics.*" *Scottish Journal of Theology* 22 (1969) 129-51.
Leftow, Brian. "Eternity and Simultaneity." *Faith and Philosophy* 8 (1991) 148-79.
―――. "Response to *Mysterium Trinitatis*: Barth's Conception of Eternity." In *For the Sake of the World: Karl Barth and the Future of Ecclesial Theology,* edited by G. Hunsinger, 191-201. Grand Rapids: Eerdmans, 2004.
―――. "The Roots of Eternity." *Religious Studies* 24 (1988) 189-212.
―――. *Time and Eternity.* Ithaca and London: Cornell University Press, 1991.
Le Poidevin, Robin. *Change, Cause and Contradiction: A Defence of the Tenseless Theory of Time.* New York: St. Martin's, 1991.
―――. "Continuants and Continuity." *Monist* 83 (2000) 381-98.
―――, editor. *Questions of Time and Tense.* Oxford: Clarendon, 1998.
Le Poidevin, Robin, and M. MacBeath, editors. *The Philosophy of Time.* Oxford: Oxford University Press, 1993.
Lepore, Ernest, and Robert Van Gulick, editors. *John Searle and His Critics.* Cambridge: Basil Blackwell, 1991.
Levinas, Emmanuel. *God, Death, and Time.* Translated by Bettina Bergo. Stanford: Stanford University Press, 1993.
―――. *Time and the Other.* Translated by Richard A. Cohen. Pittsburgh: Duquesne University Press, 1987.
Lewis, John D. "God and Time: The Concept of Eternity and the Reality of Tense." PhD diss., University of Wisconsin, 1985.
―――. "Persons, Morality, and Tenselessness." *Philosophy and Phenomenological Research* 47 (1986) 305-9.
Lewis, Peter. *The Message of the Living God.* Downers Grove, IL: InterVarsity, 2000.
Lieb, Irwin C. *Past, Present, and Future: A Philosophical Essay about Time.* Urbana, IL: University of Illinois Press, 1991.
Lindsey, F. D. "An Evangelical Overview of Process Theology." *Bibliotheca sacra* 134 (1977) 15-32.
Link, H.-G. "Life." In *The New International Dictionary of New Testament Theology.* Vol. 2, edited by Colin Brown, 474-84. Grand Rapids: Zondervan, 1986.
Lippincott, Kristen, et al. *The Story of Time.* London: Merrell Holberton, 1999.
Lloyd, G. E. R. "Views on Time in Greek Thought." In *Cultures and Time,* edited by L. Gardet et al., 117-48. Paris: Unesco, 1976.
Lochbrunner, Manfred. *Analogia Caritatis: Darstellung und Deutung der Theologie Hans Urs von Balthasar.* Freiburg: Herder, 1980.
Lodzinski, Don. "Empty Time and the Eternality of God." *Religious Studies* 31 (1995) 187-95.
―――. "Eternal Act." *Religious Studies* 34 (1998) 325-52.
Long, Brian. "Notes on the Biblical Use of *'ad ôlām*." *Westminster Theological Journal* 41 (1978) 54-67.
Löser, Werner. "Being Interpreted as Love: Reflections on the Theology of Hans Urs von Balthasar." *Communio* 16 (1989) 475-90.
Lowe, E. J. "The Indexical Fallacy in McTaggart's Proof of the 'Unreality of Time.'" *Mind* 96 (1987) 62-70.

———. *The Possibility of Metaphysics: Substance, Identity, and Time.* Oxford: Clarendon, 1988.

Lubac, Henri de. "A Witness of Christ in the Church: Hans Urs von Balthasar." In *Hans Urs von Balthasar: His Life and Work*, edited by David L. Schindler, 271–88. San Francisco: Ignatius, 1991.

Lucas, John R. *The Future: An Essay on God, Temporality and Truth.* Oxford: Basil Blackwell, 1989.

———. *A Treatise on Time and Space.* London: Methuen, 1973.

MacBeath, Murray. "God's Spacelessness and Timelessness." *Sophia* 22 (1983) 23–32.

Mackie, J. L. *The Cement of the Universe.* New York: Oxford University Press, 1974.

Mackinnon, Donald. "Some Reflections on Hans Urs von Balthasar's Christology with Special Reference to *Theodramatik* II/2 and III." In *The Analogy of Beauty*, edited by J. Riches, 164–74. Edinburgh: T. & T. Clark, 1986.

Macleod, Donald. *The Person of Christ.* Downers Grove, IL: InterVarsity, 1998.

Macmurray, John. *Persons in Relation.* New York: Harper, 1961.

———. *The Self as Agent.* London: Faber & Faber, 1957. Reprint, Amherst, NY: Humanity, 1991.

Malina, Bruce J. "Christ and Time: Swiss or Mediterranean?" *Catholic Biblical Quarterly* 51 (1989) 1–31.

Manek, Jindrick. "The Biblical Concept of Time and Our Gospels." *New Testament Studies* 6 (1960) 45–51.

Markosian, Ned. "How Fast Does Time Pass?" *Philosophy and Phenomenological Research* 53 (1993) 829–44.

Marsh, John. *The Fulness of Time.* New York: Harper, 1952.

———. "Time, Season." In *A Theological Word Book of the Bible*, edited by A. Richardson, 258–67. New York: Macmillan, 1950.

Martens, Elmer A. "Names of God." In *Baker Theological Dictionary of the Bible*, edited by Walter A. Elwell, 297–300. Grand Rapids: Baker, 1996.

Maxwell, Nicholas. "Are Probabilism and Special Relativity Incompatible?" *Philosophy of Science* 52 (1985) 23–43.

May, Gerhard. *Creatio Ex Nihilo: The Doctrine of 'Creation out of Nothing' in Early Christian Thought.* Edinburgh: T. & T. Clark, 1994.

McCall, Storrs. *A Model of the Universe: Space-Time, Probability, and Decision.* Oxford: Clarendon, 1994.

———. "Objective Time Flow." *Philosophy of Science* 43 (1976) 337–62.

McCormack, Bruce L. *Karl Barth's Critically Realistic Dialectical Theology: Its Genesis and Development 1909–1936.* Oxford: Clarendon, 1995.

McEvoy, James. "St. Augustine's Account of Time and Wittgenstein's Criticism." *Review of Metaphysics* 37 (1984) 547–77.

McFadyen, Alistair I. *The Call to Personhood: A Christian Theory of the Individual in Social Relationships.* Cambridge: Cambridge University Press, 1990.

McFague, Sallie. *The Body of God: An Ecological Theology.* Minneapolis: Fortress, 1993.

———. *Models of God: Theology for an Ecological, Nuclear Age.* Philadelphia: Fortress, 1987.

McGregor, Bede, and Thomas Norris, editors. *The Beauty of Christ: A Introduction to the Theology of Hans Urs von Balthasar.* Edinburgh: T. & T. Clark, 1994.

McInerney, Peter K. *Time and Experience*. Philadelphia: Temple University Press, 1991.
McInerny, Ralph M. *The Logic of Analogy: An Interpretation of St. Thomas*. The Hague, Netherlands: Martinus Nijhoff, 1961.
McMullin, E. "Natural Science and Belief in a Creator." In *Physics, Philosophy, and Theology*, edited by Robert J. Russell et al., 49-79. Vatican City State: Vatican Observatory, 1988.
McTaggart, J. M. E. "The Unreality of Time." *Mind* 17 (1908) 457-74.
Mechels, E. *Analogie bei Erich Przywara und Karl Barth*. Kurt Wolff: Neukirchener, 1974.
Mellor, David H. "History without the Flow of Time." *Neue Zeitschrift für Systematische Theologie und Religionsphilosophie* 28 (1986) 68-76.
———. *Real Time*. Cambridge: Cambridge University Press, 1981.
———. *Real Time II*. London: Routledge, 1998.
———. "Special Relativity and Present Truth." *Analysis* 34 (1973-1974) 74-77.
———. "Tense's Tenseless Truth Conditions." *Analysis* 46 (1986) 167-72.
Merricks, T. "On the Incompatibility of Enduring and Perduring Entities." *Mind* 104 (1995) 523-31.
Miller, L., and Stanley J. Grenz, editors. *Fortress Introduction to Contemporary Theologies*. Minneapolis: Fortress, 1998.
Minkowski, Hermann. "Space and Time." In *The Principle of Relativity: A Collection of Original Memoirs on the Special and General Theory of Relativity*, edited by H. A. Lorentz and translated by W. Perrett and G. B. Jeffery, 75-91. New York: Dover, 1952.
Molnar, Paul D. "The Function of the Trinity in Moltmann's Ecological Doctrine of Creation." *Theological Studies* 51 (1990) 673-97.
Moltmann, Jürgen. *The Coming of God: Christian Eschatology*. Translated by Margaret Kohl. Minneapolis: Fortress, 1996.
———. *The Crucified God*. Translated by R. A. Wilson and John Bowden. New York: Harper & Row, 1974.
———. *The Future of Creation: Collected Essays*. Translated by Margaret Kohl. Philadelphia: Fortress, 1979.
———. *God in Creation: A New Theology of Creation and The Spirit of God*. Translated by Margaret Kohl. Minneapolis: Fortress, 1993.
———. *History and the Triune God: Contributions to Trinitarian Theology*. New York: Crossroad, 1992.
———. *The Spirit of Life: A Universal Affirmation*. Translated by Margaret Kohl. Minneapolis: Fortress, 1992.
———. *The Trinity and the Kingdom: The Doctrine of God*. Translated by Margaret Kohl. San Francisco: Harper & Row, 1981.
———. "The Trinitarian History of God." *Theology* 78 (1975) 632-46.
———. "The Unity of the Triune God." *St. Vladimir's Theological Quarterly* 28 (1984) 157-71.
Mondin, Battista. *The Principle of Analogy in Protestant and Catholic Theology*. The Hague: Martinus Nijhoff, 1968.
Montague, George T. *Holy Spirit: Growth of a Biblical Tradition*. Peabody, MA: Hendrickson, 1994.
Moore, D. S. "Analogy and Karl Barth." *Downside Review* 71 (1953) 175-80.

Morris, Richard. *Time's Arrows: Scientific Attitudes Toward Time.* New York: Simon & Schuster, 1984.
Morris, Thomas V., editor. *The Concept of God.* Oxford: Oxford University Press, 1987.
———, editor. *Divine and Human Action: Essays in the Metaphysics of Theism.* Ithaca: Cornell University Press, 1988.
Morse, C. "Raising God's Eyebrows: Some Further Thoughts on the Concept of the Analogia Fidei." *Union Seminary Quarterly* 37 (1981–1982) 39–49.
Mounce, Robert H. *The Book of Revelation*, rev. ed. Grand Rapids: Eerdmans, 1998.
Mouroux, Jean. "Eternity and the Triune God." *Communio* 18 (1991) 127–33.
Muilenburg, James. "The Biblical View of Time." *Harvard Theological Review* 54 (1961) 225–52.
Muller, Richard A. *Dictionary of Latin and Greek Theological Terms: Drawn Principally from Protestant Scholastic Theology.* Grand Rapids: Baker, 1985.
Müller-Fahrenholz, Geiko. *The Kingdom and the Power: The Theology of Jürgen Moltmann.* Minneapolis: Fortress, 2001.
Mundle, C. W. K. "Broad's View about Time." In *The Philosophy of C. D. Broad*, edited by P. A. Schilpp, 353–74. New York: Tudor, 1959.
Nash, Ronald H. *The Concept of God: An Exploration of Contemporary Difficulties with the Attributes of God.* Grand Rapids: Zondervan, 1983.
———, editor. *Process Theology.* Grand Rapids: Baker, 1987.
Neher, André. "The View of Time and History in Jewish Culture." In *Cultures and Time.* L. Gardet et al., 149–67. Paris: Unesco, 1976.
Nerlich, Graham. *What Spacetime Explains: Metaphysical Essays on Space and Time.* Cambridge: Cambridge University Press, 1994.
Neville, Robert Cummings. *Eternity and Time's Flow.* Albany: SUNY, 1993.
Newton, Isaac. *The Principia: Mathematical Principles of Natural Philosophy.* Translated by I. B. Cohen and A. Whitman. Berkeley: University of California Press, 1999.
———. *Unpublished Scientific Papers of Isaac Newton.* Edited by A. R. Hall and M. B. Hall. Cambridge: Cambridge University Press, 1962.
Newton-Smith, W. H. *The Structure of Time.* London: Routledge & Kegan Paul, 1980.
Nichols, Aidan. "An Introduction to Balthasar." *New Blackfriars* 79 (1998) 2–10.
Nielsen, N. C. "Analogy as a Principle of Theological Method Historically Considered." In *The Heritage of Christian Thought*, edited by R. E. Cushman and E. Grislis, 197–219. New York: Harper & Row, 1965.
———. "The Debate between Karl Barth and Erich Przywara: A New Evaluation of Protestant and Roman Catholic Differences." *The Rice Institute Pamphlet* 40 (1953) 24–46.
Oakes, Edward T. *Pattern of Redemption: The Theology of Hans Urs von Blathasar.* New York: Continuum, 1994.
Oakes, Edward T., and David Moss, editors. *The Cambridge Companion to Hans Urs von Balthasar.* Cambridge: Cambridge University Press, 2004.
Oaklander, L. Nathan. "A Defense of the New Tenseless Theory of Time." *Philosophical Quarterly* 41 (1991) 26–38.
———, editor. *The Importance of Time.* Dordrecht: Kluwer, 2001.
———. "McTaggart's Paradox and Smith's Tensed Theory of Time." *Synthese* 107 (1996) 205–21.

———. "Thank Goodness It's Over." *Philosophy* 67 (1992) 256–58.

———. "Temporal Passage and Temporal Parts." *Noûs* 26 (1992) 79–84.

———. *Temporal Relations and Temporal Becoming: A Defense of a Russellian Theory of Time*. Lanham: University Press of America, 1984.

Oaklander, L. Nathan, and Q. Smiths, editors. *The New Theory of Time*. New Haven: Yale University Press, 1994.

Oden, Thomas C. *The Living God: Systematic Theology*. Vol. 1. San Francisco: Harper San Francisco, 1992.

Oderberg, David S. *The Metaphysics of Identity over Time*. New York: St. Martin's, 1993.

O'Donnell, John J. *Hans Urs von Balthasar*. Collegeville, MN: Liturgical, 1992.

———. *Trinity and Temporality: The Christian Doctrine of God in the Light of Process Theology and the Theology of Hope*. Oxford: Oxford University Press, 1983.

O'Donovan, Leo. "Evolution under the Sign of the Cross." *Theological Studies* 32 (1971) 602–26.

Ogden, Schubert M. *The Reality of God and Other Essays*. New York: Harper & Row, 1963.

O'Hanlon, Gerard F. "Does God Change?—H. U. von Balthasar on the Immutability of God." *Irish Theological Quarterly* 53 (1987) 161–83.

———. "H. U. von Balthasar and *De Deo Uno*—A New Tract." *Milltown Studies* 5 (1980) 115–31.

———. *The Immutability of God in the Theology of Hans Urs von Balthasar*. Cambridge: Cambridge University Press, 1990.

Orelli, Conrad von. *Die Hebräischen Synonyma der Zeit und Ewigkeit*. Leipzig: Lorentz, 1871.

Otte, Richard. "Indeterminism, Counterfactuals, and Causation." *Philosophy of Science* 54 (1987) 45–62.

Owen, G. E. L. "Aristotle on Time." In *Motion and Time, Space and Matter: Interrelations in the History of Philosophy and Science*, edited by P. K. Machamer and R. G. Turnbull, 3–27. Ohio: Ohio State University Press, 1976.

———. "Plato and Parmenides on the Timeless Present." *Monist* 50 (1966) 317–40.

Owen, H. P. *Concepts of Deity*. New York: Herder & Herder, 1971.

Padgett, Alan G. "Eternity as Relative Timelessness." In *God and Time: Four Views*, edited by G. E. Ganssle, 92–110. Downers Grove, IL: InterVarsity, 2001.

———. "God and Time: Toward a New Doctrine of Divine Timeless Eternity." *Religious Studies* 25 (1989) 209–15.

———. *God, Eternity and the Nature of Time*. New York: St. Martin's, 1992.

Pailin, David A., and Stewart Sutherland, editors. *God and the Processes of Reality*. New York: Routledge, 1989.

Palakeel, Joseph. *The Use of Analogy in Theological Discourse: An Investigation in Ecumenical Perspective*. Rome: Gregorian University Press, 1995.

Pannenberg, Wolfhart. *Anthropology in Theological Perspective*. Translated by Matthew J. O'Connell. Edinburgh: T. & T. Clark, 1985.

———. "Eternity, Time and the Trinitarian God." *Dialog* 39 (2000) 9–14.

———. "The God of History: The Trinitarian God and the Truth of History." Translated by M. B. Jackson. *The Cumberland Seminarian* 19 (1981) 28–41.

———. *Metaphysics and the Idea of God*. Translated by Philip Clayton. Grand Rapids: Eerdmans, 1990.

———. "Problems of a Trinitarian Doctrine of God." *Dialog* 26 (1987) 250–57.
———. *Systematic Theology*. Vol. 1. Translated by Geoffrey W. Bromiley. Grand Rapids: Eerdmans, 1991.
———. *Toward a Theology of Nature: Essays on Science and Faith*. Edited by Ted Peters. Louisville: Westminster, 1993.
———. *What is Man?—Contemporary Anthropology in Theological Perspective*. Translated by Duane A. Priebe. Philadelphia: Fortress, 1970.
Parfit, Derek. "Personal Identity." *Philosophical Review* 80 (1971) 3–27.
———. *Reasons and Persons*. Oxford: Oxford University Press, 1984.
Parsons, J. "Must a Four-Dimensionalist Believe in Temporal Parts?" *Monist* 83 (2000) 399–418.
Passmore, John A. *Philosophical Reasoning*. New York: Basic, 1969.
Peacocke, Arthur R. *Creation and the World of Science*. Oxford: Clarendon, 1979.
———. "God's Action in the Real World." *Zygon* 26 (1991) 455–76.
———. *Intimations of Reality: Critical Realism in Science and Religion*. Notre Dame, IN: University of Notre Dame Press, 1984.
Pedersen, Johannes. *Israel: Its Life and Culture*, I–II. Copenhagen: Branner og Korch, 1926.
Pedersen, O. "The God of Space and Time." *Concilium* 166 (1983) 14–20.
Penrose, Roger. "Singularities and Time-asymmetry." In *General Relativity: An Einstein Centenary Survey*, edited by S. W. Hawking and W. Israel, 581–638. Cambridge: Cambridge University Press, 1979.
Perry, J. "Can the Self Divide?" *Journal of Philosophy* 69 (1972) 463–88.
Peters, Ted, editor. *Cosmos as Creation: Theology and Science in Consonance*. Nashville: Abingdon, 1989.
———. *God as Trinity: Relationality and Temporality in Divine Life*. Louisville: Westminster, 1993.
———. "The Trinity in and Beyond Time." In *Quantum Cosmology and the Laws of Nature: Scientific Perspectives on Divine Action*, 2nd ed., edited by R. J. Russell et al., 263–89. Berkeley: The Center for Theology and the Natural Sciences, 1999.
Peursen, Cornelis A. van. *Body, Soul, Spirit: A Survey of the Body-Mind Problem*. London: Oxford University Press, 1966.
Pike, Nelson. *God and Timelessness*. New York: Schocken, 1970.
Pinnock, Clark H., et al. "Systematic Theology." In *The Openness of God: A Biblical Challenge to the Traditional Understanding of God*, 101–25. Downers Grove, IL: InterVarsity, 1994.
Pittenger, Norman. *The Divine Triunity*. Philadelphia: United Church, 1977.
Plass, Paul C. "The Concept of Eternity in Patristic Theology." *Studia Theologica* 36 (1982) 11–25.
———. "Timeless Time in Neoplatonism." *Modern Schoolman* 55 (1977–78) 1–19.
———. "Transcendent Time and Eternity in Gregory of Nyssa." *Vigiliae Christianae* 34 (1980) 180–92.
Plato, *Timaeus*. In *Plato: Complete Works*, edited by John M. Cooper. Indianapolis: Hackett, 1997.
Plotinus. *The Enneads*. Translated by Stephen MacKenna. Burdett, NY: Larson, 1992.
Pöhlmann, Horst G. *Analogia Entis oder Analogia Fidei? Die Frage der Analogie bei Karl Barth*. Göttingen: Vandenhoeck & Ruprecht, 1965.

Polk, Danne W. "Temporal Impermanence and the Disparity of Time and Eternity." *Augustinian Studies* 22 (1991) 63–82.
Polkinghorne, John, and Michael Welker, editors. *The End of the World and the Ends of God: Science and Theology on Eschatology*. Harrisburg, PA: Trinity, 2000.
Preuss, H. D. "*ôlām*." In *Theological Dictionary of the Old Testament*. Vol. 10, edited by G. J. Botterweck et al., 530–45. Grand Rapids: Eerdmans, 1999.
Price, H. *Time's Arrow and Archimedes' Point: New Directions for the Physics of Time*. New York: Oxford University Press, 1996.
Priest, G. "Tense and Truth Conditions." *Analysis* 46 (1986) 162–66.
Prigogine, Ilya. *From Being to Becoming: Time and Complexity in the Physical Sciences*. San Francisco: Freeman, 1980.
———. *Modern Thermodynamics: From Heat Engines to Dissipative Structures*. New York: John Wiley, 1998.
Prior, A. N. *Papers on Time and Tense*. Oxford: Oxford University Press, 1968.
———. *Past, Present and Future*. Oxford: Clarendon, 1967.
———. "Thank Goodness That's Over." *Philosophy* 34 (1959) 12–17.
———. "Time after Time." *Mind* 67 (1958) 244–46.
Przywara, Erich. *Analogia Entis: Metaphysik, Ur-Structur und All-Rhythmus*. Einsiedeln: Johannes-Verlag, 1962.
Putnam, Hilary. "Time and Physical Geometry." *Journal of Philosophy* 64 (1967) 240–47.
Quash, Ben. "Von Balthasar and the Dialogue with Karl Barth." *New Blackfriars* 79 (1998) 45–55.
Quine, W. V. *Word and Object*. Cambridge: MIT, 1960.
Quinn, John M. *The Doctrine of Time in St. Thomas: Some Aspects and Applications*. Washington, DC: Catholic University of America Press, 1960.
Quinn, Philip L. "On the Mereology of Boethian Eternity." *Philosophy of Religion* 32 (1992) 51–60.
Quispel, Gilles. "Time and History in Patristic Christianity." In *Man and Time*, edited by H. Corbin et al., 85–107. New York: Pantheon, 1957.
Rad, Gerhard von. *Old Testament Theology*. Vol. 2. New York: Harper & Row, 1965.
Rahner, Karl. *The Trinity*. Translated by Joseph Donceel. New York: Crossroad, 1997.
Rea, M. C. "Temporal Parts Unmotivated." *Philosophical Review* 107 (1998) 225–60.
Reihenbach, Hans. *The Direction of Time*. Berkeley: University of California Press, 1971.
———. *The Philosophy of Space and Time*. Translated by M. Reihenbach and J. Freund. New York: Dover, 1958.
Riches, John, editor. *The Analogy of Beauty: The Theology of Hans Urs von Balthasar*. Edinburgh: T. & T. Clark, 1986.
Riches, John, and Ben Quash, "Hans Urs von Balthasar." In *The Modern Theologians*, edited by David F. Ford, 134–51. Oxford: Blackwell, 1997.
Ricoeur, Paul. "Biblical Time." In *Figuring the Sacred: Religion, Narrative, and Imagination*, translated by David Pellauer, 167–80. Minneapolis: Fortress, 1995.
Rietdijk, C. W. "A Rigorous Proof of Determinism Derived from the Special Theory of Relativity." *Philosophy of Science* 33 (1966) 341–44.
Rist, John. "Plotinus and Christian Philosophy." In *The Cambridge Companion to Plotinus*, edited by Lloyd P. Gerson, 386–413. Cambridge: Cambridge University Press, 1996.

Roberts, Louis. *The Theological Aesthetics of Hans Urs von Balthasar*. Washington, DC: The Catholic University of America Press, 1987.

Roberts, Richard H. "Karl Barth's Doctrine of Time: Its Nature and Implications." In *Karl Barth: Studies of His Theological Method*, edited by S. W. Sykes, 88–146. Oxford: Clarendon, 1979.

Robinson, H. Wheeler. *Inspiration and Revelation in the Old Testament*. Oxford: Clarendon, 1946.

Rochelle, G. *Behind Time: The Incoherence of Time and McTaggart's Atemporal Replacement*. Brookfield: Ashgate, 1998.

Rogers, Katherin A. "Eternity Has No Duration." *Religious Studies* 30 (1994) 1–16.

Ross, J. F. *Portraying Analogy*. London: Cambridge University Press, 1981.

Rowan Williams, "Bathasar and Rahner." In *The Analogy of Beauty*, edited by John Riches, 11–34. Edinburgh: T. & T. Clark, 1986.

Rubenstein, Jeffrey L. "Mythic Time and the Festival Cycle." *Journal of Jewish Thought and Philosophy* 6 (1997) 157–83.

Rudavsky, T. M. "Creation and Temporality in Medieval Jewish Philosophy." *Faith and Philosophy* 14 (1997) 458–77.

———. *Time Matters: Time, Creation, and Cosmology in Medieval Jewish Philosophy*. Albany: SUNY, 2000.

Ruether, Rosemary R. *Gaia and God: An Ecofeminist Theology of Earth Healing*. San Francisco: Harper, 1991.

Russell, Bertrand A. W. "On the Experience of Time." *Monist* 25 (1915) 212–33.

Russell, Robert J., et al., editors. *Physics, Philosophy, and Theology: A Common Quest for Understanding*. Vatican City State: Vatican Observatory, 1988.

Russell, Robert J., et al., editors. *Quantum Cosmology and the Laws of Nature: Scientific Perspectives on Divine Action*. Vatican City State: Vatican Observatory, 1993.

Rust, Eric C. "Time and Eternity in Biblical Thought." *Theology Today* 10 (1953) 327–56.

Sachs, John R. "*Deus Semper Major—Ad Majorem Dei Gloriam*: The Pneumatology and Spirituality of Hans Urs von Balthasar." *Gregorianum* 74 (1993) 631–57.

———. "Spirit and Life: The Pneumatology and Spirituality of Hans Urs von Balthasar." PhD diss., Tübingen University, 1984.

Sanders, John. *The God Who Risks: A Theology of Providence*. Downers Grove, IL: InterVarsity, 1998.

Sasse, H. "aio3n." In *Theological Dictionary of the New Testament*, vol.1, edited by G. Kittel and translated by G. W. Bromiley, 197–209. Grand Rapids: Eerdmans, 1964.

Savitt, Steven F., editor. *Time's Arrows Today: Recent Physical and Philosophical Work on the Direction of Time*. Cambridge: Cambridge University Press, 1995.

Saward, John. *The Mysteries of March: Hans Urs von Balthasar on the Incarnation and Easter*. London: Collins, 1990.

Schindler, David L., editor. *Hans Urs von Balthasar: His Life and Work*. San Francisco: Ignatius, 1991.

Schlesinger, George N. *Aspects of Time*. Indianapolis: Hackett, 1980.

———. "How Time Flies." *Mind* 91 (1982) 501–23.

———. *Timely Topics*. New York: St. Martin's, 1994.

Schmid, Johnnes. *Im Ausstrahl der Schönheit Gottes: Die Bedeutung der Analogie in „Herrlichkeit" bei Hans Urs von Balthasar.* Münsterschwarzach: Vier-Türme-Verlag, 1982.

Schmidt, J. *Der Ewigkeitbegriff im Alten Testament.* Munich: Aschendorff, 1940.

Schreiner, Susan E. *The Theater of His Glory: Nature and the Natural Order in the Thought of John Calvin.* Durham: Labyrinth, 1991.

Schulman, L. S. *Time's Arrows and Quantum Measurement.* Cambridge: Cambridge University Press, 1997.

Schwager, Raymund. *Jesus in the Drama of Salvation: Toward a Biblical Doctrine of Redemption.* Translated by James G. Williams and Paul Haddon. New York: Crossroad: 1999.

Schweizer, Eduard. *The Holy Spirit.* Translated by H. Reginald and Ilse Fuller. Philadelphia: Fortress, 1980.

Schwöbel, Christoph, and Colin E. Gunton, editors. *Persons, Divine and Human.* Edinburgh: T. & T. Clark, 1991.

———, editor. *Trinitarian Theology Today.* Edinburgh: T. & T. Clark, 1995.

Scola, Angelo. *Hans Urs von Balthasar: A Theological Style.* Grand Rapids: Eerdmans, 1995.

Searle, John R. *Speech Acts: An Essay in the Philosophy of Language.* Cambridge: Cambridge University Press, 1969.

———. *Expression and Meaning: Studies in the Theory of Speech Acts.* Cambridge: Cambridge University Press, 1979.

———. *Mind, Language and Society: Philosophy in the Real World.* New York: Basic, 1998.

Seddon, Keith. *Time: A Philosophical Treatment.* London: Croom Helm, 1987.

Senor, Thomas D. "Divine Temporality and Creation *Ex Nihilo.*" *Faith and Philosophy* 10 (1993) 86–92.

———. "Incarnation and Timelessness." *Faith and Philosophy* 7 (1990) 149–64.

Sherlock, Charles. *The Doctrine of Humanity.* Downers Grove, IL: InterVarsity, 1996.

Shoemaker, Sydeny. "Persons and Their Pasts." *American Philosophical Quarterly* 7 (1970) 269–85.

———. "Time without Change." *Journal of Philosophy* 66 (1969) 363–81.

Shoemaker, Sydeny, and R. Swinburne. *Personal Identity.* Oxford: Basil Blackwell, 1984.

Sholl, Brian K. "On Robert Jenson's Trinitarian Thought." *Modern Theology* 18 (2002) 27–36.

Shults, F. LeRon. *Reforming Theological Anthropology: After the Philosophical Turn to Relationality.* Grand Rapids: Eerdmans, 2003.

Sider, T. "Four-Dimensionalism." *Philosophical Review* 106 (1997) 197–231.

Simons, John. "Eternity, Omniscience and Temporal Passage: A Defence of Classical Theism." *Review of Metaphysics* 42 (1989) 547–68.

Simons, P. "How to Exist at a Time When You Have No Temporal Parts." *Monist* 83 (2000) 419–36.

Sklar, Lawrence. *Space, Time, and Spacetime.* Berkeley and Los Angeles: University of California Press, 1974.

Smart, J. J. C. "The River of Time." In *Essays in Conceptual Analysis,* edited by A. Flew, 213–27. New York: Macmillan, 1956.

Smith, Andrew. "Eternity and Time." In *The Cambridge Companion to Plotinus*, edited by Lloyd P. Gerson, 196–216. Cambridge: Cambridge University Press, 1996.
Smith, Quentin. "General Introduction: The Implications of the Tensed and Tenseless Theories of Time." In *The New Theory of Time*, edited by L. N. Oaklander and Q. Smith, 1–14. New Haven: Yale University Press, 1994.
———. *Language and Time*. Oxford: Oxford University Press, 1993.
———. "The Mind-Independence of Temporal Becoming." *Philosophical Studies* 47 (1985) 109–19.
———. "Problems with the New Tenseless Theory of Time." *Philosophical Studies* 52 (1987) 371–91.
Smith, Quentin, and L. Nathan Oaklander. *Time, Change, and Freedom: An Introduction to Metaphysics*. London: Routledge, 1995.
Snaith, Norman H. "Time in the Old Testament." In *Promise and Fulfillment*, edited by F. F. Bruce, 175–86. Edinburgh: T. & T. Clark, 1963.
Sorabji, Richard. *Time, Creation, and the Continuum: Theories in Antiquity and the Early Middle Ages*. Ithaca: Cornell University Press, 1983.
Stead, Christopher. *Divine Substance*. Oxford: Clarendon, 1977.
Steensgaard, P. "Time in Judaism." In *Religion and Time*, edited by A. N. Balslev and J. N. Mohanty, 63–108. Leiden: Brill, 1993.
Stein, Howard. "On Einstein-Minkowski Space-Time." *Journal of Philosophy* 65 (1968) 5–23.
———. "On Relativity Theory and Openness of the Future." *Philosophy of Science* 58 (1991) 147–67.
Stoeger, William R. "God and Time: The Action and Life of the Triune God in the World." *Theology Today* 55 (1998) 365–88.
Stump, Eleonore, and Norman Kretzmann. "Eternity." *Journal of Philosophy* 78 (1981) 429–58.
———. "Eternity, Awareness, and Action." *Faith and Philosophy* 9 (1992) 463–82.
Swenson, Loyd S. Jr. *Genesis of Relativity: Einstein in Context*. New York: Franklin, 1979.
Swinburne, Richard G. *The Coherence of Theism*. Oxford: Clarendon, 1977.
Thomas, Owen C., editor. *God's Activity in the World: The Contemporary Problem*. Chico: Scholars, 1983.
Thompson, John. "Barth and Balthasar: An Ecumenical Dialogue." In *The Beauty of Christ: A Introduction to the Theology of Hans Urs von Balthasar*, edited by Bede McGregor and Thomas Norris, 171–92. Edinburgh: T. & T. Clark, 1994.
Thurman, Jerry E. "Time in the Theological Aesthetic of Hans Urs Von Balthasar." ThD diss., Catholic University of America, 1974.
Tomasino, A. "*ôlām*," and "'*ēt*." In *New International Dictionary of Old Testament Theology and Exegesis*. Vol. 3, edited by W. A. VanGemeren, 345–51 and 563–67. Grand Rapids: Zondervan, 1997.
Tomkinson, J. L. "Divine Sempiternity and Atemporality." *Religious Studies* 18 (1982) 177–89.
Tooley, Michael. *Causation: A Realist Approach*. Oxford: Oxford University Press, 1987.
———. "Causation: Reductionism versus Realism." In *Causation*, edited by E. Sosa and M. Tooley, 172–92. Oxford: Oxford University Press, 1993.
———. *Time, Tense, and Causation*. Oxford: Clarendon, 1997.

Torrance, Alan J. *Persons in Communion: An Essay on Trinitarian Description and Human Participation*. Edinburgh: T. & T. Clark, 1996.

———. "What Is Person?" In *From Cells to Souls—and Beyond*, edited by Malcolm Jeeves, 199–222. Grand Rapids: Eerdmans, 2004.

Tracy, Thomas F. *The God Who Acts: Philosophical and Theological Explorations*. University Park: Pennsylvania State University Press, 1994.

Treitler, Wolfgang. "True Foundations of Authentic Theology." In *Hans Urs von Balthasar*, edited by D. L. Schindler, 169.

Tsohatzidis, Savas L., editor. *Foundations of Speech Act Theory: Philosophical and Linguistic Perspectives*. London: Routledge, 1994.

Turetzky, Philip. *Time*. London: Routledge, 1998.

Van Fraassen, Bas C. *An Introduction to the Philosophy of Time and Space*. New York: Random House, 1970.

Van Inwagen, P. "Temporal Parts and Identity across Time." *Monist* 83 (2000) 437–59.

VanGemeren, Willem. *The Progress of Redemption: The Story of Salvation from Creation to the New Jerusalem*. Grand Rapids: Baker, 1988.

Vanhoozer, Kevin J. "A Case for Christian Panentheism? The Case Remains Unproven." *Dialog* 38 (1999) 281–85.

———. *The Drama of Doctrine: A Canonical-Linguistic Approach to Christian Theology*. Louisville: Westminster, 2005.

———. "Effectual Call or Causal Effect?" *Tyndale Bulletin* 49 (1998) 213–51.

———. *First Theology: God, Scripture and Hermeneutics*. Downers Grove, IL: InterVarsity, 2002.

———. "Human Being, Individual and Social." In *The Cambridge Companion to Christian Doctrine*, edited by Colin E. Gunton, 158–88. Cambridge: Cambridge University Press, 1997.

———. *Is There a Meaning in This Text? The Bible, The Reader, and the Morality of Literary Knowledge*. Grand Rapids: Zondervan, 1998.

———. "Providence." In *Dictionary for Theological Interpretation of the Bible*, edited by K. J. Vanhoozer, 641–45. Grand Rapids: Baker, 2005.

Verhoef, P. A. "Time and Eternity." In *New International Dictionary of Old Testament Theology and Exegesis*. Vol. 4, edited by W. A. VanGemeren, 1252–55. Grand Rapids: Zondervan, 1997.

Walker, Larry L. "Tree of Life." In *New International Dictionary of Old Testament Theology and Exegesis*. Vol. 4, edited by Willem A. VanGemeren, 1260–61. Grand Rapids: Zondervan, 1997.

Ware, Bruce A. "An Evangelical Reformulation of the Doctrine of the Immutability of God." *Journal of the Evangelical Theological Society* 29 (1986) 434–40.

———. *God's Lesser Glory: The Diminished God of Open Theism*. Wheaton, IL: Crossway, 2000.

Warnock, G. J. *J. L. Austin*. London: Routledge, 1989.

Weber, Otto. *Foundations of Dogmatics*. Vol. 1. Translated by Darrell L. Guder. Grand Rapids: Eerdmans, 1981.

Weinandy, Thomas G. *The Father's Spirit of Sonship: Reconceiving the Trinity*. Edinburgh: T. & T. Clark, 1995.

Wegener, Mogens, editor. *Time, Creation, and World-Order*. Aarhus: Aarhus University Press, 1999.

Welker, Michael. "God's Eternity, God's Temporality, and Trinitarian Theology." *Theology Today* 55 (1998) 317–28.
Wells, H. G. "Karl Barth's Doctrine of Analogy." *Canadian Journal of Theology* 15 (1969) 203–13.
Wenham, Gordon J. *Genesis 1–15*. World Biblical Commentary, vol. 1. Waco, TX: Word, 1987.
Westermann, Clause. *Elements of Old Testament Theology*. Atlanta: Knox, 1982.
———. *Genesis: A Practical Commentary*. Grand Rapids: Eerdmans, 1987.
Whitehead, Alfred N. *Process and Reality: An Essay in Cosmology*. Edited by D. R. Griffin and D. W. Sherburne. New York: Free, 1978.
Whitrow, G. J. *The Natural Philosophy of Time*. 2nd ed. Oxford: Clarendon, 1980.
———. *What Is Time? The Classic Account of the Nature of Time*. Oxford: Oxford University Press, 2003.
Whittaker, John. "The 'Eternity' of the Platonic Forms." *Phronesis* 13 (1968) 131–44.
Wierenga, Edward R. *The Nature of God: An Inquiry into Divine Attributes*. Ithaca: Cornell University Press, 1989.
Wiggins, David. *Identity and Spatio-Temporal Continuity*. Oxford: Basil Blackwell, 1967.
Wilch, John R. *Time and Event: An Exegetical Study of the Use of 'eth in the Old Testament in Comparison to Other Temporal Expressions in Clarification of the Concept of Time*. Leiden: Brill, 1969.
Williams, Arthur H. "The Trinity and Time." *Scottish Journal of Theology* 39 (1986) 65–81.
Williams, Donald C. "The Myth of Passage." *Journal of Philosophy* 48 (1951) 457–72.
Williams, Rowan, "Bathasar and Rahner." In *The Analogy of Beauty: The Theology of Hans Urs von Balthasar*, edited by John Riches, 11–34. Edinburgh: T. & T. Clark, 1986.
Willis, W. Waite, Jr. *Theism, Atheism and the Doctrine of the Trinity: The Trinitarian Theologies of K. Barth and Jürgen Moltmann in Response to Protest Atheism*. Atlanta: Scholars, 1987.
Winston, David. "The Book of Wisdom's Theory of Cosmogony." *History of Religion* 11 (1971) 185–202.
Wolff, Hans W. *Anthropology of the Old Testament*. Philadelphia: Fortress, 1974.
Wolfson, Harry A. "Patristic Arguments against the Eternity of the World." *Harvard Theological Review* 59 (1966) 351–67.
Wolterstorff, Nicholas. "God Everlasting." In *God and the Good*, ed. C. Orlebeke and L. Smedes, 181–203. Grand Rapids: Eerdmans, 1975.
———. "Unqualified Divine Temporality." In *God and Time: Four Views*, edited by G. E. Ganssle, 187–213. Downers Grove, IL: InterVarsity, 2001.
Wood, David. *The Deconstruction of Time*. Evanston, IL: Northwestern University Press, 2001.
Wright, G. Ernest. *God Who Acts*. London: SCM, 1952.
Yarnold, G. D. "Time and Eternity: What Do We Mean?" *Christian Scholar* 48 (1965) 58–71.
Yates, John C. *The Timelessness of God*. Lanham: University Press of America, 1990.
Young, Francis M. "Creatio Ex Nihilo." *Scottish Journal of Theology* 44 (1991) 139–51.
Zeh, H. Dieter. *The Physical Basis of the Direction of Time*, 3rd ed. Berlin: Springer-Verlag, 1999.

Zeilicovici, D. "A (Dis)solution of McTaggart's Paradox." *Ratio* 28 (1986) 175–95.
Zeitz, James V. "Przywara and von Balthasar on Analogy." *Thomist* 52 (1988) 473–98.
Zimmerman, Laura L. "God and Time." PhD diss., University of Notre Dame, 1983.
Zizioulas, John D. *Being as Communion: Studies in Personhood and the Church*. Crestwood, NY: St. Vladimir's Seminary Press, 1985.
———. "Human Capacity and Human Incapacity: A Theological Exploration of Personhood." *Scottish Journal of Theology* 28 (1975) 401–48.
Zwart, P. J. *About Time: A Philosophical Inquiry into the Origin and Nature of Time*. Amsterdam: North-Holland, 1976.
Zycinski, J. M. "Metaphysics and Epistemology in Stephen Hawking's Theory of the Creation of the Universe." *Zygon* 31 (1996) 269–84.

www.ingramcontent.com/pod-product-compliance
Lightning Source LLC
Chambersburg PA
CBHW071148300426
44113CB00009B/1121